T4-AVB-238

Jonathan Pond's
Financial Management Guide

Retirement Planning for Asset-Rich Individuals

Jonathan Pond

PRENTICE HALL
Englewood Cliffs, New Jersey 07632

Prentice-Hall International (UK) Limited, *London*
Prentice-Hall of Australia Pty. Limited, *Sydney*
Prentice-Hall Canada, Inc., *Toronto*
Prentice-Hall Hispanoamericana, S.A., *Mexico*
Prentice-Hall of India Private Limited, *New Delhi*
Prentice-Hall of Japan, Inc., *Tokyo*
Simon & Schuster Asia Pte. Ltd., *Singapore*
Editora Prentice-Hall do Brasil, Ltda., *Rio de Janeiro*

10 9 8 7 6 5 4 3 2 1

Library of Congress Cataloging-in-Publication Data

Pond, Jonathan D.
[Financial management guide]
Jonathan Pond's Financial management guide : retirement planning for asset-rich individuals /Jonathan Pond.
p. cm.
Includes index.
ISBN 0–13–031238–X. — ISBN 0–13–031220–7 (pbk.)
1. Finance, Personal. 2. Retirement income—Planning. 3. Portfolio management. I. Title.
HG179.P55549 1993
332.024—dc20 92-43414
CIP

ISBN 0-13-031238-X
ISBN 0-13-031220-7 PBK

Printed in the United States of America

JONATHAN D. POND

Jonathan Pond is president of Financial Planning Information, Inc., of Boston. He is the author of nine books on personal financial planning, including the *Personal Financial Planning Handbook,* considered the definitive professional reference in personal finance, *Safe Money in Tough Times, Pond's Personalized Financial Planning Guides,* a series of books for persons in various occupations, and *1001 Ways to Cut Your Expenses.* He is also a contributor to several national publications and writes the monthly newsletter *Prentice Hall's Managing Your Finances for People Over 50.* He has been recognized as an outstanding writer by the Newsletter Writers Association and the American Society of Association Executives.

Mr. Pond is widely sought as an objective and entertaining observer of the investing and personal financial planning scenes. He is a regular guest on numerous radio and television talk shows, and in the past three years alone he has made over 500 television appearances. He is perhaps best known as the financial planning commentator on the NBC *Today* Show. In addition to his work with NBC (which also includes regular appearances on WBZ-TV, the network's Boston affiliate), he has been interviewed on the following national television programs: Moneytalk, Smart Money, the Nightly Business Report, and national news segments on ABC, CBS, CNBC, and CNN. He has also been interviewed on every national radio network, including ABC, Mutual Broadcasting, American Public Radio, and National Public Radio. His weekly radio commentary, "Personal Finance with Jonathan Pond," is heard in many areas of the country. He was educated at the University of North Carolina, Emory University, and the Harvard Business School and is a CPA.

Publications by Jonathan D. Pond

Books

1001 Ways to Cut Your Expenses (Dell, $8.00)

New Century Family Money Book (Dell, $29.95)

Safe Money in Tough Times (Dell, $4.95)

Pond's Personalized Financial Planning Guide for Self-Employed Professionals and Small Business Owners (Dell, $6.99)

Pond's Personalized Financial Planning Guide for Teachers and Employees of Educational Institutions (Dell, $6.99)

Pond's Personalized Financial Planning Guide for Doctors, Dentists, and Health-Care Professionals (Dell, $6.99)

Pond's Personalized Financial Planning Guide for Sales People (Dell, $6.99)

Jonathan Pond's Guide to Investment and Financial Planning (New York Institute of Finance, $24.95)

Smart Planner—Computerized Financial Planning Review ($39.95; 617-924-6939)

Newsletter

Prentice Hall's Financial Management Letter for People over Fifty (monthly, $71.40 per year; 800-288-4745)

For the Financial Professional

Financial Advisor's Desk Reference (New York Institute of Finance, $79.95; 800-288-4745)

Personal Financial Planning Handbook (Warren, Gorham & Lamont, $195.00; 800-950-1216)

Newsline—Monthly Audiotape Series (College for Financial Planning, $165.00 per year, 303-220-1200)

Personal Financial Planning Program —Software for Financial Planners ($475.00; 617-924-6611)

What Your Over-50 Financial Management Guide Will Do for You

This *Guide* addresses the unique personal financial planning needs of affluent people over 50. These are crucial years in your financial life. Over-50s who are not retired must begin making specific plans and taking actions necessary to assure a financially-comfortable retirement. In addition, the need to plan for the future and take action to assure financial peace-of-mind doesn't end at retirement. Retirees must also devote attention to many important personal financial planning matters. After all, given today's life expectancies, many retirees can look forward to 20, 30, or even more years of retirement.

Jonathan Pond's Financial Management Guide: Retirement Planning for Asset-Rich Individuals will help you gain and maintain control over your financial future. Every important area of personal financial planning is covered, including:

- Laying the groundwork for a secure financial future
- Building and protecting wealth through wise investing
- Obtaining the right kind of insurance at the least cost
- Minimizing income taxes and maximizing tax deferred investments
- Making the most of your retirement years
- Planning your estate for the here and now as well as the hereafter
- Coping with the special trials and tribulations of later life

Opportunities and challenges abound for over-50s. Most of us can look forward to a long and active life. Those who have planned carefully during their working years will be able to enjoy a financially comfortable retirement. On the other hand, many recent trends pose challenges to both preretirees and retirees. For preretirees one unfortunate outcome of the latest recession has been a loss in the job security that many workers used to take for granted. On top of that, there is an inexorable trend toward shifting the burden of funding retirement plans to the employee rather than the employer. Once retired, we all must be wary of the tremendous toll that inflation can take over the years. Even affluent retirees must be particularly careful in planning to accumulate savings that will provide extra income in their later years to meet rising living costs. Investing our retirement savings wisely is also essential for every person over 50. Increasingly uncertain and volatile investment markets will likely make investing successfully more challenging than ever.

The *Guide* will help you understand the many changes that are taking place that affect your financial life, and provide you with the information you need to take advantage of new opportunities and avoid problems. You owe it to yourself and your loved ones to take the action necessary to assure that your retirement dreams are achieved. You'll find in these pages a lot of useful suggestions to help you reach your financial goals. You'll also discover that achieving and maintaining financial security isn't that complicated. It takes a little time and a lot of common sense. We hope that our guidance will contribute to making the second (and better) half of your life successful, comfortable, and worry-free.

Jonathan Pond

Acknowledgments

The help of several people who ably assisted in the preparation of this volume is gratefully acknowledged, including Jim Lowell, Don Carleton, and Jake Kreilkamp.

Drew Dreeland and Tom Curtin of Prentice Hall skillfully guided this volume through the editorial process.

Although I have often remarked that one key to success in personal financial planning is to avoid taking responsibility for anything that eats, I am glad to say I don't always practice what I preach. Special thanks to my wife and two daughters for coping with the long absences that are a necessary, if unwelcome, part of the book-writing process.

Jonathan D. Pond

CONTENTS

What Your Over-50 Financial Management Guide Will Do for You. vii

PART ONE—LAYING THE GROUNDWORK FOR THE TIME OF YOUR LIFE (1)

Chapter 1: How to Chart Lifetime Financial Objectives and Take Stock of Where You Stand 3

Setting Goals—3
Coping with "Life Events"—5
Minimizing Marital Money Squabbles—5
Being Happy with What You've Got—7

Chapter 2: Preretirees 9

Retirement Realities—9
It's Never Too Early or Too Late to Start Planning for Retirement—10
A Preliminary Examination of Your Retirement Planning Status—18

Chapter 3: What to Expect from Your Retirement Plan . . . 23

Major Retirement Plans to Consider—23
Retirement Plan Withdrawal Choices—29
How Pension Income Is Taxed—31
How Lump-Sum Distributions Are Taxed—31
How Lump-Sum Annuity Combinations Are Taxed—33
Should You Take a Joint and Survivor Annuity?—33
When Plans Are Over-Funded—35
How to Handle IRA Withdrawals—35
When You Have More than One IRA—35
When Your Contribution Is Nondeductible—36
You May Be Entitled to Retroactive Pension Benefits—36

Chapter 4: How to Make Sure You Get Every Penny of Your Social Security Benefits 39

Who's Covered and How the System Is Funded—40
Social Security Retirement Benefits—40

Chapter 5: Basic Insurance: Property, Casualty, Disability 53

Property and Casualty Coverage—54
Disability Insurance—61
Automobile Insurance—68
Personal Liability Insurance—69
Professional Liability Insurance—70

Chapter 6: Your Protection Against Rising Health Care and Nursing Home Costs 73

Understanding Medicare—74
Health Insurance for the Early Retiree—79
Private Insurance: Filling the Gaps in Medicare—80
HMOs: Saving on Medical Expenses—86
Trimming Your Medical Costs—87
Nursing Homes: Coping with the Cost—88

Chapter 7: Where Life Insurance Fits In 95

Life Insurance and the Preretiree—95
Life Insurance and the Retiree—97
Evaluating (and Cutting) the Cost of Your Life Insurance—99

Chapter 8: Getting Your Personal Records in Order 101

The Importance of Good Recordkeeping—101
How to Prepare Personal Financial Statements—106

Chapter 9: Using Credit Wisely 117

Basic Loans—117
Other Types of Loans—118
Credit Cards, Purchase Financing, and Deferred Payments—124
Automobile Financing and Leasing—129
Using Your Home for Credit—134
Managing Financial Difficulties—141
List of Debts—144

Chapter 10: Avoiding Scams: If It Sounds Too Good to Be True, It Is 147

"It'll Never Happen to Me"—148
Scams—150
Prime Targets—152

Part Two—HOW TO BUILD WEALTH WITH INVESTMENTS AND AVOID LOSING IT TO TAXES (155)

Chapter 11: Investing Basics 157

Understanding Investment Products—158
Pondering Investment Objectives—168
Coping with Market Uncertainty—170

Chapter 12: Constructing an All-Weather Portfolio 173

Where Do You Stand?—174
Meeting Your Investment Needs—175
Evaluating Your Fund Portfolio—176
Asset Allocation—176
Evaluating Your All-Weather Portfolio—181

Chapter 13: Cash-Equivalent Investments 183

Types of Cash Equivalents—184
Making the Most of Cash-Equivalent Investments—188

Chapter 14: Fixed-Income Investments 191

Interest-Earning Investment Strategies—192
Investing in U.S. Treasury Securities—197
Investing in U.S. Savings Bonds—198
Investing in Mortgaged-Backed Securities—199
Investing in Municipal Securities—202
Investing in Corporate Bonds—205

Chapter 15: Making Money in Stocks 209

Investing in Common Stocks—210
Advantages and Disadvantages of Common Stocks—211
Types of Common Stocks—212
Investing in Preferred Stocks—213
Stock Investment Strategies—216
Investing in Mutual Funds for Diversification and Professional Management—221
When to Sell—222
Having Your Cake and Eating It Too—223
Stock Option Strategies—224

Chapter 16: Safe Real Estate Investing in Today's Risky Market 227

Types of Ownership—228
Real Estate Investment Alternatives—234

Evaluating Real Estate Investments—238
Real Estate Investment Strategies—241

Chapter 17: Why Effective Tax Planning Is Vital 245

Tax-Deferred Investments—247
Tax-Exempt Investments—247
Mastering the Tax Game—248
Working with Your Tax Advisor—248
Year-End Tax Saving Techniques—249
Personal Interest—252
Family Matters—257
Don't Let Tax Planning Become Too Taxing—259

Chapter 18: Tax-Advantaged Investments 261

Individual Retirement Accounts—261
Self-Employed Retirement Plans—266
Annuities—267
Other Vehicles for Retirement Planning—272

PART THREE—NUTS AND BOLTS OF ESTATE PLANNING (275)

Chapter 19: Minimum Estate Planning Needs 277

Ongoing Process—278
Four Basic Documents—279

Chapter 20: How to Minimize the Death Tax Bite 299

Calculating Your Estate Tax—299
Basic Estate Tax Saving Strategies—300
Taxing Matters—302

Chapter 21: Sophisticated Strategies for Large Estates 311

Trusts—311
Reasons for Establishing a Trust—312
Types of Trusts—312
Creating a Trust—315
Choosing Trustees—316
Family Trusts—317
Qualified Terminable Interest Property (QTIP) Trusts—318
Charitable Trusts—320
Generation-Skipping Transfers—323

Chapter 22: Funeral Planning—Don't Wait Until It's Too Late 325

Without Preplanning, You Just Might Take It with You—325
Memorial Societies: A Good Place to Begin—325
Selecting a Funeral Home—326
Include Funeral Preferences in Your Letter of Instructions—326
Evaluating Funeral Alternatives—327
Religious Services—330
Financing Your Finale—331
Final Expenses and Tax Deductions—332

PART FOUR—MAKING THE MOST OF YOUR RETIREMENT YEARS (333)

Chapter 23: Choosing a Retirement Lifestyle 335

Cultivating a Hobby or Activity—335
Working in Retirement—336
Deciding Where to Live—337
Later Life Decisions—337

Chapter 24: Sorting Out Your Retirement Housing Options 339

Housing Options for Independent Retirees—341
Deciding Where You Want to Live—350

Chapter 25: Health Care—More Important than Ever ... 353

Preventive Medicine—353
Using the Internal Revenue Code to Cut Your Health Care Costs—355
The Top Ten Ways to Save Money on Healthcare—356

Chapter 26: Making Your Lifelong Travel Plans Come True 359

Plan Ahead—359
Group Benefits—360
Goodbye, Columbus—360
Getting There—368
Traveling with Grandchildren—369
Useful Government Publications on International Travel—369

Chapter 27: Working in Retirement: It's a Whole New Ballgame 373
If you Must Work to Make Ends Meet—375
Challenging Jobs for Retirees—375
The Job Search—378
Starting a Retirement Business?—379
Age Discrimination: Know Your Rights—381
How Working Affects Your Social Security Benefits—381

Chapter 28: What to Do with the Family Homestead 383
The Dollar Price—383
The Emotional Price—384
Selling Your Home—384
Maintaining Your Home—386

PART FIVE—A FINANCIAL SURVIVAL GUIDE TO THE SPECIAL TRIALS AND TRIBULATIONS OF LATER LIFE (393)

Chapter 29: Late Life Divorce and Remarriage 395
Current Attitudes Toward Divorce—395
Planning for Divorce—396
Organizing Your Life—397
Divorce Procedures and Alternatives—397
Dividing Your Assets—398
Making Sure Your Planning Reflects Your New Status—399
Tax Planning—402
Silver Lining: Remarriage—402

Chapter 30: Learning to Cope as a Widow/Widower 405
Immediate Problems—405
Budgeting and Recordkeeping—407
Insurance—412
Borrowing and Credit—414
Investments—415
Tax Planning—417
Retirement Planning—419
Estate Planning—420

Chapter 31: The Single Life 423
Unique Problems of Single People—424
Planning and Recordkeeping—425

Insurance—425
Investing—425
Estate Planning—426

Chapter 32: Choosing a Nursing Home **427**
Where to Begin—427

Index **439**

Part One

Laying the Groundwork for the Time of Your Life

1

HOW TO CHART LIFETIME FINANCIAL OBJECTIVES AND TAKE STOCK OF WHERE YOU STAND

ONE THING YOU should be doing—if you haven't already—is to establish some financial planning goals. What do you want to accomplish in your financial life? Your primary financial planning goal should be financial security. Financial security means, if you are still working, that you can live the rest of your life without having to work or if you're retired, you will not have to worry about running short of money in the face of constantly rising living costs. Many affluent people fall short of achieving true financial security. They find that they have to cut back on their lifestyle when they retire or, if they try to maintain their lifestyle, they risk running short of income in their old age.

Setting Goals

Achieving financial security requires much planning and some sacrifice because the only way you're going to be successful in reaching the universal goal of financial security (short of marrying very well or inheriting very well) is to save regularly. The only way to save regularly is to spend less than you earn which, in essence, means that you have to *live beneath your means*—even after you're retired.

Beyond the long-term goal of financial security, you probably have a variety of other financial planning objectives. Among the more common are:

- Saving more regularly
- Improving personal recordkeeping
- Making sure that savings are invested wisely
- Reducing debt
- Assuring complete insurance coverage
- Making a major purchase
- Reducing income taxes and estate taxes
- Retiring early
- Providing support for elderly parents
- Coping with health care costs when you are retired
- Making sure your estate is properly planned
- Providing for your spouse in the event of your early death
- Passing an estate on to your children or other heirs

You should be specific about your financial goals and how you plan to go about achieving them. Be sure to write them down from time to time. To encourage you to do this, Figure 1.1 is a worksheet that allows you to list your personal financial goals.

Figure 1.1. Financial Goals Worksheet

Date: ______

1. ______________________________
2. ______________________________
3. ______________________________
4. ______________________________
5. ______________________________
6. ______________________________
7. ______________________________

Coping with "Life Events." Over the course of your lifetime, you have and will experience several "life events" that will probably require you to reevaluate your personal financial status and plans. They will usually require you to make some adjustment in your planning and some may require major changes. Table 1.1 (page 6) lists those life events that most commonly require at least some modifications of the plans for those who are over 50. Note that many of the circumstances are common. In fact, you could lead a very typical life and experience many such events.

The nature and extent of changes required by these events vary. For some you will need the counsel of competent professionals, but they cannot be expected to address all necessary changes. While it is difficult to generalize about such a multiplicity of events, the following financial planning areas are often affected by the changed circumstances:

- *Budgeting and recordkeeping.* Review/revise personal budgets, prepare projections, including income tax ramifications, based on changed status.
- *Insurance.* Review beneficiary designations, adequacy of coverage, and type of coverage.
- *Credit.* Establish or reestablish credit standing, revise loan documentation.
- *Family assets.* Review holdings, change ownership designations, evaluate sufficiency of diversification.
- *Estate planning.* Review/revise estate planning documents and estate planning techniques, clarify/change bequests to heirs.

Minimizing Marital Money Squabbles

When was the last time you argued with your spouse or significant other about money? If you want to have an argument, money matters are an omnipresent and very convenient catalyst. However, money disputes are not necessarily indicative of deeper problems. Actually, the vast majority of couples agree on important, long-term family financial matters. The disagreements tend to be over smaller, day-to-day financial matters. There are several things you can do to minimize interspousal money tensions.

Table 1.1. Summary of Life Events That Usually Require a Modification in Financial Plans

Family
Marriage or remarriage
Family member with special financial needs
Aging parents
Death of a spouse or other close family member
Receipt of an inheritance
Cohabitation
Separation/divorce
Occupational
Purchasing or starting a business
Changing jobs or careers
Job subject to fluctuating income
Unemployment
Retirement
Health
Disability
Old age
Chronic illness
Terminal illness

First, you should set aside an annual date with your spouse to review your financial status and make some plans for the next year. The date you select shouldn't be around tax-return preparation time, however. That's already stressful enough on couples. Efficient and comprehensive recordkeeping throughout the year will make this "day of reckoning" much easier.

Second, you should work with your spouse to develop the financial goals that were discussed earlier in this chapter. Most financial matters don't take care of themselves. To accomplish your goals, you will have to know what they are and work toward them together.

What all this boils down to, of course, is improved communication with your spouse. Lack of communication about family finances, or for that matter, in any aspect of marriage, is a recipe for strife. But don't expect the arguments to go away entirely. Chances are you and your spouse will always have somewhat different approaches toward family money management.

Being Happy with What You've Got

There is far too much preoccupation with money these days. Most people waste a lot of time thinking they would be on Easy Street if they only earned $10,000 more than they do currently. We all want financial security, of course. Unfortunately, some people spend all they earn during their working years in the mistaken belief that they'll be able to live off Social Security when they're retired. However, Social Security will support most people for about one week each month. Assuming you'd like to provide for the other three weeks as well, you must accumulate a sizable investment portfolio by the time you retire. In order to have investments, you have to save regularly. In order to save regularly, you have to spend less than you earn.

No matter how obvious that sounds, many of us have difficulty doing it, but the best way to spend less than you earn is to be happy with what you've got. A lot of people don't like to hear this. They want a fancier car, an imported kitchen, an exotic vacation, or a larger house. After all, the advertisers tell us that we have to have these things to be happy; after all, our neighbors have some of these things and they sure seem happy. The neighbors, even the ones who do make $10,000 more per year than you do, probably feel the same way about you that you feel about them. But if you can be happy with what you've got, you'll find it a lot easier to save the money to make the investments that will allow you to achieve financial security. It's as simple as that. So at the risk of sounding like a broken record, you must learn to spend less than you earn.

2

PRERETIREES

ALL OF THE financial planning you do during your working years—from investing wisely to insuring against the unforeseen—helps you on your way to your ultimate financial goal of achieving financial security by the time you retire. Yet, retirement planning per se is all too often neglected. Sadly, even financially successful individuals overlook the importance of providing for retirement and end up working beyond their desired retirement age and/or enduring a less-than-financially-comfortable retirement.

Retirement Realities

There are other elements that affect the retirement planning process for all of us and may well influence the way you plan for your own retirement. These include:

- Affluent people have very high retirement expectations. First, and for the first time, most of us expect to retire with no diminution in lifestyle. Previous generations expected to cut back when they retired. No longer. Second, many people aspire to retire early. More and more people are realizing the dream of early retirement, although many end up (or will end up) regretting it.
- Life expectancy has increased dramatically since the begin-

ning of this century. The notion of letting people retire at age 65 was advanced at a time when few working people attained that age. Now, a person who reaches 65 should plan on living another 25 years, and many will live beyond age 90. This requires a lot of money. A professional who expects to enjoy 35-40 productive, wage-earning years must accumulate enough savings during that time to support herself for at least another quarter century.

- Higher inflation (compared to what was experienced prior to the 1970s) seems to be firmly entrenched in our economy. High inflation makes it tougher to accumulate resources in advance of retirement and makes it tougher to maintain an adequate living standard throughout a long retirement.
- Fiscal pressures on the government and employers mean that working people will have to rely less on Social Security and company pension plans and rely more on personal savings and investments to assure an adequate retirement income.

It's Never Too Early or Too Late to Start Planning For Retirement

Don't despair over your retirement prospects. However, the earlier you begin planning for retirement, the better. This chapter will show you how to:

1. Estimate how much income you will need during retirement
2. Figure out how much you will need to accumulate in order to fund a comfortable retirement
3. Take stock of your progress in meeting your retirement needs
4. Take action to close the gap between the resources you now have and the resources you will eventually need to retire.

There is no magic behind accumulating the necessary resources for retirement. You can use the investment strategies in Chapters 11 to 16 to learn how to invest wisely. Fortunately, the tax regulations still look favorably on retirement-earmarked investments. Many of these tax-advantaged plans merit your consideration (see Chapter 18).

You can use Figures 2.1 and 2.2 to help you get on the right track.

Figure 2.1. Retirement Planning Timetable

AGES 50–59

1. Continue to request your Social Security "Personal Earnings and Benefit Estimate Statement" periodically.
2. Review your status with your company's pension plan regularly.
3. Revise your retirement income and expense projections, taking inflation into consideration.
4. Confirm the beneficiary designations on life insurance policies
5. Start gradually shifting some of your IRA and other retirement-earmarked funds into lower risk investments with more emphasis on yield.
6. Join the American Association of Retired Persons (AARP) to take advantage of the many sources of information and help that it offers. The address is:
   AARP
   601 E Street, N.W.
   Washington, DC 20049

AGES 60–64

1. If you are contemplating an early retirement, discuss the advantages and disadvantages with your employer's personnel officer and the local Social Security office.
2. Collect the documents necessary to process Social Security benefits:
   –Both spouses' Social Security cards
   –Proof of both spouses' ages
   –Marriage certificates
   –Copy of latest income tax withholding statement (W-2)
3. Before taking any major actions, such as selling a house, weigh the merits of waiting until age 65 when many special breaks are available to the elderly or retired.
4. Determine the status and duration of ongoing financial commitments such as mortgages and loans.
5. Prepare detailed cash flow projections from estimated year of retirement until age 90, taking inflation into consideration.
6. Practice living for a month under the planned retirement income.
7. Consider different retirement locations. If a location other

Figure 2.1 (Cont'd)

than the present home is chosen, try living there for a while before making the move.

RIGHT BEFORE RETIREMENT

1. Establish what your retirement income will be, and estimate as closely as possible what your retirement costs of living will be.
2. Have your employer's personnel officer determine exactly what your pension benefits will be, what company or bank will send the pension, and when the first check (or lump sum distribution) will arrive; what can be done about accumulated vacation time; whether there are any special annuity benefits; and whether supplemental medical or hospital insurance is available.
3. Register with the Social Security Administration at least three months before retirement.
4. Inquire about possible entitlements to partial pensions from past jobs.

Figure 2.2. Retirement Planning Work Sheet

Use this three-part work sheet to forecast the amount of retirement income you will require and to estimate the amount of savings you will have to accumulate to meet your retirement income needs.

I. RETIREMENT EXPENSE FORECASTER

This section helps you approximate the amount of annual retirement income that will allow you to maintain your pre-retirement standard of living. First, the approximate income necessary to maintain current living standard in current dollars is calculated. Then, by reference to future value tables and by using the assumed rate of inflation, you can project this amount to your estimated retirement date.

Figure 2.2 (Cont'd)

Current gross annual income (1)	$ ....
Minus amount of annual savings (2)	(.............)
Subtotal (the amount you spend currently)	....
Multiplied by 75% (3)	X.75
Equals approximate annual cost (in current dollars) of maintaining your current standard of living if you were retiring this year	$ ....
Multiplied by inflation factor (Refer to inflation factor table below) (4)	X ....
Equals approximate annual cost (in future dollars) of maintaining your current standard of living when you retire	$ ....

INFLATION FACTOR TABLE

Number of Years Until Retirement	*Factor*
5	1.2
10	1.6
15	1.9
20	2.4
25	3.0
30	3.7
35	4.7
40	5.8

Explanations:

(1) "Current gross annual income" includes all income from all sources.

(2) "Annual savings" includes, in addition to the usual sources of savings, reinvested dividends and capital gains, and any contributions to retirement plans that are taken from your annual income.

(3) The 75% multiplier is a general rule of thumb that says, in essence, that a retiree can maintain his/her pre-retirement

Figure 2.2 (Cont'd)

standard of living by spending roughly 75% of his/her pre-retirement income. Of course, individual circumstances may dictate a higher or lower percentage. Ideally, you should prepare a retirement budget that details expected expenses. You may find a multiplier less than 75% in some circumstances (e.g., low housing costs due to paid off mortgage) or, in other circumstances, a higher multiplier (e.g., extensive travel plans).

(4) In order to project retirement expenses to retirement age, current dollar living expenses must be multiplied by a factor to account for inflationary increases. The inflation factor table can be used for that purpose. The assumed long-term inflation rate is 4.5%.

II. RETIREMENT RESOURCES FORECASTER

This section can be used to forecast pension and Social Security benefits at retirement age and then to approximate the aggregate amount of savings/investments that will be needed by retirement age to cover any shortfall between Social Security/pension benefits and your total income needs.

	Current Dollars	*Times Inflation Factor (1)*		*Future (Retirement Age) Dollars*
1. Estimated annual living expenses at retirement age (From Part I)				$ ....
2. Annual pension income (projection at retirement age available from employer) (2)	$	X	=	....
3. Plus annual Social Security benefits (projection at retirement age available from Social Security Administration) (3)	$	X	=	....

Figure 2.2 (Cont'd)

4. Subtotal projected pension and Social Security income (add lines 2 and 3)	....
5. Shortfall (if expenses are greater than income) that must be funded out of personal savings/ investments (subtract line 4 from line 1)	....
6. Multiplied by 17 (4)	x 17
7. Equals amount of savings/ investments in future dollars that need to be accumulated by retirement age to fund retirement (5)	$ ....

Explanations:

(1) Use Inflation Factor Table for the appropriate calculation.
(2) Employers usually provide pension plan projections at retirement age, expressed in current dollars. If so, the amount should be multiplied by an inflation factor to approximate benefits in future dollars.
(3) Social Security estimates are expressed in current dollars and they should be adjusted for inflation similar to (2) above.
(4) As a general rule of thumb, for every $1,000 of annual income you will need to fund at retirement age, you will need to have at least $17,000 in savings/investments in order to keep up with inflation. If you plan to retire before age 62, use a factor of 20, rather than 17.
(5) You may be dismayed by the magnitude of the amount of personal resources that you will need to fund your retirement, which can easily exceed $1,000,000 for younger persons and/or people with minimal pension benefits. Nevertheless, good savings habits combined with the power of compounding can usually close the gap between current resources and eventual needs.

III. RETIREMENT SAVINGS ESTIMATOR

This section can be used to estimate the annual amount of savings that are required to accumulate the funds necessary to

Figure 2.2 (Cont'd)

meet your retirement objectives. The amount computed on Line 7 equals the required *first year* savings. The annual savings should be increased by 5 percent in each succeeding year until you retire.

1. Amount of savings/ investments in future dollars that need to be accumulated by retirement age to fund retirement (from Part II)		$ ....
2. Minus resources that are currently available for retirement purposes (1)	$	
3. Multiplied by appreciation factor (refer to annual appreciation factor table below) (2)	X	
4. Equals estimated future value of retirement resources that are currently available (Multiply Line 2 by Line 3)		(...................)
5. Retirement funds needed by retirement age (Subtract Line 4 from Line 1)		....
6. Multiplied by annual savings		

Figure 2.2 (Cont'd)

factor (Refer to annual savings factor table below) (3) X ....

7. Equals savings needed over the next year (Multiply Line 5 by Line 6) (4) $ ....

Appreciation Factor Table

Number of Years Until Retirement	Factor
5	1.4
10	2.1
15	3.0
20	4.2
25	6.1
30	8.8
35	12.6
40	18.0

Annual Savings Factor Table

Number of Years Until Retirement	Factor
5	.1513
10	.0558
15	.0274
20	.0151
25	.0088
30	.0054
35	.0034
40	.0022

Explanations:

(1) Resources that are currently available typically include the current value of all of your investment-related assets that are not expected to be used before retirement. Don't include the value of your home unless you expect to sell it to raise money for retirement. Don't include any vested pension benefits if you have already factored them in on Line 2 or Part II of this work sheet.

(2) The appreciation factor is used to estimate what your currently-available retirement resources will be worth when you retire. The appreciation factor assumes a seven and one-half percent *after-tax* rate of appreciation.

Figure 2.2 (Cont'd)

(3) The annual saving factor computes the amount you will need to save during the next year in order to begin accumulating the retirement fund needed by retirement age as indicated on Line 5. The annual savings factor assumes a seven and one-half percent *after-tax* rate of return.

(4) The annual savings needed to accumulate your retirement nest-egg assumes that you will increase the amount of money you save by 5 percent each year until retirement.

A Preliminary Examination of Your Retirement Planning Status

How Much Income Will You Need for Retirement?

If you are still many years from retirement, estimating your income requirements at retirement age may be of little concern to you now, but you should at least pay some attention to your retirement aspirations. After all, you may well spend over one-third of your life retired. If, however, you are nearing retirement age, you must begin to think about your retirement lifestyle, including the all-important decision about where you want to live.

Once you have an idea of how you want to live in retirement, you can estimate your expenses, first in current dollars and then in future, inflated dollars. In order to maintain the same standard of living in retirement that you enjoyed during your working years, you will need annual retirement of approximately 75 percent of the amount you *spend* per year during your working years.

EXAMPLE: The Garners are going to retire in a few months. Last year, they had total income of $145,000; but they saved about $25,000 of that, including a contribution to Dr. Garner's retirement plan. Based on the 75 percent rule of thumb, they will need about $90,000 in their first year of retirement to maintain an equivalent standard of living. (The calculation is as follows: Since they saved $25,000 of their $145,000 income, they *spent* $120,000. Seventy-five percent of $120,000 is $90,000).

Depending on your circumstances and desires, you may need more or less than 75 percent of your preretirement income. If you are within 10 to 15 years of retirement, you should put pencil to paper to prepare a detailed retirement living expense budget. As best you can, try to quantify your retirement expenses. Think about how you expect your lifestyle to change. You will find that some costs decline, including work-related expenses and income taxes (but not dramatically). Social Security withholding taxes drop to zero unless you work part time. Other costs will increase, including health care (be sure to provide for health insurance) and, if you are so inclined, travel. Many people decide they would like to try alternative housing arrangements—living in a condominium rather than a single-family house, for example. Ideally, any major changes should be undertaken, or at least experienced before—not during—retirement. During retirement, when funds are limited, you don't want to realize that a lifestyle change was not at all what you wanted.

One of the biggest mistakes that people make in planning for their retirement is either ignoring or underestimating the effects of inflation. Even though inflation is much lower now than it was during the double-digit days of 1979–81, it still takes its toll on your purchasing power. Many retirees, in particular, see their purchasing power diminished by inflation since much of their income is either fixed (like many retirement annuities) or lags inflation somewhat (like Social Security). So when you project your retirement expenses, you must first consider inflation from now until you retire, and then you must factor in inflation for all of your retirement years. Now, you might ask, what rate of inflation should one assume? This is a crucial question. If you were retiring around 1970 and you looked at the inflation rate over the 1950–70 period, you may well have guessed that inflation would continue as it had—at around 2 percent per annum! Projecting inflation is a tricky business, but it must be done. Many experts now recommend that people who are making financial projections assume a future annual rate of inflation of 4 to 5 percent. Some experts think that even higher inflation rates are in the offing. Incidentally, the average annual inflation rate during the 1980s, including the high rates of the early 1980s, was 4.7%. Perhaps an expected inflation rate of 4.5% is appropriate. As the following example shows, inflation can take a heavy toll on purchasing power.

EXAMPLE: Dr. and Mrs. McCardle turned 50 this year and are now hard at work trying to figure out how much income they will need in order to be able to afford to retire at age 65. They now figure that in order to live like they want to when they retire, they will need $65,000 of income per year (including taxes) in addition to

Social Security. Of course, $65,000 would suffice if they were to retire today, but they will need more than that 15 years hence to have the same purchasing power as $65,000 of income today. In fact, at an assumed inflation rate of 4.5%, they will need over $125,000 of income at age 65 in order to enjoy the same lifestyle that $65,000 fetches today.

How Much Will You Need for a Comfortable Retirement?

Once you have estimated how much you expect to spend when you retire, you need to forecast how much you will need to accumulate personally in addition to estimated Social Security and pension benefits to provide for your needs for the rest of your life. (The so-called three legs of the retirement stool are pension, Social Security, and personal resources.) Before making the actual calculations, two important matters must be considered—life expectancy and inflation during your retirement years. Retirees are, happily, living and, hopefully, living happily for many years. But many who retired quite comfortably 20 or so years ago are struggling financially. They simply weren't prepared to fund so many years of retirement during a period of high inflation. So life expectancy and inflation *must* be considered. Whether the thought appeals to you or not, you should plan on living until at least age 90. (The current joint and last survivor life expectancy of a couple who are both age 50 is 39 years!) So if you are going to retire at age 65, you will need enough resources to tide you over for at least 25 years. By the way, I'm a strong advocate of spending it all before you and your spouse die, but don't plan to spend it all before you reach age 90.

Inflation exacts a heavy toll on retirees, particularly those whose income consists mainly of fixed annuities and Social Security.

EXAMPLE: In the previous example, the somewhat startled McCardles found out they were going to need an income of $125,000 when they retire at 65, 15 years hence to have the same purchasing power that $65,000 has today. As if this isn't bad enough, things get worse. Inflation doesn't go away when you retire. When the McCardles reach age 75, they will need just shy of $200,000 (at a 4.5 percent inflation rate) to have the purchasing power than $65,000 had 25 years earlier. Of course, inflation may end up being less than 4.5 percent (inflation affects many retirees *somewhat* less than it does working people since housing and fuel costs, which are often reduced in retirement, are major contributors to the inflation rate) . . . but it could be more.

Evaluate Your Progress in Meeting Retirement Needs

Estimating how much you will need to accumulate by the time you reach retirement age can be startling. If you are still young, this amount may seem more like the gross national product of a small country, but it is probably attainable without enduring a lot of deprivation. At this point you need to tally up the assets that you already have available that will eventually be used for retirement purposes. All of your savings (except those that are earmarked for specific nonretirement-related purposes like savings for the down payment on a home or savings for educating the children) will eventually be available to support you during retirement. Two caveats: (1) Don't include the value of your home in your retirement-related assets unless you plan to sell the house and become a renter when you retire. (2) Don't include the value of your personal property because it isn't worth anything to anyone else anyway (unless you have collectibles, which, in many instances, still don't fetch very much).

As you review your current retirement planning status, there is one other matter that you should consider—housing costs. If you can be mortgage free or have a very low mortgage by the time you retire, your living expenses will be considerably lower if you remain saddled with a large mortgage or if you rent. As part of your retirement planning, you should probably strive to be mortgage free by the time you retire.

Close the Gap Between Current Resources and the Resources You Will Need for Retirement

If you have taken the pains to figure out how much you need to be able to retire in comfort, you probably realize (if you hadn't already) that you don't yet have enough money in the kitty to meet your needs. You should take heart in the fact that very few people achieve financial independence until they are very near retirement age anyway. What is most important now is to make sure you take the action that is necessary to meet your financial needs *throughout* your retirement. Figure 2.1 serves as a reminder of important retirement planning matters. Figure 2.2 allows you to compute the annual savings required in order to accumulate the resources you will need for retirement.

3

WHAT TO EXPECT FROM YOUR RETIREMENT PLAN

THIS CHAPTER CONSISTS of two sections. The first section describes the major types of retirement plans relevant to older members of the workforce. The second section provides the information you need to make an informed decision about withdrawing money from your retirement plan(s), since there are a number of different options available to you.

Major Retirement Plans to Consider

Tax-Advantaged Retirement Plans

There are several varieties of retirement plans of which you can take advantage. While all will help give you the financial self-discipline necessary to save for retirement, some have the added bonus of being tax-advantaged. These plans range from pension plans in which your employer makes the contributions to plans where you and your employer split the contributions to plans where you make all the contributions, but where they are fully tax deductible. The least attractive plans—from a tax standpoint at least—are plans whose contributions are not tax-deductible, but the income from which is *tax-deferred* until retirement. In fact, all of the following retirement-oriented plans and investments at least have the advantage of tax deferral.

Keep in mind that there is a *quid pro quo* to making retirement-oriented investments. Your money is generally going to be tied up at least until you reach age fifty-nine and one-half. So you need to make sure that you will have ready access to some money should the need arise by keeping a portion of your investments outside of any retirement plans.

Employer-Sponsored Plans

Pension plans, employee thrift and savings plans, 401(K) plans, and 403(b) plans are for the most part either wholly or partially subsidized by your employer. For obvious reasons, if you can invest in one of these plans, you should take advantage of it without hesitation.

PENSION PLANS

If you work for a company or organization that offers a pension plan, and you stay with the company for a long time, you may retire with a pension that goes a long way toward covering your retirement needs. The important thing to do now, however, is to find out through the projections provided by your employer just how generous the plan is. You may also be permitted to make additional after-tax contributions to the plan. You should be careful, however, not to put too many eggs in one basket. In addition, if you earn a high income, your additional contributions may in fact reduce the amount your employer makes on your behalf.

If you ever leave a company in which you have vested pension benefits, you should—if your employer will pay out your vested portion—roll these benefits over into an individual retirement account (IRA). The Internal Revenue Service gives you 60 days to make transfer funds in this manner. Incidentally, chronic job hoppers, even if they dutifully roll over whatever pension benefits they receive, usually end up with far less pension income than their more sedentary colleagues. Most pension plans are designed to favor those loyal employees who put in many years of service.

EMPLOYEE THRIFT AND SAVINGS PLANS

These plans usually require you to make after-tax contributions, which are either wholly or partially matched by your employer's contributions. Even though there are no immediate tax benefits, you will still benefit from both your employer's generosity and the farsightedness of the federal government's tax policymakers: Your investment will grow tax-free and the savings will compound handsomely over time.

401(k) Plans. The 401(k) plans (also called salary reduction plans), rely primarily on voluntary employee contributions (although employers contribute to them as well). In addition to the benefit of tax deferral on the income from your 401(k) investments, your annual contributions to the plan, which are deducted from your salary, are not reported as income. Therefore, your salary reductions are the equivalent of a tax deductible contribution. There is, however, an annual cap on these tax-favored contributions that is adjusted for inflation each year. 401(k) plans are simply too good to pass up if your employer has one.

You will probably be required to manage your 401(k) plan investments by specifying the allocation of your plan assets among various investment choices, usually some mutual funds and a guaranteed investment (or guaranteed income) contract (GIC). Many 401(k) holders allocate far too much to GICs. Over the long run, a mix of stock and bond mutual funds will usually provide a superior return to a GIC, as long as you avoid an extreme investment strategy. Putting 50 percent of the plan in stock funds and 50 percent in interest earning funds (including a GIC, if you wish) is generally a failsafe recipe for achieving solid long-term results. If you have the option of investing a portion of your 401(k) portfolio in company stock, don't take an overlarge position, as good a bargain as the stock may be. While company loyalty is all well and good, diversification is better. Suppose your company fell on hard times. The stock could take a nosedive and your retirement savings could be seriously eroded. There is no need to tie yourself that closely to your company's future!

403(b) Plans. Many nonprofit organizations offer 403(b) plans (often called "tax sheltered annuities"), which are similar to 401(k)s. Contributing employees' taxable income is reduced by the amount of their contributions, and the earnings the investments are tax deferred until withdrawals commence. As with the 401(k) plan, there are limitations on the amount that can be contributed. You can, if you wish, have both a 401(k) plan and a 403(b) plan, but the total contributions to both cannot exceed the 403(b) limitations.

How you invest your 403(b) funds depends on the options that your employer makes available to you. When you have some choice, for example, stock funds, bond funds, and so forth, follow the same general investment allocation approach outlined in the discussion on 401(k) plan investments.

Self-Employed Retirement Plans

People who are self-employed, whether on a full- or part-time basis, are eligible to establish their own retirement plans. Therefore, if you earn any income from self-employment, you should consider setting up a self-employed retirement plan. There are two categories of plans to consider:

1. Keogh plans
2. Simplified Employee pension plans

Keogh Plans. Keogh plans are specifically structured to allow self-employed people—sole proprietors and partners—to set up their own retirement savings programs. Most Keoghs are designed as defined-contribution plans. Keoghs can be structured to allow you to contribute, and deduct, up to 25 percent of your net income from self-employment (actually 20 percent of your income before you make the contribution) or $30,000, whichever is less. You can tailor the plan to meet your own needs and resources. If you have employees, you must extend this benefit to them and make contributions at the same percentage-of-income level that you do for yourself. In that situation, you may well find that the net benefits of establishing a Keogh are minimal.

In some instances a *defined-benefit* Keogh plan may be a wonderful means of accumulating a substantial retirement nest egg. Generally, these plans are appropriate for high-income self-employed people who are over 50 and who have no other employees. A defined-benefit plan can be structured to allow very high annual tax deductible contributions, well in excess of the $30,000 cap on defined-contribution Keoghs.

Remember that your Keogh Plan must be established by December 31 of the tax year in which you plan to begin taking the deduction. You can, however, delay making the contribution until your tax return is filed (including extensions) in the succeeding year. (If you missed the deadline, but it is not yet April 15, you **can** set up a simplified employee pension plan, described in the following section.) People who wish to work after retirement age can continue to make Keogh contributions indefinitely as long as they report their self-employment income.

Simplified Employee Pension Plans. As the name suggests, simplified employee pension (SEP) plans are simple to set up, simple to maintain, and excellent retirement savings vehicles for self-employed workers. Instead of maintaining a separate pension plan as is required with a Keogh, SEP contributions are deposited into your (and, if applicable your employees') IRA account(s). You may establish a SEP after the end of the tax year in which you want to begin taking the deduction as long as it is set up and funded before the following April 15. Generally, the amount you may contribute is 15 percent of your gross self-employment income, up to $30,000 per annum. You can also contribute to an IRA account on top of the SEP contribution. As with Keoghs, nondiscrimination rules apply if you have employees. Finally, older workers can still contribute to a SEP as long as they wish.

Individual Retirement Accounts

Everyone who has earned income is eligible to contribute to an IRA and enjoy the benefits of tax deferral. Unfortunately, not everyone can still deduct IRA contributions. IRA deductions are restricted only for individuals who are covered by an employer or a self-employed retirement plan, or—in the case of married couples—where either spouse is covered by a retirement plan. If either you or your spouse is an active retirement plan participant, you may still make a fully-deductible IRA contribution up to the contribution limits, so long as your Adjusted Gross Income (AGI) is $25,000 or less (or $40,000 or less if filing jointly). If you're a single filer and your AGI is between $25,000 and $35,000, (or if filing jointly, between $40,000 and $50,000) you may still make a deductible IRA contribution at a reduced level. Nonetheless, no matter what their tax situation, all workers can benefit from the tax deferral that an IRA provides. For most people, pension plans and personal savings are inadequate for their retirement needs and a well-managed IRA can provide an important income supplement in the future.

Other Matters That May Need Attention

EXCESS DISTRIBUTIONS

The Internal Revenue Code imposes a 15 percent tax on so-called excess distributions from qualified retirement plans, IRAs, and 403(b) annuity contracts. If you are fortunate enough to expect an annual income from your retirement plan(s) in excess of $150,000 and/or you expect to take a lump sum distribution in excess of $750,000, the IRS will throw a bit of a wet blanket on your good fortune. Consult an income tax professional if you think you might be exposed to the 15 percent tax. The threshold amounts will be indexed for inflation, so if you are many years from retirement, you may escape being subject to this tax.

MANAGING YOUR RETIREMENT PLAN INVESTMENTS

Depending on your situation, you probably are responsible for managing part, if not most or all of your retirement plan investments. If you are managing your own retirement investments, you should summarize *all* of your investments periodically, i.e., your retirement plan investments and your personal investments. You cannot make investment decisions intelligently without knowing the status of **all** of your investments. The approach to managing retirement-earmarked investments shouldn't be any different from managing your other investments. The following suggestions may be helpful for managing your investments prudently:

- Diversify.
- Change your portfolio allocations to reflect your changing circumstances.
- Use the tax rules to your advantage.

Diversify. Your total portfolio should consist of appropriate portions of stock, interest-earning, and, perhaps, real estate investments. If you find that most of your investments are concentrated in a single investment category, you are probably either taking too much or too little risk.

Change Your Portfolio Allocations to Reflect Your Changing Circumstances. Perhaps within 10 years of retirement, you should gradually begin to increase the proportion of your total investment portfolio (not just retirement funds) to more conservative, interest-earning investments. As you age, your investment horizon narrows: you begin to have less time to make up for a downturn in the stock market, which, as we all know, happens from time to time. You still need to maintain a good-sized proportion of stocks in your retirement portfolio, however, stock investments will continue to be important well into your retirement years. Why? Inflation doesn't go away when you retire, and stocks provide the best hedge against rising prices.

Use the Tax Rules to Your Advantage. You can minimize current income taxes somewhat by loading up your retirement plan investments with highly taxed securities and concentrating your personal investments in tax-advantaged securities.

EXAMPLE: Dr. Toothman, a dentist, has $1,000,000 in investments—half in her Simplified Employee Pension plan and half in her personal portfolio. She likes to buy and hold stocks, U.S. savings bonds, and both stock and corporate bond mutual funds. Rather than mix up these investments among her SEP plan and her personal portfolio, she should load up the SEP with stock and bond mutual funds and emphasize individually-purchased stocks and savings bonds in her personal portfolio. This strategy will minimize the income taxes she will have to pay on her investment income. Although stock and corporate bond mutual funds are highly-taxed investments since they pass on dividend and interest income and realized capital gains to the investor, this income will not be taxed as long as these investments are in her SEP. However, individually-owned stocks are tax-advantaged insofar as no capital gains are paid until they are sold. Since Dr. Toothman likes to buy and hold, she can benefit from keeping stocks in her personal portfolio and letting them appreciate in value without paying any taxes. Similarly, interest on U.S. savings bonds can accumulate tax free until they mature so she is quite correct to keep them in her personal portfolio.

Retirement Plan Withdrawal Choices

Next to choosing the type of retirement plan that's best for you, your biggest decision is how you want your benefits paid out. Actually, depending on the type of plan, you may have no choice in the matter. Most pension plans, for example, pay benefits only in the form of an annuity. However, you may have a choice as to the type of annuity you want to establish.

Plans such as 401(k)s and profit-sharing arrangements, will often give you the choice of receiving your money as a lump sum or as an annuity. Each option has its advantages and disadvantages. An annuity, for instance, is a "get-it-and-forget-it" deal since it's guaranteed to last for your lifetime. However, interest on annuity payments may not keep up with inflation, thereby eroding the purchasing power of your money.

A lump sum, however, can be put into growth investments, which enables your money to keep pace with inflation. But if your investment turns sour, you could end up putting your retirement plan in financial jeopardy.

Choosing Between a Lump Sum and an Annuity

While some pension plans require you to take an annuity when you retire, your plan may allow you the option of taking a lump sum payout. There may be some advantage to taking a lump sum, but this option must be considered carefully.

If the monthly payments provided by an annuity are not adjusted for inflation (most are not), and if you are confident that you or your investment advisor can invest the lump-sum amount more profitably, then the lump-sum option may be a good choice if it is available. You'll probably be able to generate more income than the annuity and at the same time cope better with inflation. There may be a serious drawback to taking a lump sum, however. If you or your spouse should incur substantial uninsured medical expenses (e.g., a long-term hospital or nursing home stay) or should otherwise be subject to the claims of creditors or the mismanagement of money that may occur in old age, your lump-sum retirement fund may be jeopardized. In the worst instances, this could seriously erode or altogether wipe out your pension resources. This eventuality must be weighed carefully in deciding on the lump-sum option as opposed to an annuity. Money that is in an annuity is usually protected from these adverse occurrences. If you opt for an annuity, don't necessarily take the first one that's offered to you. Payout rates on so-called immediate pay annuities vary widely. Shop around for the company that offers the most attractive terms. If you take a lump sum, you have some homework to do as well. You may be able to take advantage of forward averaging to reduce the tax impact of the distribution, or, if you can afford it, you can further postpone taxes on the plan distribution by rolling it over into an IRA. This way, you won't pay tax until you begin withdrawing money from the IRA.

Combining Annuities with Lump-Sum Payments

Depending on your type of retirement plan, you may find that the most appropriate route is to take a partial lump-sum settlement and while purchasing an annuity with the remainder. For example, if your profit-sharing account balance is $200,000 at retirement, you could take $70,000 in a lump sum and use the $130,000 balance to buy an annuity that pays you fixed income for life or for a set period of years.

Whichever method you choose, you must first consider not only your own financial needs but the tax consequences as well. Here's a look at how these distributions are taxed.

How Pension Income Is Taxed

If your employer funded the entire cost of your retirement plan, then your monthly pension checks are fully taxable. However, if your plan required you to make contributions out of your own pocket to supplement the company's plan contributions, you can recover your own invested dollars without any tax cost.

How It Works

If your pension income for the first three years of distributions comes to less than the gross amount you contributed, your pension checks are tax-free until you have recovered your contributions. From that point on, all your pension is taxable.

If you don't meet the three-year rule, part of each pension check representing your employer's contribution will be taxable, and part representing your own contribution will be tax-free. Your company will let you know how much of each pension check is taxable.

Electing Out of Withholding

Your company will withhold federal income tax on your pension checks unless you elect out of withholding. If you don't, tax is withheld from your pension check as if it were your salary. In other words, the amount withheld will depend on the number of exemptions claimed on your withholding certificate.

How Lump-Sum Distributions Are Taxed

If you receive your account as a lump sum at retirement, you can take advantage of one of two tax-saving devices:

1. Forward averaging or
2. Rollover into an IRA.

Forward Averaging. If you were born before 1936 and have been a member of your plan for at least five years, you may qualify for special 5- or 10-year forward averaging. In that case, your lump sum is taxed as ordinary income. However, the tax is figured as if the income had been received over 5 or 10 years.

If you became a member of your plan before 1974, you may be able to treat that part of your payout as capital gain, and use 10-year averaging for the remainder. In that case, each portion is taxed differently.

The pre-1974 portion is taxed as long-term capital gain. The advantage here is that since it's capital gain, the amount can be offset by capital losses. The remaining, or post-1973, portion is taxed as ordinary income using the averaging rules.

IRA Rollover. The second option available to you when you receive the distribution is to roll it over into an IRA (within 60 days of payout). There is no limit on the amount of cash you can put into an IRA rollover account. The advantage to this method is that you owe no current tax on the payout. The tax is payable only as you withdraw from your IRA.

Using the rollover break enables you to earn money by investing your payout. For example, if you took a $200,000 lump-sum distribution and use 10-year forward averaging, you end up with an after-tax figure of $161,970. Invested at, say, a 9 percent return, the sum would earn you $14,577 a year.

However, if you rolled over your lump sum into an IRA, the entire $200,000 would be available for investment. At the same 9 percent interest rate, you would earn $18,000 annually.

Keep in mind that all amounts withdrawn from an IRA are taxed as ordinary income and are not eligible for special tax breaks other than five-year averaging.

Required Starting Date

Generally, distributions must begin by April 1 of the year after the year you reach age 70½, even if you're not retired. In other words, taxpayers who become 70½ in 1990 must start withdrawals by April 1991. A special rule applies if you become 70½ before 1988. You can continue working past the year you were 70½ and not start pulling down withdrawals until April 1 of the year after you retire. You follow a slightly different rule if you own 5 percent or more of the company with the retirement plan. In that case, you must start withdrawals by April 1 of the year after you reach 70½, even if you don't retire, regardless of when you become 70½.

How Lump-Sum Annuity Combinations Are Taxed

You may want your retirement plan to do two things: (1) supply a lump of cash for certain immediate financial needs, and (2) provide a source of income during retirement. You can do this, if your plan permits, by taking part of your payout in cash and part in an annuity. If so, here's how your money will be taxed.

- You can use special 10-year averaging on the ordinary income portion of the payout—generally, the payout attributable to post-1973 plan participation. This is because you are considered to have received a lump-sum payment (your entire balance) even though the annuity won't be paid until future years.
- Even though your annuity is considered to be part of a lump-sum distribution, you don't pay tax on the annuity until you receive the payments. The tax on the ordinary income portion of the distribution is computed on the cash plus the current actuarial value of the annuity. The amount of tax is then reduced by the portion of the tax attributable to the value of the annuity.

As a result, although your annuity contract is taken into account as part of the lump-sum distribution, it is not currently taxed. Instead, you pay tax on the annuity when you receive payouts.

Should You Take a Joint and Survivor Annuity?

The law requires you to take retirement plan benefits in the form of a joint and survivor annuity unless your spouse signs a waiver. With such an annuity your spouse is assured a steady monthly income if you predecease him or her.

Unfortunately, you and your spouse get a smaller monthly pension check with a joint and survivor annuity than you would with an annuity based only on your life expectancy—better known as a "single life annuity." And if your spouse dies first, you have taken the reduced benefit for nothing. There are no survivor benefits.

Alternative Method

You can get around this problem with a two-part strategy: your spouse waives the right to a joint and survivor annuity so that you can instead take a single life annuity at retirement. You then use the excess annuity payments (single life less joint and survivor) to buy a life insurance policy which names your spouse as the beneficiary.

The result of these actions is that you receive higher pension payments than you would with a joint and survivor annuity. If you survive your spouse, you can pocket the larger single life annuity payments and cash in the life insurance policy. If you don't survive your spouse, the life policy is sufficient to pay your surviving spouse an annuity equal to the joint and survivor annuity he or she would have received from your retirement plan had you not made the switch.

> EXAMPLE: Mr. Byrd is a 63-year-old employee of XYZ, Inc. Mrs. Byrd is 62. Based on current projections, Mr. Byrd will have $600,000 in his retirement plan at age 65. At 65, the Byrds would therefore be entitled to a monthly pension of $5,425 if they request a 50 percent joint and survivor annuity. If Mr. Byrd should predecease Mrs. Byrd, she would be entitled to $2,712.50 per month for the rest of her life.
>
> By electing a single life annuity, the Byrds increase their monthly benefit to $5,800. With the monthly excess of $375 ($5,800 − $5,425), the Byrds buy a $300,000 insurance policy on Mr. Byrd's life. If Mr. Byrd dies first, the life policy can buy a $2,700 monthly annuity for Mrs. Byrd—the same amount she would have received under the retirement plan's 50 percent joint and survivor option. If Mrs. Byrd dies first, Mr. Byrd can cash in the policy and pocket whatever small cash value the policy has accumulated. More important, he can keep receiving the full single life annuity payout of $5,800.

The above approach offers additional flexibility. Let's say Mrs. Byrd dies first. If Mr. Byrd decides he can get along quite nicely without having to cash in the life policy, he can make his children the beneficiaries and keep making the premium payments, providing them with an unexpected benefit.

But be wary. There are possible disadvantages to the strategy of using life insurance and waiving the right to a joint and survivor annuity. Unfortunately, these programs are heavily touted by the insurance industry, and they tend to minimize the disadvantages if they mention them at all. Some potential problems: You may not be able to keep up with the insurance payments, in which case the policy could lapse. Your surviving spouse may not be comfortable with or, at an advanced age, may be incapable of managing the life insurance windfall at your demise. Conceivably, he or she could be bilked out of the windfall. So while this alternative method may make sense for many retirees, be sure to evaluate it thoroughly before taking the irreversible plunge.

When Plans Are Over-Funded

Accumulating too much in your retirement plan can create a special problem. To limit the benefits of over-funded pension plans, Congress established a 15% surtax on the excess when distributions are more than $150,000 a year or assets add up to more than five times that sum (or $750,000). Both limits are to be indexed for inflation. There are ways to minimize the effects of this onerous surtax. Consult a tax professional.

How to Handle IRA Withdrawals

The IRS requires that withdrawals from an IRA start in the year after you reach age 70½ and that the minimum distributions be calculated using IRS life expectancy tables. There is a penalty for taking smaller payouts: you lose 50 percent of the dollars that you should have taken out.

Some rules designed to make withdrawals from an IRA easier stipulate that:

1. The first withdrawal can be made by December 31 of the year you reach age 70½ and successive withdrawals by the end of each year thereafter;
2. You can wait until the second year and make two distributions. The one for the prior year when you turned 70½ must be made by April 1, while the one for the current year need not be made until December 31.

When You Have More than One IRA

When you have two IRAs or are the beneficiary of one or more plans whose owners have died, the minimum withdrawal must be computed for each plan. However, you do not have to take out the minimum from each plan. Instead, you can continue the withdrawals and schedule the minimum payouts as you wish.

EXAMPLE: Sally has two IRAs, one with a bank and one with a mutual fund. She will be 70½ on February 1, 1994. Her minimum distributions for 1994 will be $4,000 from the bank IRA and $2,000 from the mutual fund. Thus, on March 1, 1995, she can withdraw $6,000 from either IRA or $3,000 from each or any other combination that totals $6,000. There is no penalty because the withdrawal covers the combined required distribution.

When Your Contribution Is Nondeductible

Withdrawals of nondeductible contributions call for careful bookkeeping, extra paperwork, and compliance with IRS Form 8606. This form is for reporting nondeductible contributions and the combined balance of all IRAs.

EXAMPLE. Adam, age 52, contributed $2,000 to his IRA during the years that these contributions were tax deductible. He receives a lump-sum payment from an employer-paid pension plan which he rolls over into an IRA. He continues to contribute $2,000 annually, but now this amount is not deductible because his income is above current deduction limits. Adam must report all contributions on Form 8606 with his income tax return.

At age 57, Adam withdraws $2,000 from his IRA and leaves $48,000. He cannot take out only the tax-free, after-tax contributions but must allocate his withdrawal between the nondeductible contributions and the taxable contributions. This ratio is 96 percent or $1,920 on which he has to pay as regular income tax plus a 10 percent penalty for early withdrawal. In the future, similar allocations must be made.

You May Be Entitled to Retroactive Pension Benefits

There was a time when many employers froze pension benefits for employees after they reached a certain age, usually 65. Companies that based the final amount of retirement benefits on the number of years the employee worked (a defined benefit plan) thus saved huge amounts of money because they did not have to credit older workers for the additional years they put in once they reached the designated cutoff age.

Although this was a classic case of age discrimination from an employee's perspective, it was legal until January 1, 1988 when Congress prohibited it. From that point, companies could no longer eliminate benefits on, or contributions to, an employee's pension on the basis of age.

IRA Ruling "Unfreezes" Benefits

But what about those workers who reached the cutoff age before 1988 and whose benefits were frozen even though they continued to work after January 1, 1988? The IRS has issued a notice in favor of such employees. The IRS stated that a company with a defined benefit plan has to base an employee's plan benefits on all his or her years of service, and it called for retroactive benefits for years of service before 1988. The Equal Employment Opportunity Commission (EEOC) went along with the IRS position. As a result, companies that have not already done so will have to go back and make the necessary adjustments to the retirement accounts of affected workers.

Who Is Affected?

You are affected if you worked at least one hour in 1988, you were over the "normal retirement age," and your benefit accruals were reduced or eliminated under a company's noncontributory defined benefit plan. However, if you quit or retired before 1988, your former employer doesn't have to make these retroactive calculations.

> EXAMPLE. Richard Walker, age 70, works for the AAA Company. AAA's defined benefit plan used to provide that benefit accruals would stop at age 65 so Walker's were frozen in 1983. Because of the IRS ruling, AAA has to go back and recalculate Walker's benefits to account for his years of service between 1983 and 1988. Walker will continue to accrue benefits as long as he works. However, had he retired in 1987, he would not be eligible for the retroactive calculation.

If you believe that you are affected by this IRS ruling, see the benefits manager of your company immediately. Even if you aren't sure whether your benefits or pension accruals were frozen, it pays to check to determine your status.

4

HOW TO MAKE SURE YOU GET EVERY PENNY OF YOUR SOCIAL SECURITY BENEFITS

THE SOCIAL SECURITY system was never intended to satisfy all retirement income needs, and in spite of the extraordinary amount that workers and their employers must now contribute to support the system, it will never do so. Instead, Social Security should be viewed as a supplement to other forms of retirement income that by themselves would barely keep you over the poverty level.

Your Social Security benefits represent a basic building block around which to design the rest of your retirement plan. It's one source of guaranteed income that you will never outlive. And although Social Security benefit increases don't always keep pace with inflation, neither are they fixed over your lifetime as many pension benefits are.

To make sure you get every dollar of benefits to which you're entitled and to help you forecast your other retirement income needs, it's vital to know what to expect from the Social Security system upon reaching retirement age. This chapter explains how the Social Security system works, how benefits are figured, and how you can get the biggest return on the Social Security taxes you pay into the system throughout your working years.

Who Is Covered and How the System Is Funded

Unless you've worked for the federal government since before 1984, or you work for some state and local agencies, certain nonprofit groups, or the railroad, chances are you're covered by Social Security. What this means is that a tax is withheld from your earnings (or due with your quarterly estimated tax payments if you're self-employed). By paying taxes into the Social Security system, you accumulate credit toward certain benefits.

It is a common misperception that what you put into Social Security is what Social Security will eventually pay back to you, with interest. In reality, the amount you pay in supports current retirees and other beneficiaries. Your benefits will be paid at least in part by future workers. Anywhere from 90 to 95 percent of all working Americans participate in the Social Security system, and one in six U.S. citizens is currently drawing benefits.

The Tax You Pay

During your working years, the Social Security tax is withheld from your earnings up to a maximum amount each year. Social Security does not tax anything over the taxable wage base, which is adjusted annually as average wages rise. Before 1991, the taxable wage base was the same for both Social Security and Medicare taxes. But the law was changed so that the 1.45 percent tax is now levied on a much larger amount of earnings. Taken together, the Social Security and Medicare taxes—a combined 7.65 percent rate —are known as the FICA (Federal Insurance Contributions Act) tax. FICA is the term you will find on your pay stubs and the W-2 form you get from your employer every year. If you are self-employed, you are taxed at twice the FICA rate, or 15.3%. However, half of this is tax-deductible on your income tax return.

Social Security Retirement Benefits

Social Security benefits are paid monthly, with the size of your checks based primarily on the amount you contribute to the system while working and your age at retirement. Your monthly benefit also increases after you retire because of annual cost-of-living adjustments.

Generally, people who reach age 62 after 1990 must pay into the

Social Security system for at least 40 "quarters" to be eligible for benefits. Before 1984, each quarter was any actual three-month period in which you earned a minimum amount (the quarter-of-coverage amount), which rises annually. Since then, you get credit for up to four quarters of coverage based on your earnings for the year—regardless of when during the year you earned the money.

Note that the earnings quarters do not have to be consecutive. If you leave the work force before you have enough credits to qualify for benefits, your credits will remain on your Social Security record. If you return to work later on, you can add more credits so you can qualify. However, for your family members to qualify for certain benefits, such as survivors' benefits, based on your tax contributions, you need to have both 40 quarters of coverage over your working career and be "currently insured." To be currently insured, you need to have earned at least six quarters of coverage during the 13 quarters immediately preceding your death or entitlement to benefits.

Certain groups, for example, employees of nonprofit organizations who were age 55 or older as of 1984 or anyone born before 1929, may qualify for benefits with fewer credits. And military personnel and veterans may be entitled to special credits based on their military service to help them qualify for Social Security. Contact the Social Security Administration (SSA) or Veterans Administration for full details.

Filing Social Security Claims

Social Security benefits are not paid out automatically when you reach a certain age. You must file an application or claim for benefits to initiate the monthly payment process. Unless you are receiving disability benefits, you should file a claim with your local SSA office at least three months before you would like your benefits to commence. You must apply in person or by phone, but you can do the rest by mail.

You can elect to begin receiving benefits as early as age 62, or you can postpone them until as late as age 70 for a higher monthly payment. Your actual date of retirement from your job or occupation is irrelevant, although for most people it's not a good idea to begin drawing benefits while you continue to work full-time because your earnings after you begin collecting Social Security may reduce your benefits.

To apply for benefits, you will need all of the following documents:

- Your Social Security card or a record of the number
- Proof of date of birth (driver's license, passport, birth certificate),
- Your most recent W-2 form and tax statement (so your latest earnings will be included in calculating your benefit amount),
- Veteran's discharge papers, if applicable,
- Divorce decree, if applicable,
- Checkbook or savings passbook (if you want your benefits deposited directly to your bank account—a very good idea).

You will need the originals of these documents or copies certified by the issuing office, but Social Security can make photocopies and return the originals to you. Don't delay your application because you don't have all the information. If you don't have a document you need, Social Security can help you get it.

If you aren't sure whether you qualify for a particular benefit, go ahead and apply for it. There's no penalty for trying, and Social Security will evaluate your eligibility.

How Big Will Your Benefits Be?

The amount of your benefit is based on your earnings averaged over most of your working career using a formula that places the greatest emphasis on wages in the most recent years of work. Higher lifetime earnings result in higher benefits. If you have some years of no earnings or low earnings, your benefit amount may be lower than if you had worked steadily. (See Table 4.1.)

Your benefit amount is also determined by the age at which you start receiving benefits. The earlier you start collecting retirement benefits, the smaller the size of your monthly payments for life. Once you start receiving benefits, the amount will be adjusted annually for inflation.

FREE BENEFIT ESTIMATE

The SSA will provide you with a personalized benefit estimate at your request. To find out approximately how big a monthly benefit you can expect and to check on the accuracy of SSA's record of your earnings, call 1-800-772-1213, and ask for Form SSA-7004, Request for Earnings and Benefit Estimate Statement. The SSA will send you a simple form to fill in and mail, and within three weeks or so you

Table 4.1. Projection of Approximate Monthly Benefits If You Retire at Full Retirement In 1992 and Had Steady Lifetime Earnings

		Your Earnings in 1991				
Your Age in 1992	**Your Family**	**$20,000**	**$30,000**	**$40,000**	**$50,000**	**$55,000 Or More[1]**
45	You	$ 878	$1,159	$1,302	$1,436	$1,491
	You and your spouse[2]	1,317	1,738	1,953	2,154	2,236
55	You	796	1,052	1,150	1,231	1,258
	You and your spouse[2]	1,194	1,578	1,725	1,846	1,887
65	You	748	977	1,038	1,081	1,088
	You and your spouse	1,122	1,465	1,557	1,621	1,632

[1] Use this column if you earn more than the maximum Social Security earnings base.
[2] Your spouse is assumed to be the same age as you. Your spouse may qualify for a higher retirement benefit based on his or her own work record.
Note: The accuracy of these estimates depends on the pattern of your actual past earnings, and on your earnings in the future.

should receive a statement of your complete earnings history along with estimates of your benefits for retirement at age 62, at full retirement age (which, as explained below, will be somewhere between age 65 and 67, for people age 50 and older today, depending on your age), and at age 70.

You'll also get estimates of disability and survivor's benefits that you, your spouse, and other family members might be entitled to in the event of your disability or death. These estimates can be extremely helpful in your retirement and financial planning.

What's more, it's a good idea to request these statements from SSA every few years to check the agency's record of your earnings and ensure that your earnings are being credited properly. Errors in wage reporting to SSA total billions of dollars each year.

When Should You Begin Drawing Benefits?

You can begin collecting Social Security retirement benefits as early as age 62 or as late as you like, although there's no reason to wait beyond age 70. It's important to recognize, however, that the age at which you sign up for benefits has a big impact on the size of the checks you will receive every month for the rest of your life. That's why it's vital to understand Social Security's rules on "normal" retirement age, early retirement, and delayed retirement.

NORMAL RETIREMENT AGE

Today, Social Security's normal retirement age—the age which you can begin drawing "full" or unreduced benefits—is age 65. But since people live longer today than they did when the age-65 rule was set, the law has been changed to gradually increase the normal retirement age for people born after 1937 until it reaches age 67 in the year 2027 (for people born in 1960 or later).

Thus, if you are age 55 or older in 1992 (that is, if you were born before 1938), you are not affected by the coming increase in the normal retirement age and can begin drawing unreduced Social Security benefits as soon as you turn 65. If you're between age 50 and age 55 or younger in 1992, however, you must wait a little longer to begin collecting unreduced benefits, as follows:

Year of Birth	Full Retirement Age
1938	65 years, 2 months
1939	65 years, 4 months
1940	65 years, 6 months
1941	65 years, 8 months
1942	65 years, 10 months
1943–1954	66 years

EARLY VERSUS LATE RETIREMENT

As mentioned earlier, the Social Security offers lower monthly retirement checks for early retirement. Since subsequent cost-of-living adjustments are based on your initial benefit amount, retiring before your normal retirement age means that your benefits will start low and lag farther and farther behind what they could have been. Benefits to a surviving spouse when the retired worker dies will be even lower.

The size of the early retirement benefit reduction, once again, depends on the year in which you were born and your normal retirement age for Social Security purposes. Even if your normal retirement age is later than age 65, you can still begin drawing benefits at age 62—although the penalty will be greater because you will be collecting benefits for a longer period before reaching your full retirement age. Thus, if your normal retirement age is 65, your age-62 benefit would be 80 percent of your full retirement benefit. For people born after 1959 whose normal retirement age is 67, however, the age-62 benefit is only 70 percent of the full retirement amount.

Here's a look at how the early retirement penalty works for people born before 1938 whose normal retirement age is 65:

If You Retire at This Age	You Get This Much of Your Full Retirement Benefit
62	80.00%
62 1/2	83.33%
63	86.67%
63 1/2	90.00%
64	93.33%
64 1/2	97.67%
65	100.00%

Delaying your retirement past your normal retirement age, however, currently increases benefits by 3% for each year that retirement is postponed up until you reach age 70, when delayed retirement credits stop. For people born after 1924, this delayed retirement credit will gradually be increased until it reaches 8 percent a year for those born in 1943 or later. For example, a person born in 1931 will get 105 percent of his or her full retirement benefit by delaying retirement until age 66, 110 percent at age 67 and so on. Here's a look at how the delayed retirement credit will increase in coming years:

Year You Reach Age 65	Benefit Boost per Year of Delayed Retirement
1982–1989	3.0%
1990–1991	3.5%
1992–1993	4.0%
1994–1995	4.5%
1996–1997	5.0%
1998–1999	5.5%
2000–2001	6.0%
2002–2003	6.5%
2004–2005	7.0%
2006–2007	7.5%
2008 or later	8.0%

What's the Best Retirement Age for You? Unfortunately, there's no easy answer that makes sense for everyone. Some people argue that it is advantageous to begin collecting benefits early since the aggregate amount of Social Security benefits you collect will exceed those of later retirees for many years. Drawing benefits early may make especially good sense if you don't need the money to meet living expenses and can invest it, because the return on your investments should exceed the benefit increases you would get from waiting longer to sign up for benefits.

Indeed, the most important consideration is whether or not Social Security benefits will make up a significant portion or all of your retirement income. If so, you should think long and hard about retiring early because—you may not be able to afford it over the long run, particularly as inflation begins to erode the purchasing power of the fixed portion of your retirement income. Two important tips:

1. If poor health forces you to retire early, look into Social Security disability benefits. If you qualify for these benefits, you will receive the same amount as you would for your full, unreduced retirement benefit instead of the smaller amount you collect before full retirement age.
2. Be sure to sign up for Medicare within three months of your 65th birthday—no matter when you decide to file for retirement benefits. Your monthly Medicare premiums can cost significantly more if you delay applying. (See Chapter 5 for more on Medicare.)

How Retirement Earnings Can Cut Your Benefits

The amount of unearned income you receive, such as dividends, interest, pension benefits, and the like, does not affect the amount of your Social Security benefit—no matter how old you are. However, your benefits may be taxed if your annual income exceeds certain limits, as explained below. (See also Chapter 17.)

What's more, money earned from full- or part-time employment or self-employment can take a big bite out of your Social Security benefits if you're under 70 years old. As you would imagine, this reduction—called the retirement earnings test—is extremely unpopular among working retirees. Note, however, that benefits for people age 70 and older are not reduced—regardless of income.

For beneficiaries aged 65 to 69, benefits are reduced $1 for every $3 of earnings above the annual exempt amount, which is adjusted each year as wages rise. Beneficiaries under age 65, who earn more than the exempt amount will have their benefits reduced $1 for each $2 of earnings above the limit. Starting in the year 2000, the age at which the benefit offset drops from 50 percent of excess earnings to 33% of excess earnings will increase as the retirement age increases.

HOW THE EARNINGS TEST IS HANDLED

When you first file for retirement benefits and at the beginning of each subsequent year, SSA will ask you to estimate your employment or self-employment earnings for the coming year and will base your benefit amount on that estimate. You are required to report any changes as they occur.

In January, SSA will send you an annual report (Form SSA-777) so you can compare your estimate with the amount you actually earned over the last year. If you earned more than you expected, you will have been paid too much in benefits. You can send Social Security a check for the amount you were overpaid, you can pay in installments, or you can have the amount deducted from your future benefits checks. If you earned less money than you expected, your next few benefit checks will include adjustments to make up the amount you were underpaid in the prior year.

It is generally wise to report any changes in your earnings as soon as they occur. Social Security receives a copy of the W-2 your employer sends the IRS. If you don't file an earnings report and your earnings were over the limit, or if you don't file an adjustment report and your earnings exceeded your estimate, you will owe Social Security a penalty in addition to the amount you were overpaid.

SPECIAL RULE FOR YEAR OF RETIREMENT

A special rule applies in the year you retire. Under this rule, you can receive an unreduced benefit for any month in which your wages do not exceed the special monthly limit (which is adjusted annually on the basis of average wage increases nationwide) and you do not perform substantial services in self-employment. This rule ensures that you will not be denied benefits in the months immediately following your retirement just because your earnings in the previous months of that calendar year already exceeded the annual earnings limit.

EXAMPLE: Edward Everett plans to retire on his 65th birthday, which falls on Halloween. At his current job, he earns $45,000 per year. After retiring, he will have no earned income. What benefits will Edward be entitled in November and December of the year he retires?

By the time he retires, Edward's earnings will already have exceeded the annual exempt amount. However, his retirement income will not exceed the special monthly limit. As a result, Edward is entitled to full benefits in November and December, because the monthly limit—rather than the annual limit—applies in the year of retirement.

Note that if other family members receive benefits based on your tax contributions and earnings record, their benefits will also be affected if your earnings exceed the exempt amount. However, if these other family members work, their earnings affect only their own benefits—not yours.

Benefits for Your Family

If your spouse is not eligible to receive retirement benefits based on his or her own work record, he or she can still receive monthly checks equal to up to half of your benefit amount. So together you can receive 150 percent of your individual benefit amount. If your spouse is eligible both for these spousal benefits or for benefits based on his or her own work record, your spouse will get the larger of the two—but not both.

Generally, your spouse can begin collecting these spousal benefits as early as age 62. However, your spouse's benefits will be reduced if he or she elects to receive them before his or her normal retirement age, 65. And your spouse can begin drawing spousal benefits even earlier than age 62 if a child is being taken care of who is under 16 or disabled. Note, however, that if you are age 62 or older but still working, your spouse cannot collect benefits until you begin drawing benefits, regardless of his or her age.

Other members of your family may also be eligible to receive benefits based on your work record when you retire, including:

- Your former spouse age 62 or older if the marriage lasted at least 10 years, you have been divorced at least 2 years, and your former spouse did not remarry prior to age 60 (the amount a former spouse receives will not affect the amounts you and your current spouse are eligible for);
- Dependent children under age 18;
- Dependent children age 18 to 19 if they attend elementary school or high school;
- Children of any age who were disabled before age 22;
- In certain cases, your dependent grandchildren.

No matter how many family members collect benefits based on your work record, your family's total benefits cannot exceed a Family Maximum Benefit, which is based on your benefit amount. Only your divorced spouse's benefits do not count toward your family maximum amount.

Other Benefits from Social Security

Retirement benefits for you, your spouse, and other eligible family members are only part of the package you get from your lifetime tax contributions. Social Security also provides monthly benefits should you become disabled and survivor's benefits to certain family members upon your death. The following is a quick overview of what's available. If you or your family members think you may be eligible for these benefits, get in touch with the nearest SSA office.

DISABILITY BENEFITS

Monthly income is available to those unable to work because of illness, injury, or other disabling conditions. Payments continue until age 65, at which time retirement benefits begin. For younger workers and the blind, the quarters of coverage requirements for disability benefits are less stringent than the eligibility rules for retirement benefits.

Note, however, that Social Security's definition of disability is tough. Basically, benefits are available only for people with mental or physical impairments lasting a year or more that prevent them from doing any substantial gainful work. Many private and other public disability plans set lower standards that enable disabled individuals to collect benefits when they are unable to perform their former jobs, even if only temporarily. Social Security also imposes a five-month waiting period for disability benefits, and benefits are reduced by the amount of any workers' compensation benefits received.

Table 4.2 shows approximate Social Security disability benefits for people at various ages and income levels.

SURVIVOR'S BENEFITS

Assuming you qualify for benefits based on your work record, Social Security survivor's benefits may be paid to your dependent surviving spouse, children, and even your parents in the event of your death. Survivor's benefits for your spouse are available as early as when your spouse reaches age 60 (age 50 if disabled).

Table 4.2. Approximate Monthly Benefits if You Become Disabled in 1992 and Had Steady Earnings

		Your Earnings in 1991				
Your Age	Your Family	$20,000	$30,000	$40,000	$50,000	$55,000 Or More[1]
25	You	$ 745	$ 987	$1,109	$1,231	$1,266
	You, your spouse, and child[2]	1,118	1,480	1,664	1,847	1,899
35	You	740	984	1,105	1,221	1,240
	You, your spouse, and child[2]	1,111	1,476	1,657	1,831	1,860
45	You	739	983	1,086	1,159	1,170
	You, your spouse, and child[2]	1,109	1,475	1,629	1,738	1,755
55	You	739	974	1,044	1,094	1,101
	You, your spouse, and child[2]	1,109	1,462	1,567	1,641	1,652
64	You	746	975	1,034	1,076	1,082
	You, your spouse, and child[2]	1,119	1,463	1,551	1,614	1,623

[1] Use this column if you earn more than the maximum Social Security earning base.
[2] Equals the maximum family benefit.
Note: The accuracy of these estimates depends on the pattern of your actual past earnings.

Table 4.3 shows approximate monthly benefits for the family of a worker who dies in 1991, based on the worker's age and income level.

Minimizing the Tax Bite on Your Benefits

Prior to 1985, all Social Security benefits were exempt from state and federal income taxes. Today, however, if your adjusted gross income (AGI) exceeds a certain threshold amount, you must pay tax on up to half of your benefits.

To figure the tax, add half of your Social Security benefits, all income derived from wages, taxable pensions, interest, dividends, and all other taxable income (except for certain lump-sum pension distributions taxed under five- or ten-year income averaging) plus tax-exempt interest such as from your muni bonds. If the total does

Table 4.3. Approximate Monthly Survivors Benefits if the Worker Dies in 1992 and Had Steady Earnings

		Deceased Worker's Earnings in 1991				
Worker's Age	Your Family	$20,000	$30,000	$40,000	$50,000	$55,000 Or More[1]
35	Spouse and 1 child[2]	$1,112	$1,476	$1,658	$1,840	$1,878
	Spouse and 2 children[3]	1,375	1,722	1,934	2,146	2,190
	1 child only	556	738	829	920	939
	Spouse at age 60[4]	530	703	790	877	895
45	Spouse and 1 child[2]	1,110	1,474	1,636	1,752	1,770
	Spouse and 2 children[3]	1,373	1,721	1,910	2,044	2,064
	1 child only	555	737	818	876	885
	Spouse at age 60[4]	529	$ 703	780	835	843
55	Spouse and 1 child[2]	1,108	1,462	1,566	1,640	1,652
	Spouse and 2 children[3]	1,372	1,705	1,828	1,914	1,927
	1 child only	554	731	783	820	826
	Spouse at age 60[4]	528	696	747	782	787

[1] Use this column if the worker earned more than the maximum Social Security earning base.
[2] Amounts shown also equal the benefits paid to two children, if no parent survives or surviving parent had substantial earnings.
[3] Equals the maximum family benefit.
[4] Amounts payable in 1992. Spouses turning 60 in the future would receive higher benefits.
Note: The accuracy of these estimates depends on the pattern of your actual past earnings.

not exceed $25,000 for single filers or $32,000 for married couples filing jointly, you don't owe any tax. If the total exceeds these limits, you pay tax on half of the excess or half of your benefits, whichever is less. By the way, if you're married, don't think about filing separately to lower your income. The maximum for married persons filing separately is zero, so you will have to pay tax on half of your benefits.

The only way to avoid or reduce this taxation is to reduce your "modified AGI," as the combination of regular AGI plus tax-free municipal bond interest is called. Depending on your circumstances, you may be able to accomplish this by switching from muni bonds and currently taxable investments into investments such as U.S. Savings Bonds, on which income is deferred until maturity or investment vehicles such as nondeductible IRAs and annuities that throw off no current income (or, when they do, each payment is part income and part tax-free return of your original investment).

Reducing your AGI may also make it easier for you to claim deductions for medical costs and other expenses that cannot be deducted unless they exceed a specified percent of your AGI. But don't go overboard trying to reduce your income tax liability or the quality of your investment portfolio may suffer.

Both SSA and the IRS offer free brochures and pamphlets that explain tax matters pertaining to Social Security benefits and help you determine your income tax liability.

A Note on Retiring Abroad

If you are a U.S. citizen, you can travel or live in most foreign countries without affecting your eligibility for Social Security benefits. More and more Americans today are retiring abroad so they can enjoy a lower cost of living while still receiving their U.S. Social Security and pension income.

If you're eligible for Social Security but are neither a U.S. resident nor a U.S. citizen, up to 15% of your benefits will probably be withheld for federal income tax. If you work outside the United States, different rules apply in determining if you can get your benefit checks.

Your Right to Appeal

Finally, if Social Security's records of your earnings don't match your W-2 forms, you can ask them to revise their records. And if you disagree with a decision made on your claim, you may ask the SSA to reconsider it. If you are still not satisfied, there are other steps you can take to press your claims, including, ultimately, challenging the agency in the federal courts. You also have the right to representation by an attorney or anyone else you choose. *Helpful Information:* Two fact sheets, "The Appeals Process" and "Social Security And Your Right To Representation" are available at no charge from your local Social Security office. They provide a full explanation of your rights and how the Social Security appeals process works.

5

BASIC INSURANCE: PROPERTY, CASUALTY, DISABILITY

MANY PEOPLE ARE underinsured. Many others are overinsured or inappropriately covered at a higher cost than necessary. While most people recognize how devastating a loss of life, home, or earning power could be to their families, only a few take well thought-out, informed steps to insure themselves against those possibilities. Yet having the appropriate insurance coverage can mean the difference between successfully coping with a financial emergency or being desperately ill-prepared for one.

For most people, basic insurance needs can be covered through a combination of life insurance, health insurance, homeowners or renters insurance, and automobile insurance. Working people also need to have disability insurance. And you should also consider your personal circumstances carefully to determine whether you would benefit from personal and/or professional liability insurance. For most retirees, risk coverage must be maximized to avoid jeopardizing their often fixed incomes. At the same time, however, premium payments shouldn't tax their resources too much.

This chapter focuses on property, casualty, and disability insurance coverage. Health and life insurance are discussed separately in Chapters 6 and 7, respectively, because many of the issues involved in buying life and health coverage change considerably at retirement.

Property and Casualty Coverage

Theft, fire, and natural catastrophes are ever-present risks for homeowners and apartment dwellers. Most people are aware of the importance of homeowner's insurance, but three out of four renters do not have insurance coverage.

Even if you have property insurance, you need to ensure that your coverage is adequate. For example, condominium and co-op owners should closely inspect the insurance carried by the owners' association for its restrictions and limitations, to be sure that their own condo or co-op policies leave no gaps in coverage. What's more, all homeowners and renters should review their policies periodically to ensure that your coverage keeps up with rising costs that steadily increase the replacement values of your home, furnishings, and valuables.

What's Covered

All homeowners insurance covers the same basic elements (although renter's and condominium owner's insurance, of course, does not cover the building). Basic coverage includes the following:

- The house itself, in the amount designated;
- Other structures on the property;
- Personal property and the general contents of the main dwelling, (usually up to 50 percent of the coverage on the main dewelling);
- Living costs above current expenditures incurred while repairing damages caused by an insured risk, (usually up to 20 percent of the coverage on the main building);
- Losses of personal property while away from home, including the possessions of children residing at school, (usually subject to specified limits and payable only under certain conditions);
- Personal liability up to a set maximum for each occurrence, (usually $25,000);
- Medical payment for injuries that occur on the premises, (up to a set maximum per occurrence, usually $500 per person);

- Damages to trees, shrubs, and plants, (usually up to 5 percent of the coverage on the main structure); and
- Damage to property of others, (usually up to a maximum of $250).

Of course, you can usually increase the policy limits on the various basic coverages listed above, if you need added protection albeit at increased cost.

REPLACEMENT COST COVERAGE

Your homeowners insurance should cover at least 80 percent of the *replacement value* of the home and any improvements you've made to it, while also allowing for annual inflation. However, the basic policy usually specifies that coverage is based on actual cash value or market value. Even policies that base payment on the house's market value may leave you underinsured because repair costs may rise faster than the home's market value. That's why replacement-cost protection is so important.

Insuring the house for the amount it would cost to replace it is usually 10 percent to 15 percent more expensive than the basic coverage, but it offers much more protection. Note, however, that insurers are not always willing to underwrite this insurance unless the house is covered to 100 percent of its replacement value as appraised by the company. Furthermore, such coverage on the main structure does not also cover the replacement cost of the contents. If you want to insure your possessions for their full replacement costs, that will cost you even more. Such coverage is normally available under a separate policy rider.

Replacement cost coverage for household contents is an extremely valuable option. This coverage pays to replace lost items new—rather than at their depreciated cost, known as "actual cash value." What's more, it avoids disputes with the insurer over the actual cash value of your losses and offers the peace of mind of knowing that you will suffer little or no economic loss in a claim settlement. Thus, such coverage is particularly appropriate for older people whose personal possessions are usually older and thus have a significantly lower actual cash value.

TIP: Examine your policy carefully and be sure you understand any and all restrictions. Many policies limit the amount of depreciation they will absorb to four times the actual cash value of the item. This restriction primarily affects items that depreciate quickly, such as appliances and clothing.

Standard exclusions

Household contents are normally insured up to 50 percent of the coverage on the main structure. For example, a policy that provides $90,000 of coverage on the structure would include insurance of $45,000 on household contents. This coverage may be increased to 70 percent at extra cost. And valuables are covered only up to modest limits unless you buy added coverage, usually for a marginal amount, by an endorsement (see below). The basic policy probably covers silverware up to $1,000, jewelry up to $500, and coins up to $100.

The following items are not normally covered by homeowner's insurance and should be insured separately or through riders to your homeowner's policy:

- Business-related property inside the house, including personal computers and other equipment used to run a home-based office;
- Automobiles;
- Aircraft or large watercraft;
- Rented and borrowed property or property entrusted to you for safekeeping, (except for losses resulting from fire, smoke, or explosion damage); and
- Damage from earthquakes or floods (although fires resulting from earthquakes are covered).

Injury or damage that you cause intentionally is not covered. Coverage can also be reduced or denied if you intentionally increase the risk of damage or loss. For private homes, for example, coverage can be suspended if you leave the house vacant for 30 consecutive days. The company may also suspend fire coverage or deny fire damage claims if you store an excess quantity of gasoline in the house or fail to fix a faulty gas line.

"FLOATERS" FOR VALUABLES

A so-called floater policy provides extra coverage for certain personal effects. For example, any valuables you keep at home should be professionally appraised and covered under a floater. A floater provides a specific amount of insurance for each covered object on an itemized basis, guaranteeing full replacement value and eliminating deductibles. The cost of this coverage varies from company to company but averages around $0.55 per $100 for silverware,

$1.75 per $100 for jewelry, and $0.50 per $100 for furs. Note that the coverage is likely to be more expensive in high-crime areas.

Floaters may be issued on either an "all-risk" or "named-peril" basis. Named-peril floaters provide reimbursement only for those types of loss listed on the policy. All-risk coverage eliminates the need to prove theft.

Since coverage is on an item-by-item basis, you will either need to provide sales slips for covered items or have the items professionally appraised. Unlike automobile insurance, the frequency of claims will not affect the premiums on a floater. However, the company can decline to renew a policy if it can prove excessive loss because of owner negligence.

INSURANCE FOR RENTERS AND CONDO OWNERS

The condominium association or your landlord generally insure only the structure not the contents against losses. So a renter's insurance policy is likely to be your only protection against the loss of personal belongings.

Yet only one out of four tenants buy renters insurance—even although it's among the least expensive type of personal property policies. Annual premiums should cost you between $100 and $200, depending on location and coverage. Tenant policies also provide some personal liability coverage. And tenants can expand their policy coverage by purchasing floaters and/or replacement cost coverage.

Seven Ways to Cut Your Home Insurance Costs

Premium savings are available from most major insurance carriers for policyholders who take the following steps:

1. Protect your property. Insurers give discounts for smoke detectors, alarm systems, and other security devices.
2. Tell the insurance company when you retire. If you are likely to spend more time at home during the day, the company may lower your premiums in exchange for discouraging theft.
3. Raise your deductibles.
4. Pay annually. It's usually cheaper on an annual basis than paying your premiums semiannually or quarterly.
5. Buy all your insurance from the same company. You may be able to get a package deal, but don't do it before you've comparison shopped the individual policies.

6. Quit smoking. Many insurance companies give nonsmokers' discounts on homeowners, disability, health, automobile, and life insurance. Plus, just think how much you're paying for cigarettes.
7. Don't hire a public adjuster unless necessary. This person's job is to help you evaluate your losses and settle with the insurance company. In exchange, the adjuster gets 10 to 15 percent of whatever you recover. Why not try to settle by yourself first? Then, if you have trouble with your claim or don't agree with the company's appraisal, you can hire the adjuster and pay him only for what he helps you recover over and above your initial settlement.

The Importance of Taking an Inventory

It's a common misperception to assume that if the contents of your home or apartment are insured for $100,000, the insurance company will automatically pay you $100,000 if your dwelling burns down and all contents are destroyed. In fact, the insurance company will reimburse you for losses *up to* $100,000, which is a very different thing. What this means is that it's vital to document what you own before anything goes wrong because you probably won't be able to do it from the ashes.

Your insurer should be able to supply you with suggestions on how to catalog your possessions. You should definitely take a household inventory. Record all identifying information, serial numbers and distinctive marks; the manufacturer, pattern and number of appliances and collectibles; and a complete description of all pieces of jewelry. Security analysts also recommend photographing all valuables—preferably using videotape or self-developing film so the photographs aren't processed by outsiders. A few companies offer videotaping services.

Figure 5.1, Personal Inventory Worksheet, can help you record the contents of your home. In the comments section, include information about the item's purchase price, the date of purchase, later appraisals, current condition and the like. Remember to include rugs, curtains or drapes, clothing and shoes, pots and pans, clocks and lamps, books, plants, and other easy-to-overlook items—in short, everything you would need or want to replace should you lose it all.

Most people worry more about their valuables. But if the house

Figure 5.1. Personal Inventory Worksheet

	Description	Comments
LIVING ROOM		
DINING ROOM		
KITCHEN		
BEDROOMS		

Figure 5.1. (Cont'd)

BATHROOMS

GARAGE/BASEMENT/ATTIC

PORCH/PATIO

burns down, you'll need help replacing the rest of your belongings, too. And every little bit adds up.

Disability Insurance

Disability is often the most overlooked area of insurance coverage, yet you are far more likely to become disabled than to die before you retire. Next to health insurance, disability insurance is probably your most important coverage during your working years. It replaces your wage income or a major part of it should you suffer a disabling accident or illness.

Most working people have disability coverage under Social Security. But Social Security disability benefits are difficult to qualify for and largely inadequate for people who want to maintain even a modest standard of living. And even if your employer provides long-term disability coverage, it may lack important policy features or provide insufficient benefits.

The older you get, the greater your chances of suffering a disability. So adequate disability insurance is particularly important for working people over age 50.

Naturally, your need for earnings-replacement insurance disappears after you retire. Most retirees eliminate disability insurance coverage altogether. In fact, if you have no work-related income, you cannot obtain disability insurance. But retirees who still have some work-related income often need this protection if they depend on these earnings to meet living expenses. They may need to modify or replace their former policies to ensure they will continue payments past age 65.

Here's an overview of the three primary types of disability protection—Social Security benefits, employer-sponsored coverage and private policies:

Social Security Disability Coverage

The Social Security Administration pays disability benefits under two programs: the Social Security disability insurance program and the Supplemental Security Income (SSI) program. The medical requirements for disability payments are the same under both programs and claims are handled by the same process. While eligibility for benefits is based on prior work in covered employment under Social Security, SSI disability payments are made on the basis of financial need.

Both programs pay cash benefits to people who suffer from disabling conditions that prevent them from working for a year or are likely to result in death. Benefits continue until a person is able to work again on a regular basis (or dies), and a number of work incentives are available to ease the transition back to work. Note that Social Security does not pay for partial disability or short-term disability.

WHO'S ELIGIBLE FOR BENEFITS?

You can receive Social Security disability benefits at any age. If you are receiving them when you turn 65, they become retirement benefits, but the amount will not change in most cases. Your spouse and other family members may also qualify for benefits based on your work record when you become disabled. And many disabled children qualify on their parents' records.

To qualify for Social Security disability benefits, you must have worked long enough and recently enough in employment covered by Social Security (see Chapter 3 for more on Social Security eligibility). The number of work credits needed for Social Security benefits depends on your age when you become disabled. In general, however, you must have worked 5 years out of the past 10 in covered employed, including the calendar quarter in which you become disabled.

Blind persons are subject to special rules. For example, they're allowed to earn more to supplement their benefits than other disabled persons. And even if their earnings are too high for them to qualify for disability benefits, they may also be eligible for a disability "freeze" that ensures that their future benefits will not be reduced because of relatively lower earnings during the time they were blind.

Added Protection. While Social Security disability payments are generally small (averaging $610 a month in 1992), qualifying for disability benefits automatically entitles you to Medicare after you've received monthly disability checks for two years. Medicare offers disabled people valuable protection against soaring health care costs.

HOW TO FILE A CLAIM

Social Security disability benefits commence in the sixth full month of disability. (No waiting period is required under SSI.) The claims process for disability benefits is generally longer than for other types of Social Security benefits—from 60 to 90 days. That's because it takes longer to obtain medical information and to assess the nature of the disability in terms of your ability to work.

However, you can help shorten the process by bringing certain documents with you when you apply. These include:

- The Social Security number and proof of age for each person applying for benefits. This includes your spouse and children, if they are applying for payments.
- Names, addresses, and phone numbers of doctors, hospitals, and other institutions that treated you, and the dates of your treatment.
- A summary of where you worked in the last 15 years and what you did.
- A copy of your W-2 form or your federal tax return for the past year.
- Dates of any prior marriages (if your spouse is applying).

If you are missing any of this information, the Social Security office will help you obtain it.

Remember: While Social Security disability benefits will help support you by replacing some of your former earnings, they will barely keep you above the poverty level. Thus, most people should obtain additional insurance to supplement Social Security, either through their employers, individually or both.

Employer-Provided Disability Insurance

If you're still working, you probably have some form of disability coverage at your place of employment, even if it's only workers' compensation. However, employer-provided group disability insurance, typically offers low monthly benefits and a short benefit period, (about two years in most cases). It usually does not offer adequate protection against disability by itself.

Additional long-term protection sometimes can be purchased through employers at a lower rate than would be available elsewhere. Another advantage of buying disability coverage through your employer is the generally easier standard for acceptance; a medical examination is not always required. Limited disability insurance may also be included in employer-sponsored health plans or life insurance plans.

Employer-sponsored disability insurance should be supplemented at your expense if it is not adequate to protect you and your family in the event of long-term disability. As a general rule of thumb, a policy or combination of employer and individually purchased policies that replaces 60 to 70 percent of earnings—after taxes—should be adequate. Keep in mind that disability benefits are tax-free if you pay your own premiums and taxable if your employer pays the premiums.

As you review your coverage, you should be aware that employer-sponsored policies may base the amount of disability insurance coverage on your base salary. If you have substantial income above your base salary, such as commissions and bonuses, additional disability insurance may be necessary to provide adequate income replacement in the event of long-term disability.

Also note that most employer-sponsored disability plans do not have inflation-adjustment provisions, and some lack coverage for partial disability. And if you pay the premiums yourself, you may be able to reduce your costs considerably by extending the waiting period before benefit payments begin, if this option is available. However, this tactic should be used only if you have sufficient savings to provide for the uninsured period.

Private Disability Policies

Disability insurance policies offered by private insurance companies differ widely in features and benefits. For example, some policies terminate coverage when the disabled individual can perform any occupation, while others continue paying benefits until you've recovered to the point where you can return to your former occupation. What's more, some policies offer indexed benefits that keep pace with inflation, while others do not. Indexing can make a considerable difference for someone who is permanently disabled. Private disability policies also can be structured with a rider to make additional payments equal to Social Security until Social Security benefits become available.

To help you sort through the wide variety of policy features, coverages and exclusions, here's a look at some of the most important policy terms and definitions you need to consider when shopping for private disability insurance:

KEY ISSUE: DEFINITION OF DISABILITY

Of special importance in choosing a disability policy is the definition of "disability," a concept much harder to pin down than "death" or "sickness." The wide range of definitions and the different risks associated with different occupations create a wide range of factors to evaluate in determining disability insurance needs. In general, however, disability insurance policies define disability either as the inability to perform one's own occupation or the inability to perform any occupation.

Under the first definition, disability benefits typically will be paid when the insured cannot perform the "usual and customary" duties of his of her occupation. Some policies tighten the requirements by defining disability as the inability to perform all of the duties of the insured's occupation. The distinction is crucial, for example, in the case of a computer programmer whose pre-disability income was more than $60,000 a year but who can earn only $20,000 as a consultant because of blindness.

The more stringent policies define disability as the inability to perform any job, regardless of how much income might be lost by having to accept an inferior position. For example, a surgeon who lost the use of her hands might still be able to teach, albeit at a much reduced salary. Any highly compensated professional would be foolish to purchase a policy that did not protect against the considerable loss of income he or she would likely incur in a lesser position.

That's why no matter how confusing or boring it may be it's extremely important that you read all the fine print in a disability insurance policy. And note that a policy that is offered without a medical examination requirement is likely to have the strictest definition of disability and may even refuse or terminate payment if the patient is not totally housebound. Even if you have health problems, don't purchase a policy offered without a medical examination, since there are usually better alternatives.

COVERAGE PERIOD

Very few policies start paying from the first day of disability. The usual waiting or elimination period ranges from one month to one year. Lengthening the period before benefits begin can cut your premium—sometimes substantially. It's like raising the deductibles on your auto insurance.

Since you would probably be able to make it through a short-term disability on your employee benefits, help from relatives, or your savings, it's often a good idea to lengthen the waiting period so that you can afford more coverage. Generally, the most coverage you can obtain (including your company policy, if any) is 60 to 70 percent of your income, and you should strive to obtain the maximum allowable coverage.

Most policies continue benefits until age 65, when retirement benefits usually begin. You can extend the payment period beyond age 65, but doing so will increase your premiums significantly. To reduce premiums, some policy holders reduce the payment period. But it's usually a better idea to increase the waiting period.

CAUSE OF DISABILITY

Many disability policies restrict payment based on the cause of the disability. Some, for example, cover disability resulting from accident but not from illness, even though disability is far more likely to result from illness than from accident. Your loss of income, however, is the same either way. From your point of view, it won't matter why you're no longer able to work or whether or not your disability is work-related.

> BOTTOM LINE: Try to purchase a policy that covers all disabilities—regardless of cause. Workers' compensation, of course, covers only work-related disabilities.

COST CONSIDERATIONS

As noted above, your premium costs will vary to some extent depending on the waiting and benefit periods you select and on the definition of disability used in the policy. Premium costs also depend on age, occupation, whether coverage is group or individual, and, in some instances, on your sex.

Sex-based premium variations are predicated on the fact that women are more likely than men to become disabled even when the possibility of pregnancy, abortion, miscarriage, and childbirth are excluded. However, most insurers have now developed unisex rate tables in response to consumer pressure and state laws. (Although women benefit from gender-neutral pricing on disability insurance, men benefit in life insurance.)

The odds of becoming disabled also increase sharply with age, and premium rates are set accordingly. Thus, disability coverage costs much more at age 60 than at age 50.

RENEWABILITY OF POLICIES

Since disability insurance premiums increase with age, and health conditions often worsen, a renewability clause is a valuable safeguard in a disability policy. There are three renewability classifications: class cancellable, guaranteed renewable, and noncancellable. Key differences:

- The insurance company can cancel class—cancellable policies at its discretion, provided it cancels all the policies in a given class, which may be a time or locale of issue.
- Guaranteed renewable policies are the standard choice. You will not lose your coverage, but the premiums may be increased as long as the company can prove the increase is not discriminatory.
- The insurance company cannot raise premiums or cancel coverage on a noncancellable policy.

COST OF LIVING INCREASES

Some policies adjust benefits to keep up with the cost of living. Usually this is accomplished by linking the payments to some index, such as the Consumer Price Index. Most limit the annual benefit increase to 5 percent and the total increase over the benefits payment period to 100 percent of the policy's face value. Some policies offer this feature as a rider. In a few, it's included.

TIP: If you don't plan to retire for awhile, you may be wise to pay extra for inflation-adjusted benefits. If retirement is near, or your insurance company stops payment at age 65 anyway, inflation may not be that big of a threat.

How to Compare Disability Policies

If you buy your own disability insurance, be prepared—a comprehensive policy will be quite expensive. But whether you're shopping for an individual policy or merely want to check the adequacy of your employer-provided plan, it helps to familiarize yourself with the various available features and standard limitations of disability insurance policies. The following checklist-sums up the most important issues to consider when comparing various policies:

- What's the policy's definition of total disability:
  —during the initial period?
  —after the initial period?

- Is the contract noncancellable and guaranteed renewable to age 65 with guaranteed level premiums?
- Can coverage be continued on a conditionally renewable basis to age 75 if you continue to be employed full-time?
- Is a proportional benefit included for partial disability?
- Must the number of days needed to establish disability be continuous?
- Will the policy pay "residual benefits" to supplement your income if you are able to return to work but only at a reduced level?
- Is there a presumptive total disability clause that starts on the day of a specified loss and provides for lifetime payments whether you work or not?
- What waiver of premium provisions does the policy include? (In other words, do you have to keep paying premiums if you become disabled and are receiving benefits?)
- What are the standard exclusions?
- When, if ever, does the policy become incontestable?
- Does the policy include a rehabilitation benefit?
- Are lifetime benefits for total disability included?
- Is a nonsmoker discount available?
- Are benefit payments indexed for inflation?
- Does the policy pay Social Security substitute benefits?
- Is additional regular disability coverage available on an annually renewable, increasing premium basis?

Automobile Insurance

Auto insurance rates have been skyrocketing—but maybe not as much as you think. Most people pay too much for car insurance. With a little effort (and by taking on a little more risk), you can trim your annual auto insurance bills.

THE SECRET TO SAVINGS: When your policy comes up for renewal, don't just continue the same coverage. Shop around among different insurers, and look for ways to save. Increasing your deductibles, driving a more conservative car, and dropping expensive policy options can pay off in lower premiums.

It pays, for example, to drop collision insurance on older cars. The insurer won't pay more than the car's fair market value to repair it. Also, ask about discounts for driver's education or defensive—driving courses, teetotalers, nonsmokers, off-street parking, car-poolers, low-mileage usage, public transportation users, automatic safety devices (such as airbags or seatbelts that wrap around you automatically), antilock braking, and antitheft devices.

And don't forget to tell your insurance agent about any changes in your use of your car. If you use your car to commute to work, for example, your premiums may go down when you retire. Also, if you move away from the urban area where your job was based, your rates will probably change. They'll usually be much lower in the country than in the city.

Finally, if you've ever even considered not filing a claim with your insurance company for fear it would raise your rates, ask your agent for a detailed written statement of which claims affect your rates. You may be paying for accidents that wouldn't affect your rates. Since you're already paying for them in your premiums, it's certainly worth finding out.

What's more, if the insurance company discovers you have withheld information, it could terminate your policy. Even if it doesn't, by not giving notice of an accident, you may forfeit certain policy rights, such as a legal defense, in the event of a subsequent lawsuit.

Personal Liability Insurance

Extended personal liability insurance, also called umbrella insurance, is one of the most frequently overlooked gaps in insurance coverage. The coverage is called extended because it supplements the liability coverage provided by your homeowner's or renter's policy and by your automobile insurance. Umbrella insurance is coordinated with these other policies, so you may have to increase the liability limits on them before qualifying for the umbrella. Umbrella insurance also extends your liability coverage to incidents that don't take place in your home or car.

If you don't have extended personal liability insurance, you are jeopardizing your current assets and perhaps even your future income. Here's why:

Spurred on by higher and higher awards in court actions, injured parties—whether those injuries are real or fancied—have become more willing to press claims against others for individual acts. When a defendant's assets are insufficient to pay a judgment, the court may award the plaintiff a portion of the defendant's future earnings.

Umbrella policies typically protect you and your family (including children away at college and pets) from claims such as damage or personal injury, libel, slander, false arrest and, invasion of privacy. Of course, the insurance company will pay only if the damage was unintentional—due to negligence, for example, such as when someone slips on your icy sidewalk. But if your failure to shovel the sidewalk causes injury more than once, you can be slapped with punitive damages that you (not the insurance company) will have to pay. And the insurance company could try to alter or cancel your policy. Coverage under most umbrella policies includes legal-defense costs, but it's important to understand the exclusions written into them.

Umbrella coverage is relatively inexpensive. Annual premiums for $1 million in liability insurance generally run between $100 and $200. Many insurance experts feel that $1 million in personal liability coverage is too little in this litigious age. They suggest that $2 million or even more is desirable.

> KEY POINT: Umbrella insurance is crucial for everyone—working or retired. Don't jeopardize many years of hard-earned savings by going without it.

Professional Liability Insurance

It's important to understand that personal umbrella insurance does not cover liabilities arising out of any job-related activities. You should make sure that your job does not expose you to professional liability claims.

If you're concerned about the risk, first check with your employer to see if the company indemnifies you against such claims. If not, you may need to obtain professional liability coverage. If you're uncertain, check with an insurance professional who is experienced in professional liability insurance.

Many people, particularly those who are retired, are actively involved in volunteer work. While some types of volunteer work (for example, those where you are responsible for handling money) may expose you to possible liability, most volunteer activities do not require liability insurance. Umbrella policies, however, do not cover volunteer activities.

SUGGESTION: If you're concerned about possible liability exposure from volunteer activities, check first with the organization to which you're volunteering your services. It may already have insurance.) And, if it doesn't and you're still concerned that you could become the "deep pocket" for someone injured or even dissatisfied with the organization's activities, consult with your attorney.

6

YOUR PROTECTION AGAINST RISING HEALTH CARE AND NURSING HOME COSTS

FOR A GREAT many people age 50 and over, health care heads the list of worry-inducing topics. Indeed, it appears that the physical ailments that often accompany aging cause less concern than do the financial implications of having to pay for treating those ailments. The question of how to pay for healthcare takes on particular urgency for people who lack the benefit of an employer-paid health insurance plan or a good Medicare Gap (or "Medigap") policy.

For people age 65 and over, Medicare provides relief from high healthcare costs. But Medicare often comes up short. As a result, individuals must pay a substantial portion of supposedly "covered" medical expenses. The fact is that Medicare payments have simply not kept up with rapidly rising health care costs of health care. While the health care crisis has become so acute that it has even caught the attention of our politicians, an immediate cure does not appear to be on the horizon.

The challenge for all people approaching or over age 50, then, is to ease this financial burden by learning how to supplement Medicare coverage with such other medical insurance plans as Medigap and long-term care policies. By carefully reviewing insurance coverage at retirement, you can make sure that you are paying only for the coverage you actually need and that you pay as little as possible for that coverage. If you take the time to educate yourself and plan accordingly, you can achieve maximum coverage at minimum cost.

Understanding Medicare

Whatever its deficiencies, the fact remains that Medicare is the core of most retirees' medical coverage. Ideally, the Medicare program provides healthcare benefits to every American over age 65 who is eligible for Social Security, plus certain disabled persons.

Medicare consists of two parts: Part A pays for the costs of a hospital stay—it's free for everyone who is automatically eligible for Social Security. Part B is an optional medical insurance plan designed to pay doctors' bills. Like any insurance plan, Medicare Part B participants pay a monthly premium. These premiums are automatically deducted from your monthly Social Security check.

Enrolling in Medicare

You can sign up for Medicare Part A (hospitalization) coverage any time around or after your 65th birthday. Applications for Part B, however, must be submitted within special enrollment periods. Fortunately, the Part B enrollment rules don't present a problem for most people. If you retire early on Social Security or sign up for Social Security and Medicare right before you retire, your Part B coverage should begin right when you need it. If you delay enrolling in Medicare Part B, you will likely pay a surcharge on your premiums. Furthermore, you may have to wait as long as a year or more for your Part B coverage to begin. The following Medicare enrollment policies should be familiar to every preretiree who wants to ensure full Part A and Part B coverage.

- **Enroll between the beginning of the ninth month of your 65th year and the end of the fourth month of your 66th.** The federal government gives you a seven-month window of opportunity to enroll in Medicare (generally, at age 65) called the "initial enrollment period." If you sign up during the first three months of this period, your Part B coverage will begin in the month you first become eligible for benefits. If you sign up during the last three months of this period, your coverage will begin up to three months later.

- **If you miss the initial enrollment period, you must enroll during the next "general enrollment period."** If you don't sign up for Part B during your initial enrollment period, you must wait until the next general enrollment period to apply. The general enrollment period runs from January 1 to March 31 of each year. If you sign up for Part B during this period, your coverage will begin the following July.
- **Late Part B enrollees will be penalized.** The basic Part B premium is indexed to the overall cost of healthcare as calculated by the federal government. Individuals who don't enroll within a year after first becoming eligible for Medicare benefits pay a 10 percent penalty for each year they delay signing up for Part B. Thus, a person who waits until age 70 to enroll may pay 50 percent (10 percent times 5 years) more for Part B coverage than someone who signs up at age 65. Worst of all, the premium surcharge continues for life.
- **If you retire after age 65, you may be exempt from the late enrollment penalty.** If you continue to work after you've reached retirement age, and are covered by an employee health plan, you may escape this penalty. While you continue to work, you can elect to keep the company health insurance and postpone enrolling in Medicare Part B. Essentially, you will postpone your initial enrollment period to the time you finally do retire. (Or, if your company-plan coverage is based on your spouse's employment, at the time he or she retires.) If you don't sign up during this special deferred enrollment period, you will have to sign up during the next general enrollment period. You would then be subject to the late-enrollment penalty.

Even if you plan to continue working past age 65 and will be covered by your company health plan until you retire, you might still want to enroll in Medicare Part A around your 65th birthday. After all, Part A coverage is free. You pay for it with the Social Security taxes withheld from your paychecks throughout your working years. And Medicare Part A may pay for some hospitalization costs that aren't covered under your company plan. You can then sign up for Part B—without a late-enrollment penalty—when you retire.

However, should you plan to retire at age 65, be sure to contact your Social Security office a month or more before your 65th birthday to find out exactly how the Medicare enrollment rules affect you. If you want your Medicare coverage (or Social Security retirement benefits) to begin as soon as you turn 65, file your application three months early to ensure that you don't have to wait for your benefits to begin.

What Medicare Covers

Like any private insurance plan, Medicare covers some procedures, medicines, and doctors' bills and doesn't cover others. It is important to know the ins and outs of the system to avoid unpleasant surprises.

Part A Coverage: Under Part A, you pay a one time deductible for the first 90 days of inpatient hospital care; Medicare pays the remainder of your covered costs. For days 61 through 90, Medicare pays all covered services except for a daily coinsurance charge. For hospitalization longer than 90 days, you can draw upon a lifetime reserve of 60 days of coverage. When reserve days are used, you pay a coinsurance charge. These reserve days are not renewable.

Benefits periods begin the first day you receive Medicare-covered service in a hospital, and end when you have been out of a hospital or skilled nursing facility for 60 consecutive days. If you enter a hospital again after 60 days, a new benefit period begins.

The following list enumerates the common medical expenses covered under Medicare Part A:

- **Medically necessary inpatient care in a hospital room.** Unless a private room is necessary be prepared to share a room if you plan to have your hospital stay covered by Medicare.
- **Medically necessary inpatient care in a skilled nursing facility**
- **Hospice care.**
- **All services customarily furnished by hospitals and skilled nursing facilities.** Private nursing, private rooms (unless medically necessary), or convenience items such as a telephone or television are not covered by Medicare.
- **All but the first three pints of blood received during a calendar year.** You cannot, however, be charged for blood if it is replaced by a blood plan or through a donation on your behalf, or if you have met the Part B deductible for the year.
- **Skilled Nursing Facility (SNF) Care.** Medicare Part A pays for 100 days of care in a skilled nursing facility during the

calendar year. For the first 20 days, Medicare pays 100% of the approved cost. For the next 80 days, the patient must pay a coinsurance charge.

To qualify for Medicare coverage in a SNF, an individual must have been in a hospital for at least three consecutive days, not counting the day of discharge. Generally, admission to a SNF must be within 30 days of the discharge. A physician must certify that nursing home care is necessary and will treat the same condition which originally brought the patient into the hospital. Finally, the SNF must be Medicare certified.

- **Home health care.** Part A pays the cost of medically necessary home health care for homebound beneficiaries. Covered services include:
    - Occasional visits by a skilled nurse.
    - Physical, occupational, and speech therapy and medical social services provided by Medicare-certified professionals.
    - 80 percent of the cost of physician-approved durable medical equipment.

Not covered are such services as full-time nursing care, drugs, home-delivered meals, homemaker services, or assistance in meeting personal or housekeeping needs.

Part B Coverage: Medicare Part B pays 80 percent of the "reasonable cost" of all covered physicians' services, while the enrollee pays the remaining 20 percent as coinsurance. In addition, Part B participants pay an annual deductible fee. Covered expenses under Medicare Part B include:

- **Physicians' and surgeons' services regardless of where they are provided.**
- **Home healthcare visits for persons who are not covered under Medicare Part A.** People who are ineligible for Medicare Part A can have medically-necessary covered home health visits paid for under Part B. There are no deductibles, but the enrollee must pay 20 percent of the cost of durable medical equipment supplied under the home health benefit.
- **Physical therapy and speech pathology services obtained either as an outpatient or at home.**
- **Outpatient prescription drugs furnished to hospice patients.**

- **Drugs administered by physicians and immunosuppressants provided during the first year after an organ transplant.**
- **Medical services and supplies such as outpatient hospital services, X-rays, laboratory tests, certain ambulance services, and the purchase/rental of durable medical equipment such as wheelchairs.**
- **Second opinions.** If you are ever facing the prospect of major surgery, you should always get a second opinion before going ahead with the operation. The designers of Medicare recognize this fact and will cover the cost of obtaining an informed second opinion. You can get the names of Medicare-certified physicians in your area by calling the "Medicare Hotline" (1-800-638-6833).

A vexing problem that Part B participants often encounter is the discrepancy between the Medicare-defined "reasonable cost" of medical supplies and services and what you actually pay for these items. Suppose you are charged $1,000 for a standard procedure whose "reasonable" cost Medicare has already set at $750: you will have to pay $400 of the bill yourself. (Medicare will calculate its 80 percent share on the reasonable cost—$750—leaving you to pay 20 percent of $750, or $150, plus **all** of the remaining $250.)

One way to close the gap between the Medicare-approved cost and your out-of-pocket expense is to find a doctor who accepts assignment. In that case, the doctor will agree to accept Medicare's reasonable amount as full payment for the medical procedure involved, and agrees not to bill you for anything above that amount. You can obtain "The Medicare Participating Physician/Supplier Directory" through your local Social Security Office: all the physicians listed in this booklet accept assignment. In those cases where you can't find an appropriate physician who accepts assignment, federal and state guidelines limit how much you can be charged.

What Medicare Does Not Cover

Just as with most private health insurance policies, there are a number of items that Medicare does not cover under either Part A or Part B. They include:

- Private duty nursing.
- Routine physical exams.

- Skilled nursing home care beyond 100 days per benefit period.
- Custodial nursing home care.
- Intermediate nursing home care.
- Most outpatient prescription drugs.
- Medical care received outside the United States, except under limited circumstances in Mexico and Canada.
- Dental care and dentures.
- Routine immunization.
- Cosmetic surgery.
- Routine foot care.
- Optical examinations for eyeglass fittings.
- Aural examinations for hearing aids.

DISPUTING YOUR MEDICARE BILL

If you feel that your doctor is overcharging you, call the local Medicare office to ask for a full explanation of your bill. If you find the explanation unsatisfactory, you can obtain and file a "Request for Review of Medicare Part B Claim." This automatically entitles you to a more detailed examination by the Medicare Review and Adjustment Unit which will report in 6 to 8 weeks as to whether it upholds the original decision or agrees with your viewpoint.

If the Unit turns you down and the amount in dispute is over $100, you can request a hearing before an administrative law judge in your Medicare region. Plaintiffs usually represent themselves at these hearings: Generally, there is no need to hire a lawyer, unless the sum in question is large. Disputed sums over $1,000 can be appealed to federal court.

Health Insurance for the Early Retiree

The high cost of private health insurance is a big deterrent to early retirement. If you retire before age 65—when Medicare coverage begins—you'll need to secure private coverage unless your company extends its employee health-plan to early retirees. In this day of corporate downsizing and restructurings, early retirement may often be less a choice than an order—its either accept the package or be laid off.

COBRA—Safeguard of Your Insurance Coverage

Fortunately, federal law ensures continuing group health coverage for most ex-employees and their dependents. In 1985 Congress passed the Consolidated Omnibus Budget Reconciliation Act (COBRA), which directs businesses with more than 19 employees to give employees and their family members the option of continuing group health coverage for at least 18 months after termination. (Unless, of course, the employee has been fired for misconduct). Terminated employees who elect to take the continuing coverage must pay the entire premium plus an administrative surcharge (up to 2 percent of the monthly premium). Nonetheless, even with this surcharge, group insurance rates are much lower than those of individual policies.

Should you leave your job because of disability, you must receive up to 29 months of continuing health insurance coverage under COBRA's provisions. This feature of the law protects disabled individuals until Medicare benefits become available. Social Security and Medicare benefits for disabled people under age 65 don't begin until 29 months after the onset of the disability, so COBRA plays an important role for these individuals. Disabled persons should be aware that employers do have the option of raising disabled employees' premiums by as much as 50 percent from the base price during the last 11 months of the 18-month period.

In addition, should you die while still employed, COBRA requires your employer to continue covering your dependents for the 36 months following your demise. The law also mandates that group coverage be continued for you and your dependents under a variety of other circumstances: check with your local Social Security Office to learn how the law may apply to you.

Private Insurance: Filling the Gaps in Medicare

While Medicare provides an important health care "safety net" for retired Americans, this net contains several large holes through which you might someday fall. By purchasing a supplemental Medicare Gap or "Medigap" insurance policy, however, you can ensure that whatever healthcare problems you encounter as you age, your finances will remain secure. As its name implies, Medigap insurance is designed to limit the out-of-pocket healthcare costs, including deductibles, portions of the 20 percent Plan B coinsurance charge, and other uninsured expenses.

Shopping for a Medigap Policy

Medigap insurance plans—like most insurance products—run the gamut from overpriced and fraudulent to cost-effective and ironclad. Despite the apparent plethora of products on the market, Congress has mandated that Medigap insurance be sold as one of 10 standard packages. Figure 6.1 will help you compare the 10 types of Medigap overage plans.

The best Medigap policy is your employer-sponsored insurance plan, so if you have the option of continuing it after retirement—even if you must pay the premiums yourself—by all means do so. If this option is unavailable, or if your employer's plan was unsatisfactory to begin with, however, you will have to shop around for a Medigap policy. As you evaluate the plethora of policies on the market, keep the following principles in mind.

- **Check on the quality and reputation of an insurer before buying a policy.** The events of recent years have shown that even the most apparently sound financial institutions can in fact be perilously near insolvency; unfortunately, despite their dull conservative reputation, insurance companies are not always the strong entities that they appear.
  To get a clear idea of a company's stability, simply look it up in the current edition of A.M. Best's Insurance Reports. This annually published reference work (available in most library reference rooms) evaluates the financial strength of insurers: you should think twice about buying a policy from any company that does not receive at least an "A" rating. The company should also have a high loss ratio (that is, the amount the company pays out in benefits for every dollar of premium). Federal law requires a minimum payout of 60 percent.
- **Review policy descriptions carefully.** Take the time to read those acres of grey print and obfuscation that insurers like to use. Compare the restrictions, benefits and costs of several policies to see which one comes out ahead. When reading a policy description you should note:
  - How much per day is paid for room and board in a hospital.

Figure 6.1. NAIC Model Medicare Supplement Coverage Plans

Medicare supplement insurance can be sold in only 10 standard plans. This chart shows the benefits, in addition to the basic benefits, available in each plan. Every company must make available Plan A. Some plans may *not* be available in your state.

BASIC BENEFITS: Included in all plans.
Hospitalization: Part A co-insurance plus coverage for 365 additional days after Medicare benefits end.
Medical Expenses: Part B co-insurance (205 of Medicare-approved expenses).
Blood: First three pints of blood each year.

A	B	C	D	E	F	G	H	I	J
Basic Benefits	**Basic Benefits**	**Basic Benefits**	**Basic Benefits**	**Basic Benefits**	**Basic Benefits**	**Basic Benefits**	**Basic Benefits**	**Basic Benefits**	**Basic Benefits**
		Skilled Nursing Co-Insurance	Skilled Nursing Co-Insurance	Skilled Nursing Co-Insurance	Skilled Nursing Co-Insurance	Skilled Nursing Co-Insurance	Skilled Nursing Co-Insurance	Skilled Nursing Co-Insurance	Skilled Nursing Co-Insurance
	Part A Deductible	Part A Deductible	Part A Deductible	Part A Deductible	Part A Deductible		Part A Deductible	Part A Deductible	Part A Deductible

	Part B Deductible			Part B Deductible				Part B Deductible
				Part b Excess (100%)	Part b Excess (80%)		Part b Excess (100%)	Part b Excess (100%)
	Foreign Travel Emergency	Foreign Travel Emergency	Foreign Travel Emergency	Foreign Travel Emergency	Foreign Travel Emergency	Foreign Travel Emergency	Foreign Travel Emergency	Foreign Travel Emergency
		At-Home Recovery			At-Home Recovery		At-Home Recovery	At-Home Recovery
						Basic Drugs ($1,250 Limit)	Basic Drugs ($1,250 Limit)	Basic Drugs ($1,250 Limit)
			Preventive Care					Preventive Care

Source: National Association of Insurance Commissioners (NAIC)

- How much is paid for medicines and other expenses.
- The size of the deductible.
- Whether the policy covers other family members.
- The maximum amount paid for each illness or injury.
- Whether the limits apply to future illness and injury.

Be forewarned that most Medigap policies don't pay for the extra cost of a private hospital room, routine immunization, medical expenses while traveling abroad, psychiatric care, eyeglasses, hearing aids and dental work.

If, despite your best attempts at consumer savvy, you buy a policy and then realize you've made a mistake, the law provides you with an escape hatch. Buyers of Medigap policies are guaranteed a 30-day "free look" period during which they may cancel the policy without cost.

- **Be skeptical of policies that are aggressively promoted.** Most, although not all, of the policies advertised via direct mail, radio, and TV are shoddy and overpriced products. The established insurers rely on name recognition and legions of loyal, long-time insurance sales representatives and brokers to sell their policies.
- **Buy only one policy.** Amazingly, over seven million elderly individuals own more than one Medigap policy even though the law proscribes overpayment for medical care. In other words, if one policy is adequate to cover your expenses, all the others are worthless. If you need multiple Medigap policies because none of them are comprehensive enough, you should probably find a new insurer so that you can consolidate your coverage.
- **Be accurate and truthful when filling out your application.** An incorrect or incomplete medical history will give the insurance company grounds for rejecting your application, or worse, for denying payment of your claim. List pre-existing conditions such as physical ailments for which you have received medical advice or treatment prior to applying for your MediGap policy. Some companies will not pay a claim if they can prove you knew, or should have known, about an illness at the time you signed up. One final note: Don't let the an insurance agent fill out the form on your behalf. The agent may be eager to sell you the policy and he or she may gloss over areas

where your medical record might cause problems with the insurer.

- **Never buy "dread disease" insurance.** Any policy that insures you against a specific disease, whether it be cancer, leprosy or elephantiasis should be avoided. These policies may have low premiums, but the chance you'll ever collect is even lower.

- **Check the policy's renewal terms.** A policy that is "renewable at the option of the company," is a policy that can be canceled at the whim of an insurance executive. Your policy will be more likely dropped at the order of an eagle-eyed actuary, who will cancel your coverage the moment you become a risk or liability to the company—precisely when you need the insurance the most. Buy a policy that is guaranteed for life.

- **Check out the length of the waiting period.** Most policies require a delay of six weeks before they become effective.

If you shop around for a Medigap policy only to be told repeatedly that you are ineligible, don't despair. The Blue Cross/Blue Shield in your state periodically offers an open enrollment period when every applicant must be accepted. In some states, there are also special insurance programs for people with chronic health problems. For more information about MediGap insurance policies, contact the following three agencies:

National Insurance Consumer Organization
121 North Payne Street
Alexandria, VA 22314
(703) 549-8050

Office of Beneficiary Services, Health Care Financing Administration (HFCA)
6325 Security Boulevard
Baltimore, MD 21207-5187
(410) 966-3000

Finally, if you have a complaint about a Medigap policy or the way it is being marketed, call Health Care Financing Administration's Medicare Issues Hotline toll free at 1-800-638-6833 (in Maryland, 1-800-492-6603).

HMOs: Saving on Medical Expenses

After some difficult years, health maintenance organizations (HMOs) are becoming a powerful factor in the medical care field, largely because of the vast numbers of elderly people who are enrolling in these plans. While poor management of some HMOs has slowed the growth of these health plans somewhat, they should continue to grow in importance and popularity in the 1990s.

An HMO provides for almost total health care service: doctors' appointments, hospital stays, operations, and, in some cases, prescription drugs, eyeglasses, and podiatry. Like a conventional insurance company, an HMO charges a monthly premium (some premiums are paid on an annual basis). HMO members must go to a designated health center for treatment and can usually see only physicians who are part of the HMO. HMO premiums are generally competitive with those charged for Medicare Part B.

Selecting an HMO

An HMO can be an inexpensive alternative to personal health care, but members give up a great deal of choice and flexibility. Before enrolling in a particular HMO, consider the following questions:

- **Does the HMO cover the same services and treatments as Medicare?**
- **Does the HMO pay for "extras," such as:**
    - Unlimited hospital stays
    - Annual physical exams
    - Eye care/contact lenses
    - Hearing aids
    - Foot care
- **Does the HMO cover the expense of emergency care from a non-HMO provider, especially if you require care while you are outside of the HMO's region.**
- **Does the HMO allow you to select your own doctor?**
- **Does the HMO allow you to change doctors if you're not satisfied with the service or treatment?**
- **Does the HMO cover the cost of a second opinion from an HMO doctor? What about from a non-HMO doctor?**

- **Do the HMO's doctors, therapists, and nurses make house calls for homebound patients?**
- **Does the HMO make arrangements for assistance from from visiting nurses?**
- **Does the HMO enroll individuals at any time?** If not, what are the enrollment periods? (HMOs with Medicare contracts must offer an annual 30-day enrollment period.)
- **Does the HMO allow individuals to leave the plan at any time?** Changing from an HMO to Medicare can sometimes be a slow and time consuming process.
- **Does the HMO have established procedures for redressing grievances or a hotline for customer questions and complaints?**

Trimming Your Medical Costs

Your Medicare coverage is in place. Your Medigap insurance policy is comprehensive, will continue for the rest of your life, and is in the hands of an old, solid and respected insurance company. Your health insurance safety need is strong, secure, and in good repair. Yet health care costs continue to escalate you still feel uncomfortable about the future. Is there anything you can do to fight back? The answer is yes. The following three suggestions will cut your health care bills and keep costs under control even if you or your spouse do become ill.

1. Recuperate at home
2. Self-audit your hospital bill
3. Ask for generic drugs

Recuperate at Home

In some cases you may be able to limit your hospital stays by recuperating at home with the assistance of professional home health care givers. Even with the expense of hiring a professional nurse, recuperating at home is still a medical bargain compared to staying in the hospital.

Home recuperation typically involves visits by a nurse or other health care professional who provides therapy or other medical services and monitors the patient's progress. Many health plans pay 100 percent of the cost of such care for a specified number of days each year. Some insurers waive their basic plan deductibles for policyholders who take advantage of home health care alternative. Naturally, only your doctor can authorize at-home recovery, but before you go into the operating room, consult with your physician to see whether it might be feasible.

If recuperation can't take place at home, moving to a skilled nursing facility is also an appropriate alternative to a prolonged hospital stay. Skilled nursing facilities, which are often connected with hospitals, provide round-the-clock nursing care and effective rehabilitation for far less than the cost of traditional hospital care.

Self-Audit Your Hospital Bill

Hospital bills can be long, complicated and dense, but make a point to read them over closely. Mistakes and billing errors **can** happen, and there's no point in overpaying. So if you are about to pay a lump-sum bill, don't reach for your checkbook until you first receive an itemized account of the services rendered.

If you do find a charge you can't identify or are billed for a service you can't remember, ask the hospital's billing office to explain it. If it turns out you've been overcharged, insist that the hospital accounting office correct its error.

Ask for Generic Drugs

Most health insurance plans pay only part of the cost of the pharmaceuticals your doctor prescribes—80 percent is about average. Thus, if a prescription costs $20, the policyholder usually pays about $4 out of his or her own pocket, with the insurance covering the remainder. While $4.00 here and $5.00 there may not seem like much, these expenses add up. Furthermore many medicines cost a great deal more than $20.00.

In many cases, the amount you pay for prescriptions can be cut by as much as half by using generic drugs. Generic drugs must pass the same Food and Drug Administration tests as their brand-name equivalents. Quality is not compromised by taking your medicine in generic form.

Nursing Homes: Coping with the Cost

Statistics show that 40 percent of all Americans age 65 or older will spend at least some portion of their lives in nursing homes. Moreover, half of all couples exhaust their entire life's savings within a year of one spouse's being admitted to a long-term care facility.

Even affluent retirees can be financially devastated by an extended nursing home stay. The average annual cost of a nursing home stay is $25,000, a figure that can reach $50,000 or more in some metropolitan areas. Furthermore, costs are increasing well ahead of inflation, perhaps by as much as 15 percent per year. Yet Medicare—even when coupled with private Medigap coverage—generally pays only for post-hospitalization stays in "skilled nursing facilities." Custodial and intermediate care, the kind that most people in nursing homes receive, is not covered by either Medicare or Medigap. See Chapter 32 for guidance on selecting a nursing home.

Long-Term Care Coverage: One Way to Prepare for Possible Institutionalization

Faced with these alarming costs, you may want to consider a relatively new and increasingly popular type of insurance known as long-term care (LTC) coverage. Offered by private insurance companies competing in an increasingly aggressive market, benefits have improved considerably in recent years. To be fully protected in all circumstances, a 65-year-old Medicare-eligible couple needs both Medigap insurance (either individual or employer-provided) and long-term care insurance.

Long-term care insurance is usually obtained through a separate policy, but it is sometimes available as a life insurance policy rider. These riders allow the policyholder to take the death benefit in the form of a monthly annuity if he or she is confined to a nursing home or requires home health care. If you elect to take this coverage as part of a universal life insurance contract, you may even be able to leave intact the bulk of the policy's death benefit.

WHO CAN BE COVERED

Long-term care insurance is issued to those as young as 40 and as old as 84. Level premiums are based on the current age of the insured; discounts are available for married couples. Most policies are guaranteed renewable and include a waiver of premium during the benefit period.

HOW BENEFITS WORK

Generally, a LTC policy covers four basic types of care: (1) skilled, (2) intermediate, (3) custodial, and (4) home. The first three types of care are usually provided in a hospital-like institution, with different floors or wings dedicated to different types of care.

At-home care requires the services of a paid nurse or attendant: depending on the individual's condition, the care giver might be on duty anywhere from round the clock to only a few hours each day.

Long-term care policies provide daily benefits ranging from $50 to $100 or higher for the first three types of care; benefits for home care are often about half that for nursing home care. The maximum benefit period is usually five years. In place of the deductible required by most standard medical policies, most LTC policies impose an "elimination period," a time period after admission to a long-term care facility during which no benefits are paid. Elimination periods vary from policy to policy, and some companies offer policies with no elimination period at all. The following example shows how a typical LTC policy works:

> EXAMPLE: At age 73, a male resident of New England pays $2,300 a year for a policy covering a nursing home stay including all levels of care. After an elimination period of 120 days, the policy pays $110 a day for up to four years. Starting in the second year, the benefit increases by 5 percent annually.

Policyholders can typically lower their premiums by 15 percent by waiving the inflation adjustment and hospice coverage. However, policyholders desiring lifetime coverage must pay a premium that is around 20 percent higher than that for ordinary coverage.

When the policy covers home health care, benefits amount to about half of the institutional payment. For a policyholder to qualify for the home health care benefit, a physician must periodically certify the fact that the individual suffers from disabilities that make an independent lifestyle unfeasible. Some LTC policies now cover adult day care as well.

CHOOSING AN APPROPRIATE POLICY

In evaluating LTC coverage, a number of important questions should be taken into account:

- **Does the policy cover illnesses like Alzheimer's or Parkinson's diseases?**
- **Is prior hospitalization required for nursing home admission at any level of care?**
- **Does the policy provide inflation protection that automatically increases benefits with each passing year?**
- **Is the coverage renewable for life? It should be as long as you pay your premiums.**

- **Does the premium remain the same throughout the life of the policy?** The initial premium is based on your age and should remain the same regardless of changes in age or health. Rates can only be increased for an entire class of insured people and on a per-state basis.
- **Is your premium waived after you have been receiving nursing home benefits for 90 consecutive days?**

MEDICAID: NURSING HOME COVERAGE OF LAST RESORT?

Medicaid, which is administered jointly by federal and state governments, was designed to provide medical care for the poor. Essentially by default, however, Medicaid is now the one government program that underwrites long-term custodial care for the elderly.

When it comes to long-term care, you are well advised to be either quite wealthy or utterly destitute. The very well-off can easily afford nursing home expenses and the poor automatically qualify for Medicaid. For all too many, long-term nursing home care is paid for in two stages. First, it is paid for by the individual, through his or her savings and insurance coverage, and second, by the state, once all these personal resources have been almost exhausted, at which point the nursing home resident qualifies as indigent.

Thus, before qualifying for Medicaid benefits, an elderly individual must first meet his or her state's qualifications for impoverishment. Before an application for Medicaid benefits will be approved by your state, the applicant must have "spent down" the bulk of personal assets and have little or no additional income. Given this rather grim picture, many married couples worry that one spouse's catastrophic illness will wipe out the savings of both, leaving the healthy spouse bankrupt.

In truth, however, the spousal impoverishment provisions of the Medicaid law somewhat ameliorate this otherwise cheerless situation.

"SPEND DOWN" RULES—THE GENERAL PRINCIPLES

The federal spousal impoverishment provisions essentially act as limits on the state's power to compel "spend downs" before paying Medicaid benefits. At the same time, the federal rules also keep the states from being too generous.

While the state can force a Medicaid claimant to "spend down" virtually all his or her personal assets before receiving Medicaid benefits, these assets do not necessarily include all the assets belonging to the claimant and his or her spouse. The "spend-down" requirement mandates that only all the property to which the Medicaid claimant is personally entitled must be liquidated to pay for care. This property includes all assets held in the claimant's name outright plus one-half of all "marital assets," which generally includes all jointly held property.

Thus, as far as the healthy spouse is concerned (the "community spouse," in Medicaid parlance), half of all joint property as well as all property held outright by the community spouse is unaffected by the spend-down requirement. Be aware, however, that the law places a cap on how much monthly income states can shield from spend down requirements.

Note that the states have widely differing rules for determining what is and what is not a part of the marital estate. To make matters more confusing, these rules continue to evolve. Be sure to consult a local attorney if you have any doubts about what constitutes marital assets in your state or about how the Medicaid rules are applied in your state.

HOW THE "SPEND DOWN" RULES AFFECT YOUR HOME

Under federal rules, your principal residence is generally exempt from state spend down requirements at least during the lifetime of you and your spouse. As the home is often the largest single piece of marital property, this exemption is very important.

HOW THE "SPEND DOWN" RULES AFFECT YOUR OTHER ASSETS

States are required by the federal government to exempt at least \$12,000—and may exempt as much as \$60,000—of the healthy spouse's jointly owned assets (in addition to the home). Remember, however, that these rules are irrelevant to any assets held in the well spouse's name. Assets that are solely owned by the well spouse have no bearing on the ill spouse's Medicaid eligibility.

EXAMPLE: Say your state opts to shield \$25,000 of spousal assets from the spend down requirement—well within the federal rules explained earlier. Suppose that you and your spouse have marital assets of \$35,000 (excluding your house). Without this shield, half of your joint assets, or \$17,500, would be subject to the spend down requirements. With this shield in place, however, only \$10,000 will have to be spent (\$35,000 – \$25,000 = \$10,000).

HOW THE "SPEND DOWN" RULES AFFECT INCOME

Obviously, the states have the right to set some kind of income limit above which a person cannot qualify for Medicaid. In states where the income of one spouse is considered to belong to both spouses, this means that up to half of the well spouse's income might be subject to a spend down requirement.

This is where the federal rules come into play. Under the spousal impoverishment provisions, the state spend down rules cannot reduce joint income below 122 percent of the federal poverty line income level for a couple. This minimum income level is adjusted annually. However, federal law allows states to shield as much as $1,500 per month from the spend down requirement.

Again, however, this does not necessarily mean that a well spouse's total income will be limited to $1,500 per month or less if the other spouse is to receive Medicaid. Even in states where all income is considered joint income, the well spouse still gets to keep half.

ASSET SHIFTING AND MEDICAID

Given the way the federal and state Medicaid laws are structured, asset shifting would appear to be one way of transforming one's spouse into a Medicaid-qualifying pauper in short order. Unfortunately, while sharp lawyers and accountants may try to convince you otherwise, asset shifting won't help you qualify for Medicaid unless it's done a number of years in advance.

All 50 states now have rules to limit the efficacy of asset shifting. Generally, assets shifted less than three years before claiming Medicaid benefits will most likely be considered fair game for a spend down. Benefits will usually be withheld entirely until these shifted assets have been spent down.

Where one spouse has substantial assets, and the other comparatively little, there is considerable danger that a serious illness will wipe out the family fortune. If the wealthier spouse is the one with the debilitating illness, the spousal impoverishment provisions may offer little or no protection. If you and your spouse have a high net worth, you should consider dividing all assets held by both you and your spouse into equal shares, and putting each share into a separate living trust. Using this technique, you can ensure that there are no joint assets that the state can require you to liquidate. In addition, there will be no question about who owns what.

If you are very concerned about the possibility of becoming impoverished as a result of having to go to a nursing home, you may want to speak with an attorney who is knowledgeable about your state's Medicaid regulations. But be forewarned. There are no easy solutions to the nursing home dilemma.

7

WHERE LIFE INSURANCE FITS IN

WHEN YOU FIRST embarked upon your career, and if you had a young family to support, life insurance protected your children and spouse against the income loss that would result from your death. By the time you've passed the age of 50, however, life insurance's role in your financial planning usually changes. This chapter is designed to help you deploy your existing coverage effectively and prune and/or supplement it as needed.

Life Insurance and the Preretiree

If you are like most Americans, your children will be independent adults by the time you reach your fifties. Unlike younger parents, you need not stay awake at night worrying what would happen to your children should you die. Still, when it comes to life insurance, you are not entirely out of the woods as a preretiree, especially if you have a dependent spouse or a spouse whose earnings are insufficient to continue maintaining your current lifestyle in the event of your death. Furthermore, if you think one or both of your parents may require your care or financial assistance in the future, life insurance can help provide a safety net should you predecease your parents. In addition, if you have owned a cash value life policy for some time, it may be worth a significant amount of money: You may want to consider it as part of your investment portfolio. With these "vested" policies, you have a number of options open to you. Finally, life insurance can be an important estate planning tool. (This is covered in the section, "Life Insurance and the Retiree.")

Company Insurance Policies

If you are enrolled in a group life insurance plan through your employer, don't delay finding out what happens to your policy when you leave the workforce. Unfortunately, many companies reduce their employee life insurance coverage to a token amount (say $5,000) at retirement. In some cases, you may have to acquire additional personal coverage upon retirement to avoid being underinsured.

Insurance as an Investment Vehicle

Older individuals who have faithfully paid their cash value life insurance premiums for many years will often have accumulated significant savings through their policies. Depending on your financial status it may or may not make sense to cash the policy and invest the proceeds. If you own several policies, you may want to liquidate some in this manner while owning others.

Your insurance company will offer you a variety of ways to take your policy proceeds should you decide to cash it in: Cash value life insurance has of late come into its own as an investment vehicle. Interest rates on many insurance products are competitive with those earned on bonds, certificates of deposit, and similar fixed-income investments. Assuming that the return remains competitive and the policy still meets your investment objectives in retirement, such insurance coverage could be maintained, with the added incentive of a death benefit. And with the increasing variety of special types of policies, life insurance offers new opportunities for added income in after-work years and late-life financial planning.

Insurance if You Still Have Dependents

If others continue to depend on you for support, it is as important to maintain good insurance coverage in your preretirement years as it ever was. If your wages represent your family's major source of income, you will need a policy that will provide sufficient income to offset the loss of these wages should you die. Yes, Social

Security and employer-provided survivor benefits may offset the loss of these wages, but these sources are generally a woefully inadequate source of funding. Your investment earnings, especially retirement savings, however, may represent a significant income source to make up for your earnings loss.

It's quite straightforward to approximate how much life insurance you should carry in these circumstances. First, list your expected sources and amounts of income. These would include spouse's earnings, pension benefits, income from business interests, and so forth. Then, estimate how much capital will remain after payment of estate settlement costs. Assume a reasonable rate of return on these assets (a more conservative person, for example, may wish to use only a 6 percent return). Compare the result with what you estimate your spouse will need to maintain the present standard of living. From there, decide how much capital would be needed (again using a reasonable rate of return) to meet the income shortfall, if any. The following example demonstrates how these calculations work.

EXAMPLE: Jim Voigt is age 50. His children are grown and on their own. He and his wife, Cheryl, also age 50, have an annual income of $195,000. Jim estimates that Cheryl would need approximately a $150,000 pretax income in the event of his death. At Jim's death, income would be available from the following sources:

Cheryl's earnings	$45,000
Survivor's pension	33,000
Liquid assets ($384,000) invested at 8%	30,720
	$108,720

Based on these assumptions, Cheryl would have an income "deficit" of $41,280. And she won't be eligible for Social Security survivor's benefits until she reaches age 60. Assuming that Cheryl can earn an 8 percent pretax return, she would need additional capital of $516,000 ($41,280 income needed divided by 8 percent expected investment return) to give her the desired income. Solution: Jim should maintain insurance coverage in that amount on his life.

Life Insurance and the Retiree

Upon retirement, you will—if you have planned well and prudently—be replacing wages with income from retirement plans, pensions, and your own investments. Because most of these sources will continue to provide income for dependents after you die, you may not need life insurance to protect them. If you derive a significant portion of your income from a 50 percent joint-and-survivor annuity, however, your death could create hardship for your surviving spouse. Furthermore, when a couple's (former) primary wage earner dies, total Social Security benefits will often be cut by one-third. So if either of these income sources are required to maintain your survivor's standard of living, maintaining some level of life insurance will continue to be necessary. The following examples shows how limited life insurance protection to bolster income can be necessary for a retired couple.

EXAMPLE: Adonis Feinblatt and his wife Ethyl have been retired now for six years. Their combined retirement income, including Social Security, a 50 percent joint-and-survivor pension and investment earnings, is $100,000. Adonis now estimates that Ethyl would need $80,000 of pretax income to maintain her standard of living if he were to die. Under these circumstances, the following sources of income would be available:

Social Security	$16,000
Pension	36,000
Liquid assets ($320,000) invested at 8%	25,600
	$77,600

Under these circumstances, Ethyl's income deficit would be only $1,200. That's because in retirement, Adonis's death doesn't have much impact on family income. And the impact of reduced Social Security and pension benefits is partially offset by reduced living expenses.

Being prudent, however, Adonis decides to purchase a $50,000 insurance policy on his life to provide Ethyl with the capital she needs to meet her small income shortfall and an extra "cushion."

Life Insurance as an Estate Planning Tool

Life insurance coverage may also be important to maintain for estate planning purposes. If you think that your estate might incur federal and state taxes and are concerned about having funds available to pay these taxes, life insurance can provide a solution to your problems.

Individuals with large, illiquid estates (those that include real estate or closely held businesses) will find life insurance especially useful to cover taxes and administration expenses. Life insurance will obviate the necessity for estate executors to liquidate assets to meet obligations. If your estate is large enough for these matters to be of concern, a detailed, accurate estimate of the cash needs of your estate will have to be developed in consultation with your attorney and/or accountant.

There is also a type of life insurance product designed to pay benefits only after both you and your spouse die. This "survivorship" or "second-to-die" coverage is designed to help your children or other heirs pay estate taxes when they are most likely to be due—at the death of the second spouse. When a couple buys a survivorship policy (or any life insurance policy for that matter and places it in an irrevocable life insurance trust), the proceeds are exempt from both estate and income taxes. Since an insurer has to set aside reserves for only one death benefit rather than two, the premium for such coverage is low—roughly 50 percent of what two people would pay to purchase the same amount of individual whole life coverage.

Evaluating (and Cutting) the Cost of Your Life Insurance

When it comes to insurance, most Americans are either over or underinsured: few seem to strike a happy medium. If you are paying premiums for insurance you don't need, it's time to prune your insurance portfolio. If you have a superfluous group term policy, for instance, you can elect not to replace your group term insurance coverage at retirement. You could also make a charity the beneficiary of an unneeded policy, a move that can have favorable tax consequences.

Be careful, however, not to pare your insurance coverage to the bone. It never hurts to have a cushion, so long as you are not wasting money that could be put to better use elsewhere. The following section discusses how you can reduce your insurance expenses while still maintaining adequate protection.

Is Whole Life Right for You?

If you find that you need additional life insurance to see you through retirement, it is important to buy the right type of coverage. Whether you purchase whole life or term insurance depends on how long you'll need the protection. Cash value life insurance is more expensive because it includes an investment component but, in the long run, it builds up a cash value that can reduce premiums.

As you age, term insurance, which is often attractive for

younger adults, becomes less and less of a bargain. Prices will continue to rise with age. However, because premiums will remain low compared to whole life policies, term insurance may still be attractive for pure insurance coverage.

Low-Load Life Insurance

With a little digging, you can purchase so-called low-load life insurance policies—either term or cash value. Since these policies are sold direct to you by the insurance company, the fees are much lower—no insurance agent is involved.

Tips for saving on insurance. The following tips will help you reduce your insurance costs:

- **Reduce the number of multiple policies.** When two policies have the same face value, drop the one with the higher premium. In most cases, this will be the newer one. If you are choosing between a policy from a mutual insurance company and one from a stock company, drop the stock policy if it is similar to the other policy. While that premium may be lower, the fact that the mutual policy pays dividends will probably be to your advantage in the long run.
- **Switch policies.** If your choice is between an older term policy and a newer one, the newer one may cost less. But don't drop the old policy until you know you are medically-qualified to obtain the new one.
- **Tax tip.** If you want to swap an old life insurance policy for a new one to save money or to expand coverage, you might assume that there will be no tax consequences to the exchange. Unfortunately, this is probably not the case and the swap may be a taxable event. Before you decide to make any type of exchange of life insurance policies, check with your insurance agent and, if necessary, ask him or her to seek advice on your behalf from the insurance company's home office.

8

GETTING YOUR PERSONAL RECORDS IN ORDER

SUPPOSE YOU FOUND that you needed major surgery in a few days and you would face a long period of recuperation. Would you be confident that your personal records were so well organized that your spouse or some other person could readily take charge of your financial affairs?

If you're like many people, the answer is probably "no." As modern life grows more and more complicated, we naturally accumulate greater and greater numbers of personal financial documents. Yet all too many people never get around to putting their records in order. They're making a serious mistake.

This chapter shows you why good recordkeeping habits are a must and how you can go about setting up your own straightforward and easy-to-use recordkeeping system. We will also show you how to prepare personal financial statements. These documents are essential tools for finding out where you stand financially and to help you in planning for a comfortable future.

The Importance of Good Recordkeeping

Good recordkeeping is valuable for two reasons. First, by making your financial documents easily accessible, an effectively designed system will save you time in the long run. Admittedly, setting up a recordkeeping system does take some time, especially if your records are extremely jumbled. Once your system is up and running, however, you will no longer have to spend two hours hunting for a canceled check to prove a disputed bill. Nor will you have to rifle through innumerable drawers to find a medical receipt.

Second, the process of organizing your records and documents is an excellent way to reacquaint yourself with some of the more neglected areas of your lifetime personal financial planning. In organizing your legal documents, for instance, you might find that neither you nor your spouse ever updated your powers of attorney—even though you both had assumed that the other had.

Essentially, organizing your records will force you to take stock of yourself. And to plan for your later years, you need to know exactly where you stand now. Thus, one of the most important aspects of the financial planning process is the prosaic task of getting your records in order. There are two major components of recordkeeping:

1. Developing and maintaining an effective recordkeeping system, and
2. Periodically preparing personal financial statements.

Developing and Maintaining an Effective Recordkeeping System

A good recordkeeping system is an indispensable component of sound personal financial management. Unfortunately, many people never develop sound recordkeeping habits, because they're not aware of how simple an effective recordkeeping system can be.

The advantages of a good recordkeeping system are clear:

- You will be better able to recognize problems that require attention.
- Good recordkeeping saves time in retrieving important information, such as insurance policies, brokerage advices, tax information, and other financial documents.
- A well-organized filing system eases the stress of family emergencies, particularly incapacity or an unexpected death in the family.

Good recordkeeping also serves a dual function in tax planning—it simplifies the process of preparing tax returns, whether you do your own taxes or have a tax professional prepare them, and it ensures that you have the necessary supporting documentation should the IRS audit your returns. An informal accounting system, which may consist only of a checkbook, should be maintained if you have a large number of deductible items. Kept on a daily or weekly basis, such a system allows you to record—and so, claim—more deductions, while at the same time sparing you the aggravation of a marathon at your end-of-the-year tax return preparation session.

A filing system for receipts and pertinent papers is also helpful. Finally, a notebook or appointment calendar that records miscellaneous deductible items (such as charitable contributions and unreimbursed business expenses) helps you keep track of deductions you might otherwise forget.

Note that the IRS doesn't require specific types of records, but it does require taxpayers to keep "adequate, contemporaneous records" of many types of business and other deductible expenses. For example, if you write off the business use of your car, you must keep adequate records to support the portion of automobile usage deducted for business purposes. Receipts and logbooks of automobile usage, calendars of appointments and activities, accounts of home computer use for business purposes, and other pertinent records should be maintained carefully and kept up to date to minimize potential problems with the IRS.

In general, you must keep records that support an item of income reported or a deduction claimed on a return until the statute of limitations on that return runs out—usually three years from the filing or due date. Some records must be kept for longer periods of time. For example, in many transactions involving real estate, including your own home, improvements made to property can change your tax "basis" for the property—a key figure in computing capital gain or loss for income-tax purposes. Thus, you should keep receipts of home improvements you make to your house or rental property for as long as you own the property.

KEY COMPONENTS OF THE SYSTEM

A good recordkeeping system is one that is comprehensive enough to be effective, and still simple enough to encourage regular use. In general, the more rigorous a system is, the less likely it is to be used regularly. Packaged systems are often either too complex or too generalized for most people's needs.

If you're a computer enthusiast, you can find a wide array of software programs that allow you to put your personal records on-line. Be forewarned, however, that the vast majority of home recordkeeping software sits on the shelf collecting dust.

Every good recordkeeping system has three main components: a safe deposit box, an active file kept at home, and an inactive file that can be kept either at home or in storage. In addition, you may want to keep some documents at your attorney's office, with copies kept in the home active file. Both spouses as well as one other adult family member should know where these files are located, their basic contents, and the logistics of the family accounting system.

It is sometimes desirable for each spouse to have a separate safe deposit box. Depending on the state in which a couple resides, a jointly owned box might be sealed following the death of one spouse, just when the other needs to retrieve documents or valuables. The active file should contain an inventory of all safe deposit box contents, updated whenever necessary. In fact, it's often wise to keep photocopies at home of important documents stored in the safe deposit box—at least those for which there are no other records.

The accessibility of the active and inactive files is the key to their usefulness. But keep in mind that if your files are not easy to update, they're worthless. You will end up postponing filing items—sometimes indefinitely—and so will fail to keep your vital records up-to-date. As a general rule, you should endeavor to file bills, warranties, bank statements, and other records as they come in, or collect them all together in one location and sort them periodically for filing.

And remember that home files do not need to be particularly fancy. A good fireproof metal strongbox is recommended, although desk drawers, a filing cabinet, or simple boxes work just as well. Using a separate manilla folder for each category of documents or papers should suffice. The easier the set-up is to use, the more likely it is that you will continue using it and so profit from your recordkeeping efforts.

Here's a closer look at what should go into each of the three primary components of your system:

1. *Safe deposit box:* Your safe deposit box should contain such personal papers as birth certificates and Social Security records, ownership papers such as bond certificates and deeds, contract papers such as insurance policies and estate-planning papers such as wills. The personal recordkeeping

organizer at the end of this chapter can help you in organizing your safe deposit box.

Keep two considerations in mind when renting a safe deposit box. First, appoint a deputy who has the power to open the box if you are incapacitated or otherwise unable to open it yourself. Second, keep a second copy of your estate-planning documents outside of the box—in case it is sealed upon your death.

Furthermore, if you store valuables such as jewelry in your safe deposit box, be sure to obtain a rider on your homeowner's or renter's insurance policy to insure the contents of the safe deposit box against loss. Most people don't realize that if their safe deposit box is robbed or its contents are damaged, items contained in the box are usually not insured by the bank.

2. *Active file:* The main purpose of the active file is to keep track of personal papers and important contractual obligations, and to help in preparing the current year's tax returns. The active file should also include tax working papers for the last three years, since the IRS can freely audit a return for that period. (In fact, three years is a good rule of thumb for holding most other papers as well.)

   The active file should contain a range of documents, from bank statements and recently canceled checks to loan statements and payment books to income records. In short, all papers pertaining to current matters should be kept in the active file.

   Because the active file needs to be easily accessible, it should be located in a convenient and pleasant location like a den. If the file is squirreled away in a dank basement or a stifling attic, you will be less likely to use it. If you use a desk with several drawers or a file cabinet, you could reserve each drawer for a specific class of documents—for example, one for estate-planning documents, one for insurance records, one for current bills, and one for investment materials such as prospectuses and brokers' statements.

   The personal recordkeeping organizer in this chapter will help you in organizing your active file. In addition to this active file, you would also do well to maintain a diary or appointment book to record miscellaneous medical and business expenses, expenses associated with charitable work, and miscellaneous cash contributions.

3. *Inactive file:* The main purpose of the inactive file is to hold the records necessary to back up your past tax returns, should it ever come to that. Thus, this file should contain important papers—formerly in the active file—that are over three years old. In certain instances, the IRS can examine tax returns going back more than three years, although after six years, most people can safely discard their records.

   A few other items should also be kept until after the investment is sold in the inactive file. Invoices and canceled checks pertaining to any home improvements should be kept until the home is sold. Brokerage advices should also be kept to substantiate capital gains and losses. You may also want to keep important personal papers that are not currently needed in the inactive file. Examples might include family health records and proof that major debts and other contracts have been discharged. Some people also keep canceled checks indefinitely, because they can be used to substantiate expenses long after other records have been discarded.

How to Prepare Personal Financial Statements

Personal financial statements are just as important in managing your personal finances as they are in managing a business. Of course, the better organized your records, the easier it is to prepare periodic personal financial statements.

Personal financial statements include a statement of assets and liabilities (balance sheet), a statement of past income and expenses (income statement), a statement of net worth, and a budget, which is a forecast of expected income and expenses. When regularly revised to reflect changes in your financial situation, these documents serve as important tools in evaluating and monitoring your financial picture. Without accurate personal financial statements, it's difficult to plan effectively. Only by regularly updating and revising your financial statements will you be able to chart your progress toward attaining your financial objectives.

Preparing personal financial statements and monitoring your

financial progress is particularly important for retirees and people nearing retirement. Older Americans typically have more financial resources to manage, and must be particularly prudent with the management of these resources. Sound management of your assets is crucial to assuring a financially comfortable retirement in the face of long life expectancy, inflation, and, often, investment uncertainty. Budgeting is also vitally important for older Americans, many of whom must cope with fixed or slowly rising incomes in relation to more rapidly rising living expenses.

Personal financial statements can be presented in several formats, ranging from straightforward lists of accounts and their balances to professionally audited statements that include footnoted explanations of your various accounts. The appropriate format is usually dictated by the complexity of your finances. You will probably need audited statements only if you plan to borrow money for that 200-foot yacht you've always wanted.

Again, for most of us, when it comes to preparing personal financial statements, the simpler the better.

Using Your Personal Financial Statements

The objectives of personal financial statements differ considerably from the objectives of similar statements developed for businesses. Users of business statements focus on predictions of future earnings. With personal statements, you focus on current financial conditions to plan future financial activities. Personal financial statements organize your financial "vital statistics" in a manner that enables you to:

- Assess your current financial condition, including resources (assets) and obligations (liabilities);
- Determine the changes in your net worth over time and the sources of those changes;
- Plan short- and long-term financial strategies;
- See how you obtain and spend cash; and
- Assess your ability meet your ongoing financial obligations, not only in the near future, but also many years hence.

At the end of this chapter are models and worksheets (Figures 8.1, 8.2, and 8.3) you can use to create your own statement of personal assets and liabilities and personal budget planner. The tips on pages 115 and 116 will help you in filling them out.

Figure 8.1. Personal Recordkeeping Organizer

This work sheet serves two purposes. First, you can indicate next to each item where that particular item is now located. Second, you can organize your personal records by consolidating your documents into the three "files" noted below.

I. ITEMS FOR STORAGE IN A SAFE DEPOSIT BOX

PERSONAL

1. Family birth certificates ________
2. Family death certificates ________
3. Marriage certificate ________
4. Citizenship papers ________
5. Adoption papers ________
6. Veteran's papers ________
7. Social Security verification ________

OWNERSHIP

1. Bonds and certificates ________
2. Deeds ________
3. Automobile titles ________
4. Household inventories ________
5. Home ownership records (e.g. blueprints, deeds, surveys, capital addition records, yearly records) ________
6. Copies of trust documents ________

OBLIGATION/CONTRACT

1. Contracts ________
2. Copies of insurance policies ________
3. IOUs ________
4. Retirement and pension plan documents ________

COPIES OF ESTATE PLANNING DOCUMENTS

1. Wills ________
2. Living wills ________
3. Trusts ________
4. Letters of instruction ________
5. Guardianship arrangements ________

Figure 8.1 (Cont'd)

II. ITEMS FOR STORAGE IN HOME ACTIVE FILE

CURRENT INCOME/EXPENSE DOCUMENTS

1. Unpaid bills ________
2. Current bank statements ________
3. Current broker's statements ________
4. Current canceled checks and money-order receipts ________
5. Credit card information ________
6. Copies of company expense reports ________

CONTRACTUAL DOCUMENTS

1. Loan statements and payment books ________
2. Appliance manuals and warranties (including date and place of purchase) ________
3. Insurance policies ________
   - Home ________
   - Life ________
   - Automobile ________
   - Personal liability ________
   - Health and medical ________
   - Other: ________
4. Receipts for expensive items not yet paid for ________

PERSONAL

1. Employment records ________
2. Health and benefits information ________
3. Family health records ________
4. Copies of wills ________
5. Copies of letters of instruction ________
6. Education information ________
7. Cemetery records ________
8. Important telephone numbers ________
9. Inventory and spare key to safe deposit box ________
10. Receipts for items under warranty ________
11. Receipts for expensive items ________

TAXES

1. Tax receipts ________
2. Paid bill receipts (with deductible receipts filed separately to facilitate tax preparation and possibly reduce taxes) ________
3. Brokerage transaction advices ________

Figure 8.1 (Cont'd)

4. Income tax working papers ______
5. Credit statements ______
6. Income and expense records for rental properties ______
7. Medical, dental, and drug expenses ______
8. Records of business expenses ______

III. ITEMS FOR STORAGE IN HOME INACTIVE FILE

1. Prior tax returns ______
2. Home improvement records ______
3. Brokerage advices (prior to three most recent years) ______
4. Family health records (prior to three most recent years) ______
5. Proof that major debts or other major contracts have been met ______
6. Canceled checks (prior to three most recent years) ______

Figure 8.2. Statement of Personal Assets and Liabilities

This worksheet can be used to summarize your assets and liabilities. Three columns are included so that you can periodically monitor your progress. This statement should be prepared at least once per year, and many people prepare it more frequently.

ASSETS	Date		
1. Cash in checking and brokerage accounts	$ ______	$ ______	$ ______
2. Money market funds and accounts	______	______	______
3. Fixed-income investments			
■ Savings accounts	______	______	______

Figure 8.2 (Cont'd)

■ CDs	______	______	______
■ Goverment securities and funds	______	______	______
■ Mortgage-backed securities and funds	______	______	______
■ Corporate bonds and bond funds	______	______	______
■ Municipal bonds and bond funds	______	______	______
■ Other fixed-income investments	______	______	______
4. Stock investments			
■ Common stock in publicly traded companies	______	______	______
■ Stock mutual funds	______	______	______
■ Other stock investments	______	______	______
■ Other fixed-income investments	______	______	______
5. Real estate investments			
■ Undeveloped land	______	______	______
■ Directly owned, income-producing real estate	______	______	______
■ Real estate limited partnerships	______	______	______
6. Ownership interest in private business	______	______	______
7. Cash value of life-insurance policies	______	______	______
8. Retirement-oriented assets			
■ Individual retirement accounts	______	______	______
■ Salary reduction 401(k) plans	______	______	______
■ Keogh or simplified employee pension plans	______	______	______

Figure 8.2 (Cont'd)

■ Vested interest in corporate pension and profit-sharing plans	______	______	______
■ Employee thrift and stock-purchase plans	______	______	______
■ Tax-deferred annuities	______	______	______
■ Other retirement-oriented assets	______	______	______
9. Personal assets			
■ Personal residence(s)	______	______	______
■ Automobile(s)	______	______	______
■ Jewelry	______	______	______
■ Personal property	______	______	______
10. Other assets			
■ ______________	______	______	______
■ ______________	______	______	______
■ ______________	______	______	______
11. Total assets	$ ______	$ ______	$ ______

LIABILITIES			
1. Credit cards and charge accounts	$ ______	$ ______	______
2. Income taxes payable	______	______	______
3. Miscellaneous accounts payable	______	______	______
4. Bank loans	______	______	______
5. Policy loans on life-insurance policies	______	______	______
6. Automobile loans	______	______	______
7. Student loans	______	______	______
8. Mortgages on personal residence	______	______	______
9. Mortgages on investment real estate	______	______	______
10. Broker's margin loans	______	______	______
11. Limited partnership debt	______	______	______
12. Other liabilities			
■ ______________	______	______	______

Figure 8.2 (Cont'd)

■ ________	______	______	______
■ ________	______	______	______
13. Total liabilities	$ ______	$ ______	$ ______
14. Net worth (total assets less total liabilities)	$ ______	$ ______	$ ______

Note: Assets should be listed at their current market value. Be realistic in valuing those assets that require an estimate of market value, such as your home and personal property.

Figure 8.3. Personal Budget Planner

Individuals and families should prepare budgets as businesses do. This worksheet can be used either to record your past cash receipts and cash disbursements and/or to budget future receipts and disbursements. You may want to use the first column to record your past receipts and disbursements, the second column to list your budget over the next month, quarter, or year, and the third column to compare your actual future receipts and disbursements against your budget in the second column. If you budget over a period of less than one year, be sure to take into consideration those expenses that you pay less frequently than monthly, such as insurance, vacations, and tuition. You should be setting aside an amount each month that will eventually cover those large bills.

Indicate at the top of each column whether the amounts in that column are actual or estimated past figures or budgeted future figures. Also indicate the time period in each column—e.g., "July 1993" or "Year 1994."

Indicate if actual or budget:	______	______	______
Indicate the time period:	______	______	______

Figure 8.3 (Cont'd)

CASH RECEIPTS			
1. Gross salary	$ ______	$ ______	$ ______
2. Interest	______	______	______
3. Dividends	______	______	______
4. Bonuses/profit sharing	______	______	______
5. Alimony/child support received	______	______	______
6. Distributions from partnerships	______	______	______
7. Income from outside businesses	______	______	______
8. Trust distributions	______	______	______
9. Pension	______	______	______
10. Social Security	______	______	______
11. Gifts	______	______	______
12. Proceeds from sale of investments	______	______	______
13. Other			
■ ______________	______	______	______
■ ______________	______	______	______
■ ______________	______	______	______
14. Total cash receipts	$ ______	______	$ ______

CASH DISBURSEMENTS			
1. Housing (rent/mortgage)	$ ______	$ ______	$ ______
2. Food	______	______	______
3. Household maintenance	______	______	______
4. Utilities and telephone	______	______	______
5. Clothing	______	______	______
6. Personal care	______	______	______
7. Medical and dental care	______	______	______
8. Automobile/transportation	______	______	______
9. Travel	______	______	______
10. Entertainment	______	______	______
11. Vacation(s)	______	______	______
12. Gifts	______	______	______

Figure 8.3 (Cont'd)

13. Contributions	______	______	______
14. Insurance	______	______	______
15. Miscellaneous out-of-pocket expenses	______	______	______
16. Furniture	______	______	______
17. Home improvements	______	______	______
18. Real estate taxes	______	______	______
19. Loan payments	______	______	______
20. Credit card payments	______	______	______
21. Alimony/child-support payments	______	______	______
22. Tuition/educational expenses	______	______	______
23. Business and professional expenses	______	______	______
24. Savings/investments	______	______	______
25. Income and Social Security taxes	______	______	______
26. Other			
■ ______________	______	______	______
■ ______________	______	______	______
■ ______________	______	______	______
27. Total cash disbursements	$______	$______	$______
EXCESS (SHORTFALL) OF CASH RECEIPTS OVER CASH DISBURSEMENTS	$______	$______	$______

STATEMENT OF PERSONAL ASSETS AND LIABILITIES

This financial statement, also called a *balance sheet,* is an excellent way for you to plot your financial progress. Be sure to list assets at their current market value, but be realistic when valuing real estate and personal property. If you have some common stock or real estate that has appreciated considerably in value, remember that your net worth might not be as high as it seems if you eventually liquidate those assets because, you will have to pay a capital gains tax on your profits. Also, be sure to list all liabilities. People have a tendency to understate their liabilities.

Once you have prepared an up-to-date balance sheet, you can then monitor changes in your net worth (i.e., total assets minus total liabilities) over time by periodically revising your personal balance sheet.

PERSONAL BUDGET

Budgeting is as important for individuals and families as it is for businesses. The purposes of budgeting are to define possible problems in spending patterns, to identify opportunities for overcoming these problems, and to help you plan realistically to balance spending with income. Knowing both the amount of income that you can reasonably expect and how you spend that income can go far in preventing unforseen financial problems.

The best way to prepare a budget is first to analyze your past income and expenses. Once you know past sources of income and areas of expense, you can then prepare a budget that forecasts future income and expenses.

> IMPORTANT: Be sure to include savings in your budgeted expenses. Even if you are retired, most retirees must continue to save to keep up with inflation in old age.

People over 50 not only should prepare budgets for the next year, as is most commonly the case with business budgets, but should also draw up budget estimates extending well into the future. People nearing or in retirement have the advantage of being better able to predict future income and living expenses than do younger people. Moreover, budgeting well into the future is particularly important to ensure that you do not outlive your available resources.

Taking the time to complete recordkeeping and budget worksheets well before you retire and keeping them up to date as time goes on can help you avoid unpleasant financial surprises, both now and in retirement.

9

USING CREDIT WISELY

IF YOU'VE VISITED your bank lately, you know that what used to be a sleepy, staid consumer loan department has become a varied and multifaceted loan center offering many different types of loans and loan products. You might even be a bit overwhelmed, thinking that the types of loans that are available to you have become too numerous. Take heart, they all share some basic characteristics. And, familiarizing yourself with these characteristics is more important than ever. Not only will such familiarization enable you to select the most appropriate type of loan for your particular needs, it will also help you determine and secure the best possible interest rate. This chapter explains the basics of available consumer loans, loan terms, and the use of automatic overdrafts and lines of credit—which should also be thought of as loans—in order to help you mastermind your credit management.

Basic Loans

There are two basic types of consumer loans:

1. Secured and
2. unsecured.

Secured Loans

These loans are secured by some property or asset; the two common types are car loans and mortgage loans, both of which are paid in installments. If payments are not made on time, your lender can take back the property to satisfy the loan. Other possible collateral includes savings passbooks and various acceptable investment certificates. For example, Treasury bills are accepted by commercial banks as collateral; U.S. savings bonds are not.

Unsecured Loans

No collateral is required for unsecured loans. Instead you pledge your "full faith and credit" to repay. If payments are not made on time, the lender can initiate legal action against you, and your credit rating could be adversely affected.

Both secured and unsecured loans may be repaid either in installments or in a single payment. Installments of 12, 24, or 36 equal monthly payments are common. Single-payment loans, also called term loans, are repaid in a lump sum at the end of the loan period, which can range from 30 days to several years.

Other Types of Loans

There are other, less convenient sources for loans: some offer lower interest rates than bank loans. These include life insurance policy loans; family loans; Keogh, 401(k), IRA, and pension plan loans; and brokerage account and margin loans.

1. *Life insurance policy loans.* Cash-value insurance policies build up equity through regular premium payments. The older the policy, the larger its cash value. Most policyholders can borrow the full amount of the cash value at interest rates from 5 percent to 13 percent, depending on the type of policy they carry and how old it is. This is an excellent source for emergency cash. You can generally get the money quickly, with few questions asked. In fact, it is common practice for policies to be bought with the intention of borrowing against cash values. For example, a partnership may buy life insurance to cover a buyout agreement. However, there is a limit to what you can borrow.

   Be advised that the total cost of borrowing against a life insurance policy is frequently greater than the low "net cost" quoted. Insurance companies calculate net cost by subtracting the return they pay on the account from the interest they charge on the loan. This figure ignores the opportunity cost of removing money from the cash-value account. As long as a policy loan is outstanding, the company may reduce the interest rate earned on the cash value well below its preloan rate. For a more realistic calculation of the cost of borrowing against a policy's cash account, the interest charged on the loan should be added to the difference between the pre-loan and post-loan interest rates on the cash value.

A policy loan may also adversely affect your death benefits and future premiums. Your death benefit is automatically decreased by the amount of your loan, but rises as you repay your loan. (The slower growth of the cash value during the life of the loan may reduce the potential death benefits on variable life policies and raises later premiums on policies with level death benefits to compensate for the loss of expected cash accumulation.)

2. *Family loans.* It used to be that keeping loans all in the family was in your best interest. No longer. Interest-free loans, a popular income-splitting technique, have been all but abolished. In general, interest-free loans must include an imputed interest payment, unless the loan is less than $10,000 and the borrower does not use the loan proceeds to purchase or carry income-producing assets. The rules also allow a loan of up to $100,000 to escape the interest imputation rules as long as the borrower's net investment income does not exceed $1,000. If it does, the amount of interest to be imputed is limited to the amount of the borrower's net investment income. If the purpose of the loan is tax avoidance, neither of these two exceptions apply, and interest must be imputed according to IRS regulations.

   In general, the IRS views loans to relatives, especially to children and parents, as gifts. If you are contemplating making a loan to a relative, take the same steps that would be taken in making a business loan (e.g., take a note, set a definite payment schedule, and require interest and, perhaps, collateral) so that if the loan is not repaid you may have a chance at taking a bad debt deduction. Or, if it's in your estate's best interest, why not consider "gifting" the amount?

Up to $10,000 per donee is gift tax free. (See Chapter 20 for details.)

3. *Keogh, 401(k), IRA, and pension plan loans.* A preretiree can borrow from his or her 401(k) account, with restrictions as to amount and duration. The advantage is that the interest on the loan is paid into the preretiree's own account. Ask your 401(k) manager for details.

   Technically, you can't borrow from your IRA. However, it is possible to use this account to get cash on a temporary basis. You can withdraw your money—no more than once a year—for 60 days without penalty. The cost of the loan becomes the interest not earned while the money is withdrawn. Borrowers beware: You must be very careful in using an IRA in this way. If the money is not returned within 60 days, you (the borrower) must pay income tax on the entire amount withdrawn plus a 10 percent penalty if you are under age 59½.

   Qualified retirement plan loans are subject to further restrictions. In general, the rules are intended to ensure that your plan assets are used for your retirement purposes and that loans are actually repaid and not permanently maintained by the use of balloon repayment obligations and bridge loans from third parties. Loans from pension funds to preretirees must be made at market interest rates and are subject to ceilings on the amounts borrowed.

4. *Brokerage accounts and margin loans.* Most brokerage firms allow you to borrow cash equal to 50 percent of the stocks and 80 percent of the bonds in your accounts. These are called margin loans. Traditionally, margin loans have been used to buy stock without paying full price. Investors pledge the stock they have in the brokerage house as collateral for the loan. Interest rates on these loans fluctuate with market rates. Interest paid on margin accounts is deductible only up to the extent of net investment income for the year (i.e., interest, dividends, and capital gains).

   Generally, you must maintain a minimum balance in your account. Individuals with very small portfolios should not borrow against them; if the value of the securities in a borrower's account falls, you could be forced either to pledge more securities or to pay back part of the loan. Investors have been wiped out in the past by rapidly declining stock prices. A sobering reminder—especially in uncertain economic times—of the need to use margin loans very judiciously, if at all.

Tax Aspects of Credit

The deductibility of interest depends largely on the type of loan. Home mortgage interest is still deductible but restricted, personal interest deductions are no longer permitted, while business interest (interest on debt incurred in a business, not including services performed as an employee) is generally still wholly deductible. (However, investment interest can be deducted only to the extent of net investment income.)

Because personal interest is no longer deductible from your income taxes, you should minimize this category of indebtedness and, if possible and appropriate, redeploy this debt into tax-deductible loans, such as a home equity loan.

Moreover, it is crucial that you keep comprehensive loan records; monthly credit card statements, mortgage papers, and installment loan records should be kept in your files. Keeping separate records of business, investment, home mortgage, and personal interest is essential.

Home Mortgage Interest

In general, you can deduct only interest paid on debt secured by a "qualified residence"—your primary personal residence plus a second property chosen by you (if you have more than two residences). The amount of interest that can be deducted on a refinancing is restricted to the value of the mortgage being refinanced plus $100,000, unless the proceeds are used for home improvements. Furthermore, there is a $1 million limit on acquisition indebtedness.

Qualified residence interest is deductible regardless of how the mortgage proceeds are spent.

> EXAMPLE: You draw $22,000 against your $50,000 home equity credit line to purchase a car that is used for personal purposes. The interest is deductible (assuming the loan meets all requirements to conform to the qualified residence interest rules) even though the proceeds were used for personal purposes.

Investment Interest

The amount of investment interest you can deduct is limited to the amount of net investment income (investment income less investment expenses). Investment interest is considered to be all interest on debt incurred to purchase property held for investment. Under the passive loss rules, investment interest also includes interest allocable to portfolio income or to the conduct of a business in which you do not materially participate.

Obtaining Information on Terms and Interest Rates

There are several sources for comparisons of consumer and mortgage loan interest rates. For example, the local papers in many cities list consumer credit and mortgage interest rates comparing local banks and other credit sources. Increasing competition among local lenders has also caused considerable variation in interest rates. Shopping for the optional interest rate and loan terms is therefore advisable.

Credit Bureaus

There are about 2,000 credit bureaus in the United States that serve as clearinghouses for information about your consumer debts and bill-paying habits. These credit bureaus keep files on a borrower's address, occupation, employer, marital history, moving habits, and salary. Some public-record information is also included (e.g., bankruptcies, lawsuits, judgments, and tax liens) that could affect a person's creditworthiness. The records that credit bureaus compile are just that—records, not ratings—and are subject to qualification.

Functions of Credit Bureaus

Credit bureaus sell creditors (and sometimes potential employers) the details of an individual's credit history, thus saving creditors the time and trouble of checking credit references. It is a good idea for you to check your credit records periodically with a leading credit bureau to correct possible errors before they result in the rejection of a credit or loan application. Reviewing the file is a good idea in any case; mistakes happen. Doing so is inexpensive; in addition, the Fair Credit Reporting Act of 1971 prohibits credit bureaus from charging a fee for review of a record within 30 days of being denied credit. To find the addresses of local credit bureaus, check the Yellow Pages under "Credit Reporting Agencies."

On the basis of the information provided by the credit bureau, creditors decide whether or not an applicant is a safe credit risk. Requirements vary depending on the extent of the proposed credit. A department store may be satisfied if a person is in the habit of repaying charges within 30 to 60 days. A bank, however, demands that loan installments be paid on time.

Credit Reports

Despite the fact that a credit report is not a rating (your potential creditors rate your credit applications), the reports reflect the soundness of your credit history. Not only will one's credit history appear on the report, but the agency compiling the report will also provide marginal comments on the status of various accounts, placing individuals in categories as a convenience to creditors. Comments usually indicate whether creditors perceive your history to be positive, negative, or neutral. Timely payments, of course, are perceived as positive; if you are behind in payments, the account may be neutral or negative, depending on the type of account, how far behind your payments are, and similar factors.

For each account, the report lists the creditor, type of account, terms, amount of the original debt or credit limit, and balance outstanding on the most recent report. A payment profile for the previous 12 months is made that indicates whether the individual fell behind on payments at any time during the previous year.

Generally, credit grantors are interested only in more recent information, usually for the past 12 to 24 months; many credit bureaus routinely delete older data from their files. However, bankruptcy can remain on a record for 10 years, and debts written off by creditors as uncollectible can remain for seven years.

Creditors' Rights

Under the Fair Credit Reporting Act you have the following rights:

1. To learn the name and address of the consumer reporting agency whose report hurt you in connection with a credit or job application.
2. To discover on request the nature and substance of all information, except medical, that a credit agency has on file about you.
3. To know the sources of such information, except investigative sources.

4. To get the names of all people who have received reports on you within the previous six months, or within the previous year if the report was furnished for employment reasons.
5. To have all incomplete or incorrect information investigated, and if any information cannot be found or is found to be inaccurate, to have that information deleted from your file.
6. To have a credit bureau notify all agencies of the credit bureau's mistake, at no cost to you.
7. To have your side of any controversy included in a creditor's report, if difference with that creditor cannot be resolved.
8. To have no information sent out that is more than seven years old (10 years if you have been bankrupt), with two exceptions: there are no time limits if you are applying for an insurance policy over specified limits or if you are applying for a job with a salary over specified limits.

Recent reports have indicated that a substantial number of credit bureau reports contain erroneous information. If you find incorrect information on your report, don't hesitate to demand that it be corrected—it's your right.

The government publishes many free or inexpensive guides on credit for consumers. You can obtain these booklets by writing to the following address: Consumer Information Center—Dept. Y, P.O. Box 100, Pueblo, CO. 81102.

Credit Cards, Purchase Financing, and Deferred Payments

Credit cards are a way of life for most Americans. They are a great convenience and, for those who properly manage their credit card obligations, an effective way to manage daily expenses without having to carry an inordinate amount of cash. Those who make the most effective use of credit cards understand what each type of card can and cannot do. Furthermore, they understand the nuances of credit card repayment terms.

Types of Credit Cards

You know that credit cards come in a variety of forms and are issued by banks, oil companies, retail establishments, and travel and entertainment enterprises (e.g., American Express, Carte Blanche, and Diners Club). But, are you aware that there are important differences among these types of credit cards, and all of them must be further distinguished from another card that looks like a credit card but isn't—the debit card.

Bank Credit Cards

Such cards as Visa or MasterCard are issued by banks, brokerage firms, and other organizations throughout the United States and are honored by many establishments worldwide. Typical terms for these bank cards include the following:

- Up to 36 months to pay.
- Interest rates ranging from 14 to 22 percent, depending on the state in which the card is issued.
- Small minimum monthly payments.
- Small annual fees though a few banks still issue free cards.
- Credit limits from $500 for first-time cardholders to $5,000 or more.
- No interest on new charges that are paid within 20 to 30 days of receipt of the bill.

Not all Visa or MasterCard cards are the same. The difference in interest rates, in how they are computed, and in annual fees can be substantial from one bank to another and from state to state. Comparative information on bank credit card interest rates is published in *Barron's* and may also be available in local newspapers.

Visa and MasterCard issue premium cards as rivals to the American Express Gold Card. Interest rates for premium cards are similar to those for regular cards, but annual fees may be more than twice the amount. In addition to higher credit limits, these premium cards often include no-fee traveler's checks, higher cash-advance and check-cashing limits, and free credit life insurance.

Whichever card is decided on, it is important for you to read the applications carefully. Read the fine print and if the interest rate is not apparent, ask about it.

Although most cards offer 20 to 30 days' grace without incurring interest charges, some have shorter grace periods, and others have none. Again, the fine print should disclose this information. Some cards also have transaction fees or other fees that are similar to check-writing fees that are charged each time the card is used. Be aware of the variable interest rate and how it is adjusted. The variable rate at some banks might have a floor of 18 percent, whereas the rate at others might have a ceiling of 18 percent.

Cash advances are available to Visa and MasterCard cardholders, but such advances should not be considered free money. Loan fees are charged, usually 2 percent of the loan amount, and interest on the loan begins to accumulate as soon as the advance is made. However, these cash advances do offer an important source of funds in an emergency.

Travel and Entertainment Cards

American Express, Diners Club, and Carte Blanche are the major travel and entertainment cards. On balance, the American Express card offers the most advantages and is accepted at more establishments than any other travel and entertainment cards. These cards are honored at some establishments that do not honor regular bank cards, such as prestige clothing stores and upscale restaurants.

Travel and entertainment cards, when compared to other credit cards, often charge higher annual fees. (Unless you need the higher line of credit or check-cashing privileges that go with such premium cards as the American Express Gold and Platinum cards, they probably are not worth the extra annual fees.) Moreover, there is an additional fee for extra cards for a spouse or children, and payment in full must be made within 20 to 30 days of receipt of the bill. There are limited exceptions to this policy: There is no interest if charges are paid on time, but credit privileges may be canceled if they are not. There is no spending limit, but eligibility requirements are much stricter than with other cards. Technically, these cards are charge cards, not credit cards; their main purpose is convenience not credit.

Nevertheless, if you are planning a trip, travel and entertainment cards offer some advantages over regular bank cards. An airline ticket, hotel, and meal charges might combine to quickly exhaust the credit line on a Visa or MasterCard, whereas travel and entertainment cards have no spending limits.

Debit Cards

Many banks issue MasterCard, Visa, or their own debit cards. Debit cards look like regular credit cards; however, instead of sending monthly bills, the bank transfers payments directly from your checking, savings, or asset management account as soon as it receives notice of the charge.

Because the cards are directly linked to your bank accounts, you must monitor them as closely as you do your checkbook. Debit cards offer some convenience in paying bills but on balance they don't have any outstanding virtues.

Maximizing Credit Care Usefulness

There are various factors that can affect the way you are billed for your credit card balances. Use them to your advantage. If you know the billing cycle, use your cards on days that will give the longest use of the money without interest. If fact, you can obtain six to eight weeks of free credit by buying just after the billing date and paying in full just before the due date. One card may actually be cheaper than two because of the break point: For example, if the APR is 18 percent on the first $500 and 12 percent on amounts over that, it is better to charge $1,000 on the same card. (If your cards are issued by the same bank, it is advisable to ask the bank to combine the billing and charge the lower combined rate.)

Retail establishments pay high charges to credit card companies for providing customer convenience of using cards. Often, however, such charges are tacked on to retail prices. Unfortunately, the person who pays the cash or check still pays the extra charge. A customer who might otherwise use a credit card should ask if there is a discount for paying cash. Occasionally, a retailer is willing to give the cash customer a small discount.

Card issuers are trying to lure customers by augmenting their cards with incentives known as enhancements. Such enhancements may include cash advances, luxury suites, toll-free message services, check-cashing services, card and travel insurance, and even small rebates of amounts purchased with the card, for example, the Discover Card. Think twice before signing up for these enhancements. Some of them are of little value to begin with (e.g., credit card insurance). Even if the issuer doesn't charge for these services directly, you will probably end up paying for them through larger annual fees and higher interest rates. No matter what, remember that prompt payment of credit card bills is in your best interest.

Safeguarding Cards

The fraudulent use of credit cards and bank ATM cards is a prevalent problem though it is often avoidable if you follow some basic rules. These are discussed in the following sections.

Credit Cards

If a card is fraudulently used, under Federal Reserve rules the cardholder is liable for only $50 of all purchases made. Nevertheless, the episode may be held against you should you decide to apply for a higher credit limit. It is also an inconvenience to be left without a card for several weeks, or even months. Precautions can be taken to avoid these problems.

First, keep alert during all transactions. Make sure your card is used on only one sales slip and check to see that the card returned is your own. Second, be discreet about credit card numbers. Never throw away receipts without first tearing them up; counterfeiters use these numbers to duplicate cards. Furthermore, never give out a card number over the phone, except when calling a reputable merchant to order goods or services. (A legitimate bank or credit company would never call and ask customers to give out their card numbers.) Third, adopt thorough clerical procedures. Scrutinize monthly bills to ensure that all charges are valid. Also, be advised to make a list of all your cards and account numbers and check every so often to make sure that your cards are all there. Finally, carry as few credit cards as possible.

Bank ATM Cards

In the event of fraudulent use, there may be greater liability with bank ATM cards than with standard credit cards. There is a $50 maximum charge if the bank is notified within two business days of discovering the loss; after that, the liability increases to $500. If you receive a bank statement showing unauthorized charges and fail to report them within 60 days, then liability for future charges becomes unlimited.

Two simple precautions can help prevent bank card fraud. First, never select an obvious number. Given the option of selecting a card identification number, never choose your Social Security number, birthday, or any other number that might appear in your wallet or pocketbook. (Those are the first numbers a pickpocket will try.) Second, your card identification number should never be written on the card or kept in a wallet or pocketbook. It sounds elementary, but in an informal survey, one bank found card identification numbers written on 25 percent of its ATM cards!

Lost or Stolen Cards

Anyone who has credit cards should keep a list in his or her file (not his or her wallet or pocketbook) of all the account numbers. That way, if a card is lost or stolen, you can promptly notify the proper issuers. There are companies that offer such a notification service; the user registers the charge cards with the company. However, because the maximum liability on lost credit cards is $50 and because some companies charge a small annual fee, the need for these services is questionable.

If a card is lost or stolen and you have not kept a list of your card numbers, the account number can be identified on a recent charge account statement.

Automobile Financing and Leasing

In the 1960s, the typical American spent about two months' gross salary to purchase a new car. Today, it is not unusual for someone to pay as much as 12 months' income on a new car. As if things weren't bad enough, high financing costs make the situation even worse. Shopping for car financing is therefore just as important as shopping for the car itself.

For many consumers, money that used to go into savings and investments is now being spent to finance automobiles. While this may be acceptable financial misbehavior for a youngster, it's hardly so for the over-50 consumer! Longer-term auto loans (they now average more than four years, and some banks finance luxury cars for up to nine years) simply exacerbate the problem. Nevertheless, many over-50s buy new cars more frequently than their younger counterparts. Tip: Shop wisely for automobile financing in order to help minimize your overall costs. Also, consider buying less expensive cars and keeping them longer. The benefits of doing this can easily be demonstrated by comparing the cost of trading a car every few years with that of keeping and maintaining a car for 7 to 10 years.

Those who are in the habit of financing cars long-term while trading cars frequently will find (because these loans are calculated by the add-on method) that a large portion of principal remains unpaid when they get ready to trade in the car.

The following facts pertain to the cost and convenience of a car loan and should be understood and considered carefully:

1. The total finance cost is the exact amount in dollars that is to be paid to finance the car.
2. APR is the cost of the loan expressed as the yearly percentage of the amount still unpaid. In comparing loans with the same repayment period, the loan with the lower APR should be chosen.
3. The shorter the repayment period, the lower the total finance cost but the larger the monthly payments. In general, a car should be financed over a short period, ideally 24 months or fewer. The reason is that it can be both financially and psychologically discouraging to be incurring repair bills and making car payments at the same time.
4. The dealer should specify the exact dollar amount of the down payment. The dealer's percentage figure, which could appear to be a percentage of just the price of the car, might actually include the sales tax and license and registration fees as well. Also, beware of "no down payment" loans; they cost more in the long run because you are financing the car's entire purchase price.
5. A monthly due date should be selected that puts the least strain on your family budget, so that all bills are not due at the same time of the month.
6. Penalties for late payments or prepayments are included in some contracts. Look for loans without prepayment penalties and with low late fees.
7. Some loan sources require credit life and disability insurance, which would pay off the loan if you die or become disabled before the final payment. Any insurance offered by the finance source is usually expensive and should be avoided.

Collateralized Loans

For collateralized car loans, the car is used as security; the borrower does not legally own it until the final payment is made. Payment periods usually extend from 12 to 60 months. These loans can be obtained from several sources, including credit unions, banks, automobile dealers, and finance companies. Credit unions often offer the lowest rates, and loan requests from members are seldom rejected. Stay active in your credit union even after you've retired. Bank interest rates are typically one to three percentage points higher than those of credit unions.

Automobile dealers offer financing through the car manufacturing or local financing outlets. All terms are negotiated with the dealer, including the interest rate and repayment conditions; the rate is often higher than your bank's rate. Periodically, dealers or manufacturers do advertise very low interest rates; however, the lower rate is almost always offset by a smaller discount from the automobile list price, and a substantial (20 to 30 percent) downpayment. Of course, if you can afford the downpayment, you might well be better off taking this route.

Finance company rates are usually much higher than those of banks. The option of a loan from a finance company should be considered only if all other sources are *not* available.

Automobile Brokers

A broker can provide you with a car, with any options desired, for an average of $125 above dealer cost on domestic cars and approximately $1,000 over invoice on imports. The broker usually arranges for you to pick up the car through a nearby dealer, where you can also have it serviced.

There are several types of car brokers. Full-service brokers handle every aspect of the deal, from arranging the financing to testing the radio. You need only go to the dealership and sign the necessary papers. This level of service can cost $200 or more. At the other extreme, for as little as $20, some less comprehensive services will provide you with a computerized price list comparing a dealer's invoice price with the retail price. "Consumer Reports" offers this service, for example. Some brokers are actually referral services that provide you with the names of dealers who, under an arrangement with service, will sell cars at a specific dollar or percentage level under the manufacturer's suggested retail price. You must negotiate with the dealer on prices of options and must also set up financing and handle any trade-in.

The obvious advantage of using a broker is that you get the right car, and the right price with a favorable warranty. A full-service broker offers buying without the concerns of automobile financing. One disadvantage, however, is that you do not get to test drive or even see the car until it is delivered. Another major drawback is that the credit terms are generally very stiff; lower interest rates are often available at a bank. Some brokers insist that a buyer finance the car with them and purchase expensive insurance and extended warranties; rarely a good deal.

Check out a prospective broker company with the Better Business Bureau to see if there are any complaints lodged against it. Some states require brokers or buying services to be licensed or bonded. If your intended broker is a member of the National Automobile Dealers Association, chances are that he or she is a safe bet.

Arranging for foreign purchase of luxury automobiles can be risky. Most deals require cash months before the automobile is delivered, and there are some unscrupulous operators who will pocket your money and disappear. Furthermore, the automobile must be retro-fitted to meet U.S. emission standards, which costs several thousand dollars and carries the possibility of severely damaging the car. Be wary of these arrangements.

Noncollateral Loans

When you purchase an automobile with a noncollateral loan, it cannot be repossessed in the case of default. If you have a strong credit capacity, but you can't pay cash, you might want to consider the following types of loans.

Passbook Loans

Deposit-account (i.e., passbook) loans from banks are not direct car loans. The bank lends you an amount of money equal to the balance of your savings account, and these savings must remain on deposit while the loan is repaid. They continue to earn interest during this time. Interest rates on passbook loans are very good, usually two percentage points higher than what the money is earning in a savings account. This does not mean that a borrower with a deposit-account loan at 11 percent and a savings account paying 6 percent faces net interest of only 5 percent. The rate is still 11 percent; interest earned on the savings account has no direct bearing on this.

Insurance Policy Loans

Insurance companies offer loans to their policyholders. If you are a whole life policyholder, you can borrow from the cash value of your policies at rates that are usually considerably less than commercial automobile loan rates. Borrowers are billed for the interest, but they can repay the principal on their own time. If a borrower dies before the loan is repaid, the amount he or she owes is deducted from the face value of the policy before the company pays the beneficiary.

Signature Loans

Signature loans are unsecured bank loans for automobile purchases. Because these loans are unsecured, their interests rates are higher than the rates the same banks would charge for car loans.

Leasing

Leasing an automobile, usually from one to five years, is becoming a more popular and attractive option. Leasing is convenient; everything can be taken care of from license plates to insurance, and a maintenance contract covering repairs can also be included.

Two types of leases are available: closed end and open end. In a closed-end agreement, the car is leased for a specific amount of time, at the end of which the car is returned to the dealer, ending one's obligation. However, payments are based on expected mileage, agreed on at the inception of the contract. A lessee who exceeds this figure can face an additional per-mile fee. With an open-end lease, the car is assessed at the time that the lease is signed. Upon its return, the car is sold. If it brings less than the dealer originally estimated, the lessee is liable to pay the difference, up to a maximum of three times the monthly payment in accordance with the Consumer Leasing Act. If it brings more than estimated, however, the lessee is entitled to a refund.

Among the advantages of leasing an automobile are the following:

- The cost of leasing and operating the automobile can be deducted if it is used for business purposes.
- The lessee can afford a more expensive car. Most monthly lease payments are lower than purchase payments, because the lessor usually gets the car back at the end of the lease period. (The wisdom of purchasing a more expensive car should be assessed.)
- Leasing can cost only a few hundred dollars more than buying if the lessee usually keeps a car for fewer than five years.

- No down payment is required if the lessee's credit history is very favorable. If the credit rating is less than sterling, a small down payment might be requested, usually equal to two monthly payments.

The disadvantages of leasing include the following:

- The more expensive the car that is leased, the more the lessee "saves" buying. Thus, leasing can encourage some over-50s to obtain more expensive cars than may be needed.
- Leasing tends to encourage trading automobiles more frequently than may be economically desirable. When the leasing agreement is ended, the lessee must lease again, and lease payments can continue forever. However, the longer one owns a car, the cheaper it is to operate, because it physically depreciates less each year. Financing a car short term and keeping it well beyond the loan period makes more sense for most people. Over the long run, leasing arrangements are almost always more expensive than buying the car and financing it.

Using Your Home for Credit

Many financial institutions offer a line of revolving credit ("equity lines of credit") with your home as collateral. These types of financing plans are designed for people who have accumulated substantial equity in their homes or who have seen the market value of their homes appreciate but have not realized any of the gain. For the most part, over-50s fit this bill.

Other programs, such as the reverse annuity mortgage (RAM), provide the older retiree with a monthly check resulting from the partial conversion of their home equity. Homeowners facing major expenses can also take out a second mortgage.

Because the deductibility of consumer interest has been eliminated, home equity loans have become an attractive alternative for obtaining credit. Nevertheless, there are potential problems. If you fall behind on your payments, your home is at risk. Moreover, variable interest rates on most home equity loans mean that if interest rates rise, payments will rise, too—perhaps dramatically. This is especially true of lines of credit with no cap on or maximum increase in the interest rate. In addition, although most home equity loans no longer charge points, many require fees. Finally, rules regarding home equity loan interest deductibility are complicated. The result: Home equity financing should not be seen as an easy and painless way to generate cash. The decision to convert home equity should be made only after a meticulous review of your options. An imprudent plan could be devastating.

Even if you manage your home equity credit lines reasonably well you may find that, rather than enjoying your retirement years with little or no mortage indebtedness (a very desirable financial planning objective), you will be saddled with substantial mortgage payments well into your retirement years. Therefore, evaluate the long-term as well as the short-term implications of adding to your home indebtedness.

Home Equity Conversion

Even affluent retirees may eventually face the problem of being cash poor, having limited income to cope with medical expenses, an increased cost of living, or other financial problems. Home equity conversion plans allow retirees to supplement their incomes by converting some of their home equity into cash. These plans differ basically in the amount of cash they provide.

Reverse Mortgage

With a conventional mortgage, you repay the lender over a specified time period, at the end of which you (i.e., the borrower) own the home. Under the reverse mortgage plan, however, the borrower owns a home and the lender, typically a bank, issues a loan based on a percentage (usually 20 to 60 percent) of your home equity. You receive periodic (monthly or quarterly) payments from the lender, based on an annual calculation, or receive a lump sum. Usually, the retirement of the debt entails the selling of the home.

The size of the cash flow to you resulting from a reverse mortgage is determined by property value, interest rates, and age. The property value and your equity determine the size of the loan. Your age is a determinant of the loan term (i.e., the time over which the cash flow is spread), and the interest rate affects the actual amount. Therefore, a combination of high interest rates and long life expectancies may not yield a cash flow great enough for you to consider taking out the reverse mortgage. For example, monthly payments to you from a reverse mortgage, assuming a $50,000 balance and a 12 percent interest rate, would be $612.22 with a five-year term, $217.35 with a 10-year term, and only $50.54 with a 20-year term.

The reverse mortgage is ideally suited for the retiree who expects to move soon but needs money in the interim or for the retiree who does not expect to outlive the mortgage. Current income from a reverse mortgage is maximized when interest rates are low and especially when the loan term is short. This short loan term, which makes the mortgage most attractive for those wishing to increase their income, is also the greatest danger of the reverse mortgage. If the loan comes due and you have insufficient funds to repay, the bank may foreclose, leaving you with no other housing options. Or, the retiree who outlives the mortgage may be forced to sell the home and move, an experience that can be traumatic. The reverse mortgage, then, must be carefully written to provide you with enough income for a sufficiently long period of time.

Reverse Annuity Mortgages

The RAM is similar to the reverse mortgage, but with a RAM you're guaranteed a home and income for life. Consequently, the income stream is smaller than that from a reverse mortgage. The RAM is an income supplement, not an income generator, a boost in a retiree's monthly income.

To obtain a RAM, you first take out a mortgage from a savings and loan institution. With the proceeds, you purchase an annuity from an insurance company. The insurance company subtracts the interest due on the mortgage from each annuity payment and sends it to the lending institution. The remainder is sent to you. The subtracted interest remains constant for the duration of the RAM because the loan is not repaid. When you die, the home is sold and the mortgage principal is repaid—any remaining proceeds go to your estate.

The size of the annuity payment depends on interest rates, the property's value, your age, and your marital status. Because the insurance company is taking on a mortality risk and wants to ensure a profit for itself, the annuity payment is going to be smaller than a straight reverse mortgage payment over a fixed term.

The main disadvantage of the RAM is its *tax effects*. To determine the amount of the annuity that must be declared as income, a complicated calculation is necessary. Suffice it to say that you may wind up paying taxes on money you have never received. Just as for a reverse mortgage, the interest rate plays a key role in determining the feasibility of this financing plan.

Private Annuities

With a private annuity, you sell your home to a private party (often your children) or to a corporation and in turn receive an annuity for life. In addition to the cash flow impact, the private annuity has both estate planning and tax ramifications that must be weighed.

The private annuity removes the home or other asset from your estate. Assuming you will spend the income from the annuity, the transfer has the effect of lowering the total value of your estate.

There is an emotional advantage to keeping the home in the family. However, the private annuity may be difficult to arrange. Children may be reluctant to assume ownership of the home, may not be able to agree with their siblings as to the arrangement, or may not have the resources to do so.

Retirees should investigate the possibility of a private annuity because it combines the advantage of the RAM—the guarantee of continued living in one's present house—with an increased cash flow.

If used wisely, a private annuity has many tax savings, but the tax advantage can be a double-edged sword. No capital gain is immediately realized on the transfer of property (for income tax purposes), and no fair value can be placed on the unsecured promise of a person to pay the annuity. The price of this tax advantage is an unsecured promise that the person to whom you sell your home will, in fact, make the stipulated payments to you for the rest of your life.

Refinancing

Methods of using your home's equity to generate cash include refinancing an existing mortgage, taking out a second mortgage, or taking out a home equity loan. With these techniques, the equity is not converted, as it is in the plans previously described. Rather, the equity is used as collateral for a cash loan. Refinancing, then, is often not suitable for the retiree because it imposes an extra debt. Moreover, refinancing may be unwise for any retiree who may eventually need Medicaid. Equity in a home does not disqualify you from

Medicaid, but the cash proceeds of refinancing may have to be exhausted before you can qualify for it.

Nevertheless, if you face major expenditures and have substantial equity in your home, you can borrow against this equity. As always, become familiar with the different plans to locate the one that best fits your needs.

Refinancing Existing Mortgages

Refinancing an existing mortgage is the process of taking out a new mortgage large enough to retire the old mortgage and provide the needed extra funds. The costs involved makes this plan unsuitable for many, because a complete new house closing, with all associated costs, must be undertaken. In addition, the interest rate may be higher than the interest rate on the existing mortgage, so the monthly costs will be greater. Therefore, refinancing is most effective when the existing mortgage is almost paid off or when the current interest rates are lower than the original rate, often as little as one to two points lower. Before refinancing a mortgage, however, compare the costs of the new mortgage versus the existing mortgage, taking into consideration the incremental closing costs. It is important to note that the IRS states that points paid in *refinancing* a mortgage are no longer immediately tax deductible. Instead, they must be spread over the life of your new loan. In addition, home mortgage interest that can be deducted on a refinancing is limited to the value of the mortgage being refinanced plus $100,000 unless the proceeds are used for home improvements.

Second Mortgages

Taking out a second mortgage is another means of drawing on your home's equity. Usually, you can borrow up to 80 percent of equity, and the interest rate on the second mortgage may be either fixed or adjusted periodically. The adjustable-rate second mortgage is risky, but it is also less expensive at first and it could remain less expensive if interest rates during the mortgage lifetime are low.

The main drawback of a second mortgage is the burden of the additional debt and often higher interest rates. If you are still paying a first mortgage, you may have difficulty with a second mortgage added. Nevertheless, the second mortgage might be a flexible method for financing large expenditures.

Home Equity-Secured Credit

Home equity-secured credit is essentially a credit account, secured by a second mortgage, that operates like a checking account. Generally, the line of credit is 70 to 80 percent of the appraised value of the house less what is owed on it. For example, a house worth $200,000 with $80,000 still unpaid on the mortgage might qualify for a $90,000 line of credit (75 percent of $200,000 less $80,000). Usually, the amount of credit allowed depends on your income. (The length of the loan may range from 5 to 12 years, or longer at some institutions.) It is wise to shop among local lenders, because interest rates, origination fees, and maintenance costs can vary substantially.

A home equity line of credit is a convenient, flexible way to borrow that can preserve the deductibility of interest under the current tax laws. Once your line of credit is in place, you are not required to fill out a loan application again. However, because such credit draws on the equity built up in your home (i.e., the difference between the value of your home and what you owe on it), it should be used only for major expenditures and worthwhile purposes, such as home improvements, grandchildren's education expenses, major purchases (e.g., an automobile) and debt consolidation.

Home equity-secured credit usually offers a lower interest rate than other lines of credit because it is secured by the equity in your home. Most home equity lines of credit have a variable interest rate, which is usually based on the prime rate or a government Treasury bill rate index. This allows you to secure the best rate available at a given time. However, these rates will fluctuate over time, sometimes raising monthly payments. Make sure you can afford this flexibility.

When evaluating and selecting a home equity loan, review the following list of considerations:

- Is a home equity loan most suitable for your needs?
- Are there application fees? Annual fees? Closing fees?
- What is the minimum monthly payment? How much of it will go toward paying off principal?
- Do minimum monthly payments go up with variable interest rates? How much?
- Are there conditions under which monthly payments can be reduced?

- Can the bank demand refinancing of outstanding credit? Can any of the credit terms be changed without your approval?
- Is there an option to convert the line of credit into a fixed-term installment loan? If so, at what interest rate and over what period of time?
- If income or the amount of available equity increases, can your line of credit be increased?

Choosing a Plan

When choosing an option to finance a large expenditure, consider which plan best meets your long- and short-term needs. The second mortgage has a shorter repayment period and therefore, probably a lower total cost. If you take out a second mortgage, you have to choose between a fixed-rate mortgage, a variable-rate mortgage, and a credit line secured by a second mortgage. The fixed-rate mortgage is more expensive but is more secure than a variable-rate mortgage. The home equity credit line, if available, is attractive because it simplifies the financing procedure into a something akin to a checking account. A key determinant: the interest rate.

Proper Use of Financing

Home equity loans, reverse mortgages, and other related plans give you more financial freedom. However, despite the attractiveness of these new forms of borrowing, you should use them with discretion, and only for productive purposes. At any time in your life, but especially once you've passed the 50-year-mark, it is downright foolish to risk sinking into debt or losing your home because you want money for an extravagant gift or a luxury item. Appropriate purposes include maintaining home improvements, perhaps financing grandchildren's education (although refinancing should not be used for this purpose until all other sources of education financing have been considered) and providing needed income late in life so long as you will be able to continue making loan payments for the rest of your life.

Home equity loans can represent an excellent source of credit. They are flexible, and the interest on them may continue to be tax deductible. Proper use of financing, however, remains essential. You could jeopardize your home as a result of abusing this relatively easy and heavily marketed form of credit. In essence, proper management of home equity loans is no different from debt management of a business entity. The loan principal should be paid off over a time period consistent with the use of loan proceeds.

Home equity loan borrowers, like businesses, typically borrow for short-term purposes (e.g., vacations, home maintenance and repairs, and payment of estimated income taxes), intermediate-term purposes (e.g., automobiles), or longer-term purposes (e.g., major home improvements and payment of college tuition bills). Short-term loans should be paid off within a year, intermediate loans should be paid off over a few years at most, and longer-term loans should be paid off over a maximum of 10 to 15 years.

If you lack the self-discipline to manage your borrowing properly, particularly when you have such easy access to a large credit line, then don't tempt yourself. Financial institutions are already beginning to note a disturbing increase in the rate of home equity loan foreclosures! A typical case of misuse: borrowing for a car through a home equity credit line and not making any payments against principal and then purchasing another car a few years later by simply adding to the existing indebtedness. Keep this pattern up and you too could eventually be faced with serious credit problems.

Some lenders offer interest-only payments, which may be appropriate when special circumstances make it difficult or undesirable for you to pay down the principal. Generally, however, it is preferable to pay down at least some principal to retire the debt. If you are making only the minimum monthly payments on your home equity loan, take it as an early warning sign of potential credit problems.

With some plans, interest-only payments lead to a balloon payment at the end of the loan term. This arrangement may be appropriate for you if you can predict that you can pay off your loan at a future time (e.g., if you are planning to sell the home). For others, it may be entirely inappropriate. In general, despite the potential pitfalls, if you can repay your home equity borrowing over an appropriate period of time, it can be a very effective tool for credit management.

Managing Financial Difficulties

Although credit has recently been more difficult to obtain, the easy availability of credit in the past has burdened many over-50s with debt. That debt may take years to pay off. Others have encountered financial difficulties not of their own making. For example, increasing numbers of professional and managerial-level workers are losing their jobs because of organizational downsizing, mergers, weak business or economic conditions—all of which add up to an unexpected but necessary early retirement.

How much is too much debt? One guideline is not to owe more than 15 to 20 percent of one's yearly after-tax income (excluding home mortgage). Another is not to owe more than one-third of one's yearly discretionary income, which is income leftover after such basics as food, clothing, and shelter are paid for. However, an acceptable debt level depends on your particular circumstance. Also, it is important to remember that very few people manage to get through life without experiencing a period of some financial difficulty. Hopefully, that period is behind you.

Warning Signs

People of all ages, occupations, and income levels run into credit trouble. The problem is even increasing among upper-income people who are trying to maintain their standard of living while taxes and inflation are reducing their discretionary income. Be watchful for the first signs of credit abuse:

- Amount owed on various charge accounts are rising steadily, so you are never out of debt to local stores.
- Before you have finished paying last month's bills, this month's are stacking up. Payments are always late, and you are regularly receiving notes about delinquent accounts and perhaps some notices threatening legal action.
- You are continually lengthening the repayment periods on installment purchases and putting down smaller initial payments.
- You are taking cash advances on credit cards or using savings to pay basic monthly bills (e.g., rent or utilities).
- So many separate bills are received each month from so many sources that you borrow from a lending institution to have one consolidated loan. Yet credit buying continues, adding more and more new bills to this one big debt.
- An ever-increasing portion of your net income goes to pay debts.
- You are using large credit lines (e.g., a home equity loan), to

pay for current living expenses or to make frivolous purchases.
- You are making only the minimum required monthly repayments on credit cards or a home equity loan.

Getting Out of Debt

If an unexpected expense is causing a short-term credit problem, you may be able to juggle your bills. Current living expenses (e.g., rent or mortgage) must be paid first; phone and utilities can be delayed somewhat. Next, pay the minimum allowed on the bills that affect your credit ratings. Bills that do not affect your credit rating can probably be held off a month or two without jeopardizing the account.

What should you do if you are over your head in debt beyond the ability to work it out in a few months? First, discuss the situation with each creditor and try to work it out. Explain why you are overextended and arrange a repayment loan. Many creditors will go along with a reasonable plan under which they will receive their money slowly, if you show that you are trying to pay debts as opposed to avoiding them. Most creditors prefer doing this to trying to repossess the goods or taking the debt to court, which is expensive and time-consuming. Also, you should do everything possible to avoid repossession, litigation, or having an account turned over to a collection agency.

If an arrangement cannot be made directly with your creditors, credit counselors may provide the answer. Bankruptcy should be viewed as a last resort.

Debt Counseling

If you have financial problems that you can't resolve, the next step is to consult a credit counselor, provided the problem is not a psychological or legal one. There are various institutions that offer such counseling, including the following:

- Many banks and credit unions offer formal or informal debt counseling for their customers or members.
- Hundreds of family service agencies throughout the country can provide financial counseling or will make referrals to an appropriate professional.
- Nonprofit consumer credit counseling organizations backed

by local banks and merchants provide services to anyone, particularly to overextended families or individuals. If you are slightly overextended, the agency will usually help you develop a repayment plan for a nominal monthly fee. The agency may take monthly payments from you and distribute them to your creditors. The agency also talks to the creditors and often gets them to agree to a delayed or reduced payment. Because these groups are backed by local merchants, they will do everything possible to get you to repay debts and may not advise bankruptcy even if the situation seems to warrant it. In addition, the fact that one has used this service is reported to credit bureaus and noted on one's credit record.

Budget Realistically

No matter what the cause of the financial difficulty, it is essential to continue to prepare a realistic budget. The first step is to put away all credit cards until all debts are settled. If you lack willpower, destroy your cards. Next, income should be determined and the possibility of additional income should be explored. You might cash in some investments to take a temporary second job. Then, the entire family should identify exactly how the money is spent, dividing expenses into categories and deciding which are essential and which are optional. What obligations must be met? What can be put off or given up? The resulting budget should be practicable; if it is too harsh, it is unlikely to be followed. Failure to follow your budget will almost always lead you down the path toward financial travail. But if you can stick to your budget, you will be well on your way to firm financial footing.

List of Debts

Figure 9.1 can be used to evaluate your current indebtedness. It represents a simplified way to keep track of your less complicated debts.

Figure 9.1. Evaluating Current Indebtedness

Creditor	Type of Loan	Date of Last Payment	Maturity Date	Monthly Payment	Total Amount Due
....	....	....	....	$.......	$.........
....	....	....	....	....	....
....	....	....	....	....	....
....	....	....	....	....	....
....	....	....	....	....	....
....	....	....	....	....	....
....	....	....	....	....	....
....	....	....	....	....	....
....	....	....	....	....	....
....	....	....	....	....	....
....	....	....	....	....	....
....	....	....	....	....	....
....	....	....	....	....	....
....	....	....	....	....	....
....	....	....	....	....	....
....	....	....	....	....	....
....	....	....	....	....	....
....	....	....	....	....	....

Total Monthly Payments $.......

Total amount owed $.........

10

AVOIDING SCAMS: IF IT SOUNDS TOO GOOD TO BE TRUE, IT IS

IT'S BEEN SAID countless times: If it sounds too good to be true, it is. Yet, surprisingly, countless numbers continue to neglect its basic truth. In fact, so many people fall victim to fraudulent schemes that P.T. Barnum's estimation of consumer savvy, "there's a sucker born every minute," needs to be revised. According to the Council of Better Business Bureaus, which admits that it can't even begin to quantify the *actual* number, a more appropriate estimate would be that *1,700* suckers are born every minute. This figure should give even the most experienced over-50 investor and homeowner reason to be guarded about future money transactions. For the novice over-50 investor—cash rich, but knowledge poor—the statistic should be downright sobering.

This chapter is intended to be your wake-up call to investment scams and other types of fraud. It should help you know what to look out for, and what sources you should trust for questions and guidance concerning businesses and individuals who are interested in giving you that clever sounding but ill-fated "once in a lifetime deal." Of course, the burden of insuring yourself against becoming a victim of one scheme or another is up to you. Fortunately, there are many sources at your beck, if you have the sense to call.

"It'll Never Happen to Me"

"New and improved:" The credo of a product's progress. Yet, how many times have you actually purchased a product because of such a claim? Most of us, since we've been active consumers for many decades, aren't convinced that a dazzling new package and a glitter of rhetoric translates into substantial improvements in an old product. Nevertheless, when it comes to investments that cost more than a bread box—a new roof for our home, a land investment in a sunny climate, or the chance to get in on the bottom floor of a new stock of a company we have never heard of—we prove time and again that we're gullible. Granted, there isn't always an easy warning signal like the catch phrase "new and improved." However, the following phrases are prevalent in most financial schemers vocabulary:

"Unconditional lifetime money-back guarantee"

"Big savings"

"Will last forever"

"It's now or never"

"If at any time you're not completely satisfied"

"You can't lose"

If someone comes knocking at your door, or starts talking a mile a minute to you on your phone, or is sending you glitzy mailgrams which tell you that you are a "definite, absolute, guaranteed winner if only you . . .", politely shut the door, hang up the phone, and/or make good use of your circular file. Believe me, bunk is bunk, no matter how pretty the wrapping or flowery the words. In fact, the prettier the wrapping and the more flowery the words the greater the likelihood that you're being duped. So, if it sounds too good to be true, it probably is. If it all sounds too simple to be believed, it is probably much more complex. If you think you are being misled, you probably are. And, if you feel you're being pressured, you most likely *are* being pressured. The scam artist knows how to tell a tall tale, and make it sound convincing. Some themes that could embroil you in the leading role of your own financial tragedy are:

- Anything that requires up front cash to get rich quick. (The only person who stands to get rich quick this way is the person who is pitching the scheme to you.)
- Anything that requires you to pay for the secrets of someone else's success. (We all like secrets, but how secret can it be if it is broadcast every morning on your local T.V. station? The true secret to such success lies in the ability to sell the products which the expensive T.V. advertisement is pushing on you.)
- Anything that promises to make you or your house the envy of your neighbors. (Does a fake brick facade really enhance the look of your home more than a decent paint job? The price, usually with the temptation to finance the project, often leaves you twice as much in debt for your newly adorned, fake brick castle.)
- Anything that costs you money in order to save you money. (If a new gas furnace is what an "inspector" who came to your home unannounced and offering a free furnace inspection ordered, with the attendant reasoning that a new furnace will save you hundreds of dollars over the next several years, simply ask what if anything is wrong with the old one. Chances are, the cost of the new furnace will not save you enough money to make up the difference of your "inefficient" old one. A brand new furnace will lead you to the poorhouse faster than the perfectly competent one you now have. The same goes for water filtration systems.)
- Anyone who tells you that rather than working for your money, you should let your money work for you. (Making your money grow is the hardest, albeit the most rewarding work you'll ever do.)
- Anyone who doesn't tell you in plain English what it is you're putting your money into. (If you can't easily understand what you're being told to buy, don't buy it.)
- Anyone who doesn't have the time, inclination, or willingness to let you get a second opinion about the proposed investment idea. (What's the rush? A good investment should always be long lived.)

From tragedy to philosophy: forewarned is forearmed. It was

the Greek philosopher Socrates who affirmed that a knowledgeable person was distinguished as such by knowing what he or she didn't know. In financial matters, this should be your philosophical maxim: Know what you don't know. The reason: It will help you avoid whimsical or impulse investing. (Never buy on impulse, especially from a complete stranger. The likelihood of disaster, no matter how safe it seems, is almost guaranteed.) Before you open your wallet or checkbook again, repeat the following credos to yourself:

know the product
know the salesperson
know the company
know when to say **"NO!"**

Scams

In the end, the only way to be 100 percent positive that you will never be the victim of a scam that leaves you cash short is to never buy or invest in anything at all. However, since abstinence is far from a reasonable proposal, it is best to familiarize yourself with the scam artist's array of temptations.

Some of the most common examples of scams seem as simple as a stone, but prove to be complex webs of deception whenever they're turned over and examined. The most common scam is called a pyramid scheme. A close relation, in structure and use, is called a Ponzi scheme.

Pyramid Schemes

The most common scam going, pyramid schemes are something that many of us have first hand knowledge of. The racket: a letter arrives promising untold riches that will materialize if only you would participate and pass it on. Participation is simple; you only have to remove the name at the top of a list of, say, six people, send the person whose name you removed $1 to $100, and then put your name at the bottom of the list. You then send the revised letter to the same number of people on the list; six new unsuspecting lambs. When your name hits the top of the list, you have success. For example, say a list of six names comes to you. You remove the name at the top, insert your own, and send it along to six new people. At the end of the day, a day that never comes, you will receive your original amount multiplied to the sixth level—or 279,936 people participating. By the time the letter reaches the tenth level, 362,797,056 people would have to be participating. Sound too good to be true? It is. Pyramid schemes always fall apart, leaving you, and the majority of the beguiled participants with less money and potentially fewer friends.

Ponzi schemes are named in honor of Charles Ponzi, a 1920s scoundrel. Although he didn't pioneer the scheme, he certainly popularized its use. In a Ponzi scheme, a victim is asked to give the scam artist a sum of money today which, the scam artist promises, will be returned with substantial interest in only 30 days. And what do you know, in 30 days the scam artist delivers on his word and returns your money, with substantial "interest" applied, to your eagerly outstretched hand. The victim is then asked if he or she would like to do the same transaction for another 30 days, and, of course, he or she consents. Often, they will "loan" even more money the second time around. But how the money grew so quickly is never disclosed. The reason: it grew as a result of the scam artist's ability to recruit a second tier of investors whose money he used to pay off the first tier. By the time the second tier's money is due, the scam artist will have a third tier (comprised of the repeat first tier and new recruits) signed on. But sooner or later he or she will just close shop and walk off with three or more tiers of willing investors' cash. It's one of the oldest, yet most successful investment schemes going. Chances are you know someone who has fallen prey to it.

Land Investment Schemes

"Private getaway with water views" (swamp land), or "Your own Ponderosa in the heart of the Old West" (treacherous mountain land with no water or sewer lines, and no access nine months of the year due to avalanches). Less than greener pastures gussied up in promotional advertising campaigns which look too professional not to be believed, convert many a sane person into a money spending dupe. If the land is inexpensive, there's probably a good reason for it. Usually it relates to zoning laws that prohibit building on it, or something as basic as no running water. But, who hasn't heard of Florida real estate that ended up being nothing but an acre of some uninhabitable alligator swamp? Aren't we all the wiser? Most of us are "wise" enough not to let on that we have been so swindled. The fact is that those who are swindled seldom tell the tale. The reason? Vanity and the dislike of being seen as someone who has been taken to the cleaners. But if you have been victimized why not tell your friends? At the very least you'll get some sympathy, and you could be doing them a world of good. The scam artist's greatest ally is the silence of his or her victims. If you think you are being swindled in a land "deal", contact the Interstate Land Sales Registration Division in Washington, D.C., (202) 708-0502.

Home Improvement

Undertaking home improvement projects can often lead to sleepless nights and financial nightmares. So what if your home isn't your neighborhood's showplace? Everyone's paint cracks sooner or later, everyone's gutters spout at the seams at least once, and, yes, it's conceivable that the color of your roof isn't what it used to be. Be wary of anyone who drops by unannounced touting some kind of home improvement service. Many home improvement scamsters are so subtle that their victims don't have any idea they've been taken until it's much too late. If your home is in need of maintenance or repair, you'll undoubtedly know it without any assistance from some stranger who shows up on your doorstep. When the time is right, summon reputable (check and double-check their references) home improvement contractors to do the necessary work.

Prime Targets

If you're over 50, you're a prime target for one scam or another. Moreover, the older you are, the greater the likelihood that someone out there is going to test your financial and mental mettle. Why are retirees the preferred target? The simple reason is that they tend to have the most amount of readily available cash—usually placed in easy-to-access savings accounts. This, combined with the fact that retirees have more time to listen, and often more willingness to do so, provide the scam artist with the best possible motive for targeting over-50s. Another likely factor: Retirees are concerned with maintaining the value of the property they have. That translates into a concern for maintenance, which in turn plays nicely into the hands of a home improvement scamster. A concern particular to affluent over-50s is insuring the value of their estate for future generations, which requires actively investing at least part of their retirement dollars. Again, it is the attitude of concern which the scam artist can easily prey upon. But in this day of thousands of legitimate mutual funds, the blame of investing in shadow rather than substance falls on you. There is simply no reasonable excuse for it.

One way to ensure a margin of safety is to double check with your children or trusted friends before plunking down large chunks of your retirement cash—a large chunk should be considered to be anything over $1,000. While it may be difficult for you to discuss your misgivings, it is in your best interest to do so.

Also, check with all the appropriate consumer protection agencies, or check with as many as you need to know about the product, the company, and the salesperson. It's time consuming, but it's also the only way you can be guaranteed that you will not be swindled. In the end, most of us will have, or have already been taken advantage of by one scheme or another. For the most part, it will have been a relatively harmless reminder that, when it comes to financial decisions, we should always let prudence be our guide.

PART TWO

How to Build Wealth with Investments and Avoid Losing It to Taxes

11

INVESTING BASICS

A PENNY SAVED, a penny spurned. That's what happens—no matter how frugal a person you may be—if you don't put your capital to work for you. The reason: inflation. If your money doesn't grow at least at the same rate as the consumer price index, you might just as well be feeding $50 bills into your furnace. Thus, the first principle of effective investing is: invest in that which will provide you with a total return greater than or at least equal to the rate of inflation.

In our inflationary age, investing is more than a financial survival tool: It is an essential implement for building and preserving wealth; you need to make it a top priority if you want to assure a comfortable retirement. Suppose, for instance, you earn $50,000. In today's dollars, you would need to have aggregate investments of $850,000 to guarantee the same income in retirement and still be able to reinvest enough to keep up with inflation.

You may be thinking pension and Social Security benefits will provide some steady retirement income. But, for most people, these two sources alone are woefully inadequate. In short, providing for your retirement is your own responsibility, and judicious investments are the route you'll need to take. Investing wisely and protecting capital are even more important for people over 50 whose retirement is just around the corner because you have less time to make up for investment mistakes.

You have already built up a portfolio? Now is the time to reevaluate your investment goals, especially if you haven't done so recently. You are at an age where changes may be necessary. If, for example, your children have been put through school and the mortgage is mostly paid off, you should start concentrating on accumulating enough capital for retirement. If, however, one or more of your children are still college-bound, you may well have to defer *some* of your retirement-oriented investing for a few years.

The amount of attention you need to focus on wealth building—creating a retirement nest egg—depends on the success you have had in saving and investing during your younger years. Ideally, of course, a savings and investment program should have started while you were in your twenties or early thirties. Unfortunately, most of us weren't thinking about retirement at that age. (At 30, we tend to believe that thinking about retirement is what you do when you're retired. Passing 40, thoughts of retirement planning begin to take root. At 50, those thoughts have blossomed into major concerns.)

This chapter presents some important investing basics pertinent to the over-50 investor.

Understanding Investment Products

If you haven't already done so, you need to familiarize yourself with what's out there. At first glance, it's a jungle of investment products vying for your dollars. Table 11.1 describes commonly used investment alternatives. The field *is* a crowded and diverse, with products ranging from CDs to money market mutual funds to bond funds to real estate limited partnerships. The following sections will assist veteran and novice alike in sorting out and understanding the numerous investment vehicles.

Cash-Equivalent Investments

Cash-equivalents are income-earning investments with maturities of less than a year. They include money market funds, Treasury bills, and short-term CDs. Most individual investors who invest in cash equivalents own them indirectly through money funds, or purchase CDs from banks. Cash-equivalents have the advantages and disadvantages of cash: they're highly liquid, but don't generate much return. In fact, their low returns rarely stay abreast of inflation after taxes are paid. For this reason, cash-equivalents should be viewed as a temporary place to invest your money (especially when you cannot confidently identify attractive fixed-income, stock, or real estate investments.) Nevertheless, there are times when short-term interest-earning securities should be the investment of choice—an uncertain economy is one—and they are a good place to keep cash reserves for emergencies. (For a detailed discussion of cash-equivalents, see Chapter 13.)

Fixed-Income Investments

Fixed-income investments, including Treasury, municipal, and corporate bonds, are interest-earning securities with maturities greater than one year after their issue date. Backed by the "full faith and credit" of the federal government, Treasury bonds and notes are considered the safest fixed-income investments. Next in safety are municipal bonds: while they aren't guaranteed by the Federal government, they are backed by state and local governments. And, although cities and towns can default, they very rarely do. (Defaulting would seriously impair the issuer's credit rating.) Least secure are corporate bonds. Because these bonds are only backed by the company that issues them, their degree of safety is directly related to the company's health. If a firm goes bankrupt, the bonds can become worthless. Thus bonds issued by "blue chip" corporations are the safest. Junk bonds, however, offer very high yields to lure investors to provide money-hungry companies with badly needed credit. While most investors should steer clear of junk offerings, there is possibly a place for *some* junk bond mutual funds in more aggressive portfolios.

The bellweather yield on long-term Treasury bonds is an easy-to-obtain indicator of relative yields on interest-earning securities. Yields tend to move in tandem with the long-term Treasury yield. In recent years, long-term Treasury yields over 8 percent have often signaled attractive returns from many interest-earning securities. When the long Treasury yield is between 7 and 8 percent, you may still be able to find decent returns on fixed-income securities as well. The interest rates on long Treasuries, as well as other interest-earning securities, are available in the *Wall Street Journal* and other financial publications. (For a more detailed discussion of fixed-incomes, see Chapter 14.)

Table 11.1. Commonly Used Investment Alternatives

Investment	Description	Advantages	Possible Disadvantages
Stock Investments			
Common stock	Security that represents ownership in a company	Potential for high rate of return through capital gains; many pay dividends	Risk of market decline; not protected by government; value fluctuates daily
Convertible preferred stock	Preferred stock that may be exchanged by owner for common stock	Combines usually attractive dividend payout with potential of capital appreciation of common stock	Lower yield than bonds; sells at a premium to conversion value of the common stock
Futures contracts	Contracts covering the sale of financial instruments or commodities for future delivery; includes agricultural products, metals, Treasury bills, foreign currencies, and stock index futures (i.e., Standard & Poor's (S&P) 500)	High potential return through use of leverage	Highly speculative and volatile; favorite of investment "scamsters"

Options	The right to buy (call) or sell (put) a stock at a given price (strike price) for a given period of time	Inexpensive way to speculate; possible high return for small investment; covered option writers can add income with low risk	Option buyers usually lose entire investment
Preferred stock	Stock sold with a fixed dividend; if company is liquidated, it has priority over common stock	Fixed rate of return; safer than common stock dividends	Dividend is usually never increased; stock price appreciation potential may be limited
Stock mutual fund	Investment trust in which your money is pooled with those of other investors and invested in stocks by professional managers	Professional management; diversification reduces risk; can switch from one fund to another within a family of funds; wide selection; low costs; low investment minimums	Not federally insured; subject to fluctuations in the stock market
Unit investment trust (stocks)	Fixed portfolio of securities deposited with a trustee; offered to public in units	Diversification; professional selection; usually can redeem units	Portfolio is not managed actively; subject to price fluctuation
Warrant	Gives holder right to purchase a given stock at stipulated price over a fixed period of time	If underlying shares rise in value, so will warrant; can exercise warrant at any time	If warrant expires, value of investment is lost

Table 11.1. (Cont'd)

Investment	Description	Advantages	Possible Disadvantages
Interest Earning Investments			
Bond mutual fund	Investment trust in which your dollars are pooled with those of others and invested by professional managers in various bond issues	Professional management; diversification reduces risk; can switch from one fund to another within a family of funds; wide selection; low costs; low investment minimums	Not federally insured; subject to fluctuations in interest rates
Certificate of deposit (CD)	Receipt for money left in bank for set period of time at an agreed-upon interest rate; at end of period, bank pays deposit plus interest	Insured up to certain limits by federal government; competitive interest rates	Penalty for early withdrawal; interest rates may rise while your money is locked in
Convertible bond	Bond that may be exchanged by owner for common stock of same company	Combines safety of bonds with potential for capital appreciation of common stock	Lower yield than similar quality nonconvertibles; sell at premiums to the conversion value of the common stock
Corporate bond	Debt obligation of corporation	Receive fixed return over specified time; assured return; low risk with highly rated bond issues	May be called prior to maturity, particularly if interest rates decline

Money market deposit account	A type of money market fund at a bank or savings and loan association; has limited checking privileges	No federal regulation of rates: banks set their own rates; insured by federal government up to certain limits; no withdrawal penalties	Minimum balance required; limited check writing; rates often lower than money market mutual funds
Money market mutual fund	An investment company which buys short-term money market instruments	High short-term interest rates; no withdrawal penalties; handled by professional money managers; check-writing privileges	Usually not insured; no capital growth potential
Mortgage-backed securities	Securities representing a shared ownership in pools of mortgages; backed by federal, state, or local governments; include Ginnie Maes, Fannie Maes, Freddie Macs, etc.	Backed by government or government agencies; high yields; liquidity; receive regular monthly income	Prices decline if interest rates increase; payments dwindle as mortgages are paid off
Municipal bond	Debt obligation of state, city, town, or their agencies	Interest earned is tax-free at federal level and in state and city where issued	Subject to price fluctuations; after-tax return may be lower than other bonds
NOW account	Negotiable order of withdrawal; interest-bearing checking account	Funds in account earn interest; unlimited checking; federally insured up to certain limits	Interest rates are low; must maintain minimum balance

Table 11.1. (Cont'd)

Investment	Description	Advantages	Possible Disadvantages
Savings account	Account in which money deposited earns interest	Federally insured up to certain limits; guaranteed yield; can be used as collateral	Low interest rates
Treasury bills	Short-term U.S. Treasury securities; maturities: 13, 16, and 52 weeks	Backed by U.S. government; interest earned is exempt from state and local taxes	Rates often lower than other short-term investments
Treasury bonds	Long-term U.S. Treasury securities; maturities: 10 years or more	Backed by U.S. government; interest earned is exempt from state and local taxes	Value declines if interest rates rise
Treasury notes	Medium-term securities of U.S. Treasury; maturities: not less than 1 year and not more than 10 years	Backed by U.S. government; interest earned is exempt from state and local taxes	Value declines if interest rates rise
Unit investment trust (bonds)	Fixed portfolio of securities deposited with a trustee; offered to public in units; categories include municipal bonds, corporate bonds, public utility common stocks, etc.	Diversification; professional selection; usually can redeem units; available in small dollar amounts	Portfolio is not managed; most have 25–30 year maturities

U.S. savings bonds	Debt obligation of U.S. Treasury	Backed by U.S. government; if held 5 years, return is 85% of the average yield on 5-year Treasury security with a 6% minimum guaranteed; exempt from state and local income taxes; may defer federal tax; registered, so it can be replaced if lost or stolen	Generally lower rate of interest than available elsewhere
Zero-coupon bonds	Debt instrument; sold at discount from face value with no (zero) annual interest paid out; capital appreciation realized upon maturity	Low initial expenditure leads to balloon payment upon maturity; you know exact amount you will receive	Yields lower than for regular bonds; must pay taxes annually as though you received interest unless invested in tax-deferred account
Real estate investments			
Income-producing real estate	Do-it-yourself real estate investing involving the purchase and management of properties ranging from apartments to commercial and industrial buildings	Total control over the acquisition, management, and sale of the property; opportunity for significant tax-favored wealth accumulation	Expensive to get into; risk of loss through vacancies or declining prices; management of property can be a hassle

Table 11.1. (Cont'd)

Investment	Description	Advantages	Possible Disadvantages
Real estate investment trust (REIT)	REITs invest in or finance real estate projects including offices, shopping centers, apartments, hotels, and so on; REITs are sold as stock and trade on the stock exchanges	Provides participation in real estate with small amount of money	Subject to fluctuations of real estate and the stock market
Real estate limited partnership	A real estate ownership arrangement involving one or more general partners and limited partners; liability is generally limited to the extent of actual investment; can invest in all kinds of real estate	Provides participation in real estate with small investment; limited partners are relieved of chore of managing the property	Potential for profits is limited vs. buying property yourself; many deals have soured over past years
Undeveloped property	Do-it-yourself investment in raw land that, hopefully, will eventually be developed	Well-situated property can appreciate a great deal; minimal management responsibility	Good raw land is very expensive and difficult to finance long term; lack of income requires ability to commit money over a long period of time

Stock Investments

Of all investment vehicles in the public consciousness, stocks loom largest. Even though the bond markets have grown immensely in both importance and volatility over the past decade, if you ask the average American what one word comes to mind at the mention of financial markets, he or she will undoubtedly say "stocks."

Paradoxically, many Americans never take advantage of stock investments. They should: Stocks can provide both regular income (in the form of dividends) and appreciation (rise in value over time). They are an important part of every portfolio. Contrary to popular belief, retirees need to maintain a healthy proportion of stocks in their portfolios as a hedge against future inflation. Stock investments are best made when prices are depressed or at least not unusually high. One measure of relative stock market prices is the price to earnings (P/E) ratio of a stock or index of stocks. A P/E ratio is the number derived by dividing the price of a share of stock by that stocks' annual dividend. If a stock's P/E is well over its own historical average or the historical average for a major stock index, chances are that the stock is overpriced. If the P/E ratio is lower, the stock may be a good buy. (For a more detailed discussion of stock investing, see Chapter 15.)

Real Estate Investments

The most complicated form of investment is real estate. Evaluating a property's potential investment income, resale value and tax liability is a daunting task in itself, let alone monitoring—and if you buy the properties yourself, managing—the property once it's purchased. Opting for a passive form of real estate ownership, through a limited partnership considerably simplifies the process of real estate investing, but it in no way safeguards your investment from real estate slumps. The easiest way to participate in the real estate market is to buy shares of real estate investment trusts (REITs) or real-estate limited partnerships, but returns are usually far less than you could attain by buying individual properties.

Evaluating Potential Real Estate Investments

The following discussion provides some rules of thumb that can help you assess the financial viability of income-producing real-estate investments. (These evaluation methods are equally valid for direct real estate and limited partnership investments.) The simpler method involves comparing the total selling price with the current gross annual rental. A property that is selling much more than 7 or 8 times gross annual rental is likely to yield a negative cash flow, and should therefore be avoided.

The second method is calculating the capitalization rate, usually referred to as the *cap rate.* The cap rate is determined as follows:

$$\text{Capitalization rate} = \frac{\text{Net operating income}}{\text{Total amount invested}}$$

For example, a limited partnership investment in an apartment building requiring a total investment of $3.5 million has an estimated net operating income of $300,000. The cap rate is $300,000/$3,500,000 or 8.6 percent. A cap rate of 8 or greater is considered desirable.

Also, be aware that undeveloped land is particularly difficult to evaluate. Generally, land with significant appreciation potential is well situated and, therefore, very expensive. Cheap land usually remains cheap. (For a more detailed discussion of real estate investing, see Chapter 16.)

Pondering Investment Objectives

What should your investment objectives be? It depends on your individual circumstances. But, don't forget that a key objective is to beat inflation over the long term.

Since income and capital-gains taxes take a bite out of investment income, investments must show a positive return after both inflation *and* taxes. (If this fact is overlooked it will prove to be a costly oversight.) Assuming a 5 percent rate of inflation, a 10 percent annual return will provide the investor with only 1.7 percent after a combined federal and state tax rate of 33 percent. However, when funds are placed in a retirement-oriented account that isn't taxed until funds are withdrawn, the investor gets the advantage of returns which compound pre-tax income. A reasonable long-term investment objective for your total portfolio is to beat inflation by 3 percent after taxes have been paid.

Allocating Investments

Ideally, most portfolios should contain a balanced combination of the various types of investment vehicles discussed earlier, interest-earning investments (both cash equivalent and fixed incomes), stocks and, perhaps, real estate. As an over-50 investor you should generally be somewhat more conservative in your investment allocation than your younger counterparts. The reason? You need to minimize the possible adverse effects of being caught in a protracted down-turn in the stock or real estate market: You don't have as much time to regain lost ground. The strategy: gradually begin to increase the proportion of your portfolio that is invested in safer interest-earning securities (although most people over 50 should still have 40 percent or more of their investments in stocks and, if they are actively involved in real estate, in real estate.)

Once you have determined how to apportion your portfolio, decide whether to directly, or indirectly, own your investments. Owing individual stocks is a form of direct investing whereas investing in mutual funds is an increasingly popular means of indirect investment. Remember that diversification is always necessary. With respect to stock investments you would probably be best served by investing part of your portfolio in specific company shares and part in mutual fund shares.

Deciding how much to place in indirect as opposed to direct investments requires a great deal of judgment. For purposes of illustration, assume that you want to maintain a 50/50 percent split between total stock investments and total interest-earning security investments. A possible allocation might be:

	25%	in directly owned common stocks
	25%	in stock mutual funds
Subtotal	50%	in stock investments
	25%	in directly owned, interest-earning investments
	25%	in interest-earning mutual funds
Subtotal	50%	in interest-earning investments
Total	100%	

Once you have distributed your assets among directly and indirectly owned investments, you will need to divide these investment categories into specific industry, market, and/or fund categories. Directly owned, interest-earning investments might consist of short-term investments (money market accounts, certificates of deposit), municipal bonds, corporate bonds, and Treasury bonds. If you also decide to invest in interest-earning mutual funds, you might consider immediate-term municipal bond and/or convertible bond funds.

Finally, you will need to select specific investments within each of the industry or mutual fund categories that you have identified. Perhaps the most important attribute of successful investing is to be your own investment manager—don't rely solely on someone else to make your investment decisions for you. It's certainly acceptable for others to make suggestions, but you should have the final say. By familiarizing yourself with the array of commonly used investments, you can become an excellent investor yourself.

Coping with Market Uncertainty

Many investors overreact to unexpected market fluctuations. Some jittery types dump all of their stock and bond investments, and retreat to the safety of cash-equivalents. Yet the yield on cash-equivalent investments rarely keeps pace with inflation after taxes have been paid on the interest. The following tips will help you invest successfully in the face of market uncertainty:

- Maintain a balanced portfolio
- Diversify
- Buy quality
- Stagger the maturities of your fixed-income investments
- Opt for mutual funds that have superior long-term track records
- Use stop-loss orders on stocks
- When in doubt, seek safe havens
- Doing nothing is often the best response to crisis
- Avoid investing with borrowed money
- Take a long-term investment perspective

Maintain a Balanced Portfolio

Your investment portfolio should consist of common stock investments *and* fixed-income investments, and perhaps real estate. Otherwise, you will risk having a substantial portion of your assets eroded by unfavorable market conditions.

Diversify

Once again, it pays to follow this most basic and time-honored investment truism. All too many people have too much of their portfolio invested in the stock of one or a very few companies or in a single mutual fund. One reason for lack of diversification is caused by participation in employee stock purchase plans. Although such participation is usually advisable, there is always the danger that the price of the particular shares involved will collapse. If you can't afford the risk (and most people can't), liquidate some of your single-issue portfolio.

Buy Quality

While it is true that the market is driven by rumors and unfounded fears, and that short-term changes in stock prices often have little to do with companies' underlying value or financial health, shares of quality, dividend-paying companies with no or low debt are favored during volatile markets. Investors should realize that these companies have more staying power, if, in fact, market conditions deteriorate. You should be concentrating on long-term performance anyway: unlike day-to-day price fluctuations, long-term stock performance is a direct function of a company's viability.

Stagger the Maturities of Your Fixed-Income Investments

If your interest-earning investments mature simultaneously, you will find yourself rather abruptly burdened with a lot of cash. This situation can easily be avoided if you pick fixed-income investments with varying maturities. You will be better served if your fixed-incomes mature periodically; this strategy will allow you to insulate your investments somewhat from the effects of fluctuating interest rates.

Opt for Mutual Funds That Have Superior Long-Term Track Records

Stock mutual funds have typically performed abysmally during bear markets. Some investors are surprised to discover that the value of most bond mutual funds decline when interest rates rise. Nevertheless, some funds, usually those with strong long-term performance records, have proven to be better suited at coping with adverse market conditions than their competitors. Conversely, today's high flier is often tomorrow's crash victim.

Use Stop-Loss Orders on Stocks

A stop-loss order will help protect your stocks against sharp and/or rapid market drops. They are not foolproof, however. For example, in a volatile market, you may be sold out of a stock that subsequently rebounds in price.

When in Doubt, Seek Safe Havens

If you are totally daunted by market conditions, park at least some of your capital in safe cash-equivalent investments like money market funds, Treasury bills, and short-term certificates of deposit. While you may not be earning a particularly attractive return, at least you are protecting your assets.

Doing Nothing Is Often the Best Response to Crisis

Most investors who react to suddenly adverse market conditions almost always do the wrong thing. They will sell, for instance, when they should be holding, if not buying. In general, you should not sell into weakness. Wait until things settle down. Also, be very wary of the opinions experts offer immediately after the crisis. Ask yourself, "If they're such experts, why didn't they predict this situation in the first place?"

Avoid Investing with Borrowed Money

The investors who were really hurt by the 1987, 1989, and 1990 market downturns were generally those who had invested "on margin": they used borrowed money to invest. The only way for them to cover their margin calls was to sell their stock holdings at a most inopportune time. While the judicious use of margin investing can be an effective means of leveraging a stock portfolio, fully margined investors expose themselves to considerable risk.

Take a Long-Term Investment Perspective

The 500-point, single-day drop in the Dow Jones Index (Dow) on October 19, 1987 did not provoke another Great Depression. Indeed, the total decline during the October 1987 market erased only one year's gain in the Dow. Flat (if not down) 12-month stock markets are not that uncommon, yet few people remembered this fact during the 1987 post-crash hysteria. Invest for the long term—it is a principle equal in importance to diversifying.

12

CONSTRUCTING AN ALL-WEATHER PORTFOLIO

MANY EXPERTS PREDICT that the volatility in the world stock, fixed-income, and real estate markets that was so prevalent in the late 1980s will become the norm of the 1990s. Your portfolio must reflect this possibility through greater diversification and more attention to asset allocation. In addition, you will have to learn to cope with continuing, rather than sporadic, market volatility.

This chapter focuses on building, maintaining, evaluating, and monitoring an all-weather investment portfolio. It is designed to help you design a portfolio that will help you achieve your financial objectives. If you are not yet retired, a key objective will be to accumulate sufficient personal investments to be able to supplement your pension and social security income. If you are already retired, you should structure your portfolio so that it will provide you with needed income during your retirement to be able to provide for ever-increasing living expenses. Therefore, a retired person's portfolio must typically consist of both income-oriented investments and capital-appreciation oriented investments.

Where Do You Stand?

One of the first things you must do is discover where you stand in your portfolio. To find out how, you should follow these steps:

1. Project your investment requirements
2. Evaluate your current portfolio holdings
3. Determine an appropriate allocation of investment assets
4. Devise a portfolio redeployment program
5. Regularly monitor your portfolio composition and performance
6. Coordinate your portfolio with other financial planning areas

Project Your Investment Requirements

You need to be clear about what you want to accomplish with your investments in order to construct a suitable all-weather portfolio. Common reasons for investing include providing an emergency fund for unforeseen contingencies and/or meeting major expenses like a home renovation and, most importantly, funding a comfortable retirement while accumulating an estate for future generations.

Evaluate Your Current Portfolio Holdings

Reviewing and evaluating your current investments is one of the most important components of portfolio planning. Often, you'll find you have not paid sufficient attention to your investments, both from a standpoint of asset allocation and from the standpoint of selecting appropriate individual investments. You should also be sure to consider *all* investments over which you have control either as to individual security selection and/or asset allocation. (Most of us tend to review our investment accounts separately when they should be evaluated in their totality.

Determine an Appropriate Allocation of Investment Assets

After you have evaluated your investment objectives and needs, and have determined the asset allocation of current investment holdings, you can begin to consider long-term asset allocation parameters. Asset allocation decisions are complex and highly judgmental, but are nevertheless an essential component of a comprehensive portfolio creation and maintenance process.

DEVISE A PORTFOLIO REDEPLOYMENT PROGRAM

More often than not, your comparison of your current asset allocation with a target or desired asset allocation will reveal substantial differences. Many people tend to invest in extremes often resulting in either too much or too little investment risk. Similar to the asset allocation decision itself, devising a portfolio redeployment strategy requires a good deal of planning and judgment. Generally, if you find the need to make a significant restructuring in your portfolio, shift your assets gradually. Don't make a major reallocation hastily.

REGULARLY MONITOR YOUR PORTFOLIO COMPOSITION AND PERFORMANCE

Managing your investment portfolio is a dynamic process and you should therefore monitor your portfolio composition and performance on a regular basis. The extent of your involvement may range from periodically reviewing holdings to being actively involved in investment selection.

COORDINATE YOUR PORTFOLIO WITH OTHER FINANCIAL PLANNING AREAS

Coordinate your investment portfolio plan with the other functional areas of your financial planning such as tax planning, retirement planning, and estate planning. Always keep your objectives firmly in mind. That way, you'll be better able to resist the temptation to make a major—and often ill-advised—revision to your investment program as a result of changes in market condition or, worse, the opinion of some "expert."

Meeting Your Investment Needs

For most people, accumulation and management of personal investments is the most important aspect of personal financial planning. As you grow older, this side of financial planning only grows in importance. Letting excess funds lie idle or investing them inappropriately is inefficient and, over time, can lead to substantially less accumulated capital. For example, a 30-year-old investor who begins making his or her individual retirement account (IRA) investments on the first day of each tax year, rather than just before the April 15 deadline for making IRA investments for the previous year, will accumulate over $50,000 in extra IRA Funds (at a 10 percent rate) by age 60. Using the right instruments efficiently, therefore, not only puts money to work but also facilitates the achievement of your long-term financial security.

Evaluating Your Fund Portfolio

Once you have put together a mutual fund portfolio, you will need to evaluate it periodically from the standpoint of the allocation of the total portfolio and individual fund performance. With respect to the portfolio as a whole, you will need to determine how the total fund assets are allocated. Is the allocation in line with your parameters? If not, perhaps some reallocation is necessary. If stock prices have risen sharply, the proportion of stocks in relation to the total portfolio is probably higher than you had originally determined was appropriate. If so, you should sell some stock funds and buy additional interest-earning funds. (Follow the opposite course should stock prices fall.) The disciplined approach to fund evaluation forces you to sell stock funds when prices are high and buy stock funds when prices have dropped. This is exactly the approach that most investors should take, but few have the discipline, and most do the opposite. How often should you reallocate? Certainly no more frequently than once per quarter and probably less frequently unless there has been a precipitous change in stock or bond prices.

Beyond having to sell certain funds as part of a portfolio reallocation, periodically make an objective evaluation of each fund in the portfolio. If you selected good funds in the first place, you're probably better off holding onto the funds even if they post a disappointing few months or quarters. If a particular fund consistently turns in below average results for its fund category, consider replacing it with a better performing fund. This shouldn't happen too often, however. Most important, don't fret over short-term fluctuations in either market conditions or in performance of funds in your all-weather portfolio. Buy and hold good funds for the long-term rather than trying to strike it rich from the get-go. You'll be more likely to come out ahead.

Asset Allocation

The regular review of the allocation of investment assets in your portfolio is one of the most important parts of the financial planning process. It is a particularly challenging task, because the asset allocation decision hinges on so many disparate and potentially volatile factors, including stock market conditions, interest rates, economic prospects, tax regulations, investment product availability, and your financial status, objectives, and preferences. Unfortunately, all too often, insufficient attention is directed toward asset allocation. It is easier to focus on individual investments (e.g., a stock mutual fund, municipal bond, or real estate limited partnership) than to step back and look at your current and expected portfolio in its totality.

Asset allocation involves up to four steps. First, the appropriate percentage of total available funds that should be invested in each of the four major investment categories (cash-equivalent, fixed income, stock, and real estate) must be determined. If you are not interested in real estate investments, the allocation will be among stock and the two categories of interest-earning securities.

The second step involves evaluating which general kinds of investment vehicles within each category are suitable (e.g., direct ownership of stocks, bonds, and real estate or indirect ownership by means of mutual funds or partnerships). Most often, the appropriate course is one of diversifying across investment vehicles. For example, with respect to equity investments, you may be best served by having some of your equity portfolio invested in specific company shares and some of it invested in mutual fund shares.

The third step in the asset allocation process further breaks down the general categories of investment into specific industry, market, or fund categories. Appropriate directly owned cash-equivalent investments might include money market instruments and Treasury bills; fixed-income investments might include municipal, government, and corporate bonds. Assuming that you should also be invested in fixed-income mutual funds as is usually the case, you might want intermediate-term municipal bond funds, long-term bond funds, and convertible bond funds. The percentage or dollar amount of each investment in each specific category must also be determined.

The final step consists of selecting specific investments within each of the industry or fund categories delineated in the third step (e.g., a particular bond or stock issue or mutual fund).

Figure 12.1 depicts the asset allocation process. The information that should be placed in each "cell" becomes more specific with each succeeding step in the asset allocation process.

Figure 12.1. Investment Allocation

Method of Ownership	Investment Category		
	Stock	Interest-Earning	Real Estate
Direct Ownership			
Indirect Ownership (Mutual Fund/ Partnership)			

Asset allocation decisions are complex, highly judgmental, and dynamic. It is impossible to provide specific recommendations; however, the following guidelines may be helpful in evaluating the balance, or lack of balance, in an existing portfolio and in suggesting appropriate asset allocation strategies.

- **Preretirees who are within, for example, 10 years of retirement should begin a gradual shift of an aggressive portfolio into more conservative investments.** This tactic minimizes the possible deleterious effects of being caught in a protracted downturn in the stock or real estate markets. An appropriate allocation depends on many factors, particularly how heavily you need to rely on your personal portfolio for retirement purposes. A typical preretiree who will need the portfolio to help pay living expenses might eventually consider an appropriate portfolio balance to consist of at least 40 percent equities and the remainder fixed income and cash equivalent investments. If the retiree owns investment real estate, his or her portfolio might consist of 30 percent equities, 20 percent real estate, and 50 percent interest earning investments.
- **Retirees often fail to realize the importance of capital appreciation in their portfolios.** Many erroneously think that as long as they preserve capital and this capital provides sufficient current income to meet living expenses, their financial needs will be met. Yet new retirees have a long life expectancy (a married couple both 65 years old have a joint and

last-survivor expectancy of 25 years). Many are finding that inflation has so eroded their fixed income that they are having to curtail their living expenses, or worse, are running out of money. Therefore, it is important to remember the importance of maintaining stock or other inflation-hedge-potential investments during your retirement years.

- **Certain major life events such as the loss of one's job, disability, divorce, or the death of a spouse often require a change in the portfolio allocation mix.** Divorce, for example, often materially alters the financial condition and financial outlook of each spouse, thereby reducing the proportion of assets that should be placed at risk (See Chapter 31).
- **The investment portfolio has many uses in a well-diversified financial life.** The security portfolio can be used to balance any risk factors that affect your most important investment (your job) or your most important asset (your house). For example, someone with an adjustable-rate mortgage who owns a car dealership is already subject to a disproportional amount of interest rate risk. A heavier weighting in stocks that are not particularly interest-rate sensitive, and lighter weighting in real estate and long-term bonds may be an appropriate way to use the investment portfolio to protect against the risk factors of their other assets.
- **The amount of money you have to invest influences the extent to which direct versus indirect investments should be considered.** For example, if you have $10,000 to invest on a long-term basis you should probably select indirect investments (mutual funds) almost exclusively. If you have a $100,000 portfolio, however, you should consider mutual funds and directly purchased stock and fixed-income investments. For example, a desirable mix that incorporates a 50 percent equity allocation and 50 percent fixed-income allocation might consist of equal portions of directly owned stocks, directly owned fixed-incomes, stock mutual funds, and fixed-income mutual funds. Investors with substantially more than $100,000 to invest on a long-term basis could consider real estate investments, either directly owned or limited partnerships, in addition to mutual funds and directly owned stocks and fixed-income investments.

- **The key to successful asset allocation and personal portfolio management is beating the rate of inflation on an after-tax basis over the long term.** An after-tax return on investment that exceeds the inflation rate by 3 percent is an appropriate objective for most investors. Exceeding inflation by 4 percent over the long term is considered very successful. Beating long-term inflation is easier said than done, however. As the following example indicates, if you have a combined federal and state tax burden of 33 percent, you'll have to earn a 12 percent return on a taxable fixed-income investment (e.g., a corporate bond) to beat an assumed 5 percent inflation rate by 3 percent after taxes.

Most investors do not pay sufficient attention to the impact of taxes. Investors have been greatly attracted to fixed-income securities whenever interest rates reach 10 percent. Yet, as the example in Table 12.1 shows, they were staying just ahead of inflation on an after-tax basis. However, these rates may be very attractive for retirement-oriented accounts, because income on retirement funds is not taxed until the money is withdrawn at retirement.

Finally, once you have your allocation portfolio in place, remember that successful individual investors are inevitably those who take a patient, prudent, long-term view of asset allocation and portfolio return. You also need to review periodically where your portfolio stands. That is the subject of the next section.

Table 12.1. After-Tax Returns on Investment and Inflation Premiums on a $10,000 Taxable Investment

	Annual Rate of Return	
	10%	12%
Pretax income	$1,000	$1,200
Federal income tax (28%)	(280)	(336)
State income tax (5%)	(50)	(60)
Total tax	(330)	(396)
After-tax income	$670	$804
After-tax return on investment	6.7%	8.0%
After-tax inflation premium (assuming 5% rate of inflation)	1.7%	3.0%

Evaluating Your All-Weather Portfolio

Once you have put together an all-weather portfolio, you should periodically evaluate both the overall portfolio composition and the performance of specific securities and mutual funds. With respect to the portfolio as a whole, you need to determine how your total assets have been deployed. Have they been allocated in line with your investment parameters? If not, perhaps some allocation is necessary. If stock prices have risen sharply since you last reviewed your portfolio, the proportion of the portfolio's net worth that equity investments represent may be larger than you'd like. In such a situation, you might want to sell some of the appreciated stock and purchase some fixed-income investments with the proceeds. (The opposite course would be appropriate should stock prices fall.) Taking a disciplined approach to portfolio evaluation forces you to sell high and buy low, a route that most investors should take, but one that most lack the will to follow.

How often should you reallocate your portfolio? Certainly no more than once per quarter and probably less frequently unless there have been major price changes in the securities markets.

In addition, you should periodically evaluate each individual security in your portfolio. If you selected quality investments in the first place, you're probably better off holding onto them even if they post a disappointing few months or quarters. With respect to mutual funds, don't consider dumping a product until it has turned in below average results in its fund category over two consecutive years. Don't fret over short-term fluctuations in either market conditions or the performance of securities and funds in your all-weather portfolio. Buy and hold good investments for the long-term rather than trying to strike it rich from the get-go. In the long run, you'll come out ahead.

13

CASH-EQUIVALENT INVESTMENTS

To many over-50 investors, cash-equivalent investments (like Treasury Bills and money market accounts) represent safety. For these investors, increasingly concerned with financial stability and security, cash-equivalent investments provide a priceless return: peace-of-mind. Yet, as you read in Chapter 9, too much safety can be as injurious to your prospects for long-term financial security as too much risk.

Cash-equivalents do have a place in your portfolio. In fact, they provide a most important ingredient—liquidity—funds that can be readily accessed in the event of an unexpected expense or financial emergency. They also provide an appropriate portion of security in your portfolio just in case the sky does fall in. Moreover, when short-term interest rates are high, cash equivalents can be attractive investments in themselves.

There may be substantial differences in yield among short-term investments, particularly on an after-tax basis. Thus it is advisable to check prevailing rates regularly. Remember, however, that over the long-term, the yield on cash-equivalents will never match the returns of stocks and/or longer-term interest earning securities. Short-term investments will, at best, barely beat inflation on an after-tax basis. Therefore, these investment vehicles should therefore generally be viewed as a temporary parking place for money pending more attractive investment alternatives.

When investing in cash-equivalents, your goal should be to find those that provide an acceptable level of yield. However, never allow your quest for high cash-equivalent yields to degenerate into yield chasing. Whenever interest rates decline you are probably going to be encouraged by some salesperson to switch into higher yielding investments. Recently, several types of mutual funds purporting to be just as safe as money market funds have been heavily marketed. Among the most heavily marketed products: global income, adjustable rate mortgage (ARM), and prime rate funds. Like money-market funds, these mutual funds invest in bank and government debts and obligations. But, while their portfolios are safe, they are prone to greater volatility than their domestic, money market fund counterparts. These funds may play a role in your portfolio, but they should not be considered a substitute for a money market account.

Types of Cash Equivalents

Not too long ago, the only place for investors to earn interest while maintaining a relative measure of liquidity was a low-yielding passbook savings account. Today, you can choose from a wide variety of interest-earning investment products. This section describes the most common cash-equivalent investments.

Certificates of Deposit

The most familiar cash equivalent is a certificate of deposit (CD). There is often some confusion as to whether or not a CD is a cash-equivalent or a fixed-income investment. Generally, CDs with a maturity of one year or less are considered cash equivalents; greater than one year, fixed incomes. A CD is a receipt for funds deposited at a financial institution at a specified interest rate for a specified period of time. There are a variety of CDs designed for individual investors with varying interest rates, maturities, and minimum deposits (e.g., some institutions offer a minimum deposit of as little as $500 for a 6-month CD.)

CDs, purchased from banking institutions, are essentially loans from investors to banks. Unlike loans, however, the bank does not pay back principal over the life of the CD. Instead, like bonds, CDs have a fixed life span, or maturity, at the end of which the investor receives his principal in a lump sum. CD maturities range from 90 days to 10 years, although investors should have a medley of maturities—some of 1 year or less, others for longer terms—in order to provide liquid funds for emergencies. The reason: There is usually an early-withdrawal penalty if the investor liquidates his or her CD before it has reached maturity.

Like checking or savings accounts, CDs are generally insured by the FDIC. (CDs may be insured by either a private insurance company, a state insurance fund, or a federal agency.) Federal agency-insured institutions are safest. A prudent investor will limit his or her CD investments to them. The federal deposit insurance limit is $100,000 of a depositor's combined accounts—savings and checking accounts, NOW accounts, money market deposit accounts, and CDs—per bank. (Higher limits can be achieved with multiple accounts using different family members as owners or co-owners.) But, you need to be vigilant. Give the federal deposit insurance limits a regular check up—Congress may change them, and you don't want to get caught short. Many over-50 people put their finances at risk by keeping deposits at one bank far in excess of the FDIC limit. If you are one of them put some of your money in another institution.

Money Market Mutual Funds

In the early 1970s, money market rates climbed far above the rates offered by banks and thrifts. The money market fund, invented in the mid-1970s, was aimed at investors who wanted to profit from the money market's high return and liquidity. These funds were designed to appeal to the small investor who found the substantial capital required for direct investment in money market securities a barrier to his or her participation. Because mutual fund transaction costs were very small, they could purchase a broad range of securities with relatively low credit risk. The same holds true today. Remember that money market funds are not risk-free. Money market funds are managed so that their shares are always priced at $1.00 each. Shares are generally redeemable at any time either through the mail or by telephone. Many funds even offer check writing privileges.

Most mutual fund companies offer three types of money market funds.

1. *General purpose funds* invest in a wide range of quality money market instruments that typically have a maturity of 30 to 40 days.
2. *U.S. government short-term funds* invest in treasury securities and U.S. government agency issues.

3. *Tax-exempt money market funds* invest solely in short-term municipal securities and are exempt from federal income taxes.

Some single-state tax-exempt money funds are available free of both federal and state income taxes. However, because of their tax deductibility, tax-exempts have a lower yield than the other two types. Since money market fund yields fluctuate constantly, you should periodically check to see which category of money fund—taxable, tax-exempt, or if available in your state, single-state tax-exempt—provides the highest *after-tax* yield. Figure 13.1 is a worksheet that can be used to make a yield comparison.

Money Market Deposit Accounts

These accounts are offered by banks which are free to pay any interest rate they choose. Unlike CDs, Money Market Deposit Accounts (MMDAs) have no maturity date, and because their interest rate varies, a set yield is *not* guaranteed. When compared to money market funds, the disadvantages of MMDAs include generally lower interest rates, a generally higher minimum balance, limited check-writing privileges, and the inconvenience of going to the bank to transfer or withdraw funds. However, unlike money market funds, money market accounts offered by FDIC insured financial institutions are insured up to $100,000.

Treasury Bills

T Bills are the safest cash equivalents. They are the only short-term debt instruments guaranteed directly by the "full faith and credit" of the U.S. government. Moreover, investment returns from these debt instruments are exempt from both state and federal taxation. T Bills are negotiable, noninterest-bearing securities with an original maturity of 1 year or less. Currently, T Bills are offered in minimum denominations of $10,000 and increments of $5,000 thereafter. The investor purchases a T Bill at a discount from its face value. When the bill reaches maturity, the federal government redeems the bill at its face value. The difference between the purchase price and the redemption constitute's a T Bill's investment return. T Bills can be purchased directly from the Federal Reserve or, for a nominal charge, through a bank or brokerage firm. Similar to Treasury notes and bonds, T Bill interest is federally taxable, but is exempt from state and local taxes.

Figure 13.1. Tax-Exempt Money Market Yield Comparison

This work sheet can be used to compare periodically the after-tax yields on selected taxable, tax-exempt, and, where applicable, single-state tax-exempt money market funds. Relative yields on these accounts vary, and, therefore, you should evaluate money market rates regularly.

Name of Fund					
1. ________________	(taxable money market fund yield)	times	(1 minus your combined marginal federal and state income tax rate)	equals	After tax yield on taxable money market fund
	(............)	×	(..............)	=	........%
2. ________________	(tax exempt money market fund yield)	times	(1 minus your marginal state income tax rate)	equals	(After tax yield on tax exempt money market funds
	(............)	×	(..............)	=	.......%
					Yield on selected single-state tax-exempt money market fund
3. ________________					.......%

Municipal Notes

State and local governments issue interest bearing muncipal notes with maturities ranging from one month to one year. They are secured by the issuer's pledge of credit, a pledge that does not absolutely remove debt risk, as it is possible that a municipality might default on its securities. Municipal notes' primary attraction is that interest income on them is exempt from federal taxation, and from state taxes as well if you are a resident of the state where the notes are issued.

Making the Most of Cash-Equivalent Investments

Finding the Highest Rates

Many over-50, income-oriented investors spend a great deal of time shopping for interest rates. This is not always the most efficient use of your investing time—if you are really interested in attractive returns, spend more time looking at bond or stock investments, and less time trying to gain an extra tenth of a percent from a CD.

Nonetheless, it does pay to shop around, and there is no point in always purchasing a CD from your usual bank if a competing bank can give you a better return. Remember, however, that markedly higher returns are always predicated on higher risks, even in cash-equivalent investments—high-yielding money funds often invest in corporate paper, which while still very safe, is a step up in risk from T bills.

Local newspapers (especially the Sunday business section) and financial publications provide extensive coverage of rates offered on CDs, money market accounts, and T Bills. Interest rates on CDs vary not only from one local bank to another, but also from one region to another. CDs are often advertised nationwide, and you can make the purchase by mail or through your stockbroker via so-called brokered CDs. However, be sure that the bank or savings institution is federally insured.

Competition for your money is often intense—and you will be the beneficiary. Local banks may engage in price wars to attract money. Mutual fund companies may temporarily waive all or part of their fees in order to attract investors' cash. So keep abreast of conditions in the short-term investment markets by periodically calling and comparison shopping the banks in your area. Don't restrict yourself to one particular kind of cash-equivalent investment. You may be foregoing some opportunities for better returns, or you may be well rewarded for your efforts.

Be sure to compare the after-tax yields on taxable short-term investments, like CDs and ordinary money market accounts. Also remember that T bills are exempt from state and local taxes, so if you live in a high tax area, you may benefit. It's not very difficult to measure after-tax return; simply deduct any taxes that would be due from the total interest received on any short investments that you are considering. The key amounts to compare, are these investments' *after-tax* (both federal and state) yields. You may well find that you'll be better off with a tax-exempt money market fund, although conditions do change periodically. So compare rates of return on cash equivalents regularly.

Selecting Convenient Features

Short-term investments vary in the number of convenient features they offer. In general, money market mutual funds are the most convenient and flexible, but it is up to you to decide which, if any, of the following conveniences will make your financial life a little easier:

- Check-writing privileges
- Immediate confirmations and regular statements
- Low investment minimums
- Telephone transactions
- Quick redemptions
- Timely resolution of problems

By keeping up-to-date on cash-equivalent investment market conditions, you will be better prepared to take advantage of the most suitable investment opportunities when you next need to invest some short-term money.

14

FIXED-INCOME INVESTMENTS

WHILE THE ATTENTION of many investors was riveted to the stock market during the latter half of the 1980s and the early 1990s, bonds and other interest-earning investments were undergoing revolutionary changes that would make them more complex, more volatile, and at the same time, more attractive as investment vehicles. Today, investors can choose from a wide variety of taxable, tax-exempt, and tax-deferred bonds, as well as a variety of other interest-earning (often referred to as fixed-income) investment securities, such as fixed-income mutual funds, unit trusts, and mortgage-backed securities. A separate classification of short-term investment, known as cash equivalents is discussed in Chapter 13.

Common stocks, of course, have long been viewed as one of the better hedges against inflation, Yet, fixed-income investments also have a place in the portfolios of investors who are seeking attractive, inflation-beating rates of return with moderate risk. Despite the dramatic descent in interest rates since the early 1980s, bond yields after inflation is taken into account are actually more attractive now than they were during that period.

With the attractive interest rates available today, however, comes increased volatility in the prices of most fixed-income securities. Until the 1970s, when interest rates moved slowly, bonds were considered a safe, stable haven for income-oriented investors. Today, when interest rates can fluctuate several percentage points within the course of a year, price volatility is a factor that must be taken into account in planning and selecting these investments.

You need to evaluate how fixed-income investments fit into your overall investment portfolio (including your retirement account investments) and then decide the kinds of securities that are most suitable. It is safe to say that fixed-income investments belong in every portfolio. However, the proportion as well as the type of investment vehicles will vary considerably among investors. For example, someone who is retired or is nearing retirement will, in all likelihood, require a larger proportion of interest-earning investments in his or her portfolio than a younger individual.

Many considerations must be taken into account when selecting an appropriate fixed-income security. One of the most important is the tax treatment of interest and capital gains or losses, particularly if you live in a state which levies a high tax on interest income. The lowering of federal income tax rates as well as the inclusion of some tax-exempt interest in the alternative minimum tax, are relatively new developments that must be kept in mind. Maturity, quality, relative yield, liquidity, and call features are other important factors in the selection process.

Fixed-income investing will almost certainly continue to be a somewhat complex, yet potentially rewarding, investment arena throughout the 1990s. The popularity of the myriad of fixed-income investments which have come on the scene in the last decade will prompt a new, even more diverse crop of products. Changes in tax laws will continue to play a major role in evaluating the relative attractiveness of tax-exempt and tax-favored securities and investment vehicles.

As you plan the fixed-income investment portion of your investment portfolio, don't overlook the many benefits of bond-mutual funds. Over the past decade, bond fund managers have proven themselves adept at managing their portfolios efficiently and effectively in both stable and volatile interest rate environments. Some specialized categories of fixed-income securities, such as foreign bonds, should be purchased through professionally managed mutual funds with proven expertise in a specialized types of securities.

Interest-Earning Investment Strategies

Volatile interest rates combined with the proliferation of many different kinds of interest-earning securities have discouraged many investors from taking the plunge into these investments. Instead, they are content with short-term cash-equivalent securities such as money market funds. Yet, with a little effort, you can increase your investment returns by taking advantage of the many attractive fixed-income investment vehicles that are available to individual investors. The following suggestions will help you become a better investor in fixed-income securities:

- Become familiar with the many fixed-income securities that are currently available
- Monitor prevailing interest rates
- Don't speculate on interest rate changes
- "Ladder" the maturities of your fixed-income investments
- Compare interest rates on various types of securities
- Make mutual funds a part of your interest-earning investment portfolio
- Consider the tax effects of each investment
- Don't chase yield
- Make fixed-income investments one part of a well-balanced portfolio

Become Familiar with the Many Fixed-Income Securities That Are Currently Available

The following is a list of many of the commonly available securities. They can be purchased either directly or through a mutual fund and many can be acquired with a very small initial investment.

- U.S. Treasury Notes
- U.S. Treasury Bonds
- U.S. Savings Bonds
- U.S. Government Agency Debt
- Mortgage-Backed Bonds
- Municipal Notes
- Municipal Bonds (Uninsured and insured)
- Certificates of Deposit
- Zero Coupon Bonds—Corporate
- Zero Coupon Bonds—Municipal
- Zero Coupon Bonds—U.S. Treasury
- Corporate Bonds
- Convertible Bonds

- Foreign Bonds
- U.S. Government Bond Mutual Funds
- Corporate Bond Funds
- Mortgage-Backed Bond Funds
- Municipal Bond Funds
- International Bond Funds
- Unit Investment Trusts
- Closed-End Bond Funds

Chances are that some of the above securities can benefit you now or some time in the future. Be aware, however, that some of these securities may have various risks that may make them inappropriate for your needs.

Monitor Prevailing Interest Rates

You should make it a habit to keep up-to-date with interest rates. Develop some rules of thumb that help you decide what interest rates are attractive to you. For example, you may find that fixed-income securities are attractive when they beat inflation by a couple of percentage points after taxes are taken out. Many individual investors monitor the yield on long-term Treasury bonds to get an idea of the level of interest rates.

The key to investing successfully in interest-earning investments is to purchase longer-maturity securities when you think interest rates are high and are likely to fall in order to lock in high returns. Conversely, you should purchase shorter maturity securities (or cash equivalent investments) if you think prevailing interest rates are likely to rise.

Don't Speculate on Interest Rate Changes

Many investors don't understand the volatility of interest-earning investments until they find that their bond or bond mutual fund holdings have lost value. Fixed income security prices can, in fact, be more volatile than stock prices. This risk, which is shared by all long-term fixed-income securities, is called interest rate risk. Simply stated, interest rate risk means that the principal value of a fixed-income investment will decline if interest rates in general rise. Fixed-income mutual funds have this risk, although many fund managers are adept at handling interest rate risk over the long run. Some individual investors perceive themselves as experts in predicting the direction of interest rates and, therefore, buy individual interest-earning securities with the intention of selling them before they mature. Many such armchair speculators risk losing a great deal of money on a supposedly safe investment. The only way to avoid this risk is to hold onto these securities until they mature. Thus, you are better off buying individual fixed-income securities with the intention of holding to maturity, even though you may end up selling them early anyway to meet living expenses or to take advantage of an increase in the value of your investments caused by a decline in interest rates. The lesson here is to leave interest rate speculation to the professionals.

"Ladder" the Maturities of Your Fixed-Income Investments

Smart investors do what is known as "laddering" or "staggering" the maturities of their fixed-income investments. Rather than investing in a single issue or in several issues with roughly the same maturity, you should opt for a variety of maturities—some short term, some intermediate term, and some long term. In that manner, if there is a significant change in interest rates, you will avoid having placed a heavy, and perhaps incorrect, bet on a single maturity. Simply stated, laddering maturities minimizes the risk in your interest earning security portfolio. Don't forget to time some of the maturities to coincide with times when you may need the money, for instance to meet college tuition bills or to provide money during your first few years of retirement. If you invest in fixed-income mutual funds you can also vary the maturities held by these funds by investing in an array of short-, intermediate- and long-term bond funds. (See "Make Mutual Funds a Part of Your Interest-Earning Investment Portfolio.")

Compare Interest Rates on Various Types of Securities

You'll probably be amazed at how different interest rates are on various fixed-income securities. For example, over the past several years, interest rates on tax-exempt bonds have been very attractive compared with the after-tax returns on Treasury securities and corporate bonds. Rates on medium-grade bonds are sometimes much higher than on high-grade bonds even though the risk of default on medium-grade bonds is not much higher than the blue chips, for example, high-quality issues of financially strong companies or municipalities. Thus before making an investment, compare returns. Your efforts will be well rewarded.

Make Mutual Funds a Part of Your Interest-Earning Investment Portfolio

Fixed-income mutual funds are an excellent way to participate in the many attractive interest-earning investment opportunities. Most investors are not aware of the wide variety of mutual funds that are available, including Treasury funds, mortgage-backed securities funds, tax-exempt bond funds, corporate bond funds, and even foreign bond funds. Within most of these categories, you can often select funds that invest in high-, medium-, or low-quality issues. Finally, you can often select funds that concentrate on long-duration securities or intermediate- or shorter-duration securities.

Consider the Tax Effects of Each Investment

You can probably increase your investment returns by carefully examining the tax effects of alternative interest-earning investments. Some are fully taxable, Treasury securities are federally taxable but exempt from state taxes, and municipal obligations are usually exempt from state taxes. It is important to remember that the most heavily taxed (and usually higher yielding) securities should be placed in your tax-deferred retirement accounts. On the other hand, tax-favored investments should be placed in your taxable portfolio.

Don't Chase Yield

A fixed-income investment that pays 14 percent when prevailing rates are 8 percent is trying to tell you something. This is a junk bond. Yet, many investors erroneously think that the higher the yield the more attractive the investment. This is just not true. As many junk bond holders discovered, some of these bonds went down the tube. Some portfolios can benefit from speculative investments, but if you do decide to include them in your portfolio, don't risk too much money in these investments.

Make Fixed-Income Investments One Part of a Well-Balanced Portfolio

Some people invest too much money in fixed-income investments because they are afraid of stocks. Others think stocks are the ultimate investment and have too little money in fixed-income securities. What everyone needs is balance, and a well-balanced portfolio consists of generous proportions of stocks, fixed-income investments, and, if you are so inclined, income-producing real estate.

Investing in U.S. Treasury Securities

High interest from the federal government! Great tax breaks! No commission charges!

No, this isn't a pitch for another new and improved investment product. But if the U.S. government ever decided to create a hard-sell ad for Treasury securities, it would probably read something like this. While other investments may earn better returns at times, Treasury securities consistently appear in a wide variety of investment portfolios.

U.S. Treasury issues—which, along with U.S. savings bonds, are the only types of securities that are direct obligations of Uncle Sam—have long been classic, bread-and-butter investments. Their appealing features include:

- **High liquidity.** Individual investors must often pay higher fees when buying municipal and taxable bonds because the market for small blocks of securities is limited. But the treasury arena is so huge that an investor with $1,000 is on the same footing as someone with $100,000.
- **Noncallability.** Many investors who think they've locked in high yields for decades on corporate and municipal bonds get a rude awakening when an issuer redeems its bonds before they reach maturity. This won't happen with Treasuries, though, since most of them cannot be called.
- **Tax exemption.** These issues are exempt from state and local taxes. As states continue to raise their tax rates, Treasuries become ever more attractive.
- **Low or no sales commissions.** It costs nothing to purchase bonds through a local branch of the Federal Reserve Bank. You can also pay a small sales charge when you buy them through a broker. In addition, because brokers maintain an active secondary market in Treasury issues, they are easy to sell before maturity.

There are several species of Treasury issues. Treasury bills come in minimum denominations of $10,000 and mature in one year or less. Treasury notes mature in 1 to 10 years and have a minimum purchase requirement of $1,000 (except for 2- and 3-year notes, which have a $5,000 minimum investment requirement. You can also invest in U.S. Treasury issues through a U.S. government-only mutual fund. However, the interest on these may be subject to state and local taxes. Be sure that you understand how owning shares in a government fund will affect your tax situation before you invest in one.

Investing in U.S. Savings Bonds

Savings bonds occupy the territory between cash-equivalents and interest-earning investments. Unlike the other vehicles described in this chapter, U.S. savings bonds are not fixed-income investments: they pay a variable interest rate, the amount of which is recalculated every six months. This interest rate is set at 85 percent of the benchmark 5-year Treasury yield, with 6 percent floor which limits how far the bonds' yield can sink downward. (For bonds purchased before November 1986, this floor is set at 7.5 percent.) Finally, while investors are guaranteed their principal back when the bonds reach maturity, they will incur stiff penalties by cashing in U.S. savings bonds before five years have elapsed.

Series EE bonds sell for half their face or redemption value, which ranges from $50 to $10,000. The bonds must be held for at least 5 years to receive the full rate which is never less than 6 percent. Accrued interest is subject to federal, but not to state and local taxes.

Transaction Tips

Keep copies of the issue dates and serial numbers of U.S. Savings Bonds in a safe place separate from your bonds. This will make it easier to replace them if they are lost or stolen. Make large purchases in small denominations so you have the option of gradually redeeming a large purchase at your local bank. It is possible to redeem part of a Series EE bond with a denomination of $100 or more, but the transaction will have to be handled through your local branch of the Federal Reserve Bank. To avoid a heavy tax bill at redemption, you may want to consider rolling U.S. savings bonds over into Series HH bonds. Because they are taxed on the basis of their current, semiannual interest payments, you can receive current income from your bonds and continue to avoid further taxes until redemption. The main drawback of this is the low interest rate, which has remained at 6 percent for several years. Even though you may purchase your bonds at a bank, you should direct important questions elsewhere, since banking personnel are often not well versed on the particulars of U.S. savings bonds. It is safer to get your information from the Savings Bond Division of your local branch of the Federal Reserve Bank.

Since bonds are credited with interest for the entire month in which they are bought. It is best to purchase them at the end of the month. Similarly, it is best to sell them at the beginning of the month so that you will receive the interest earned during the preceeding month. (Before redeeming the bond, you should find out when the interest is credited. Older savings bonds are credited only once every six months, and if you cash in one of these bonds a day early you will lose six months' interest.)

You can call the Savings Bond Information Office at (304)420-6112 to obtain further information about investing in savings bonds.

Investing in Mortgage-Backed Securities

Mortgage-backed securities are collateralized by mortgages and are designed to be long-term investments that attract funds to the mortage industry. These securities originate with loans provided by banks and other lending institutions to prospective homeowners. These loans, collaterized by mortgages, are sold by the lending institutions to issuing institutions, who pool them. Investors then purchase portions of these pools and receive principal and interest payments as the homeowners pay off their loans.

Mortgage-backed securities are issued by federal, state, and local governmental agencies and private institutions. They offer high yields and safety, but they differ in the predictability of their income and maturity dates.

Mortgage-Backed Pass-Through Securities

Mortgage-backed pass-through securities provide payment of both interest and principal by passing through the homeowner's loan payments to the investor. Unlike the case with most fixed-income investments, both interest (taxed as ordinary income) and principal are paid on a regular, monthly basis. In essence, the investor receives no money back on maturity. Although most mortgages have 30-year maturities, pass through obligations usually last about 12 years. This discrepancy results from the prepayment of mortgages following the sale of a home and from homeowner refinancing when interest rates decline. Examples of these securities include:

- Ginnie Maes
- Freddie Macs
- Collateralized mortgage obligations
- Fannie Maes

GINNIE MAES

The Government National Mortgage Association (GNMA) guarantees the best-known of these mortgage-backed securities: the GNMA pass-through, or Ginnie Mae. Because the GNMA is a government agency, Ginnie Maes are considered the safest of mortgage-backed securities. The mortgages are insured by the Federal Housing Administration or the Veterans Administration, and the investor cash flow itself is secured by the full faith, credit, and taxing authority of the federal government. Although Ginnie Maes are the highest yielding of all government-secured investments, they are still relatively low earnings compared with other mortgage-backed securities.

Homeowners' loan payments are separated from payments to investors by a 45-day cushion, which prevents late loan payments from directly affecting payments to investors.

A minimum investment of $25,000 provides the investor in Ginnie Maes with a liquid security that has an active secondary market. The price of these securities on the secondary market rise less than those of bonds because most investors are not willing to pay a premium for an instrument that returns a portion of their principal each month. When interest rates rise, however, mortgage-backed security prices fall as severely as bond prices. Like stock investment prices, the prices of Ginnie Maes fluctuate.

Ginnie Mae investments offer the advantages of relatively high yield and guaranteed return. Investors who need a large monthly income might find reinvesting the returned principal an added headache, especially if interest rates are declining. The problem is less bothersome if interest rates are rising.

The most significant problem with Ginnie Maes concerns the unpredictability of both income and maturity. Mortgage prepayments and refinancing have shortened many investments, and because payment depends on how quickly homeowners pay off their mortgages, investors can never be sure how much they will receive or for how long. To compensate for the uncertainty, interest rates are usually one to two points higher than those of comparable Treasury securities. Another major drawback of the GNMA pass-through is what investment advisers call the "double whammy." When interest rates rise, the investor can probably get better returns elsewhere; however, when interest rates fall, more homeowners refinance their mortgages, and as a result, the investor's interest income declines.

An increasing number of people use Ginnie Mae trust accounts for their IRA or Keogh plans and thus qualify for tax-exempt status. In addition, Ginnie Mae mutual funds and unit trusts now being offered can provide the individual investor with an opportunity to participate for as little as $1,000.

FREDDIE MACS

Unlike Ginnie Maes, Freddie Mac pass-through bonds are not guaranteed by the U.S. government but are privately insured by the Federal Home Loan Mortgage Corporation (FHMLC). These securities require a minimum investment of $25,000 and guarantee timely payment of interest. Unlike Ginnie Maes and Fannie Maes, Freddie Macs do not ensure regular payment of principal: If homeowners do not make their mortgage payments on time, investors could wait as long as a year to receive the appropriate amount of principal. Because of the added risk and uncertainty, Freddie Mac interest rates have historically been higher than those of the Ginnie Maes.

COLLATERALIZED MORTGAGE OBLIGATIONS

Investors who dislike the unpredictable income streams that often accompany mortgage-backed securities might be attracted to collateralized mortgage obligations (CMOs). Technically, a CMO is a mortgage-backed security that represents a share in an organized pool of residential mortgages. Principal and interest payments are passed through to shareholders.

CMO pools are often divided into four shares classes that correspond to the maturities of underlying mortgages, which may range from 5 to 20 years. Therefore, an investor can receive payouts in 5, 10, 15, or 20 years. Other types of CMO pools channel principal repayments to a redemption fund that randomly pays off CMOs at par value as cash in the redemption fund builds. This scheme delivers unpleasant surprises to investors who get their money back sooner than expected. Of course, the pace of redemptions speeds up when interest rates drop and homeowners rush to refinance.

Another type of CMO is the companion CMO, which is sold

mainly to individuals. These CMOs form part of a CMO issue consisting of planned-amortization bonds, which are favored by large institutional investors that seek to engineer income flows. Companion CMOs are junior to other securities in the same issue, and if interest rates in general drop, companion CMOs will be called first. Therefore, the prepayment risk inherent in mortgage-backed securities is even greater in companion CMOs. In a rising rate environment, companion CMOs also suffer; regular redemption payments are directed to institutional investors, who can then reinvest at higher prevailing rates.

FANNIE MAES

Fannie Mae securities are long-term, privately issued bonds guaranteed by the Federal National Mortgage Association (FNMA). Like Ginnie Maes and Federal Macs, Fannie Maes are pass-throughs (i.e., the principal of the mortgage is paid monthly along with the interest).

Fannie Maes are general-obligation debentures that require a $10,000 minimum investment for older issues and a $25,000 minimum for newly issued certificates. Semiannual interest is paid by coupons, which can be redeemed through the mail or exchanged at federally chartered banks; both timely payment of interest and principal are guaranteed. The FNMA also issues guaranteed short-term discount notes in various denominations between $5,000 and $1 million.

Although Freddie Macs and Fannie Maes lack the unconditional guarantee the federal government offers to Ginnie Maes, the FHLMC and the FNMA are both chartered by Congress. So although income streams to investors are privately insured, the corporations' close association with the federal government makes it unlikely that these agencies would default and not receive federal assistance. To compensate for the slightly higher risk, however, Freddie Macs and Fannie Maes still typically yield from 0.25 to 0.5 percent more than Ginnie Maes.

Investing in Municipal Securities

Municipal securities are promissory obligations issued by cities, towns, and villages; states, territories, and possessions of the United States; and housing authorities, port authorities, and other quasi-independent agencies. Bondholders or noteholders supply the issuing authority with the capital needed to provide goods, facilities, and services within the authority's jurisdiction. Many municipal securities generate interest income that is tax-free, making them especially attractive to the affluent investor. Most are exempt from state and local taxes if the bondholder or noteholder resides within the issuing state or municipality. Minimum denominations generally range from $5,000 to $10,000, and maturities vary from 1 month to 30 years. Investors may also select from numerous tax-exempt securities mutual funds.

Municipal Notes

The types of municipal securities may be categorized by maturity or by purpose. Municipal notes have maturities ranging from one month to three years, but they generally mature within one year. The notes are sold at a discount below par at face value on maturity, with the difference between the purchase price and the redemption price serving as interest. These short-term debt instruments are used for construction lending and cash flow provisions. Municipal notes are further divided according to their means of financing. Bond anticipation notes (BANs) are long-term debt instruments that are eventually paid off through new bond issues. Analyzing a municipality's long-term borrowing capacity is critical in determining the strength of a BAN. Tax anticipation notes (TANs) are secured by the issuer's expected tax income or by any other unencumbered revenue. When evaluating TANs, investors and advisers should scrutinize the municipality's taxing authority. Revenue anticipation notes (RANs) receive their backing from revenue sources other than taxes, such as federal and state aid. Project notes, issued by housing authorities, finance urban development and renewal projects and are considered the safest of all municipal securities, because they are backed by the full faith, credit, and taxing authority of the federal government.

Municipal Bonds

Municipal bonds differ from notes in that they generally mature anytime between one and 30 years. Used to finance long-term projects, the bonds provide semiannual interest payments by means of coupons. The principal is paid on maturity. Bondholders may purchase either general obligation securities (GOs) or revenue bonds. GOs are backed by the full faith, credit, and taxing power of the issuing authority and are initially secured by any unclaimed revenues received by the municipality (i.e., tax receipts and federal or state aid). Revenue bonds provide funding for specific projects, and interest payments are made from the revenues of that project.

TAX IMPLICATIONS

The tax treatment of municipal obligations depends on the purpose for which the bond is issued. Bonds issued after August 1986 fall within one of three categories:

1. **Public-purpose bonds.** These bonds are generally tax-exempt and include bonds issued directly by state or local governments or their agencies to meet essential government functions, such as highway construction and school financing.
2. **Nongovernmental-purpose bonds.** These include bonds issued to finance qualifying housing and student loans. There are limits on the amount on nongovernmental-purpose bonds an authority may issue. Interest on these bonds is tax-free for regular income tax purposes but is a preference item to be added to taxable income if the taxpayer is subject to AMT. Because of the AMT factor, nongovernmental-purpose bonds may pay slightly more interest than public-purpose bonds. Therefore, they may be a sound investment for clients who are not subject to AMT tax or whose AMT liability is small. Bonds issued before August 8, 1986 are not affected by these rules.
3. **Private activity bonds.** Bonds issued after August 31, 1986 for nonessential purposes are subject to federal income tax but may be exempt from state and local taxes in the state in which they are issued. Generally, private activity bonds are those whose proceeds are used in the trade or business of persons other than the state or local governments, such as industrial development bonds. Certain private activity bonds are exempt from these restrictions, including small-issue industrial development bonds.

Tax-exempt securities represent one of the few remaining genuinely tax-sheltered investments. Because of the tax-exempt feature, however, yields are lower than on similar taxable investments. Nevertheless, tax-exempt securities may offer attractive yields in comparison with after-tax yields on corporate, government, and other interest-earning investments. Experts expect tax-exempt securities to continue to provide attractive yields in order to remain competitive in the marketplace.

OTHER CONSIDERATIONS

Although the municipal securities market is attractive to a growing number of investors, the municipal market is currently much more speculative than it was in the past. Financially weak municipal issuers could delay or fail in paying interest because of unanticipated low tax revenues or unprofitable income-generating projects. Worse, default on principal repayment, though rare, is not unheard of. The strength of a municipal security can be determined by consulting its Moody's or Standard & Poor's municipal bond rating. Although these ratings are not infallible, they are indicators of bond quality.

Diversification is another factor that you must keep in mind. Municipal bond portfolios should contain several different securities, and industrial municipal bonds should be diversified across an array of local industries in order to be less vulnerable to shifts in the business cycle.

Insured bonds, insured bond funds, and insured unit trusts guarantee timely payment of interest and return of principal on maturity, and backing from an independent insurance company automatically enhances their ratings to AAA, which Moody's describes as "the best quality, carrying the smallest degree of investment risk." Insured bonds do not protect against losses incurred because of market depreciation, however. The yield on these securities is usually one-fifth to one half percentage point below noninsured equivalents, though some insured bonds rated AAA are yielding more than their uninsured counterparts. This discrepancy arises because many institutional buyers are not certain that the bonds warrant their high-quality rating: the adequacy of the insurance remains untested.

Investing in Corporate Bonds

Corporate bonds are generally riskier than municipal or Treasury securities and thus exact a higher yield, though the risks vary with the type of backing and the various features the bond provides.

Corporate bonds may be secured with specific collateral or may be unsecured (without specific backing). Secured bonds may appear as mortgage bonds, which are backed by real estate or plant and equipment; by collateral trust bonds, which are backed by non-real estate collateral (e.g., stock in another corporation or promissory notes); and by equipment trust obligations, which are secured by specific pieces of equipment.

Debenture and Mortgage Bonds

Unsecured bonds, or debenture bonds, are not backed by any specific collateral but are secured by the good faith of the issuing corporation; their unsecured status does not necessarily make them riskier investments. On the contrary, healthy and well-established corporations usually issue debenture bonds that can be traded without any additional security. Bonds backed by specific collateral usually need this extra asset to attract investors. This added protection does not always work however. The Penn Central bankruptcy demonstrated how even strong corporations can fail under adverse financial developments.

Convertible Bonds

Convertible bonds are bonds that can be converted into stock at a predetermined price. They are more attractive to some investors than debenture bonds because they enable investors to gain from the appreciation of common stock. However, this conversion privilege costs one or more percentage points in yield. Corporations intend convertible bonds to be delayed sales of stock, and they can force investors to convert into stock whenever the market value of such converted stock is equal to or greater than the call price of the bonds. The fact that convertible bonds may easily be called should be considered when an investor is planning short- and long-term investment goals. Investors could be forced either to redeem their bonds at a small premium and lose their former income or to buy shares of company stock.

Junk Bonds

Junk bonds, also called high-yield bonds, are those rated BB or lower by Moody's or Bb or lower by Standard & Poor's. They are highly speculative, behaving more like stock than like debt. Junk bonds tend to rise when the economy is on an upswing or when the issuing company experiences good fortune. These instruments represent companies in unfavorable industries, those with weak financial structures, or those that are well managed but young and highly leveraged. Junk bonds can also be the products of a corporate takeover.

The extra risk can pay off in a high return, however. Junk bonds generally yield at least three percentage points higher than Treasury bonds. For investors holding lower-quality bonds, a strong economy could present a great opportunity to cash in on high total returns. A resurgent economy allays fears of bankruptcy and thus can stimulate price increases for these lower-quality bonds. If they are sold, the capital gain plus the high yield could result in an attractive total return. However, a weakening economy can be disastrous for highly leveraged companies, which all too often end up defaulting on their debt obligations. Therefore, these bonds are suitable only if you can afford the added risk.

15

MAKING MONEY IN STOCKS

ALTHOUGH SOME PEOPLE over 50 are reluctant to own any stocks, almost every affluent person should have stocks in his or her portfolio. As you approach retirement age, you may want to consider gradually moving a greater percentage of your investments into more conservative interest-earning investments, but you still need to have a generous portion of your investments in stocks so that your income will be able to keep up with inflation during your retirement years. Over almost every ten-year period in the past, stocks have outperformed other investment alternatives. In fact, although stocks are riskier than many other investments, the Dow Jones Industrial Average, the most widely used index of stock prices, rose in 20 of the last 29 years (1963-1991). During the 1980s, the stock market increased in eight years of the decade—including 1987, when the infamous stock market crash occurred.

Many retirees falsely believe that they should restrict their investments almost exclusively to interest-earning securities, but most retirees can look forward to a long life expectancy, certainly long enough to take advantage of the appreciation potential of stocks. It is also a long enough period for inflation to erode your purchasing power if you don't keep some money in securities that have appreciation potential; that is, they can increase in value to provide a steadily increasing source of income to meet higher living costs.

In the last few years, many people have abandoned the stock market in the face of dramatic declines in stock prices (remember October 19, 1987?). Nevertheless, most employee pension plan managers keep half or more of the plan's assets invested in stocks. If that's what the professionals think is the best way to optimize return on investments earmarked for retirement, don't you think you should consider it?

All this doesn't mean that the same stock issues are appropriate for you and your grandchildren, and it doesn't mean that you should take any undue risks, but it does mean that a balanced investment portfolio, with a portion invested in a diversified group of high-quality, dividend-paying stocks or stock mutual funds, is still your best bet in your golden years.

Fortunately, you don't have to be an expert to be a good stock investor. All it takes is a little time to familiarize yourself with the stock market and, depending on whether you want to buy stocks directly or through mutual funds, with individual stocks or stock mutual funds. Don't be misled into believing that you have to stay on top of the market or your investments every day. If you buy high-quality stocks and stock mutual funds, you can and probably should hold onto them for a long time without worrying about short-term price fluctuations.

This chapter introduces you to both the various kinds of stocks that are available and strategies most commonly used by successful professional investment managers and individual investors.

Investing in Common Stocks

The types of stocks you select depends in large measure on your investment objectives (see Chapter 11). Growth stocks are relatively risky but are good investments for over-50 investors aiming for long-term capital appreciation. However, income stocks are less risky and, as their name implies, can provide stable sources of income. Such stocks are most appropriate if you need an income supplement.

Common stocks offer a liquid element to a portfolio because, unlike some kinds of investments such as real estate and collectibles, they can be turned into cash readily, usually within a week. However, the forced sale of stock to meet unexpected family expenses may result in unintended capital losses or adverse tax consequences. Common stocks, in principle, serve as a hedge against inflation; that is, they have tended to provide returns (appreciation in value plus dividends) that equal or exceed rises in general price levels when held over a long term. The shortcomings of common stocks are the volatility of stock prices in general and the possible instability of underlying corporate earnings and dividends for specific stocks that you own. The advantages and disadvantages of common stocks are described in more detail in the next section.

Advantages and Disadvantages of Common Stocks

Stock investments have several advantages. The most common are:

1. Regular income,
2. tax deferral,
3. liquidity, and
4. dividend reinvestment.

Most well-established corporations distribute quarterly dividends to their stockholders; some have been doing so for more than a century and a half! These dividends can be a source of income for the over-50 investor who requires additional income to meet living expenses. Stocks that you own directly (as opposed to mutual funds) that rise in market value can also be viewed as tax-sheltered investments, because taxes on the gains are deferred until the securities are sold. For example, a 28 percent tax bracket investor who puts $25,000 into an 8 percent certificate of deposit (CD) pays $560 in federal taxes each year plus any state taxes. Conversely, a $25,000 stock investment that increases 8 percent in market value incurs no tax liability as long as the stock is held and not sold. Of course, the 8 percent increase in market value is far from certain, but in the long run, stock investments have produced attractive returns.

Many companies also offer *dividend reinvestment plans* in which you not only can have your dividends automatically converted into more shares of stock (if you don't need the cash), but you can also buy additional shares directly from the company.

The risks of owning common stock include declines in the stock's price and reduction or suspension of dividend payments. A severe impairment of a company's financial structure could result in a rapid decline in the price of its stock and/or a suspension of dividends, but financial risk is reduced if you limit your holdings to several larger, established corporations. A decline in a stock's earning power or future stream of dividends also causes its price to fall. Changes in competition, demand, costs, or management all can affect the amount of business risk to which any stock is subject. You can avoid large losses from such events by being watchful and acting quickly, perhaps through the use of stop-loss orders. Even when a corporation's earnings power does not change, the price of its stock can fluctuate extensively. The causes of these price changes are varied, but they include intermittent transactions by buyers and sellers, and investors' periodic preferences for different types of investments, not to mention moves in the stock market as a whole.

Types of Common Stocks

Many types of common stock are available. An informal classification system identifies stocks that have common or similar characteristics and puts them into one of the five following categories:

1. income stocks,
2. growth stocks,
3. blue chip stocks,
4. cyclical stocks, and
5. speculative stocks.

Income Stocks

Income stocks are usually bought for current income, as they have a higher than average dividend yield. Companies whose stocks fall into this category are typically in fairly stable industries (e.g., telecommunications and electrical utilities), have strong balance sheets, and pay out a substantial portion of their earnings in dividends. Income stocks may be particularly appropriate for retirees, who are more dependent upon stability of principal and steady dividend income.

Growth Stocks

Investors buy growth stocks for capital appreciation. Because most growth companies are growing rapidly and are involved in research, most or all of their earnings are reinvested in the company for future expansion. Thus, while growth stocks have the prospect of increased market value, they have little, if any, dividend return. The prices of growth stocks usually go up faster than do those of other stocks, but they can fluctuate widely in both directions.

Blue Chip Stocks

Blue chip stocks are considered the highest quality of all common stocks and they generally have the ability to pay steady dividends in both good and bad years. These companies hold dominant positions in industries that generally are not overly vulnerable to cyclical market swings.

Cyclical Stocks

Cyclical stocks include issues of companies whose earnings tend to fluctuate sharply with their business cycles. When business conditions are good, a cyclical company's profitability is high and the price of its common stock rises; but when conditions deteriorate, the company's sales and profits can fall sharply. For example, the housing and steel industries suffer when interest rates are high because of the inverse relationship between industry revenues and interest rates. Thus, the correct timing of transactions is crucial to a successful investment in cyclical stocks.

Speculative Stocks

In a sense, all common stocks are speculative stocks, since they offer a variable rather than a fixed return, but some stocks are more speculative than others. Speculative stocks typically have high price to earnings (P/E) ratios, extensive price fluctuations, and a high risk factor. "Hot" new issues, high-flying glamour stocks, and penny mining stocks are speculative stocks. The average investor should avoid them unless he or she can easily afford the loss; they usually are traded successfully only by expert investors.

You can select stocks in one or several categories depending on your age, income, preferences, financial situation, and experience in stock market investing. Retirees might want to concentrate on income and blue chip stocks; they're less exhilarating, but often as rewarding.

Investing in Preferred Stocks

Preferred stocks have been frequently called hybrid securities because they have features of both bonds and common stocks. For instance, a preferred stock is like a bond in that it usually has a fixed-percentage dividend and it is similar to a common stock because its share price fluctuates and you cannot receive a dividend unless it is declared by the corporation. Although preferred stock legally represents a portion of ownership in a corporation, you normally do not have voting power, as do holders of common stock. Preferred stock issues also offer an opportunity for price appreciation (or depreciation) although they generally do not fluctuate in value as much as common stock.

Should a company be liquidated, the preferred shareholders receive priority over the common shareholders in the distribution of its remaining assets. Some corporations create more than one class of preferred stock; such classes may rank in sequence (first, second, third, and so on) in priority of claim or they may be equal in this respect.

Preferred stock that is traded on the stock market is usually less volatile and more interest rate sensitive than is common stock. For example, assume a certain preferred stock, at purchase, has a dividend yield of 9 percent: a $2.60 dividend on a $29 share. Later, interest rates in general rise. In order for the stock to remain competitive with the bond market, the market value of the shares theoretically must fall until the price returns a rate higher than 9 percent. In short, the market value can fluctuate inversely with the change in market interest rates.

Advantages and Disadvantages of Preferred Stocks

Preferred stocks offer *stability* to your investment portfolio. They are similar to bonds in that they provide a fixed rate of return, but they have two advantages over bond investments. First, they can be bought with a smaller amount of money. Second, preferred stocks offer the possibility of greater price appreciation than that offered by bonds.

Different types of preferred stocks can add flexibility to a portfolio. For instance, convertible preferred stock gives the holder the option of converting those shares into common stock, which is useful if you see a solid capital gains opportunity in converting.

In general, preferred stock offers two particular advantages to the over-50 investor: (1) Preferred stockholders enjoy a fixed dividend rate, as the possibility of dividend payout dropping with the economy (as common stock dividends could) is low; and (2) preferred stocks protect capital better than common stocks do because their owners have a priority claim on corporate assets.

The major disadvantage of preferred stock is that its dividends do not rise with the firm's profits. Also, as with any stock issue, preferred stocks can and do decline in value.

Types of Preferred Stocks

Preferred stocks are not all alike; in addition to the question of priorities in the event the company liquidates, they may be straight, voting, callable, convertible, cumulative, or participating; they may have some of these features or none of them; and they may or may not have still other features. Be familiar with the rights and privileges of any preferred stock you now own or contemplate buying.

STRAIGHT PREFERREDS

Straight, or nonconvertible, preferred stock simply yields a fixed dividend rate without other options or privileges.

VOTING PREFERREDS

There currently is a trend toward full voting rights for preferred shares although most older issues are nonvoting.

CALLABLE PREFERREDS

Most modern preferred stock is callable or redeemable; that is, the corporation reserves the right to pay it off at specified prices and retire it. Usually, you must be notified two or three months before the call date. This feature is seldom an advantage to you because it enables a prosperous corporation to retire high-dividend-rate preferred stock. The absence of a call feature in a preferred stock does not necessarily guarantee that you can keep it indefinitely, however, as mergers or recapitalizations sometimes result in the substitution of a new security that may be callable.

CONVERTIBLE PREFERREDS

About one third of all preferred shares are convertible, at the option of the shareholder, into the company's common stock. If you're a holder of a convertible preferred share you can benefit from this feature when the price of the common stock rises to a point where the common stock is worth more than the preferred stock that you would tender to obtain the common. Of course, you must weigh the income advantages of the preferred stock against the capital gains advantage of the conversion. Thus, the conversion option permits you, as a holder of preferred stock, to participate more fully in the company's success if it prospers, but allows you to retain your preferred position if it does not.

CUMULATIVE STOCKS

Cumulative preferred stock assures that any dividends that cannot be paid in a particular year will accumulate and must be paid before any dividends can be paid on the company's common stock. Most modern issues are cumulative, although sometimes junior or lower-ranking preferred stock is noncumulative (e.g., third preferred) when the senior preferred is fully cumulative. Clearly, cumulative preferred stock is a more satisfactory investment vehicle than noncumulative. Sometimes even strong companies must omit preferred dividends temporarily, and it is better for you that the dividends are merely deferred rather than lost.

PARTICIPATING STOCKS

A few preferred issues receive participating status, which means that if other shareholders receive large dividend increases or special benefits, then you, as a preferred shareholder, participate in the benefits too. Participating stocks allow for the possibility of dividends being paid on the preferred stock in excess of the fixed amount.

Most preferred issues combine some of the above features and some contain even newer features. Standard and Poor's *Stock Guide*, available by subscription or in most well-stocked libraries, offers helpful information about the character of preferred stocks.

Stock Investment Strategies

The following well-respected strategies are among the most commonly used for investing in stock. This is not a compendium of esoteric or high-risk investment techniques. The vast majority of over-50s should not take a lot of risk with their money. Instead, it summarizes some basic strategies for achieving long-term stock investment success. These strategies are not just for selecting new stocks to add to your portfolio, but they can also help you to evaluate your existing stock portfolio or contemplate a change in your overall investment strategy.

Never Buy Stocks Indiscriminately

Many investors buy stocks haphazardly simply because they have money to spend. Investments should be made only when you have a good reason to buy a particular stock. If possible, you should keep some cash available to take advantage of new opportunities as they arise.

Select a Promising Industry

At any given time, most industries in the economy are either on the upswing or the downswing with respect to earnings potential. When choosing a stock to buy, you should start by selecting a promising industry. You'll do better if you have a good reason for selecting an industry and a company within it whose future looks promising.

Diversify

Try to own stocks in several different industries, because different forces drive different sectors of the market. There's also the too-many-eggs-in-one-basket problem. Overdiversification on a small amount of money is unwise, however, because you may have difficulty keeping track of individual stock holdings, and you may incur higher-than-necessary brokerage commissions if you buy or sell stocks in groups of less than 100 shares. Mutual funds are a convenient way for persons with large or small investment portfolios to achieve broad diversification.

Buy Low and Sell High

So you've heard this before? Then it may surprise you to hear how many people never get this right. You should condition yourself to buy stocks when stock prices are down and sell them when prices are up. Stocks can rebound when prices are low, and major selling opportunities come when stocks are hot and prices are high. How do you know when stock prices are high or low? Since most individual investors are usually wrong in their assessments of market conditions, the next time your bridge or golf partner says that stocks are the only place to be since the opportunity to reap enormous profits is assured, you can be assured the market has peaked and is headed downwards. Conversely, if your friends are getting out of stocks, chances are that the market is poised for a rebound.

Use Dollar-Cost Averaging

Dollar-cost averaging is a conservative method of investing in the market that attempts to screen out the whims and hunches that cause many investors to buy high and sell low. Instead of trying to time the highs and lows, you buy the same amount of equity in a stock or a mutual fund at regular intervals over a long period of time, often reducing the average price paid per share.

Stay Abreast of General Market Trends

It is always important to look at general trends in the market. A stock that has already risen in value might be a good candidate for continued gains if the market is still rising. Conversely, a stock that does not respond to a general market rise might be a poor investment.

Use Dividend Reinvestment Plans

Dividend reinvestment plans (DRPs) are a useful way for investors to reinvest their dividends until they begin to need the income to meet living expenses. Investors purchase modest amounts of stock in companies that they intend to hold onto and have all their dividends reinvested (with no sales commission) to purchase additional shares regularly. You do have to pay taxes on the dividends even though you don't receive them in cash. You can also augment your holdings by making additional optional purchases through the DRP, usually with no brokerage charge and sometimes at a slightly below-market price.

Buy Good Performers

Always try to buy value. Companies with strong balance sheets (valuable assets and little or no debt) and solid earnings growth are consistently better long-run performers.

Look for Regular Small Stock Dividends

You may want to consider buying stock in companies that habitually pay regular small stock dividends. A small stock dividend (20 percent or less) often does not result in a lower stock price consistent with the dilution of ownership. This strategy therefore allows you to increase the value of your holdings with no current income tax effect.

Buy Low P/E, High-Dividend Stocks

A stock's P/E is the ratio of its price to its earnings: the current market price divided by its per share earnings over the past 12 months. Many successful long-term investors use the investment strategy of purchasing common stocks of companies with low P/E ratios and high dividend yields. As long as the company is fundamentally sound, the dividend yield of such stocks is relatively attractive. The stock may appreciate as the market discovers its undervaluation, and then it might increase its dividend to maintain an attractive yield. Investors in these shares enjoy a win-win situation—capital appreciation and increasing dividend income.

Know the Risks of Short Selling

Short selling is a very risky approach to playing bear markets; most investors are usually wrong in predicting them. In fact, the odd-lot short sale index has been one of the most consistent contrary indicators of future market performance. In other words, an increase in odd-lot short selling activity almost certainly means a bull market. For most bearish investors, buying put options is preferable to short selling although most option buyers end up losing their money. All investors should think twice before investing in any way in which your losses are not limited by the amount of your investment, which includes selling short. Persons over 50 should think three times. In fact, don't waste your hard-earned money on any investment vehicles or strategies that are unfamiliar to you, such as commodity futures, rare coins, art or collectibles—don't stray from mainstream investments.

Write Covered Call Options

Writing call options on stocks in your portfolio provides additional income from the premiums received. A conservative covered call-writing program can be implemented with minimal risk (see the following section).

Diversify Overseas

There is always a bull market somewhere in the world. Foreign companies account for over 70 percent of the world's stock market capitalization, compared with 50 percent just 10 years ago, and many foreign markets have consistently outperformed the home team. If you haven't already, commit some of your stock investment money, perhaps 10 to 20 percent, to foreign stocks. The best way to play the foreign markets is to buy a good international mutual fund. Avoid single country funds or single region funds. Look for broad-based international funds that scour the world for the best investment opportunities.

One thing to keep in mind as an international investor is the effect currency fluctuations can have on your investment returns. When the dollar rises against foreign currencies, earnings of overseas companies translate into fewer U.S. dollars and overseas holdings are worth less to U.S. investors. When the dollar declines however, foreign earnings are enhanced when translated into U.S. currency and foreign holdings are worth more to U.S. investors. Some portfolio managers buy currency futures and other esoteric instruments to hedge the currency risk in their funds. Before investing in an international fund, you should examine its prospectus to see what kind of hedging, if any, the fund engages in. Hedging can protect your investment when the dollar rises, but you'll pay for it when the dollar falls. You certainly wouldn't want to try it on your own, but if you approve of the fund's hedging policy go ahead and invest in it.

Invest with a Long-Term View

Although brokers may not like this, the buy-and-hold strategy of investing usually produces much better results (for the investor) than an actively traded portfolio. Studies have shown that over most holding periods of 10 years or longer, investors in stocks have enjoyed returns well in excess of inflation; shorter holding periods generally produce lower returns. Also, if you take a long-term perspective, you will certainly fret less over shorter-term market vacillations.

Buy Quality

Quality investments offer a good measure of protection, particularly in times of market volatility and investment uncertainty. Stocks and bonds of well-established companies have greater staying power when market conditions deteriorate.

Don't Borrow to Invest in Anything Except Real Estate

The investors who are really hurt by adverse bond and stock market conditions are almost always those who borrowed on "margin" to increase their investments. The only way for them to cover their margin calls was to sell their holdings at an inopportune time. While borrowing for real estate can be an effective means of increasing investment returns, heavily margined stock and bond investors expose themselves to considerable risk.

Avoid High Risk Investments

While you may think they offer you a one way ticket to nirvana, such investments as commodity futures, coins, and buying stock options are, for the most part, suckers' games. If you want to make high risk investments, feel free so long as you use only a small portion of your portfolio. Just be prepared to lose the money because, more often than not, lose it you will.

Avoid New Investments

Don't buy anything new like a new stock issue (you probably aren't important enough to your broker to be offered an issue that will rise in value), a new closed-end fund (they almost always go down in value because the price you pay for the new fund is considerably greater than the value of the assets in the fund), or a "new and improved" type of security.

Investing in Mutual Funds for Diversification and Professional Management

Although many investors look down on mutual funds because they aren't very exciting, they are a wonderful place for your stock investment money. Why? First, you get instant diversification with a stock mutual fund, and diversification is crucial in any market. Second, you get full-time, inexpensive professional management: you pay someone a very nominal sum (about one percent per year) to worry about your investments. Mutual funds are easier to evaluate and compare than many other types of investments, so it's easier to pick ones that will do well, and it's easier to follow them once you've bought. Since this is so easy, you can do it yourself and buy straight from a no-load (meaning no sales commission) or low-load (meaning low commission) mutual fund company like Dreyfus, Fidelity, Neuberger Berman, T. Rowe Price, Scudder, Twentieth Century, and Vanguard.

You can add to your fund investment or get out of it any time you want. Most mutual funds offer a variety of shareholder services. For example, most funds allow you to have all your dividend and capital gains distributions automatically reinvested in additional fund shares, add to the fund automatically by having funds transferred from your checking account on a regular basis, or have the fund send you a set amount every month.

There are over 3,000 mutual funds, and they vary widely in investment objective, policy, and services. The most important thing about picking a fund is making sure that its objectives match yours. A fund is required to send you a prospectus before you invest, and this document explains what securities the fund buys and what it's trying to get from them (i.e., growth, income, or some combination). You aren't looking for the one "best" fund, there are probably dozens that would serve you well. Besides, you can spread your bets even further by choosing a few mutual funds. You don't need to be a millionaire to own a few funds; you can start an account with most of them for $500 to $2,500, and once you have the account, you can add to your fund investments in even smaller amounts. Some funds don't have any minimums at all.

Numerous publications provide excellent and timely coverage on mutual funds. *The Wall Street Journal* and *Barron's* have many articles about mutual funds and interviews of leading investment managers. You can also use the advertisements in these publications to find out the 800 telephone numbers of some fund companies, most of whom would be pleased to send you some brochures on investing and on their funds. Your local library should have the *CDA/Wiesenberger Investment Companies Service* or *Morningstar* which provide unparalleled coverage on mutual funds. These publications offer a wealth of written and statistical data to keep readers abreast of ongoing mutual fund industry trends, short- and long-term performance, and dividend payouts. Keeping up-to-date on investment matters takes some time and some initiative, but you will be well-rewarded for your efforts.

When to Sell

Ideally, the answer is never. If you did your research carefully, you're hoping to find a stock or stock mutual fund that'll continue to serve you well for years after you buy it. Unfortunately, this isn't always the case: companies' fortunes change, your investment needs change (e.g., you may need more income to meet living expenses when you're retired), and sometimes you don't make the right choice to begin with.

The Company Is No Longer Appealing

You should be able to explain why you think the stock should be profitable. If you bought the stock because you thought it would do well for a specific reason, and that reason has not materialized, then it might be a good time to sell. If what you anticipated has come to pass and will no longer affect the stock price, maybe you should take your gains. If it hasn't and no longer looks as though it will, maybe you should take your losses. For example, suppose you buy a pharmaceutical company stock because you expect the FDA to approve a miracle drug it was testing. If the drug turns out to be a dud, and that was the only reason you bought the stock, sell. Already owning a stock is not usually a good reason to continue owning a stock. If you don't have reason to believe it will appreciate, you should probably sell.

Your Stock Is Doing Worse than Other Companies in Its Industry

If you still have reason to believe it will do well, hold onto it. If you don't, sell.

Your Stock Isn't What It Appeared to Be

If the company's quarterly earnings are below what they were last year or are lower than expected for two consecutive quarters, or if profit margins start to narrow, the stock might be a dog.

Your Mutual Fund Has Performed Worse than Other Funds with Similar Policies for Two Consecutive Years

Maybe the manager has just lost the golden touch that made you choose that fund. Maybe someone else has taken over. You gave it a chance to make up a temporary setback and it didn't do it. Don't sell a fund just because it underperforms for a quarter or two, however. If you had reason to buy it, give it a chance to prove its worth.

Having Your Cake and Eating It Too

Many people find it much harder to decide to sell than to buy. If the price has gone up, they're afraid they'll miss out on future gains. If the price has gone down, they can't believe it won't come back up. If you have a good reason to sell or you don't have any good reason to hold, sell. If you wouldn't buy the same stock now, it might be time to dump it. One way to make buy and sell decisions easier is to average in and out of your stocks instead of committing all your resources (or dumping all your stock) at once. Remember, almost nothing in investing (or financial planning, for that matter) is either-or. If you aren't sure whether you should hold onto a stock or dump it, why not sell half? If the price goes up, you'll still catch some of the profits. If the price falls, you won't lose your shirt or blouse.

Stock Option Strategies

A stock option is a contract to buy or sell stock at a particular price. The exchange-listed options quoted each day in the financial press are standardized so that each contract establishes the right to buy or sell 100 shares within a fairly short period of time. All exchange-listed options have a designated expiration date—generally one to six months from the date of issue. Longer term stock options have also begun to be offered.

Options can be used either to "hedge" an existing stock holding (i.e., to reduce your risk), or to speculate, in which case your risk is magnified. In effect, a hedge is a form of insurance, and you buy this insurance by paying a premium. This premium is the sacrifice of certain profits you would have made had you kept the stock and not optioned it.

Options afford those willing to take the risks of speculation a high degree of leverage in the sense that a small investment of capital can go a very long way. Just as a mortgage lets you realize all the increase in value of a real estate investment without having to pay full price for the asset, a stock option lets you pick up all the increase in the value of a stock while investing only a small fraction of the stock's current value.

In contrast to real estate, however, the leverage that stock options afford is not the result of borrowing money. The leverage flows from the fact that an option is only a right in an asset, and a limited one at that. But just as borrowing can get you into trouble when the asset appreciates less than the cost of borrowing, so can speculation in the right to purchase or sell shares at particular prices.

Most option strategies don't make sense for most individual investors. Transaction costs (commissions) and taxes can eat up any gains—and for most option buyers, gains are few and far between. There is one strategy that often makes sense, however. This is setting up a so-called covered-call-writing program. Writing an option puts you on the opposite side of the transaction from the person who buys an option. Writing a "call" option obliges you to deliver a specified number of shares of stock at a specified price by a specified date (if the call option is exercised by the investor who bought it;

that is, if the option holder "calls" the stock away from you), and writing a "put" option obliges you to buy a specified number of shares of stock (presumably shares that you want to buy anyway) at a specified price by a specified date (if the put option is exercised). The idea behind writing options is that if most people who buy options lose money, you can make money by selling them.

A covered option is one in which the seller (also called the writer) of the option owns the underlying security; its opposite is an uncovered (also called a naked) option, where the writer does not own the underlying stock. *Naked* option writing is one of the most dangerous ways to invest. You can lose a tremendous amount of money almost over night. The purpose of a covered-call-writing program is to generate income on stock you own and plan to keep. The risk you take on in exchange for earning extra income on your stock is that you may forgo a portion of your potential profit if you end up having to deliver your shares to the investor who bought your option at a price that is less than the market price. In other words, the option buyer wins and you lose, a bit, at least.

> EXAMPLE: Patrick Paladin owns 100 shares of ABC stock, currently trading at $98 per share. He writes an option contract on the shares giving the option holder permission to buy them for $99½ in October. The premium for the option is 4¼ so he receives a total of $425 (less commissions). If the stock price rises and the option is exercised, he will be assured of an effective selling price of 102.25 (98 + 4¼). If, instead, the stock price declines, he can "walk down" the option by buying in the call and writing another one at a lower exercise price. Should the market price of the stock continue to decline, he can replace the second option with one whose exercise price is even lower.

Before you start such a program, however, you should plan what you will do if the stock rises or falls more than you anticipated when you wrote the call. Writing covered options is certainly less risky than writing naked ones, but it isn't for everyone. Be sure you understand all the risks before you undertake any investment strategy involving derivative securities (options, stock index futures, etc.)—or any securities for that matter.

16

SAFE REAL ESTATE INVESTING IN TODAY'S RISKY MARKET

REAL ESTATE HAS traditionally been one of the best ways for long-term investors to create wealth. But it is also possible to lose a lot of money in real estate, as many owners of soured limited partnerships and short-term speculators can attest.

During much of the 1980s, real estate was widely considered a "can't lose" investment. Today, overbuilt, sluggish markets in many areas of the country, combined with less attractive tax incentives, have made real estate investments somewhat less alluring, at least in the short term. Yet, carefully chosen real estate remains a worthwhile component of a well-balanced investment portfolio.

There are ways to own real estate without having to endure the headaches of managing it, although the people who get rich on real estate usually buy and manage individual properties. This chapter discusses the opportunities and drawbacks of real estate as an investment. Home ownership is discussed in Chapter 24 and Chapter 30.

The tax reforms of the 1980s had a dramatic impact on the entire arena of real estate investment. Less generous depreciation schedules, as well as new restrictions on using most real estate tax losses to offset other income, have severely curtailed investment in tax-loss-generating properties.

Today, wise investors must look for real estate investments that can stand on economic merit alone—in other words, properties that generate a positive or close to positive cash flow. While weak real estate markets in many areas of the country may be viewed as an opportunity to make real estate investments, caution is essential in view of the possibility that prices may continue to fall in some markets. Also, high vacancy rates in many areas of the country will plague even cheaply purchased rental properties.

Real estate investment and ownership decisions are never easy, but they are particularly difficult for retirees and people nearing retirement. Many investors who purchased real estate during their working years, some of whom made their first investments after age 50, have found that it provides a secure and inflation-protected source of retirement income.

Yet retired people who own real estate often face hard financial choices and have to decide whether to hold onto their properties or partnership interests or to sell them. These are particularly difficult decisions that usually have significant tax, cash-flow, and estate planning ramifications. Later on in this chapter, you'll find tips both on buying investment real estate—and on when to sell.

Types of Ownership

There are three common ways to invest in real estate. The first is to "do-it-yourself" by purchasing properties directly. Investors who lack the time, inclination, or capital to buy and manage real estate on their own can purchase interests in real estate limited partnerships. Finally, real estate investment trusts (REITs) allow investors to participate in large real estate projects for relatively small amounts by purchasing shares of these publicly-traded corporations.

Here's a closer look at the pros and cons of each of these three investment approaches:

Direct Ownership

For those who have the resources to purchase and the inclination to manage real estate on their own, direct ownership is the most lucrative way to invest in real estate. Two categories of investment are available: income-producing real estate and undeveloped land.

Income-producing real estate can range from a two- or three-family owner-occupied home to small apartment buildings to commercial and industrial properties. Undeveloped land is a more expensive way to invest in real estate because land with strong appreciation potential is very costly and difficult to finance.

Buying and managing income-producing properties yourself is the surest way to create wealth in real estate, but you have to weigh the risks and rewards. This method normally requires a substantial time commitment and a personality that can deal effectively with tenants. Many older individuals and couples, who are settled in their careers and finances, have found that for the first time in their lives they have the money and time to make and manage real estate investments.

The key to successful investing in owner-managed real estate is to find the right property—at a cost-effective price. When a property can be purchased at the right price (so that it carries itself on a cash-flow basis) and offers a strong likelihood that it will stay fully rented, there's money to be made over the long haul despite periodic weak real estate markets. Why? Because the rental income alone will cover the expenses of owning and maintaining the property, so you aren't relying on rapid capital appreciation to make money on the property. Note, however, that these properties aren't easy to find, and successful real estate investors are prepared to wait a long time—years perhaps—rather than pay too much for a parcel.

Limited Partnerships

In real estate limited partnerships, a group of investors pools their money and invests in new construction or existing commercial or residential property, including apartments, office buildings, and shopping centers. Shares in a partnership are offered to potential limited partners by a general partner in order to attract additional capital. The liability for losses of the limited partners is usually limited to the amount of their investment.

The general partner, who organizes the partnership and is involved in the day-to-day management of the investment, receives a share of the profits, plus fees and commissions. Usually, the partnership disbands after a period of time, ranging from a few years to more than 10 years, and the partnership proceeds are distributed to the investors.

The various types of programs available allow you to shop for a real estate partnership that best suits your financial situation. Be sure to examine the offering memorandum or prospectus carefully and pay special attention to the information about risks and returns of the investment and about the general partner's background and experience.

You should also look for independent sources of information about similar limited partnerships. It never hurts to ask someone else—an accountant, attorney, or acquaintance who has some experience with similar kinds of investments—to provide a second opinion on a contemplated investment. Frankly, the people who sell these investments tend to emphasize the positives and gloss over the negatives, so you can't look to them for an objective opinion.

ADVANTAGES OF PARTNERSHIPS

Advantages to investment in real estate limited partnerships include:

- Ease of buying in. While direct ownership requires a complex system of transfer, an investor in a limited partnership needs only to complete some documentation and send a check to the general partner. The partnership's prospectus gives you access to information necessary to make a reasonably quick decision.
- Fixed cash requirements. After you make your initial payment, you will usually not be responsible for financing any further cost overruns.
- No management responsibility. This is often a blessing to older investors. The general partner is responsible for finding tenants, maintenance, bookkeeping, tax reporting and all other management duties.
- Limited legal liability. As a limited partner, your maximum legal liability is limited to the total amount you have invested in the partnership. Thus, your other assets are not at risk, as they are when you own and manage property yourself.
- Smaller initial investment. In most deals, you need to invest as little as $5,000 (less if you invest through an IRA or other retirement plan) to receive the benefits of a large real estate project.
- Lower overall risk. Diversification and professional management can make limited partnership investments less risky than direct ownership.

PARTNERSHIP DISADVANTAGES

Naturally, there are also disadvantages to investing in real estate limited partnerships. These include:

- No acquaintance with the manager and restricted knowledge of the deal. You usually must base your knowledge of the general partner on secondary sources. So despite the information available in the prospectus, there's always the chance you might fail to identify hidden risks associated with the deal. What's more, your best interests will not always coincide with those of the general partner.
- Less control. A limited partner has no say in the management of the property, nor can he or she dictate when or to whom the property is sold.
- Lower overall return. This is due to fees and commissions paid to set up the partnership, to operate the property, and upon liquidation of the partnership.
- Limited tax-saving opportunities. Under current tax rules, many of the tax shelter opportunities that once made limited partnerships so attractive to high-income investors are either severely restricted or eliminated altogether.
- Illiquidity. Because there's little demand for existing limited partnership investment units, they typically sell for far less than the original investment—if they can be sold at all. This could be a major drawback for retirees who may need to sell the investment on short notice to provide income or who want to remove illiquid investments from their estates.

The degree of risk of owning an interest in a real estate limited partnership is affected by three different factors: the amount of leverage used, the percentage specified, and the type of property and investment.

- Leverage. Highly leveraged investments—those financed with large amounts of borrowed money—require larger cash flows to make payments on the debt and are thus riskier. If cash flows decline to the point where debt payments are interrupted, the property may be foreclosed upon.
- Percentage specified. A general partner may sell limited partnership shares before selecting all properties. A deal with 0 percent specified—a so-called "blind pool"—is the riskiest kind, since you cannot examine and evaluate the investment beforehand (although a general partner with a strong track record might not present too high a risk, even with a blind pool). A further risk connected with blind pools is the possibility that, in a robust real estate market, the sponsor might be

forced to lower his or her standards and make riskier investments in order to get the partnership up and running.

- Type of property. Investments in existing property will have more information available, because of the property's operating history. Commercial property and established residential property will probably (but not always) be more secure investments than hotels or undeveloped land.

Most of the limited partnerships on the market today stress income and capital gains because of decreased tax incentives. Nevertheless, investors should be very wary of limited partnerships in the current environment of real estate instability. Investors in older partnerships have suffered billions of dollars of losses. And while some of the more recent deals have been attractive, they are a distinct minority of the real estate limited partnerships being offered today.

Also keep in mind that limited partnerships are generally not advisable if you may need access to your money in the near future, since selling the shares on the secondary market before the partnership is liquidated will usually result in substantial losses. Senior citizens should be particularly wary of the lack of liquidity inherent in limited partnerships. Always assume that your money will be tied up in the partnership indefinitely. Although the deals are structured more sensibly than they were when they were primarily tax-shelter investments, most still rely on price appreciation to turn a profit, even though prices are flat or moving downward.

BEST ADVICE: Avoid making any new partnership investments until the real estate market turns around. And never invest in a real estate limited partnership if there's the slightest chance you'll need the money in the foreseeable future.

The people who sell you these partnerships may tell you that the market has already turned around, that the partnership will be liquidated in just a few years, and that, if necessary, you'll be able to sell your interest readily on the secondary market if you need to. Don't let any of these assertions influence your decision to purchase a limited partnership interest.

Real Estate Investment Trusts (REITs)

REITs are the least expensive and most liquid way to invest in real estate. REITs are publicly traded stocks that invest in real estate projects and/or mortgages. Since they generally trade on the major stock exchanges, they are as easy to sell as any widely held stocks.

REITs are an excellent way to participate in real estate with a small investment—for three reasons: (1) All capital gains realized through the trust go directly to the shareholders, (2) the diversified portfolio minimizes risks, and (3) the ability to trade provides greater liquidity than other real estate investments.

REITs, like mutual funds, bring the advantages of centralized, professional management to individual investors. REITs are subject to strict regulations and thus tend to be well-managed.

The current outlook for REITs is guarded, however. Many REITs invest in major commercial properties, and overbuilt real estate markets are adversely affecting the leasing environment. In addition, many REITs are suffering from major cash-flow problems, both as a result of overbuilding and recent low inflation. Finally, the specter of the Resolution Trust Corporation's vast holdings of real estate flooding an already depressed market has cast a pall over the REIT industry and held down share prices.

If you want to play the real estate market, the REIT route may still be your best bet. It certainly is the cheapest way to get your feet wet. Better still, you can sell your investment and receive cash in a matter of days.

What's more, REITs have traditionally provided a rich dividend yield.

Real estate investments are renowned for their extreme boom/bust cycles, and it's at the perceived bottom of a cycle that experienced real estate professionals jump in and reap extraordinary returns. The REIT vehicle was legislated into existence specifically to enable the smaller investor to participate in such gains. Since REIT prices have been beaten down so badly, such an opportunity might present itself.

> TIP: If you want to take the plunge, look for REITs that specialize in apartments or cater to older people and retirees. As you well know, the demographics for this market is good and improving all the time. Thus, such projects should hold up relatively well even in the toughest economic times.

ONE MORE CHOICE

There is one other way you can invest in real estate, albeit indirectly. How indirectly? By buying stocks of companies that have substantial undervalued real estate holdings on their balance sheets.

Investment professionals often cite the large paper companies and some retailers that own a lot of their outlets as attractive "real estate-rich" companies.

Real Estate Investment Alternatives

No matter which form of real estate investment you are considering, there are a range of types of real estate available for purchase.

Undeveloped Land

Undeveloped land is the most speculative real estate investment. It has both the greatest potential for appreciation—and the greatest risk. The key to making money in undeveloped property is to purchase land that's currently undervalued relative to the surrounding properties but that seems likely to increase in value.

The four most important factors in determining raw land value are the physical conditions of the property and surrounding area, and governmental, economic, and sociological factors. For example, a piece of land that's too small or irregularly shaped could discourage development. Just as important as physical conditions are government rules and regulations affecting the property. Restrictive building codes and zoning could prohibit development and limit profit. Local tax laws and environmental regulations may also have significant implications for development.

Economic factors such as local employment rates, interest rates, and inflation must also be considered. The more employment growth and diversification evident in a community, the more promising an adjacent raw land purchase might be. Growing populations with shrinking household sizes are favorable demographic trends, indicating a need for more residential housing. To understand the effect of all these various forces on a potential undeveloped land purchase, an investor should consult a local broker, attorney, and perhaps an engineer or land surveyor—before you buy.

The chief advantage of undeveloped land is the potential for sizable appreciation. Disadvantages include the lack of current income from the property and an accompanying reluctance on the part of bank lenders to finance undeveloped land investment (because of the lack of income). Also, since few comparative appraisals are available for raw land, and industry standards are not well established, some land may be overpriced. Often, land with the lowest price is located in areas where values are unlikely to increase substantially or at all in the foreseeable future.

Residential Rental Property

Residential property's greatest benefit as an investment is that it produces current income, which lessens out-of-pocket costs while the property (hopefully) increases in value. Location, type of structure, and available utilities all may affect the property's value, as can local population trends and zoning changes. The primary categories of residential property are single-family homes, condominiums, multifamily dwellings, and apartment buildings.

SINGLE-FAMILY HOMES

Investments in single-family units can be attractive for investors because such properties are relatively affordable and provide immediate rental income, although the income may not be sufficient to cover the expenses of owning a single-family rental.

On the down side, a single-family unit requires active management. The most important factor in determining value is the property's neighborhood. Availability of recreational facilities, transportation, and shopping are all important.

One approach that can be very profitable is to purchase at low cost in a "transitional" neighborhood that seems ready to improve. This technique is, of course, highly speculative and, thus, isn't advisable for inexperienced investors.

The potential for capital appreciation with single-family units is great. Such properties have been good insulators against inflation. In addition, small investments in cosmetic improvements can substantially improve the residence's selling price.

However, single-family residences provide relatively low cash flow, and tend not to be self-supporting. Most of the return will be realized through value appreciation. Probably the most important factor in single-family residential investment is location. Avoid areas where property values are not rising. Also, keep in mind that prospective tenants must be carefully screened for their ability to pay rent reliably.

CONDOS AND CO-OPS

Condominiums usually command lower prices than single-family homes and often have collectively owned amenities, such as a swimming pool and parking facilities. Cooperatives differ from condominiums primarily in the way liability is assigned. Since a condominium's apartment units are individually financed, remaining owners need only assume a defaulting owner's share of operating expenses. A cooperative, however, usually takes out a blanket mortgage on an entire building. So, when an owner (technically, a shareholder) defaults, the remaining owners must assume the extra share of carrying costs.

Condominiums and cooperatives are a viable investment in areas where rents can be increased significantly over time. In recent years, however, many areas of the country have been overbuilt with condos and co-ops, causing price declines.

RESORT HOMES

Although the IRS has restricted the tax breaks that once applied to vacation homes used for rental purposes, vacation homes still offer some of the tax benefits of primary residences—plus rental income to help offset your costs. Remember, however, that in most resort areas of the country, prime rental season is limited to a few months of the year. So the opportunity for rental income may be limited, especially if you want to use the property yourself during the peak season.

All the same, many Americans find the idea of owning a vacation home appealing, especially now that depressed prices of vacation properties in many areas of the country mean that good buys can be had. The best way to evaluate a vacation home, however, is to assume that it will garner no rent. Don't believe for one minute the assertions of real estate agents or home sellers about a property's rental potential.

> BOTTOM LINE: If the vacation home passes your personal financial muster assuming that you will not be able to rent it, then it may well be worth considering. At the least, it may provide you with some well-deserved psychic income.

TIME-SHARE UNITS

Time-sharing, or interval ownership, is particularly suited to resort areas because owners can pay a smaller price for a piece of a more expensive property. Time-sharing deals typically fall into two categories:

Simple-fee ownership, in which an owner purchases a piece of the property and owns total rights to it, offers many of the same advantages as regular home equity. Right-to-use ownership grants a right to use a property for a specified period of time, after which point the possession of a property reverts to the "real" owner. Right-to-use owners are usually prohibited from transactions that simple-fee ownership allows.

Time-sharing property is marketed very aggressively because developers need to find many owners for each unit. Unfortunately, some unscrupulous time-share salespeople and developers have preyed on older Americans. While many time-share owners have been pleased with their investments, a lot of these projects are of dubious quality. And since the time-share resale market is almost nonexistent, the vast majority of these projects should not be considered investment-quality. However, as larger, more established companies begin to enter this business, time-sharing may become a more viable investment.

DUPLEXES AND APARTMENTS

Multifamily units and apartments offer investors greater opportunities for tax breaks and positive cash flow than single-family structures. Included in this category are small two-, three-, and four-family homes that are often owner-occupied. Although multifamily dwellings require a greater initial investment, the cost per dwelling unit usually is lower.

Multifamily units are relatively easy to finance for investors with sufficient resources, as lenders see the potential rental income as protection on their loans. However, a major problem with large apartment units in some communities is the presence of rent-control restrictions (either present or potential). Other drawbacks include the possibility of overbuilding in a community and the illiquidity of the investment.

As with any other real estate, the property's location can make or break the investment. So prospective buyers should avoid areas of depreciating property values. Proximity to main avenues of transportation and to shopping, recreation, schools, and work is particularly important to apartment dwellers. If the physical condition of the property has been neglected, the costs of repair could erode profits. Owners can be hit with large unexpected expenses such as re-roofing or replacing the electrical, plumbing or heating systems of a building. Thus, investors in apartment buildings must have adequate reserves to meet such contingencies.

Commercial Property

Office buildings, shopping centers, other retail property, and industrial real estate are attractive to investors with substantial resources. However, as potential rewards from owning substantial properties increase, buying and managing such properties become more complicated, so you should be especially well-informed about the specifics of the purchase.

SUGGESTION: With the exception of very small, well-located, and fully occupied properties, commercial real estate is best left to the experts. If you want to participate, do so through real estate limited partnerships or real estate investment trusts that invest in commercial properties.

Evaluating Real Estate Investments

Experienced real estate investors are always on the lookout for reasonably priced properties. In order to do a quick initial evaluation of a property, savvy investors typically use simple formulas that compare selling price to expected income from the property. If the price-income relationship seems reasonable, they will then conduct a more detailed analysis. A couple of commonly used real estate evaluation formulas are described below. They can be useful whether you're considering the purchase of a property yourself or through a limited partnership.

Rent Multiplier

The simplest formula involves comparing the total selling price with the current gross annual rental:

$$\text{Rent multiplier} = \frac{\text{Selling price}}{\text{Gross annual rental}}$$

For example, say a duplex selling for \$180,000 generates \$15,000 in annual rent. The rent multiplier is calculated as follows:

$$\text{Rent multiplier} = \frac{\$180{,}000}{\$15{,}000} = 12$$

In other words, the property is selling for 12 times annual rental. A property that is selling for much more than seven times the gross annual rental is likely to yield a negative cash flow. In the above example, until rents can be raised significantly, which may take years, you're probably going to be pouring more cash into the investment after you buy it. Of course, you could put a sizable cash downpayment into the property to assure a positive cash flow. But, you would only be fooling yourself because there's an opportunity cost associated with tying up a lot of cash that could otherwise be earning interest.

Similarly, if a real estate limited partnership pays more than seven times the gross annual rental to buy a property, the partnership is probably paying too much, unless it can reasonably expect a dramatic increase in the value of the property (for example, immediate condo conversion). Of course, the salespeople always expect great things out of the deal, although a less optimistic prognosis would often be more accurate.

Capitalization Rate

A second real estate evaluation formula is the capitalization rate, usually referred to as the "cap rate." The formula is simple:

$$\text{Capitalization rate} = \frac{\text{Net operating income}}{\text{Total amount invested}}$$

For example, a limited partnership in an apartment building requiring a total investment of \$3.5 million has an estimated net operating income of \$300,000. The cap rate is calculated as follows:

$$\text{Capitalization rate} = \frac{\$300{,}000}{\$3{,}500{,}000} = 8.6\%$$

A cap rate of 8 percent or greater is considered desirable. And whether you invest in real estate yourself or through a limited partnership, make sure the amounts that go into the cap rate formula are realistic. For example:

- "Total amount invested" includes both the downpayment and the borrowed money necessary to buy the property.
- "Net operating income" is the total rental income (allowing for vacancies) less all the expenses except debt service. A favorite trick of real estate agents and general partners is known as "bumping to market," which means raising rent projections from what they currently are to a supposed market level in order to make the deal look more attractive.

The above formulas are simply rules of thumb, and just two of many important considerations that go into making sensible real estate investments. In some instances, a promising location may outweigh a low cap rate. Or tax advantages available to owner/managers who meet certain income criteria may compensate for a high rent multiplier.

Figure 16.1 on the next page, the Rental Property Income and

Expense Worksheet, can help you summarize past income and expenses and project future budgets for a rental property.

Those who are most successful in real estate investing, whether they do it themselves or through limited partnerships, share one characteristic—patience. When they believe that real estate is overpriced, they're happy to wait until market conditions meet their criteria.

Figure 16.1. Rental Property Income and Expense Worksheet

Planning and budgeting are essential for any business, including the business of owning rental property. If you own rental property, the following worksheet can be used to summarize past income and expenses and budget future income and expenses.

Property location and description: ....

....

Assumptions used in projecting income (e.g., occupancy rate, level of rent increases): ....

....

Assumptions used in projecting expenses (e.g., general rate of inflation of expenses, unusual or nonrecurring repairs and maintenance): ....

....

		Budget		
	Prior Year Actual	**........ Year**	**........ Year**	**........ Year**
Income:				
Rental	$.......	$.......	$.......	$........
Other	....	....	....	....
Total Income	....	....	....	....
Expenses:				
Advertising	$.......	$.......	$.......	$........
Automobile and travel	....	....	....	....
Bank charges	....	....	....	....
Cleaning and maintenance	....	....	....	....
Commissions	....	....	....	....

Figure 16.1. (Cont'd)

Insurance	....	....	....	....
Interest	....	....	....	....
Legal and professional	....	....	....	....
Management fee	....	....	....	....
Repairs and maintenance	....	....	....	....
Salaries and wages	....	....	....	....
Supplies	....	....	....	....
Taxes	....	....	....	....
Telephone	....	....	....	....
Utilities	....	....	....	....
Depreciation	....	....	....	....
Other	....	....	....	....
Total Expenses	....	....	....	....
Income (Loss)	$	$	$	$........
Other information:				
Principal payments:	$	$	$	$........
Property improvements:	$	$	$	$........

Real Estate Investment Strategies

In many areas, the real estate industry has been in such a weakened condition that even experienced investors are justifiably reluctant to make real estate commitments. There still are opportunities for the venturesome, but given the likelihood of continued downward pressure on prices and the difficulty of obtaining bank financing, the real estate industry seems certain to flounder in many regions of the country for some time to come. If you're considering real estate investments, the following suggestions can come in handy:

PURCHASE CLOSE TO HOME

Since real estate is so closely tied to local economies, those who are familiar with the local real estate market enjoy a significant advantage over those who try to purchase real estate in unfamiliar locales.

But be forewarned. Real estate conditions vary from region to region and from one type of property to the next. In general, apartments seem to have the most potential in the early 1990s, due to the aging population and the growth of single-parent households. Commercial properties seem sure to lag because of past overbuilding and oversupply in many markets—although, again, it all depends on the community.

EXAMINE "BARGAINS" CAREFULLY

Distressed properties in many regions of the country have lured investors into trying to purchase properties at foreclosure auctions or through the Resolution Trust Corporation (RTC), the agency charged with disposing of the foreclosed properties of defunct savings and loans.

Both methods of acquiring property are fraught with difficulty and risk, however. Buying at auction requires extensive research before bidding, and the properties are generally sold "as is," without warranty or contingencies for inspection. Foreclosed properties sold at auction are often in poor condition and foreclosed development projects are typically awash in red ink. There may be liens on the property or clouds in the title. What's more, dealing with the RTC can be a time-consuming bureaucratic nightmare, although a local real estate broker may be able to assist you.

USE REAL ESTATE TO DIVERSIFY YOUR PORTFOLIO

In spite of the many pitfalls of real estate investing, is it still feasible for pre- and recent retirees to make real estate investments? Yes, so long as the investments make sense both from a financial and personal standpoint.

For example, many preretirees find that for the first time in their lives, they have both the money and the time necessary to purchase and manage parcels of income-producing real estate. Such investments have the potential to provide a steadily rising income that's so necessary to keep pace with inflation during retirement. And the equity build-up of the real estate can be tapped later in life to provide substantial additional capital for retirement or estate-transfer purposes. Investors who aren't inclined to become landlords may find some opportunities in carefully selected limited partnerships, although the pickings in the early 1990s are slim at best.

So, real estate often does play an important role in an older person's well-diversified investment portfolio.

Deciding When to Liquidate Real Estate Investments

Recognizing the appropriate time to sell a property is as important to your investment success as the decision to buy. Generally, the decision to sell is based primarily on financial considerations—for example, a more attractive investment alternative becomes available.

For older people, the decision to sell directly owned properties may be motivated by a number of reasons, including a desire to alleviate the management headaches, the need for a higher level of income than the real estate investment provides, the desire to become "more liquid," and the need to remove illiquid investments from the estate for estate planning purposes—to ease the eventual transfer of the estate to heirs. These decisions are difficult at best, and in most instances should be made only after you obtain professional counsel, particularly in the areas of tax, estate, and overall financial planning.

The professional should evaluate the soundness of your reasons for wanting to sell your real estate or transfer it to heirs during your lifetime, your strategy for selling the property, and the timing of the sale. It's best to plan for the sale of directly-owned properties well in advance—years in advance if possible. Advance planning will lessen the risk of having to sell on short notice or during a slump in the real estate market. Just as successful real estate investors take time to make the right investments, successful real estate sales take time as well.

Older people who have limited partnership investments can expect a lot of difficulty liquidating these investments before the partnership itself is liquidated. While there is a secondary market for limited partnerships, most sell at a sharp discount—if they can be sold at all.

Most big brokerages will try to find buyers for partnership units they sold their clients originally. But if you're in a hurry to sell, you may come out ahead by getting in touch with one or more of the many small firms around the country that specialize in matching limited partnership sellers with buyers. Some firms, such as Bigelow Management (New York), EquityLine Properties (Miami), and Partnership Securities Exchange or PSX (Oakland, California), act as principals and buy partnership units—often at a discount—for their own accounts. Others act as brokers or agents and collect commissions from either the buyer or the seller. Still others, such as National Partnership Exchange (Tampa, Florida), conduct auctions of partnership units. Keep abreast of any regulatory changes in the secondary market for partnership exchanges.

Generally, it's better to hold onto them, unless you need to sell fast in a financial emergency. Of course, if you foresee liquidating your real estate holdings within the next several years, you should avoid purchasing any new limited-partnership interests or making any more direct real estate investments. Opt for REIT investments instead if you want to maintain the diversification that real estate provides.

17

WHY EFFECTIVE TAX PLANNING IS VITAL

IT'S AMAZING HOW obsessed people are with concocting elaborate schemes to avoid paying taxes. Nevertheless, figuring out ways to save on taxes is as American as apple pie. Even the law has consistently upheld this American right. In the words of Judge Learned Hand: "Over and over again courts have said that there is nothing sinister in so arranging one's affairs as to keep taxes as low as possible. Everybody does so, rich or poor; and all do right, for nobody owes any public duty to pay more tax than the law demands; taxes are enforced exactions, not voluntary contributions."

Just because there are legal ways to pay Uncle Sam less doesn't mean those options are always preferable. Billions of dollars have been invested over the past decade in tax sheltered limited partnerships that have proven worthless, millions of dollars have been given away without taking advantage of available deductions, and estates have diminished rather than increased as a result of misguided tax savings strategies.

A significant part of tax confusion was generated by the tax reform of the 1980s (there were seven major pieces of tax legislation enacted during the decade). As a result, we often tend to lose sight of the fact that Congress retained intact the one "tax shelter" that, in my experience, has been responsible for the vast majority of family wealth accumulation in this country. We can still buy and hold capital assets free of taxation on the unrealized accretion in value. In plain English, this means you can buy stock and real estate, and, so long as you hold on to it, you will not pay any capital gains taxes on the increase in its value. Time and time again as I have reviewed the portfolios of some very wealthy families, I find the same pattern. They either bought a lot of real estate and have held on to it for many, many years, or they bought a lot of common stock and have held on to it for many, many years. The annual returns they have enjoyed on their original long-held investments are often 20 percent, 30 percent, or more of their original cost basis. Why? Because, in the instance of real estate, they have been able to increase rents and, over time, have reduced operating expenses and reduced, if not eliminated, mortgage payments. In the instance of stocks, these families have invested in blue chip stocks of good companies with strong dividend paying records (I refer to them as "the Generals," like General Electric and General Motors), companies that have consistently increased their dividend rates over the years. Mind you, all of this has been enjoyed without any payment of capital gains tax. If these investments are held until death, capital gains taxes may be avoided altogether since the heirs will receive a "stepped-up" basis upon the death of the owner. (Estate taxes, however, may have to be paid.) This is wealth creation at its best, and there is no reason why you can't do the same thing. As the saying goes, "One way to get rich is to look at what rich people do, and do the same thing." While I don't want you to spend like rich people, you will be delighted if you invest like them.

One key to wealth building that no financially fit person or family forgets is the role that strategic tax planning plays in their investment portfolio. Tax planning is an important part of personal financial planning, but *it is just one part.* Any investment or financial decision should include an evaluation of its tax ramifications, but none should be regarded solely or even primarily on that basis. There are many cases in which the option that results in a lower cut for Uncle Sam also results in a lower cut for you! Other tax-saving strategies simply aren't worth the effort.

Whether you are in the work force or not, don't allow your savings strategies to be guided by grandiose tax-saving schemes. Often, these lack economic substance (in spite of what the colorful brochures tell you). Many people also rely too heavily on their tax preparers, who, while they may provide you with sound advice, are obviously not as familiar with your own needs as you are, particularly over the long term. In fact, effective tax planning often takes years to accomplish. One final note: The Tax "Complification" Act of

1986 reduced the marginal tax rates so significantly that "tax shelter" is no longer a significant issue. Things were a lot different when you were taxed at 40 or 50 cents on the dollar, but many over-50 people still haven't realized the changes in thinking that are required for the current income tax rate environment. The more you say, "What is the income tax impact of this transaction," the more likely you are to become so tax driven that you literally sacrifice savings potential and retirement income.

Tax-Deferred Investments

Tax deferral, most often in the form of retirement-oriented accounts—IRAs, KEOGHS and deferred annuities—is an important component of the investment and retirement planning process (even those who work for organizations that already have pension plans). Many of them are designed to force you to save, or at least strongly discourage you from spending, because if you contribute money to them it accumulates with no tax liability until it is withdrawn, whereas if you withdraw it prematurely it incurs stiff penalties. In addition, when you contribute to some of these plans you can deduct the amount you contribute from your current earnings. Chapter 18, which deals with tax-advantaged investments, contains explanations of tax-deferred retirement plans and investments. If it's difficult to choose among them, don't worry. You can set up as many as you can afford. The one thing you do sacrifice is liquidity, so you really shouldn't put any funds in these accounts that you might need before retirement.

Tax-Exempt Investments

Tax-exempt investments can also be a smart way to invest, but they are subject to the same principles by which you would evaluate any other investment. Over the past several years, the yield on many long-term tax-exempt bonds often has not been much less than the yield offered by taxable long-term Treasury bonds. When you consider that you don't have to pay federal income tax on the interest, tax-exempt bonds begin to look like a pretty good addition to a diversified investment portfolio. For example, an investor in the 31 percent federal tax bracket would have to earn almost 12 percent on a taxable bond to match an 8 percent tax-exempt yield on an after-tax basis. Single-state municipals (or municipal obligations of Puerto Rico) can provide exemption from both Federal and state income taxes. An alternative to buying individual municipal issues is to invest in municipal bond mutual funds and unit investment trusts that offer tax-free compounding, diversification, and professional securities selection for a low price. Tax-exempt bonds are one of the few alternatives left that protect current income from taxes and are still generally a good investment, but you must be careful to weigh your alternative minimum tax position before investing in them. The interest on some municipal bond issues that are used to finance activities that are not related to the issuing government are subject to the AMT.

Mastering the Tax Game

Tax planning isn't just a year-end issue: It's a multiyear issue. Sound tax-saving techniques usually take years of planning and often take years to develop fully. One of the best things about multiyear tax planning is that you eventually learn to avoid making mistakes that you have made in the past.

It doesn't take a big time commitment to become "tax aware," it just takes commitment, and you're sure to benefit. Remember that "tax aware" doesn't mean "tax driven." Your days of tax-motivated transactions have, mercifully, come to an end. In spite of an incredibly complex Internal Revenue Code, we are better off at least to the extent that you are better off by making investment decisions primarily on the basis of their economic merits, and while you need to be aware of the tax implications of your day-to-day personal and business activities, they should no longer be motivated by their impact on your personal tax status.

Working with Your Tax Advisor

Now that you know some general tax and investment rules, you need to figure out how to develop and implement them. The first question becomes, do you need a tax advisor? Many of the best-prepared tax returns from the standpoint of accuracy and tax minimization are prepared by the individual taxpayer. Many people don't mind doing their own taxes because they have the time to become informed about tax-saving matters. If your individual tax situation isn't too complicated, there's nothing wrong with doing your own taxes. It will also save you some money that you, in turn, can save.

However, for many working and retired people, tax preparation and planning is intimidating, frustrating, and downright unpleasant.

The extensive tax reforms of the 1980s have managed to confuse just about everybody, and as soon as you begin to feel that you understand the current rules, Congress is probably going to change them. A good tax advisor can be a lifesaver. He or she will help you minimize your tax bill by keeping you informed of strategies you can use and by knowing how different expenses and income are treated. Also, a good tax advisor will help you stay up-to-date on tax saving techniques and the latest changes in tax law.

But, you have to work with your tax advisor because *only you are fully aware of your financial situation.* You shouldn't expect your tax advisor to be a miracle worker who can make sense out of an unorganized mass of receipts and forms you give him or her around April 1st. You should organize your records, keep them organized throughout the year, and always keep tax considerations in mind before making any financial transaction. Simplify your tax life and your tax advisor's job as much as you reasonably can. Consolidate investments, keep the best and most complete records you can, and *avoid all sorts of supposed tax shelters.* Keep a notebook handy to record miscellaneous deductible expenses such as costs associated with medical care and volunteer activities. Remember, tax minimization and tax planning is a year round process, so expect your advisor to advise you throughout the year, and listen to the advice. A good tax advisor will be available year round not only to answer your questions but also to review the tax implications of contemplated investments and suggest tax-saving strategies.

Whether you prepare your taxes yourself or have a tax advisor, you will benefit from obtaining IRS publications that pertain to your situation. (Figure 17.1 provides a list of IRS publications.) Figure 17.2, Income Tax Return Summary, can help you monitor your year-to-year income and tax trends. Figure 17.3, Tax Planning Action Plan, will help you assess which areas of tax planning need your attention.

Year-End Tax Saving Techniques

You realize that tax planning is a long-term and ongoing process. However, sometimes things just don't work out the way you've planned them. If you realize it's already November and you haven't started to plan at all, take heart. There are a few tricks you can use between Halloween and New Years to help cut your current year's tax bill and start planning the next year in advance. And, while

Figure 17.1. IRS Publications

These publications, which are available free from the IRS, can be very helpful in understanding income tax matters that pertain to you.

Publication Number	*Title*
1	Your Rights as a Taxpayer
17	Your Federal Income Tax
54	Tax guide for U.S. Citizens and Resident Aliens Abroad
448	Federal Estate and Gift Taxes
463	Travel, Entertainment, and Gift Expenses
501	Exemptions, Standard Deduction, and Filing Information
502	Medical and Dental Expenses
503	Child and Dependent Care Credit
504	Tax Information for Divorced or Separated Individuals
505	Tax Withholding and Estimated Tax
508	Educational Expenses
510	Excise Taxes
514	Foreign Tax Credit for Individuals
516	Tax Information for U.S. Government Civilian Employees Stationed Abroad
520	Scholarships and Fellowships
521	Moving Expenses
523	Tax Information on Selling Your Home
524	Credit for the Elderly or the Disabled
525	Taxable and Nontaxable Income
526	Charitable Contributions
527	Residential Rental Property
529	Miscellaneous Deductions
530	Tax Information for Homeowners (including Owners of Condominiums and Cooperative Apartments)
533	Self-Employment Tax
534	Depreciation
535	Business Expenses
536	Net Operating Losses
537	Installment Sales
538	Accounting Periods and Methods
539	Employment Taxes
541	Tax Information on Partnerships

Figure 17.1. (Cont'd)

544	Sales and Other Dispositions of Assets
547	Nonbusiness Disasters, Casualties, and Thefts
550	Investment Income and Expenses
551	Basis of Assets
552	Recordkeeping for Individuals and a List of Tax Publications
554	Tax Information for Older Americans
555	Community Property and the Federal Income Tax
556	Examination of Returns, Appeal Rights, and Claims for Refund
559	Tax Information for Survivors, Executors, and Administrators
560	Retirement Plans for the Self-Employed
561	Determining the Value of Donated Property
564	Mutual Fund Distributions
570	Tax Guide for Individuals in U.S. Possessions
575	Pension and Annuity Income
584	Nonbusiness Disaster, Casualty, and Theft Loss Workbook
586A	The Collection Process (Income Tax Accounts)
587	Business of Your Home
589	Tax Information on S Corporations
590	Individual Retirement Accounts (IRAs)
593	Tax Highlights for U.S. Citizens and Residents Going Abroad
594	The Collection Process (Employment Tax Accounts)
596	Earned Income Credit
721	Tax Guide to U.S. Civil Service Retirement Benefits
901	U.S. Tax Treaties
904	Interrelated Computations for Estate and Gift Taxes
907	Tax Information for Handicapped and Disabled Individuals
908	Bankruptcy and Other Debt Cancellations
909	Alternative Minimum Tax for Individuals
910	Guide to Free Tax Services
911	Tax Information for Direct Sellers
915	Social Security Benefits and Equivalent Railroad Retirement Benefits
916	Information Returns
917	Business Use of a Car
919	Is My Withholding Correct?

Figure 17.1. (Cont'd)

924	Reporting of Real Estate Transactions to IRS
925	Passive Activity and At-Risk Rules
926	Employment Taxes for Household Employers
927	Tax Obligations of Legalized Aliens
929	Tax Rules for Children and Dependents
934	Supplemental Medicare Premium
936	Limits on Home Mortgage Interest Deduction
1004	Identification Numbers Under ERISA
1048	Filing Requirements for Employee Benefit Plans
1212	List of Original Issue Discount Instruments

these efforts can't take the place of sustained, long-term planning, they can start you off on the right foot come next year.

Personal Interest

KNOW YOUR AMT LIABILITY

Alternative minimum tax (AMT) liability must be considered before implementing any tax saving strategies. Unfortunately, many high-net-worth individuals cannot escape the AMT. Try to determine whether or not you will be subject to the AMT either in the current year or the next. It can levy an additional tax against your regular income tax with "tax preferences" added back, and certain deductions canceled. In general, you try to accelerate deductions into the current year and defer income to the next year, but AMT provisions disallow certain itemized deductions and may tax income at a higher rate than it would otherwise be subject to. Itemized deductions that are treated as exclusion items for AMT purposes should be shifted to years in which you will not be subject to AMT. These include state and local taxes, and most miscellaneous itemized deductions. If you are subject to AMT in the current year but will not be in the next, the acceleration of income could result in tax savings depending on the nature of the AMT preferences and/or adjustments.

KNOW WHAT YOU'RE WITHHOLDING

Make sure your withheld and estimated taxes will equal or exceed either last year's tax bill or 90 percent of what you'll owe for the current year. If you think you'll come up short, there may still be time to compensate if you're still working by increasing your with-

Figure 17.2. Income Tax Return Summary

Use this work sheet to record key numbers from your past tax returns. This is a convenient means of monitoring your year-to-year changes in income, deductions, and income tax burden.

	Year					
	.....	.....	.....	.....	......	.....
Income:						
Wages	$....	$....	$....	$....	$....	$....
Interest	.....	.....	.....	.....	......	.....
Dividends	.....	.....	.....	.....	......	.....
Personal business	.....	.....	.....	.....	......	.....
Capital gains	.....	.....	.....	.....	......	.....
Pensions	.....	.....	.....	.....	......	.....
Rents, royalties, partner-ships, and trusts	.....	.....	.....	.....	......	.....
Other	.....	.....	.....	.....	......	.....
Total income	.....	.....	.....	.....	......	.....

Note: The following items are not additive; simply indicate the amounts from the appropriate lines on your federal and, in the case of the last line, on your state/local income tax returns:

Total adjustments to income	.....	.....	.....	.....	......	.....
Total itemized deductions	.....	.....	.....	.....	......	.....
Taxable income	.....	.....	.....	.....	......	.....
Federal income tax	.....	.....	.....	.....	......	.....
State/local income tax	.....	.....	.....	.....	......	.....

Figure 17.3. Tax Planning Action Plan

Current Status		
Needs Action	*OK or Not Applicable*	
[ ]	[ ]	1. Familiarize yourself with the tax-saving techniques.
[ ]	[ ]	2. Carefully analyze any investment or transaction that is being recommended to you or that you intend to make primarily on the basis of tax saving.
[ ]	[ ]	3. Coordinate your income tax planning with other important personal financial planning areas, including investments, retirement planning, and estate planning.
[ ]	[ ]	4. Don't lose sight of the role of "old-fashioned" tax-advantaged investments like tax-exempt bonds and buying and holding stock and real estate.
[ ]	[ ]	5. If you, like many affluent over-50 people, may be subject to the AMT, you should incorporate AMT considerations in your tax planning.
[ ]	[ ]	6. Maintain complete and well-organized income tax records throughout the year. Your tax record keeping should be coordinated with your personal recordkeeping system.
[ ]	[ ]	7. Effective income tax planning is both a year-round process and a multiyear process. Spend some time after tax season with your advisor, if applicable, or yourself planning your income tax strategies over the next five years.
[ ]	[ ]	8. Take full advantage of one of your best investment opportunities—tax deferred investments. (See Chapter 18.)

holding for the rest of the year. If you make estimated state income tax payments, rather than paying the last installment in January, you may want to pay it in late December so that it can be deducted this year. Make sure your tax deduction will exceed the amount of interest lost by paying early, however. Also, this strategy won't work if you are subject to the AMT this year.

DIVIDE AND CONQUER

Set up separate bank accounts for business, personal, investment, and real estate activities. Interest deductibility depends on your activity. If you use just one bank account, it's hard to tell where the money came from and where it went.

REMEMBER YOUR TAX DEFERRED INVESTMENTS

If you have any net income from self-employment, you can open up a Keogh account and tuck away up to 20 percent of those earnings tax free. Many people mistakenly assume that they can't have a Keogh plan for their moonlighting income if they participate in an employer-sponsored pension plan. Although you can contribute to your Keogh plan up to the time you file your tax return, the plan itself must be set up by December 31. An alternative to the Keogh is the Simplified Employee Pension plan, which is more limited in the amount that can be contributed but which can be set up and funded as late as April 15 of the following year.

If you're past the age of 70, remember to make at least the minimum withdrawals from your IRA and other retirement plans.

MIND YOUR OWN BUSINESS

Many business expenses are deductible. For example, the cost of operating and maintaining an automobile used for business purposes, dues paid to professional societies, even attending business conventions and the costs of subscriptions to professional journals or information services bought in connection with the performance of your professional duties are normally deductible as a business expense, and so are contributions to qualified pension plans. Even educational expenses may be deductible business expenses if certain conditions are met. The expenses are deductible if the education maintains or improves skills required in the professional's trade or business or meets the express requirements of the professional's employer. If the educational expenses meet these requirements, reimbursements by the employer to the employee do not need to be reported by the employee and such reimbursements are not considered wages for purposes of Social Security taxes, unemployment taxes, or income tax withholding. However, if the education being sought is a minimum educational requirement for qualification in a profession or part of a program of study that will lead to qualifying an individual for a new profession, trade, or business, expenditures are not deductible. Moreover, for the education to be considered as maintaining or improving professional skills, you must be actively engaged in the profession at the time you take the course.

CONTROL YOUR OWN INVESTMENTS

Controlling when you receive investment income can help your tax situation. One way to defer investment income is to transfer funds from instruments that pay current interest, such as money market funds, into Treasury bills or certificates of deposit that mature within a year or less and that won't pay interest until next year. You also have control of when you realize capital gains and losses on stocks and real estate. You may want to consider realizing capital losses to offset any capital gains in a specific year. In addition, you can use net capital losses in excess of capital gains to offset up to $3,000 of other income on a dollar-for-dollar basis. If you plan to make a large charitable contribution in a year in which you intend to recognize a capital gain in securities, you'll get a double tax benefit by making the gift with the securities although you may need to consider alternative minimum tax (AMT) consequences. Generally, you get a deduction for the full value of the securities you donate, and you won't owe tax on their appreciation. When you borrow money to invest, any interest you pay on the loan is deductible but only against investment-related income. If you paid investment interest this year, try to produce enough investment income to offset it. Capital gains count as investment income for this purpose. Talk to your securities broker about bond (or stock) swaps. You may be able to realize a capital loss by selling a security in which you have a loss and then buying a similar but not identical one. You must be careful not to buy the same instrument, which could subject you to the wash sale rules.

BE GOOD

The end of the year is the season to yield to your charitable impulses. Don't forget that donations of such tangibles as old clothing, furniture, and books are deductible at fair market value. Keep track of any expenses you incur driving your famous chocolate royale pound cake to the church bake sale—your mileage is deductible at 12 cents per mile. Donations of appreciated stock are often even better than cash, since in addition to your income tax deduction for fair market value you can avoid paying tax on the capital gain.

BE DETAILED

Since miscellaneous expenses are deductible only to the extent that they exceed 2 percent of your adjusted gross income, you should tally them up prior to year end to see how close you are to the 2 percent hurdle. Miscellaneous expenses include professional dues, tax preparation fees, unreimbursed employee business expenses, and certain educational costs. To the extent permitted by the regulations, you can either bunch more miscellaneous expenses into the current year or defer them into the next, depending on where you stand. Similarly, you may want to check on whether your taxable income is nearing a higher tax bracket. If so, you should consider deferring income, to the extent permissible. However, postponing income isn't always a great idea. If you expect to be in a higher tax bracket next year, then you would try to do the opposite—to accelerate earnings into the current year. In order to decide when to receive the income, you generally have to have a pretty good picture of your tax situation for this year and next.

Family Matters

KNOW WHO YOUR MEDICAL DEPENDENTS ARE

Many people pay medical expenses for other loved ones, but don't realize that these expenses qualify for a medical deduction. A "medical dependent"—a relative, young or old, whose shelter, food, and medical expenses you pay at least half of—entitles you to include their medical expenses as part of your own medical deduction. Sandwiched between the continuing cost of contributing to the financial stability of young adult family members and meeting the expense of elders who require both standard and specialized medical care doesn't have to be a financial nightmare as well as a psychological burden.

KNOW YOUR MEDICAL DEDUCTIONS

Medical expenses can be debilitating. Knowing what medical deductions you qualify for can help you revivify your financial condition. Your medical expenses above 7.5 percent of adjusted gross income are deductible. Just as with miscellaneous expenses, try to bunch them up. If you're close to exceeding 7.5 percent for one year, pay any outstanding bills and prepay any medical procedures that you will be having the next year. If you aren't going to come close to the 7.5 percent floor, however, put off as many of these expenses as possible because perhaps next year your medical expenses will be higher.

The following is a list of major and miscellaneous deductions which you and your medical dependents can qualify for:

- A nursing home's entrance fee requirements.
- A nursing home's lump-sum fee for anticipated medical care.
- The entire cost of a nursing home, including room and board, if and only if your relative is incapacitated and requires full-time care.
- The entire cost of necessary full-time medical care.
- The cost of prescription drugs and insulin, and medically prescribed vitamins.
- The extra cost of a prescribed special diet if it is solely for the treatment of a medical problem and in addition to normal nutritional needs (such as organic foods and high protein meals for hypoglycemia).
- The extra cost of a special mattress designed to alleviate an arthritic condition.
- Acupuncture, if it is used to alleviate a specific ailment.
- The cost of a program that prevents or relieves a specific ailment or illness, including programs prescribed to reduce or alleviate hypertension, obesity, or hearing problems.
- Medicare B premiums, which pay for supplemental medical coverage.
- The value of the room and board you provide a nurse who stays in your home, including the Social Security tax that you pay on the nurse's wages.
- The extra cost of orthopedic shoes.
- The cost of a wig or toupee, if it's required to relieve severe mental distress.
- The cost of long-distance medical travel, even if similar treatment is available closer to home.
- The cost of bringing a necessary campanion along on a medically related trip. (Deductible expenses include up to $50 per person per day for lodging, as well as transportation costs.)
- The cost of a visit to a psychotherapist—even if that therapist is not licensed.
- The cost, above the increase in value to your home, of a home health spa that relieves an illness.

- The installation and monthly cost, on the advice of a dentist, of a fluoride device for your home water supply.
- The cost of computer storage of your medical history.
- The initial cost and the repair costs for special telephone equipment that allows a deaf person to communicate over the phone.
- The initial cost and repair costs of a specially equipped TV that provides subtitles for the deaf.
- The cost (that exceeds the value of regularly priced books) of braille books and magazines.
- The cost and care expenses of a guide dog or other animal to a assist a blind, deaf or physically disadvantaged person.

Don't Let Tax Planning Become Too Taxing

While I advocate educating yourself about the tax saving strategies, I know there are times when confusion takes hold. If this happens, consult a qualified tax planner. Also, remember that at this stage in your life, income tax planning and estate planning often become interrelated. A good income tax planner (or a good estate planning attorney) can guide you in these often complex matters.

18

TAX-ADVANTAGED INVESTMENTS

Tax-advantaged investments are, for the most part, associated with retirement savings plans. Dividends, interest, and capital gains earned on so-called tax-deferred investments grow free of taxes until the money is withdrawn, usually when you're retired. Avoiding taxes along the way can prove very beneficial. Think about it. A taxable investment that returns 7 percent per year will barely beat inflation after Uncle Sam and your state legislators get finished taking out their piece of the action. (For example, a taxpayer in the 28 percent federal tax bracket and whose state taxes are 5 percent will net, after taxes, just 4.7 percent on the "7 percent" investment.) But an investment that grows tax free at 7 percent provides you with an attractive, inflation-beating buildup of retirement-earmarked savings. Note to retirees: The longer you can postpone withdrawing your tax-deferred investments (IRAs, etc.), the more time these resources will have to grow free of taxes. Before we get into the nitty gritty about tax-advantaged investing, don't forget to review the benefits of tax-free municipal bonds which are described back in Chapter 14.

Individual Retirement Accounts

In spite of their popularity, there are many misconceptions about individual retirement accounts (IRAs). First, IRAs are not the dull and boring investment most people think they are. In fact, you should manage your IRA account(s) with as much diligence and persistence as you do your other investments. Secondly, while everyone with job-related income can contribute to an IRA, not everyone can deduct his or her IRA contribution: Level of income and participation in your company's pension plan are determining factors. Many people use the excuse of not being able to deduct their IRA contribution as a justification for not making one. This is a shortsighted rationalization. Finally, as with most investments, your IRA is not tax-free—when you withdraw your funds you will be taxed. But it *grows* tax free, and this is a big plus.

Managing Your IRA Funds

You can shift your IRA from one investment to another, perhaps in response to changes in market conditions and your specific needs. There are two ways in which funds can be shifted: direct transfer (the most common), and rollover.

When you want to transfer funds directly into a new account, you sign a form that the new custodian sends to the old custodian, who then transfers the funds. A possible disadvantage of direct transfers is the delay. Sometimes the old custodian delays the transfer, being reluctant to let go of the account, or you may encounter the ever-present red tape of administrative inertia. Transfers within "families" of mutual funds avoid this problem.

A number of problems may arise during a transfer. The custodian may not know the correct procedure, and the paper work and red tape increase the chances of a mistake being made. Some vehicles, such as limited partnerships, are simply very difficult to transfer. Certain steps can be taken, however, to help prevent these problems. Make certain preparations beforehand, such as getting instructions—from both custodians—on how to carry out the transfer, and find out from the old custodian exactly whom the new sponsor should contact. (Misdirected paper work is often a source of delay.) You should also be aware of any fees incurred because of the transfer. In fact, when an IRA is set up, the sponsor must provide a disclosure statement of all fees, commissions, transaction charges, penalties, and projected growth of investment (although many sponsors are remiss on the last point). Finally, be sure to get an estimate of how long the transfer should take. Follow up and keep good records.

Rollovers usually occur when your pension funds are transferred into an IRA or when you yourself (rather than a custodian) transfer existing IRA funds from one account to another.

In the first circumstance the rollover is used to place pension funds in a new or existing IRA. Many, if not most people who receive a payout of their vested pension benefits should roll them over into an IRA. Check with an accountant or other tax professional to find out if an IRA rollover is your best course of action and do so long before the 60 day rollover limit ends.

In the second circumstance you personally transfer your IRA funds by withdrawing all or part of the investments from the existing custodian and reinvesting them with another. The advantage of this rollover method is that you are totally in charge of the transfer, and, therefore, there is less likelihood of a delay. The disadvantage is the risk of penalty that is incurred if the money is not reinvested within 60 days. The former custodian must be specifically notified of your intention; otherwise it must withhold the 10 percent penalty when the funds are withdrawn. You are entitled to only one personal rollover in a 12-month period, whereas direct transfers may be made as often as desired.

You can, in effect, make personal use of your IRA funds for up to 60 days per year while rolling over your account(s), but this "opportunity" can easily be abused. For example, you may succumb to the temptation of investing your IRA money on the basis of a "hot tip" on some stock that doesn't pan out. On the other hand, one possible beneficial use of a personal transfer, if you are short of cash, would be to use the money to fund a new IRA before the April 15 deadline by using old IRA money. (Of course, you'll have to come up with $2,000 in new money within 60 days to refund your "borrowed" IRA.)

Withdrawing Funds

Because of the time and attention spent on investing in IRAs to ensure the largest nest egg possible upon retirement, planning for the actual withdrawal of funds is often forgotten. However, with good withdrawal planning, you stand to gain handsomely.

You may begin withdrawing from your IRA at age 59½, or earlier if you become permanently disabled. Any other withdrawals before age 59½ are subject to a 10 percent penalty tax in addition to the withdrawal generally being fully taxed as regular income. Retirees *must* begin making IRA withdrawals by April 1 of the year after turning age 70½. (Failure to do so can cost you a whopping 50 percent penalty from the IRS.) All withdrawals (except the principal portion of any nondeductible IRA contributions that you made) are taxed as regular income, and special forward averaging treatment is *not* available for IRAs. Minimum withdrawals must be made each year for those over 70½, taking into account your life expectancy or, with married couples, your joint life expectancies.

For some, taking the whole IRA in one lump sum may be preferable. By doing this, one eliminates any risk of the 50 percent penalty for falling behind the withdrawal schedule. The money can be reinvested in non-IRA vehicles, which will probably be taxable. However, because most IRA money is taxed as regular income on withdrawal (with the exception of nondeductible contributions) taking it out in a lump sum may create a large tax bill. If you're going to take the money out in a lump sum, it may be preferable to make one withdrawal in December and another in January to spread the tax impact over two years. Unless you actually need your total IRA accumulation all at once, it is almost always better to withdraw the money gradually, over a period of many years.

To compute minimum withdrawals for each year, simply multiply the IRA's total assets by the fraction of one over the single- or joint-life expectancy as indicated in the IRS life expectancy tables. For example, a single person, age 70, with a 15-year life expectancy would take out one-fifteenth of his or her IRA savings upon reaching age 70½. The next year he or she would take out one-fourteenth of the remainder, and so on. It is now possible to lower withdrawals by refiguring life expectancy every year: Because with each passing year that you're fortunate enough to survive, the age to which you are expected to live increases. So refiguring makes the amount you have to withdraw somewhat smaller. Thus, your IRA funds are depleted more slowly which maximizes the amount that can continue to grow tax free.

Another possibility is to base withdrawals on the joint life expectancies of you (the IRA owner) and your spouse or other beneficiary. But check the IRS restrictions on this before going ahead.

One of the advantages of following the minimum withdrawal schedule is that the funds left in the IRA continue to accumulate tax free. The following table shows how much this can actually increase the funds that will be received during your retirement. The table calculates total withdrawals of $67,314 over 19 years. If you took this IRA in a lump sum, you would receive $25,000 in the first year; if, instead, the money is withdrawn in installments and the withdrawal schedule is re-figured each year by a changing life expectancy, the accumulation is greater. For the highest accumulation, it is best to take out the smallest amount possible while allowing for your financial needs. The table assumes 10 percent interest on an account with minimum withdrawals:

Figure 18.1. Sample IRA Minimum Withdrawal Schedule

		Minimum Withdrawal	
Year	***Beginning Year Balance***	***Fraction***	***Amount***
1	$25,000	1/19	$1,315
2	26,052	1/18	1,447
3	27,065	1/17	1,592
4	28,021	1/16	1,751
5	28,896	1/15	1,926
10	31,025	1/10	3,102
15	24,983	1/5	4,996
19	7,315	remainder	7,315

Remember, if the minimum withdrawal schedule is not followed the IRS is allowed to take 50 percent from every dollar in the IRA that falls behind the withdrawal schedule. (This penalty is rarely waived.) Also, note that the above table is only a minimum schedule and that after age 50½ withdrawals can be as large as you desire.

If your IRAs are spread among more than one account, the minimum withdrawal schedule will be the same, but you may decide from which accounts the withdrawals will be taken.

IRA Annuities

As a retiree, you may also use your IRA to purchase an annuity. Buying an annuity that begins regular payments by age 70½ satisfies the IRS' withdrawal rules. It can be purchased for your life expectancy or jointly for the combined life expectancies of you and your spouse. One advantage of this option is that it guarantees payments for your lifetime or, in the case of a joint annuity, for the lifetime of both you and your spouse. There may also be a provision in the annuity that provides for payments to heirs. On the other hand, experienced investors can generally do better than annuities, although inexperienced investors and those who have little else to rely on for retirement other than IRA funds should consider the safety of an annuity.

Designating Beneficiaries

Designating beneficiaries is an important matter that is often not given sufficient attention. The rules and choices governing the receipt of IRA funds by the beneficiary in the case of the IRA owner's death are important, as they can significantly affect the beneficiary's tax liability.

When you open your IRA account, you designate a beneficiary —your spouse, estate, another person, or a group of people. Unlike you, however, your beneficiary has fewer options for withdrawing the funds. An individual other than the decedent's spouse who inherits an IRA may not treat it as one established on his or her behalf. The result: The IRA distribution is taxed as ordinary income. However, if your designated beneficiary is your spouse, he or she can take over the IRA as the equivalent of an IRA rollover. In this case, the same rules apply as to a regular IRA; that is, your spouse cannot withdraw funds without penalty until age 59½ and can delay withdrawals until the time when he or she would have turned 70½. Finally, the unlimited spousal deduction means that any bequests to a spouse are not subject to federal estate tax. (They may be subject to state death taxes, however.)

Self-Employed Retirement Plans

Keogh Plans

The Keogh plan (also called an HR-10 plan) was introduced in 1964 by the Congressman after whom it is named. The purpose of the Keogh plan is to provide the opportunity to self-employed individuals to establish a private pension fund for their own retirement. These plans are now available for unincorporated self-employed persons and their employees. Even if you participate in a pension plan at your place of employment, you may also set up a Keogh plan if you have earned income from outside work. Money that is put into a Keogh plan is tax deductible and the savings grow tax free until withdrawal. More information on Keogh plans can be found in Chapter 3.

Simplified Employee Pension Plans

Instead of maintaining a separate pension plan as is required with a Keogh plan, SEP contributions are deposited into your IRA account(s). The same tax deduction and tax-deferral features of

Keoghs apply to SEPs. You may establish a SEP after the end of the tax year in which you want to begin taking the deduction. See Chapter 3 for more details on SEPs.

Further information on self-employed retirement plans may be found by contacting the IRS and requesting IRS Publication 560, *Tax Information on Self-employed Retirement Plans.*

Annuities

An annuity is an investment contract in which you, the annuitant (the purchaser of the annuity) receive regular payments from a life insurance company for a certain period of time or, more commonly, for the remainder of your life in exchange for a previously paid sum. Annuities may have a variety of tax advantages for people who are saving for retirement and retirees who must decide how they will receive the income from their retirement plans.

Deferred and Immediate-Pay Annuities

Annuity payments can be deferred or paid immediately. *Deferred* annuities may be purchased in one of two ways. Single-premium annuities are purchased with a lump sum, and then the insurance company begins paying out the money to the annuitant in regular installments at a future date. (You may also have the alternative of withdrawing a lump sum rather than taking the annuity.) Flexible payment annuities can be purchased with installment payments over a period of many years. Since the money placed in a deferred annuity accumulates free of taxes, it is a very popular tax-advantaged investment vehicle for retirement-earmarked money. Also, as opposed to an IRA there are no limits as to the amount of money that can be placed into deferred annuities.

Immediate-pay annuities guarantee a fixed amount every month (or quarter or year) to be paid to the annuitant until death. They are funded with a lump-sum payment (e.g., the proceeds of a pension plan).

Distribution of Benefits

The way in which you receive the benefits from annuities is a difficult and crucial decision. Therefore, it must be very carefully evaluated. The following section describes and evaluates alternative ways to receive benefits.

Straight-Life Annuities provide payments to you until your death. A straight-life annuity has a win or lose aspect. You can win by living longer than was forecast in the original calculations, or you can lose by dying prematurely and thereby stopping the payments before the expected sum has been paid out. (Heirs get nothing under these arrangements.) Remember that insurance companies want to make a profit and also have a great deal of experience in working with mortality tables. There is a better-than-ever chance of losing at least part of the money that you invested in the straight-life annuity.

Life annuities with certain installments provide a way of overcoming the risks of straight-life annuities. They resemble straight-life annuities in that they guarantee regular payments until death. In addition, a certain number of payments are guaranteed: If death occurs before many payments have been made, the balance of the guaranteed payments will be paid to your survivors. Most commonly, the guaranteed payments are for a period of 10 years, which is usually shorter than the expected life expectancy at retirement. Thus, early death results in a smaller monetary loss with this type of annuity than with straight-life annuities.

Refund annuities alleviate some of the risk inherent in straight-life annuities by guaranteeing that the retiree or his survivors will receive back as much money as was originally paid into the purchase. Therefore, if the retiree dies prematurely, the balance will be paid to his beneficiaries. This balance can be paid either in one lump sum (a cash-refund annuity) or in regular installments (an installment-refund annuity).

It is important not to misunderstand the meaning of the term "refund." Refund does not mean that the money originally paid can be returned at any time, but only upon the annuitant's death. There is still a risk of loss in this annuity, as money is tied up in the annuity and may not be used for personal investing to create more income. Both refund annuities and life annuities with certain installments offer lower annuity payments than straight-life annuities do.

Joint-and-survivor annuities guarantee that neither you (the annuitant) nor your spouse or other beneficiary will outlive the income. Payments will continue to your spouse even after you die, should you die first, although the survivor will typically be paid smaller installments than both received previously. Also, because the annuity is intended for a longer period of time, the regular payment to both spouses will be smaller than with a straight-life annuity.

Variable and family annuities. Variable annuities are used to protect against inflation. The monthly payment is based not on a fixed payment but on the value of a pool of common stocks and other investments in which the annuity's trustees have invested. The value of this is that the bite inflation can take out of a fixed income is somewhat alleviated by the growth of these stocks, although there is also the risk of their losing value, in which case your monthly payments will be decreased. Also, insurance companies that sell variable annuities may charge participants two kinds of fees. One is a sales fee that is deducted from each contribution to the annuity. Many variable annuities may be purchased with no sales fee. Another type of fee is called a periodic fee for investment management and maintenance of the account, which usually is charged annually. Many people divide their annuity purchases between fixed and variable annuities; these are called balanced annuities.

Family annuities are another way of dealing with the potential in other types of annuities for loss of money due to premature death. Family annuities are purchased from the family rather than an insurance company. To do this, you transfer a portion of your property, such as a family business or real estate, to one or more of your heirs in exchange for them paying a certain monthly installment until your death. Family annuities have complex income and estate tax implications, so consult your tax professional.

Evaluating Annuities

It's easy to become confused when evaluating an annuity. That's why it's important to compare the annuity payouts among several companies. Comparison shopping is particularly important when making a permanent commitment of your money. You'll be surprised at how much different the payouts are among otherwise identical annuities. Take advantage of the competition for your money among the insurance companies.

Additional Annuity-Planning Considerations

Remember, even though annuities have many advantages for your retirement-planning program they do pose risks and often an investment-wise pre-retiree or retiree can do better managing his or her own funds. Additional considerations:

- **Protection.** Protection of the annuity varies from state to state. Some states, like New York, strictly regulate annuities and maintain a guaranty fund to cover any default; other states have no guaranty fund and do not have the staff to police the annuities under their jurisdiction. State insurance officials can tell what protection a given state offers, if any.

- **Diversity.** Because annuities are not federally insured, most people are well advised to invest in a few smaller policies, with different insurance companies, rather than one large one. With this kind of diversity, the risk of losing all your savings is significantly reduced.
- **Company's financial strength.** As with any other purchase, check the financial strength of the company offering the annuity. Sources of information include the annual stockholder's reports, if the company is public, and *Best's Insurance Reports.*
- **Inflation.** Annuities (with the possible exception of variable annuities) do not rise with inflation. By providing alternative plans that allow the annuity holder to transfer money between funds without withdrawal penalties, some insurance companies enable the annuity holder to take advantage of changing interest rates.
- **Fees.** Fees, commissions, and penalties have been a major drawback of annuities. While some companies have dropped their charges to more reasonable levels it still pays to compare fees.
- **Early withdrawal.** Having a change of mind can be costly in annuities, as there are usually contractual penalties for early withdrawal. There may also be adverse tax consequences; that is, taking cash from a deferred annuity can be viewed as a premature distribution of assets, subject to a penalty. Exceptions to this penalty apply, however, under the following circumstances:
  —The policyholder has reached age 59½ or has become disabled.
  —The distribution is a payment under an annuity for life or at least 60 months.
  —The payment is to a beneficiary (or estate) after the policyholder's death.
  —The payment is from a qualified retirement plan (i.e., one purchased as part of a tax-deductible IRA, Keogh, or company pension plan).

—The payment can be allocated to investments made before August 14, 1982.

The penalty is 5 percent of the amount that is includible in income. For annuity contracts issued before January 19, 1985, the penalty applies only to investments made within 10 years of receipt of the cash withdrawals.

Advantages and Disadvantages

Annuities are complex, often entail a permanent commitment, have certain tax advantages mainly for pre-retirees, and are heavily touted by comissioned salespeople. As indicated previously, the purchase of annuities should be approached with caution, not because they are inappropriate retirement investments. Rather, it's because often there are preferable investment strategies. For example, you could gain many of the same advantages of annuities, and fewer of their disadvantages, by purchasing U.S. Savings Bonds.

The main concerns: Annuities have a relatively low yield; the purchasing power of fixed annuity payments will erode with inflation; the high fees, commissions, and penalties; and the possible loss of a substantial part of an estate as a result of your premature death. Nevertheless, an annuity is an alternative worth considering. Tax-deferred annuities offer some preretirees an excellent opportunity to shelter the income earned from after-tax contributions to the annuity. If you have a high discretionary income because of few family expenses and a high overall income, compare the disadvantage with the advantages. If, on the other hand, you are not, or do not plan to remain, an active manager of your investments, and you could use the additional funds for your retirement, then a deferred annuity may be a good choice. Similarly, an annuity may be a good choice for a retiree and his dependents who are neither financially secure upon retirement nor capable of managing and conserving money: The annuity ensures them an income, which, in these circumstances, may be important.

DON'T BUY WITHOUT SHOPPING

Whether you are buying a deferred annuity or an immediate-pay annuity, be sure to shop carefully and thoroughly. This is a very competitive business, so those who do their homework will be amply rewarded for their efforts. Don't rely on a single salesperson to do your shopping. Obtain quotations form several companies, not just the one your agent represents, including ones that your agent does not represent. If you are considering taking an annuity as part of a payout from a pension plan or deferred annuity, chances are you can get a better deal through another insurance company rather than continuing with the same company that has been accumulating your money.

Other Vehicles for Retirement Planning

401(k)—Salary Reduction Plans

Known as 401(k) plans, salary reduction plans allow a worker to defer a percentage of his or her pretax income—typically 2 to 10 percent of total compensation, which accumulates tax-free. Moreover, many companies make matching contributions. These plans are very popular among large corporations, and are becoming increasingly popular among smaller companies. The following are the primary features of 401(k) plans:

- **Tax advantages.** Because money in a 401(k) plan is deferred compensation, as opposed to a deductible IRA contribution, the 401(k) money never shows up on the W-2 form and thereby escapes federal income tax and Social Security taxes (with possible exceptions), and most state and local taxes. (For those with incomes over the maximum income from which Social Security is withheld, the Social Security tax savings are nil.) It should be noted that you may have a 401(k) plan and still take advantage of an IRA.
- **Withdrawals.** The regulations governing withdrawals from 401(k) plans are more lenient than those for IRAs. Money normally cannot be withdrawn before age 59½ unless the worker dies, retires, quits, or becomes disabled. If the employee experiences financial hardship, however, most companies allow him or her to withdraw from the 401(k) plan.
- **Benefits.** Because company pension benefits are often based on compensation during the last three to five years of employment, you may want to continue to receive your full compensation rather than defer it and consequently lower your company benefits. The solution to this problem depends on whether predeferral income or the W-2 figure is used as the base in determining company benefits.
- **Loans.** Loans from 401(k) funds are permitted for up to half the account balance up to $50,000, whereas loans of less than

$10,000 may exceed one half of the balance. Such loans must be for a stated interest rate and have a predetermined repayment schedule. Except for home loans, the maximum loan period is five years.

Deductible Employee Voluntary Contributions

In lieu of making an IRA contribution, a preretiree may make a deductible contribution to his or her company's pension plan, which will be lumped in with the employer's contribution. The company, however, must decide to allow these employee contributions and must account for them separately. The preretiree employee should also know that such contributions will be deducted from the amount allowable in his or her IRA contributions. The time limit for such contributions is April 15, unless the employer chooses another time limit. Finally, know that although, as an employee, you will be able to take advantage of the management expertise of the pension plan's directors, you will also retain less control over your investments.

Housing Equity

In order to take advantage of the equity built up in your home over the years without selling or moving during retirement, a retiree can either set up a charitable remainder trust or contract to sell the home to a tax-exempt organization.

Tax advantages can accrue to people who donate their homes to a charitable remainder trust. The charity sets up an annuity for the former owners based on the market value of the donated property. The owners may continue to live in the home until they die, and they also enjoy substantial tax deductions. The charity sells the home, but neither the charity nor the former owners pay capital gains tax.

Under a second option, a tax-exempt organization (e.g., the Red Cross or the Girls Scouts) buys your house at a bargain price. You continue to live in the house; you do not pay real estate taxes and make no mortgage payments. In addition, you receive a substantial charitable deduction for income tax purposes. When you and your spouse die, your house goes to the charity. For more information on charitable remainder trusts and bargain sales, see Chapter 21.

One more point: be aware of the tax advantages of the sale of a home if you are over age 55. See Chapter 28.

PART THREE

Nuts and Bolts of Estate Planning

19

MINIMUM ESTATE PLANNING NEEDS

EFFECTIVE ESTATE PLANNING doesn't have to be complicated to help you achieve many valuable objectives, including:

- Minimizing the problems and expenses of probate to avoid potential family conflicts;
- Providing your spouse with as much responsibility and flexibility in estate management as desired, consistent with potential tax savings;
- Providing for the conservation of your estate and its effective management following the death of either or both spouses;
- Minimizing taxes at time of death as well as income taxes after death;
- Avoiding leaving the children or other heirs too much, too soon;
- Providing for adequate financial resources immediately after death to cover taxes and other expenses;
- Providing for estate management in the event either you or your spouse become incapacitated;
- Assuring that your wishes are carried out in the event you become terminally ill;

- Coordinating your personal estate plan with all business arrangements;
- Organizing all important papers affecting your estate plan in a spot known to all family members and reviewing them at least annually, and
- Informing family members about the overall estate plan.

Yet many of us fail to complete even the most basic estate planning documents. Or, we neglect to review and revise our estate plan periodically to reflect changes in personal circumstances or new laws and regulations. While it's unpleasant to contemplate our own mortality, it can be a tremendous relief to organize your estate and know that your plan is up to date. Chances are, your personal records will also be better organized if you get your estate in order.

In addition to a will, most people also need a durable power of attorney or living trust, living will and letter of instructions. Beyond these basics, there are several sophisticated planning techniques that most affluent individuals will find necessary to include in their estate plans.

Ongoing Process

As we get older, we tend to accumulate more and more assets and our past investments grow in value. Thus, your estate may well be worth more than you realize. And even if you have prepared an estate plan in the past, the makeup of your estate or your feelings towards its disposition may have changed since you last revised it.

For example, have you had any children or grandchildren since you last revised your will? Have any of your intended heirs died, married, divorced or become disabled since you wrote your will?

Such events might require a revision of your estate planning documents. It's certainly worth a little time and possible expense to update an out-of-date estate plan, and your heirs will be grateful.

Finally, Congress is beginning to pay more attention to estate and gift taxes as a means of raising additional revenue, which doesn't bode well for affluent families. According to many experts, the tightening of the estate and gift tax laws will probably not affect many of the estate plans already in effect. This is all the more reason to attend to important estate planning matters sooner rather than later.

Four Basic Documents

Estate planning need not be complicated to be effective. A simple estate plan can save legal fees, prevent unnecessary delays and ensure that your estate will be distributed according to your wishes. It may also have some positive effects while you are still alive.

Single people should also plan their estates because state laws governing intestacy (dying without a will) may not distribute the estate the same way you would have. For example, you may want to leave at least a portion of your estate to a friend or to charity, but intestacy laws generally leave everything to blood relatives. The relatives who end up with your estate may not be people you would have chosen to enjoy the fruits of your savings and labor.

A minimum estate plan usually consists of four documents:

Valid and Up-to-Date Will

Everyone knows the importance of preparing and maintaining a will, yet many older adults do not have wills. Your will should specify exactly how your estate is to be divided, including, if appropriate, a list that indicates which heirs are to receive specific items of personal property. This will avoid disputes over these properties. Such disputes, unfortunately, are common among heirs—even those who seem most able to work things out amicably.

And don't forget that intestate estates incur higher than necessary legal fees and unnecessary delays. Worse, a judge will decide how your estate is to be distributed—you will have no say in the matter. Changing your will to reflect changes in your personal circumstances (moving to another state, getting married or divorced, birth of children or grandchildren) or changes in state and federal laws is also essential and often overlooked.

At a minimum, the following items should be included in a will:

- Your full name and the location of your principal residence.
- Statement that the document is a will.
- Date.
- Statement revoking all previous wills.
- Instructions with respect to disposal of your body and funeral arrangements.
- Specific bequests with provisions for the death of the named

beneficiaries. Specific bequests are for the transfer of a particular piece of property to a named beneficiary.

- General bequest, which does not specify from which part of the estate the property is to be taken, with provisions for the death of the named beneficiaries.
- Instructions for dividing the residuary, which is the amount of the estate remaining after these specific and general bequests have been made.
- Provisions for trusts, including the names of selected trustees and successor trustees.
- Statement of who should be presumed to have died first (either husband or wife) should both die in a common accident. This allows both wills to be processed without undue complications or unwanted tax effects.
- Names of guardians and alternative guardians for minor children, if necessary, or for any handicapped adult or child under your care.
- Designation of what resources or assets are to be used to pay death taxes.
- Names of the executor and substitute executor.
- Signature. The will should be signed in the presence of all of the witnesses.
- Any major changes should be made in the form of codicils. These, too, must be witnessed and signed, as was the original will.

IMPORTANT: Have your will drawn up and/or revised by a lawyer. An experienced lawyer can help you draw up a will to specify exactly how you want your estate divided. While do-it-yourself wills, will-drafting kits and even computer software programs that draft wills are becoming increasingly common, they're usually no substitute for the services of a competent legal professional.

Note that your will does not prevent you from doing whatever you like with your property while you're still alive. And while it's recommended that you discuss your wishes with your heirs and survivors before your demise, you do not have to do so. Until you die, your will is a private document whose contents do not need to be known to anyone other than you and your lawyer. Of course, your two signing witnesses must see you sign the document and must know you intend the document to be your will. But even they do not need to know the contents.

WHERE TO KEEP YOUR WILL

There should be only one original copy of a will at any given time, although you may want to give unsigned photocopies to your lawyer, heirs, or financial advisor. Deciding where to keep the original copy of the will can be a vexing problem. Options include a home safe, a business safe, a bank safe deposit box, your lawyer's office or a trust company, if you named one as executor. Or a clerk of the local probate court can hold it for safekeeping in a sealed envelope.

State and local probate law is a major factor in deciding where to store your will. For example, some states automatically seal safe deposit boxes when their owners die, so if the will was inside it will be inaccessible pending a court order. Also make sure that wherever you keep the will, you tell the appropriate people where it is!

JOINT WILLS

Sometimes married couples or other related parties write "joint wills" in which they leave everything to each other or to specified beneficiaries if they die together. Although this might seem to simplify the whole process, in reality it's not a good idea.

Reason: Joint wills can create problems and unexpected litigation. Questions arise as to whether one person can change the terms of the will without the other. Some joint wills oblige the survivor to make bequests to specific persons, which may be regarded by state law as not qualifying for the marital deduction. What's more, circumstances may change after the first spouse's death and the survivor may want to change the distribution of his or her will. The joint will makes this difficult.

> KEY POINT: Everyone should have an individual will. Even persons who think they don't have enough property to bother arranging for its disposal should prepare a will in case their circumstances change. Whatever your financial circumstances, you will be doing your loved ones a big favor by having a will. So, unless you dislike your family, have a will prepared and keep it up-to-date.

CHOOSING AN EXECUTOR

The executor is the individual or institution responsible for the management and distribution of your estate after your death. You should name an executor and an alternate in your will in case your first choice is unable or unwilling to serve. Choose carefully on the basis of competence, concern for your family and your wishes, and availability. The executor's duties include:

- Investing the estate assets until they can be distributed under the terms of your will;
- Collecting any debts due the deceased, including death benefits from pension plans, insurance and Social Security;
- Paying the estate's outstanding debts;
- Dealing with insurance, trusts and other assets not controlled by the will;
- Distributing property according to your wishes; and
- Paying all estate, income and inheritance taxes out of the assets of your estate.

SUGGESTION: It may be wise not to pick the person closest to you as your executor as this person may be distraught after your death. Many people prefer to pick someone trusted but less intimate, for example, a sibling instead of a spouse. Other common options include your lawyer, your bank trust department or a business associate.

It's also often a good idea to pick someone younger than you who has the time to fulfill his or her responsibilities as executor. And whether you choose an individual or an institution, the executor is entitled to certain fees for managing your estate, although many individuals, particularly interested parties, choose to waive those fees. By the way, it also may be desirable to choose an attorney who is younger than you to handle your will and other estate planning documents to assure that he or she will still be practicing law when you are retired.

Durable Power of Attorney

If you ever become incapacitated (through accident, illness or just plain aging) and unable to handle your own affairs, a court order may revoke your right to manage your own money and appoint a guardian or conservator. It's possible that the court may not appoint the guardian that you would have chosen, and even if it does, the process of securing court approval of the guardian will be subject to unnecessary red tape and confusion. The simplest way to protect your assets and ensure that they will continue to be managed as you see fit is to appoint a guardian for yourself through a durable power of attorney.

Assigning a durable power of attorney ensures that someone

you trust will act in your behalf in the event you become unable to manage your own financial and personal affairs. A power of attorney may be either special, applying only in certain situations, or general, giving the attorney-in-fact virtually limitless control over the principal (the person who created the arrangement). General powers of attorney can be dangerous because they're subject to abuse. What's more, they're usually unnecessary.

If you use special powers of attorney, you can give different people responsibility for different jobs. For example, you may want one person to make decisions regarding your health care and housing, but another to manage your finances. A power of attorney may also be either indefinite or for a specific length of time. No matter how it is assigned, it may be canceled at any time, and it terminates immediately upon the death of the principal.

THE LIVING TRUST ALTERNATIVE

An alternative to a durable power of attorney is a living trust. Living trusts can provide a variety of estate planning advantages, such as avoiding probate and keeping your financial matters private. You can also specify in a living trust the person or institution you want to take over your financial affairs if you become incapacitated.

Living trusts may be preferable for residents of some states. Check with an attorney who can objectively advise you on the efficacy of living trusts. For more information on living trusts, see Chapter 21: Sophisticated Strategies for Larger Estates.

Living Will

You may be aware of the dilemmas surrounding terminally ill patients and the importance of trying to accommodate the patient's wishes. If you are concerned about these matters, you should consider drafting a so-called living will, informing family members and physicians of your wishes to forgo or to receive artificial life-prolonging care under certain circumstances. You can spell out these circumstances as specifically as you wish.

Thus, a living will permits you to direct your own terminal care and it protects your physician from liability for withholding or terminating care in accordance with your wishes. Living wills are legally recognized in most states. And even where they are not, they may assure your family and the court of your wishes if the need to make these difficult decisions arises.

If you've already prepared this key document, it's a good idea to review and revise or re-sign your living will from time to time. Not only will a recent reaffirmation carry extra weight with doctors, hospitals and judges, but it will also force you to reconsider your position as your circumstances change.

> IMPORTANT: The living will must be written and executed while you are competent and of sound mind. Choose two adult witnesses who are not related to you, are not entitled to any part of your estate, and are not your doctor. And be sure to have the document notarized.

To ensure that your living will is truly effective, you should also draw up a health-care proxy. In fact, some states may not recognize the validity of a living will if it is not accompanied by this document. Your attorney can advise you about the legal situation in your state. A health-care proxy designates the person who—should you ever become incapacitated—will make health care decisions on your behalf. Should you neglect to draft this important document, questions could arise as to who has the authority to carry out the wishes you enumerated in your living will.

Letter of Instructions

A letter of instructions is an informal document (you don't need a lawyer to prepare one) that gives your survivors information concerning important financial and personal matters. While a letter of instructions is not as important as the will, living will and durable power of attorney, many people think it's the best thing you can do to make things easier for your survivors during a difficult time. You'll certainly be doing your heirs and survivors a big favor by preparing one.

Although it does not carry the legal weight of a will, the letter of instructions is very important because you can clarify any further requests to be carried out upon death and provide essential financial information, thus relieving the surviving family members of needless worry and speculation.

The most common areas to cover in a letter of instructions are listed below, although you can modify this list to meet your individual needs. (A work sheet to help you prepare a letter of instructions can be found at the end of this chapter.) The typical letter of instructions includes:

- Instructions on whom to contact and what to do immediately. Include a contact at work for final paycheck and benefits, your lawyer and your life insurance agent.
- Instructions for the funeral and disposition of remains.

- Directions for handling other matters such as cancelling credit cards or converting them to a single name, cancelling subscription and memberships, and changing ownership designations on joint accounts.
- Inventory and explanation of assets, as well as a list of where to find key documents, records and financial statements. Include account numbers, brokers' names and telephone numbers, and locations of passbooks and safe deposit box keys.
- Personal wishes. Although this is not a binding legal document, it may be the place to express your wishes about the education of your children, how your heirs spend their inheritances or anything else. You can also explain the reasoning behind your will or leave any other last words.

Obviously, your survivors will benefit if you prepare a letter of instructions. But you will, too. A well-prepared letter of instructions is a great way to organize your records. Also be sure to keep it up-to-date since the information in it is likely to change. Finally, make sure your heirs know where the letter is.

The four documents described in this chapter are the essential components of a basic estate plan. In order to meet your estate-planning goals, however, you will probably need to use other planning techniques, including trusts, gifts to relatives and strategic property ownership designations. These techniques are discussed in more detail in the next two chapters.

Figure 19.1. Estate Planning Review Checklist

	Yes	No	N/A
1. Have you clearly articulated your wishes regarding the ultimate disposition of your estate?	☐	☐	☐
2. Do you have an up-to-date will that is consistent with your personal wishes and individual circumstances?	☐	☐	☐
3. Has an appropriate executor been named? (Your spouse or children may not be the best choice for executor.)	☐	☐	☐

Figure 19.1. (Cont'd)

	Yes	No	N/A
4. Have you prepared an up-to-date letter of instructions?	☐	☐	☐
5. Have you provided an appropriate adult guardianship arrangement (such as a durable power of attorney or living trust) in the event you should become incompetent?	☐	☐	☐
6. Have you designated personal and financial guardians for children and other dependents?	☐	☐	☐
7. Have you considered preparing a living will?	☐	☐	☐
8. Have you estimated the size of the taxable estate?	☐	☐	☐
9. Have provisions been made to provide adequate estate liquidity upon your death?	☐	☐	☐
10. Have you evaluated the impact of estate taxes on the estate?	☐	☐	☐
11. Are the property ownership designations (single ownership, joint ownership, etc.) pertaining to your assets appropriate from an estate planning standpoint?	☐	☐	☐
12. Married people often assume that one spouse, typically the husband, will predecease the other spouse. Have you imagined the personal and estate planning effects if the assumed order of death does not occur?	☐	☐	☐
13. Are your gifts to children or charities consistent with your financial condition and estate planning program? (Gifting programs by the elderly are sometimes too generous.)	☐	☐	☐
14. Have appropriate provisions been made in your estate planning process if you own property in more than one state?	☐	☐	☐
15. Have trusts been considered as part of the estate planning process?	☐	☐	☐

Figure 19.1. (Cont'd)

	Yes	No	N/A
16. If you have a closely held business, have provisions been made for its disposition that are consistent with estate planning requirements?	☐	☐	☐
17. Have you considered the possibility that you may incur substantial uninsured health care costs in retirement?	☐	☐	☐
18. Does the estate plan include provisions for any heirs or dependents who may have special needs?	☐	☐	☐
19. Do you have a clear understanding of what employee benefits will be paid/available upon death?	☐	☐	☐
20. Have you clearly articulated your funeral wishes for your survivors?	☐	☐	☐
21. If you have elderly parents and/or grandparents, are you aware of any gap or omission in their estate plan?	☐	☐	☐

Figure 19.2. Letter of Instructions Worksheet

EXPECTED DEATH BENEFITS

1. From employer:
   - Person to contact: .... Telephone: ....
   - Life Insurance: $ ....
   - Profit sharing: $ ....
   - Pension plan: $ ....
   - Accident insurance: $ ....
   - Other benefits: ....
2. From insurance companies—total amount: $ ....
3. From Social Security—lump sum plus monthly benefits: ....
4. From the Veterans Administration—amount: $ ....
   VA must be informed.
5. From other sources: ....

Figure 19.2. (Cont'd)

FIRST THINGS TO DO

1. Call: ....
2. Notify employer. Name and telephone: ....
3. Make arrangements with funeral home. (See "Cemetery and Funeral" section.
4. Request at least 10 copies of the death certificate. (Usually, the funeral director will get them.)
5. Call lawyer. Name and telephone: ....
6. Provide the following newspapers with obituary information: ....
   ....
7. Contact local Social Security office. (See "Social Security" section.)
8. Retrieve and process insurance policies. Policy locations are listed in "Life Insurance" section.
9. Notify bank that holds home mortgage.
10. Notify the following acquaintances and organizations: ....
    ....

CEMETERY AND FUNERAL

CEMETERY PLOT

1. Location: ....
2. Date purchased: ...., 19...................
3. Deed number: ....
4. Location of deed: ....
5. Other information (e.g., perpetual care): ....
   ....

FACTS FOR FUNERAL DIRECTOR

This list should be brought to funeral home, as well as the cemetery deed if possible.

1. Full name: ....
2. Residence: ....
3. Marital status: .... Spouse's name: ....
4. Date of birth:................., 19 .... Birthplace: ....
5. Father's name and birthplace: ....
6. Mother's maiden name and birthplace: ....

Figure 19.2. (Cont'd)

---

7. Length of residence in state: .... in United States: ....
8. Military record: ....
   When: ....
   Bring veteran's discharge papers, if possible.
9. Social Security number: .... Occupation: ....
10. Life insurance
    Bring policy if proceeds will be used for funeral expenses.

Insurer	Policy Number
....	....
....	....
....	....
....	....

SPECIAL WISHES

1. ....
2. ....
3. ....
4. ....

PERSONAL EFFECTS

The following personal effects should be given to the named person:

Item	Person
....	....
....	....
....	....
....	....
....	....

LOCATION OF PERSONAL PAPERS

1. Last will and testament: ....
2. Birth and baptismal certificates: ....
3. Communion, confirmation certificates: ....
4. School diplomas: ....

Figure 19.2. (Cont'd)

5. Marriage certificate: ....
6. Military records: ....
7. Naturalization papers: ....
8. Other (e.g., adoption, divorce): ....

SAFE-DEPOSIT BOX*

1. Bank name and address: ....
2. In whose name: .... Number: ....
3. Location of key: ....
4. List of contents (if extensive, attach separate inventory): ....
   ....

POST OFFICE BOX

1. Address: ....
2. Owners: ....
3. Box number: ....
4. Location of key or combination: ....

INCOME TAX RETURNS

1. Location of all previous returns (federal, state, local): ....
   ....
2. Tax preparer's name: .... Telephone: ....
3. Location of estimated tax file: ....
   Check to see if any estimated quarterly taxes are due.

DOCTOR'S NAMES AND ADDRESSES

1. Doctor's name: .... Telephone: ....
   Address: ....
2. Dentist's name: .... Telephone: ....
   Address: ....

*In the event of death of a safe-deposit box owner, state law may require the bank to seal the deceased's box as soon as it is notified of his or her death, even if the box is jointly owned.

Figure 19.2. (Cont'd)

---

3. Children's pediatrician's name: .... Telephone: ....
   Address: ....
4. Children's dentist's name: .... Telephone ....
   Address: ....

CHECKING ACCOUNTS

Attach a separate summary if there are multiple accounts.

1. Bank name and address: ....
2. Name(s) on account: ....
3. Account number: .... Type: ....
4. Location of passbook (or certificate receipt): ....
5. Special instructions: ....
   ....

CREDIT CARDS

All credit cards in the deceased's name should be canceled or converted to the survivor's name.

Provide the following information for each card.

1. Company: .... Telephone: ....
   Address: ....
2. Name on card: .... Number: ....
3. Location of card: ....

LOANS OUTSTANDING

Provide the following information for each loan other than mortgages.

1. Bank name and address: ....
2. Name on loan: ....
3. Account number: ....
4. Monthly payment: ....
5. Location of papers and payment book (if any): ....
6. Collateral (if any): ....
7. Is there life insurance on the loan? ☐ Yes ☐ No

Figure 19.2. (Cont'd)

DEBTS OWED TO THE ESTATE

1. Debtor: ....
2. Description: ....
3. Terms: ....
4. Balance: $..
5. Location of documents: ....
6. Comments on loan status/discharge: ....

SOCIAL SECURITY

1. Name: .... Number: ....
   Location of Social Security cards: ....
2. File a claim immediately to avoid possibility of losing any benefit checks. Call local Social Security Administration (SSA) office for appointment and follow SSA's instructions as to what to bring. SSA telephone: ....
3. Expect a lump sum of about $........., plus continuing benefits for children under age 18, or for full-time students until age 22. A spouse may receive benefits until children reach age 18, between ages 50 and 60 if disabled, or if over age 60.

LIFE INSURANCE

To collect benefits, a copy of the death certificate must be sent to each insurance company.

Provide the following information for each policy.

1. Policy no: .... Amount: $..................
2. Location of policy: ....
3. Whose life is insured: ....
4. Insurer's name and address: ....
5. Kind of policy: ....
6. Beneficiaries: ....
7. Issue date: ...., 19 .... Maturity date:......, 19 .....
8. How paid out: ....
10. Other options on payout: ....
11. Other special facts: ....
12. For $....... in veteran's insurance call local Veteran's Administration office. Telephone: ....

Figure 19.2. (Cont'd)

OTHER INSURANCE

ACCIDENT

1. Insurer's name and address: ....
2. Policy no. ....
3. Beneficiary: ....
4. Coverage: ....
5. Location of policy: ....
6. Agent (if any): ....

HOMEOWNERS/RENTERS AND AUTOMOBILE

Provide the following information for each policy.

1. Coverage: ....
2. Insurer's name and address: ....
3. Policy number: ....
4. Location of policy: ....
5. Term (when to renew): ....
6. Agent (if any): ....

MEDICAL

Provide the following information for each policy.

1. Coverage: ....
2. Insurer's name and address: ....
3. Policy number: ....
4. Location of policy: ....
5. Through employer or other group: ....
6. Agent (if any): ....

HOUSE, CONDO, OR CO-OP

Contact local tax assessor for documentation needed or more information.

1. In whose name: ....
2. Address: ....
3. Lot: .... Block: .... On map called: ......
4. Other descriptions needed: ....

Figure 19.2. (Cont'd)

---

5. Lawyer at closing: ....
   Address: ....
6. Location of statement of closing, policy of title insurance, deed, land survey, and the like: ....
7. Mortgage
   a. Held by: ....
   b. Amount of original mortgage: $ ....
   c. Date taken out: ...., 19 ....
   d. Amount owed now: $..
   e. Method of payment: ....
   f. Location of payment book, if any (or payment statements): ....
   g. Is there life insurance on mortgage? ☐Yes ☐No
      - If so, policy number: ....
      - Location of policy: ....
      - Annual amount: $..
8. House taxes
   a. Amount: $..
   b. Location of receipts: ....
9. Cost of house
   a. Initial buying price: $ ....
   b. Purchase closing fee: $..
   c. Other costs to buy (e.g., real estate agent, legal, taxes): ....
   d. Improvements: Total: $..
10. House improvements
    Provide information for each improvement.
    a. Improvement: ....
    b. Cost: $ .... Date: ...., 19 ....
    c. Location of bills: ....
11. If renting, is there a lease? ☐Yes ☐No
    a. Lease location: ....
    b. Expiration date: ...., 19 ....

HOUSEHOLD CONTENTS

1. Name of owners: ....
2. Form of ownership: ....

Figure 19.2. (Cont'd)

---

3. Location of documents: ....
4. Location of inventory: ....
5. Location of appraisals: ....

AUTOMOBILES

Prepare the following information for each car.

1. Year, make, model: ....
2. Body type: ....
3. Cylinders: ....
4. Color: ....
5. Identification number: ....
6. Title in name(s) of: ....
   Title to automobiles held in the deceased's name must be changed.
7. Location of papers (e.g., title, registration): ....

IMPORTANT WARRANTIES, RECEIPTS

Item	Location
....	....
....	....
....	....
....	....

INVESTMENTS

Provide the following information. If necessary, attach a separate sheet.

STOCKS

1. Company: ....
2. Name on certificate(s): ....
3. Number of shares: .... Certificate number(s): ....
4. Purchase price and date: ....
5. Location of certificate(s): ....

BONDS/NOTES/BILLS

1. Issuer: ....
2. Issued to: ....

Figure 19.2. (Cont'd)

3. Face amount: $.............. Bond number: ....
4. Purchase price and date: ....
5. Maturity date: ....
6. Location of certificate: ....

MUTUAL FUNDS

1. Company: ....
2. Name on account: ....
3. Number of shares or units: ....
4. Location of statements, certificates: ....

OTHER INVESTMENTS

For each investment, list amount invested, to whom issued, issuer, maturity date, and other applicable data, and location of certificates and other vital papers.

....
....
....
....
....
....
....
....

Figure 19.3. Death Certificate and Funeral Preference Information Form

DEATH CERTIFICATE AND FUNERAL PREFERENCE INFORMATION FORM

This brief form can be used to specify information regarding the death certificate and funeral. This is not, however, a substitute for a letter of instructions.

1. Full name: ....

Figure 19.3. (Cont'd)

2. Upon death, please contact:
   Name: .... Relationship: ....
   Address: .... Telephone: ....
3. Important papers are located at: ....

INFORMATION FOR DEATH CERTIFICATE AND FILING FOR BENEFITS

1. Address: ....
2. Citizen of: .... Race: ....
3. Birthplace: .... Date of birth: .., 19 ....
4. Social Security number: ....
5. Occupation/type of business: ....
6. If veteran, rank: .... Branch of service: ....
   Serial number: ....
   Date and place entered service: ....
   Date discharged: ...., 19 ....
7. Marital status: ☐Never married ☐Married ☐Widowed ☐Separated
   ☐Divorced ☐Remarried
8. Spouse's full name: ....
9. Name of next of kin (other than spouse): ....
   Relationship: .... Address: ....
10. Father's full name and birthplace: ....
11. Mother's maiden name and birthplace: ....

FUNERAL PREFERENCES

1. Donate these organs: ....
2. Autopsy if doctor or family requests ☐Yes ☐No
3. Simple arrangements: ☐No embalming ☐No public viewing
   ☐ The least expensive burial or cremation container
   ☐ Immediate disposition

4. Remains should be:
   ☐Donated: Arrangements made on ...., 19. with.
   ☐Cremated and the ashes ☐Scattered ☐Buried at ....
   ☐Disposed of as follows: ....
   ☐Buried at ....

Figure 19.3. (Cont'd)

5. The following services:
   ☐Memorial (after disposition) ☐Funeral (before disposition)
   ☐Graveside
   To be held at: ☐Church ☐Mortuary ☐Other: ....
6. Memorial gifts to: .... Omit flowers: ☐Yes ☐No
7. Prearrangements have been made with the following mortuary: .....
   ....

Signature: .... Date: ...., 19 ....

20

HOW TO MINIMIZE THE DEATH TAX BITE

TWO SAYINGS ALWAYS come to mind when the subject of death and taxes are mentioned: the certainty of both, and the fact that, if you haven't prepared your estate for the event, you just might end up taking a substantial portion of it with you. This chapter targets both lifetime transfers and after death transfers that should help minimize estate taxes. While this may be a complicated task, requiring sophisticated strategies (many of which are discussed in detail in Chapter 21), what follows should enable you to begin to make appropriate, prudent financial planning decisions relative to your estate and the death tax.

Remember, gift and estate taxes are not income taxes, but excise taxes on the right to transfer property. The burden of payment, therefore, rests with the donor, not the donee. As you probably know, gifts and inheritances are not included in the taxable income of your beneficiaries.

Calculating Your Estate Tax

If you haven't recently estimated your possible estate tax liability, use the worksheet and tax rate schedules at the end of this chapter (Figures 20.2 and 20.3) to find out what your estate may owe. Once you have calculated your tentative net estate tax, you can begin to consider strategies to reduce it. But remember, each strategy, along with the reduction in estate taxes it brings, has its own "cost."

Lifetime gifts, for instance, can play an important role in reducing the size of your taxable estate. The first $10,000 in gifts made to any one person during each calendar year is not taxable. The number of exclusions is not determined by the number of gifts, but by the number of donees. For example, a parent can give $10,000 every year to each of his or her three children, for a total of $30,000 in gifts per year. If the spouse joins in, this amount could be doubled tax free. Even more could be "gifted"—and removed from the estate—by making gifts to children's spouses and even grandchildren.

Of course, before you decide to give anything "away," whether to reduce estate taxes or for any other reason, be mindful of the effects such gift giving will have on your own financial well-being. For example, you might think you're being clever by reducing your taxable estate substantially (and your children won't complain) but what happens if you later run out of money? Counting on longevity is a good idea: it's becoming increasingly common for people to live to a ripe old age. Just ask Willard Scott of the NBC *Today* show. So use this chapter to develop a wise estate-tax strategy, one that will benefit your heirs while allowing you to enjoy the full benefit of the assets you have worked so hard to accumulate.

Basic Estate Tax Saving Strategies

A will may be the first step in a sound estate plan, but it won't reduce your estate tax liability. To achieve the maximum tax savings possible, you have to construct a solid estate plan that joins together several planning strategies. The following estate planning tools will go a long way toward helping you develop a sound plan.

- **Property ownership.** The estate tax treatment of property owned in sole tenancy, in joint tenancy, or as community property differs greatly. Forms of property ownership that were appropriate during your younger years may no longer be appropriate when you've reached the point where you are ready to begin the estate tax planning process.
- **Trusts.** Trusts are widely used and can take many forms. Some shift the tax burden to lower-bracket beneficiaries to

decrease the total tax assessment, and others can help you—as the grantor—avoid estate taxation altogether.

- **Gifts.** Property given to future heirs during your lifetime is eligible for gift tax exemptions. Gifts of cash and other assets to relatives are tax-free in amounts up to $10,000 per beneficiary per year (or $20,000 annually for a couple giving jointly).
- **Spousal transfers.** The unlimited marital deduction allows one spouse to pass his or her entire estate to the other, completely free of federal estate taxes; the regulations regarding marital deductions in individual states vary. However, this may not always be the best method of transferring property between spouses.
- **Charitable gifts.** Charitable gifts made during your lifetime provide a dual tax advantage. First, a lifetime gift creates an income tax deduction, and second, when such a gift is made, its value, (plus any future appreciation) is removed from the estate. There is a restriction on the amount of the income tax deduction that can be taken with a lifetime gift either of 50 percent or 20 percent of adjusted gross income, depending on the type of charity. Moreover, for charitable contributions of appreciated property, the excess of fair market value over the basis of such property may be a preference item for alternative minimum tax (AMT) purposes.

If you make a charitable gift under the terms of your will, your estate will earn a deduction equal to the gift's fair market value; there are no limitations. Charitable giving can also be carried out through a remainder trust. For example, in a remainder trust agreement, the ownership of a farm or personal residence can be turned over to a qualified charity while the donor still maintains the right to live on the property and claim all revenues it generates. Upon the donor's death, the property passes directly to the charity. With such an agreement, the donor can earn an income tax break at the time of the initial arrangement as well as a deduction from the estate of the property value.

General Guidelines

The following guidelines may be helpful in deciding on an appropriate estate-planning strategy:

- If your estate is below the federal estate tax exemption limit, federal estate tax savings are of little concern, although in some states the state estate tax burden might need to be considered. A proper combination of joint ownership agreements between you and your spouse along with a will, and, perhaps, a living trust, should provide for an uncomplicated settling of the estate. Testamentary trusts can also be used if there are minor children, other dependents, or unusual circumstances.
- For estates just above the amount of the federal estate tax exemption, an appropriate combination of lifetime gifts (if you can easily afford to part with the money) should bring the estate value closer to, if not below, the exemption limit. Such planning, along with joint ownership agreements between the spouses, plus a will, should reduce taxes and simplify probate proceedings.
- For estates valued well above the exemption limit, any combination of methods may be used to achieve estate-planning objectives (e.g. a marital deduction trust). For the largest estates, plans can be complicated and should be drafted by an experienced estate-planning attorney.

Taxing Matters

Federal Estate Tax

Federal estate taxes take a sizable bite out of estates worth more than $600,000. Nevertheless, properly devised estate-planning strategies can reduce your federal estate tax liability. You should also realize that if you have an existing plan, changes in the federal tax code may require changes in it. Any or all of the following five items pertaining to federal estate tax regulations may affect your own estate plan.

1. *Unlimited marital deduction.* The unlimited marital deduction has lifted any restrictions on the value of gifts that can pass from one spouse to another free of federal taxes. When married couples buy property jointly or make lifetime or testamentary gifts to each other, no federal gift tax is levied, regardless of the amount of each spouse's contribution to the asset's acquisition. Use of the unlimited marital deduction defers tax payments until the death of the second

spouse but can result in a large estate tax because of the increased size of estate upon the death of the surviving spouse. To really pare down the estate tax, it is often advisable not to take the full advantage of this deduction but instead use another planning tool, such as the qualified terminable interest property (QTIP) trust.

2. *Taxation of jointly held property.* Property jointly held by married couples is assessed for 50 percent of its value upon each spouse's death, regardless of the relative contributions of each. Thus, it is imperative that both spouses have separate wills and estate plans. Inheritance between spouses is not automatic, and if one spouse dies intestate, the judgment of the probate court may not reflect the wishes of the surviving spouse. If the joint owners are not married, the property in question will be assessed for 100 percent of its value upon the death of each and every owner.
3. *Unified credit.* The maximum size of nontaxable estates is $600,000, reflecting the federal credit for gift and estate taxes, or unified credit. The unified credit is an estate tax credit subtracted directly from the estate tax calculated from the rate table. An estate of $600,000 will incur a tax of $192,800. In the same year, the tax credit given to each estate will also be $192,800, so that the net tax on this estate will be $0. However, if the decedent has transferred gifts during his or her lifetime in excess of the annual gift exclusion, any gift tax incurred will also be charged against the unified credit so that the credit may be less at death. The unified credit sets the ceiling on the amount that anyone can pass to heirs tax free, both during his or her lifetime and after death (hence the term "unified"). Because the IRS now takes into account the lifetime transfer of gifts and treats them in much the same manner as property transfer upon death, the importance of inter vivos gifts has declined. Those who wish to use lifetime gifts to transfer property should know that gifts yielding the highest amount transferred at the lowest possible tax cost to the donor are those that have the maximum potential for appreciation. By transferring stocks, real property, and other appreciable gifts, say, 20 years after death, the donor has in effect transferred—tax free—20 years' worth of appreciating value.

4. *Tax-free gifts.* The limit on tax-free gifts is $10,000 per year per donee ($20,000 for couples). A program of lifetime annual giving to heirs can reduce your taxable estate, often considerably. The annual gift exclusion is also advantageous if you wish to contribute trust funds on a yearly basis and thus escape having the gift charged against the unified credit. However, only gifts of a present interest qualify for the annual exclusion: many trusts set up for the beneficiaries' future interest do not qualify for the exclusion, requiring the donor to pay a gift tax on any contribution made to the fund.
5. *Estate tax rates.* At this writing, the Clinton Administration has proposed maintaining the maximum federal estate tax rate at 55%. It had been scheduled to decline to 50% beginning in 1993. Furthermore, current rules phase out the benefits of the graduated estate and gift tax rates and unified credit for transfers over $10 million. Under rules effective at the end of 1992, the tentative tax computed with the rate table (Figure 20.1) is increased by an amount equal to 5 percent of the taxable amount that is over $10 million but less than $21,040,000 ($18,340,000 in the case of decedents dying, and gifts made, after 1992). If the taxable transfer exceeds $21,040,000 or ($18,340,000 after 1992), a flat rate applies to the entire transfer. Be sure to keep up-to-date on any changes that are likely to be made in the federal estate tax rates and regulations.

State Estate Tax

A second important tax consideration in estate planning is state taxation, which varies considerably among the states and may become a burden even if your estate escapes the IRS. Indeed, if you have a high net worth, your decision on where to establish legal residency may be influenced by local estate tax rates. Tests of residence vary, but most states consider an individual a legal resident if he or she pays income tax, votes, does banking business, registers a car, obtains a driver's license, and has primary residence in the state. If you don't clearly establish legal residence, however, two or more states may tax the estate you leave.

Even when legal residency has been clearly established, more than one state may still lay claim to the decedent's estate. Intangible assets such as stocks, bonds, and insurance proceeds are taxed in the state of legal residency. Taxable assets—such as real estate, automobiles, boats, and household goods—are taxed in the state where they are located. Therefore, if you have residences and/or business interests in several states, you should consider all the state tax laws applicable to your estate.

Figure 20.1. Estate Tax Rate Schedule

The following schedules are for decedents dying and gifts made during the following years.

1988–1992

Amount		Tentative Tax		
Over	But Not Over	Tax +	Percentage	On Excess Over
$ 0	$ 10,000	$ 0	18%	$ 0
10,000	20,000	1,800	20	10,000
20,000	40,000	3,800	22	20,000
40,000	60,000	8,200	24	40,000
60,000	80,000	13,000	26	60,000
80,000	100,000	18,200	28	80,000
100,000	150,000	23,800	30	100,000
150,000	250,000	38,800	32	150,000
250,000	500,000	70,800	34	250,000
500,000	750,000	155,800	37	500,000
750,000	1,000,000	248,300	39	750,000
1,000,000	1,250,000	345,800	41	1,000,000
1,250,000	1,500,000	448,300	43	1,250,000
1,500,000	2,000,000	555,800	45	1,500,000
2,000,000	2,500,000	780,800	49	2,000,000
2,500,000	3,000,000	1,025,800	53	2,500,000
3,000,000	10,000,000	1,290,800	55	3,000,000
10,000,000	21,040,000	5,140,800	60	10,000,000
21,040,000		11,764,800	55	21,040,000

Figure 20.1. (Cont'd)

1993 and Thereafter

(Be alert to any changes that are likely to be made in Federal estate tax regulations. At this writing, this schedule is accurate, but the Clinton Administration has proposed an entirely new rate schedule for years beginning in 1993.)

Amount		Tentative Tax		
Over	But Not Over	Tax +	Percentage	On Excess Over
$ 0	$ 10,000	$ 0	18%	$ 0
10,000	20,000	1,800	20	10,000
20,000	40,000	3,800	22	20,000
40,000	60,000	8,200	24	40,000
60,000	80,000	13,000	26	60,000
80,000	100,000	18,200	28	80,000
100,000	150,000	23,800	30	100,000
150,000	250,000	38,800	32	150,000
250,000	500,000	70,800	34	250,000
500,000	750,000	155,800	37	500,000
750,000	1,000,000	248,300	39	750,000
1,000,000	1,250,000	345,800	41	1,000,000
1,250,000	1,500,000	448,300	43	1,250,000
1,500,000	2,000,000	555,800	45	1,500,000
2,000,000	2,500,000	780,800	49	2,000,000
2,500,000	10,000,000	1,025,800	50	2,500,000
10,000,000	18,340,000	4,775,800	55	10,000,000
18,340,000		9,362,800	50	18,340,000

Figure 20.2. Work Sheet to Estimate Your Estate Tax

1. Gross Estate:
   a. Property in which you have an interest

   $...

Figure 20.2. (Cont'd)

---

b. Transfers with retained interest

$...

c. Certain gifts made within three years of death

$...

d. Annuity proceeds

$...

e. Life insurance proceeds

$...

f. Property with general powers of appointment

$...

g. Dower or curtesy interests

$...

h. Other

$...

i. Gross estate (total of lines a-h)

$...

2. Deductions:

j. Funeral expenses

$...

k. Administration expenses

$...

l. Income taxes

$...

m. Estate indebtedness

$...

n. Losses from casualty or theft

$...

o. Marital deduction

$...

Figure 20.2. (Cont'd)

p. Charitable deduction

$...

q. ESOP deduction

$...

r. Total deductions (total of lines j-q)

$...

3. Taxable estate (line i minus line r)

   $...

4. Taxable gifts made after 1976

   $...

5. Tentative tax base (line 3 plus line 4)

   $...

Figure 20.3. Computation of Federal Estate Tax

6. Tentative tax on amount on line 5

   $ ....

7. Gift taxes paid on gifts made after 1976 that are not includible in gross estate

   $ ....

8. Tentative estate tax before credits (line 6 minus line 7)

   $ ....

9. Unified credit*

   $ ....

* Large estates are subject to phaseout of unified credit.

Figure 20.3. (Cont'd)

10. Credit for state death taxes

    $ ....

11. Other credits including foreign death taxes

    $ ....

    Net Estate Tax (line 8 minus lines 9, 10, and 11)

    $ ....

21

SOPHISTICATED STRATEGIES FOR LARGE ESTATES

PERHAPS THE MOST interesting and significant aspect of estate planning, albeit the most complex, is that of trusts. There are many different types of trusts, all of which are designed to help asset rich individuals—and their estates—adapt to lifetime events that are unforeseen (e.g., becoming incapacitated) and foreseen (e.g., dying). For over-50s, trusts are especially important to consider: lacking a trust can in some instances impair your estate's well-being and, as a result, your family's financial well-being. This chapter examines a variety of trust arrangements, how they function, and which type of trust might be appropriate for you.

Trusts

Trusts are a special form of ownership. Trusts transfer ownership of your property to a third party, the trust, while allowing you to retain control by appointing yourself, another individual, or a financial institution as the trustee(s). A trust is established by you (the grantor), overseen by a trustee, and reserved for the benefit of the beneficiaries. Each of these roles can be held by separate persons, or all three can be held by the same person.

Reasons for Establishing a Trust

The most important advantage of establishing a trust is that it can help you avoid the costs associated with owning property outright. Unlike other forms of ownership, a trust can ease the chore of managing your estate, shelter your assets from lawsuits and creditors, allow for a speedier inheritance, and, in some cases, reduce the tax burden at the same time. Most importantly, a trust can be created to shift the burden of management to a trusted third party, to transfer properties to minors without the need to appoint a guardian, to safeguard the inheritor's principal against unwise or extravagant spending, or even as a retirement tool to ensure you and/or your spouse of a well-managed fund should you become incapable of managing it yourself.

Many advantages can be gained by establishing a trust. As the grantor, you can allow a trustee to exercise as many or as few powers as you wish. In fact, you can appoint a trustee with powers as broad as those available to the sole owner of property.

The trustee's powers of action can include the following rights:

- To retain, sell, exchange, and dispose of the trust assets.
- To invest or reinvest trust assets within the guidelines designated by you.
- To participate in joint ventures.
- To manage and dispose of real property.
- To consent to and participate in corporate action.
- To appoint and retain agents, investment counsel, attorneys, and other professional advisors.
- To exercise options or allow them to lapse.
- To buy, sell, and allocate income and resources for the trust and to make other adjustments between income and principal.
- To settle claims.
- To distribute properties.
- To exercise any additional powers specified by you.

Types of Trusts

There is a wide variety of trust arrangements. In general, trusts are classified as being either irrevocable or revocable. Further, trusts are either established during your lifetime or upon your demise. These classifications are discussed below.

Revocable vs. Irrevocable Trusts

Revocable trusts offer no tax advantages to you and therefore should be considered mainly for nontax reasons. Irrevocable trusts, however, significantly restrain your powers and freedom of action and therefore are considered primarily in the context of estate taxes. An irrevocable trust is a completed gift at the time of the property's transfer into the trust. You retain no reversionary interest and little power to control the trust.

In general, an irrevocable trust is advisable when your primary concern is to transfer part of your assets before death so as to reduce estate taxes. The property placed in the trust should be likely to appreciate in value, as the appreciation will not be subject to gift or estate taxes. Rather than, or in addition to, establishing an irrevocable trust to reduce the amount of your taxable estate, you may want to take advantage of the annual gift exclusion which can be as much as $10,000 per donee (or $20,000 with your spouse's consent).

A revocable trust, on the other hand, should be used when you are primarily concerned with nontax advantages and prefer to retain control over the trust. As the name implies, a revocable trust can be changed during your lifetime. You can avoid the probate process—and thereby the delay created by the process—by transferring assets into the trust. This assures the payment to beneficiaries of proceeds from life insurance, pension and profit-sharing plans, and other benefit plans without going through probate. A revocable trust also reduces vulnerability to post-death contest among the heirs and reduces access of creditors and claimants to the low estate *after* your death. Your financial affairs remain private, as the trust plan is not subject to public inspection. Competent management by professional trustees assures that your will be adhered to. At times, grantors have created a revocable trust as a "test run" for creating an irrevocable trust, to measure both the competence of the chosen trustees and the viability of the trust.

Living vs. Testamentary Trusts

A living trust, often called an inter vivos trust, is one created during your liftime; a testamentary trust is one created according to your will. Creating a trust by specifying it in your will has some advantages over leaving property outright. First, it allows you, rather than your inheritors, to control the disposition of your estate. Second, a testamentary trust may reduce estate taxes for married couples. The death of the first spouse incurs no federal estate tax, but the death of the surviving spouse incurs an estate tax that may be substantial if the entire first estate is included in the estate of the second to die. With a testamentary trust such as a marital deduction trust, however, you can choose whether to include the property in your estate or in your spouse's estate. This may lead to substantial tax savings. Third, a testamentary trust may provide superior management of your estate after your death. Finally, it can eliminate or reduce the need to sell estate investments for distribution among the heirs and to select an estate manager.

The major drawbacks of testamentary trusts, as opposed to living trusts, are their inclusion in the probate process and estate tax assessment. Because the testamentary trust can be created only by a will and all wills are subject to probate, a testamentary trust can be created only after the probate process. Sometimes an improperly drawn will that has been thrown out of court blocks the testamentary trust altogether. The property in the trust also is considered as part of your estate and thus is subject, after your death, to estate taxation. (An irrevocable living trust, however, would not be included in your taxable estate.)

A better alternative might be to create an inter vivos (living) trust during your lifetime, which can achieve all the advantages of the testamentary trust and other significant ones, too. A living trust's immediate advantage is that it can circumvent probate; if all your assets are held in the trust, there is nothing to transfer through the will. The trust is not obligated (in most states) to pay any remaining debts, and it ensures continuous management of the assets, uninterrupted by your death. If, at any point, you become disabled or otherwise unable to make an important decision concerning the assets, your cotrustee can take responsibility. (If you simply do not want to manage all your assets during the remainder of your life, you can appoint a cotrustee.) A trust, as compared to a will, provides more assurance that your desires will be carried out; a trust document can specify exact conditions about the distribution of your assets (such as at what age a child will receive an inheritance), and can allow the trustee the discretion to withhold or distribute extra assets if prudent or necessary.

Your trust can serve as a receptacle for estate assets and death benefits from your employee benefit plans and life insurance. Also, it can unify in one location all your assets and thus avoid administration of the estate in different places. When compared to a testamentary trust, this trust is protected from public inspection, and may be less vulnerable to attack on grounds of fraud, incapacity, or duress.

Moreover, if your living trust is revocable, it permits you to alter it as necessary or desired. Unfortunately, a revocable trust provides no tax savings. An irrevocable living trust's chief virtue is that it is not includable in your estate for estate tax purposes. If, however, you die without revoking a revocable trust, it automatically becomes irrevocable. Remember that the savings of future probate costs afforded by a revocable living trust may be offset by the costs of preparing and administering your trust.

Creating a Trust

A trust should be drawn up only by your lawyer, if he or she is experienced in trust-planning, or by a lawyer who does have tax and trust-planning expertise. Whether the trust has been made for tax or nontax purposes, only a properly written agreement can fulfill your intentions. The following should be included in the provisions of your trust:

[ ] Identify the individual(s) or institution(s) with fiduciary duties and specify provisions for the appointment of successor trustees in the event of the death, resignation, or incapacity of your designated trustees.

[ ] Identify your primary and contingent beneficiaries.

[ ] Describe the trust capital or corpus, authorize any additional contributions, and provide for the corpus distribution. "Pourover" provisions can direct property from your will or from a source outside the testamentary estate into the trust.

[ ] Set up the conditions under which the beneficiaries will receive income distribution from the trust. The trustees can be empowered either to distribute the income on a fixed schedule at a fixed rate or to "sprinkle" the income among the various beneficiaries as deemed appropriate.

[ ] Specify the trustees' powers in administering the trust.

[ ] Provide for the appointment of a guardian for beneficiaries who are minors.

[ ] Set up safeguards so that beneficiaries cannot transfer their interest to a third party and so that their interest cannot be subject to future creditors' claims.

[ ] Specify the trust's time limit. (It cannot be longer than 21 years after the death of the last surviving beneficiary who was alive at the time the trust was created.)

[ ] Provide for the payment or waiving of fees for the trustee.

[ ] Provide for the bond or security or waiving of such bond and security for the trustee.

Choosing Trustees

Because the trustee is considered your personal representative, your designation may be the most important decision in drawing up your trust. You can name any person or institution, including yourself, a member of your immediate family, or the beneficiary(ies), as the trustee. Although a relative is a good choice in some circumstances, it may not be in others.

To secure any tax benefits, the trustee cannot retain the right to sprinkle income among the adult beneficiaries, nor can he or she add new beneficiaries during the trust's duration. However, if *you* are the trustee, you can change the corpus beneficiaries (distribution of the capital to another beneficiary) without including the trust in your income, as long as such power is limited by a reasonably definite standard. You can also temporarily accumulate income rather than distribute it, provided that this income will ultimately be paid to the same beneficiary from whom it was withheld. If the beneficiary is under age 21 or is legally disabled, you will have more leeway to distribute the trust's income to parties other than the beneficiary or to add the retained income to your trust capital.

The IRS defines a "related or subordinate party to the grantor" as the spouse if living with you (the grantor); any member of the grantor's immediate family; an employee of the grantor; an employee of a corporation, or the corporation itself, in which the grantor has "significant" voting power; or a subordinate employee of a corporation in which the grantor is an executive. Most state laws prohibit the sole beneficiary from being the sole trustee.

In general, it is not advisable to name the grantor or the beneficiary as the trustee if the main reason for drawing up the trust is to reduce income and estate taxes. Also, it is not advisable to name as the trustee someone who is related to you or the beneficiary. If a related party to the beneficiary is named as the trustee and he or she then uses the trust's capital or income to discharge his or her legal support obligation to the beneficiary, the trust will be included in that trustee's estate.

From a tax perspective, appointing an independent party as a trustee—an unrelated business partner or a bank or trust institution—is your best alternative. However, with such a third party, the factor of disinterest must be added to your concerns. Furthermore, many bank and trust institutions prefer to deal only with trust funds of more than $100,000. A common compromise: appoint your spouse as a co-trustee along with an independent third party. From a tax standpoint, as long as the spouse can be outvoted by the other trustee(s), the trust is considered sufficiently independent not to be included in the grantor's income and estate tax return. This arrangement is an especially popular alternative when the trustee is empowered to "sprinkle" income among the beneficiaries. The spouse's concern and knowledge about the beneficiaries' welfare can then be combined with the management expertise of the bank or trust corporation without forfeiting the tax advantage you worked so hard to provide.

When choosing a bank or trust institution as a trustee, you should first examine the institution's trust department. How long has the trust department been in existence? How qualified are its personnel? What rate of income and growth has the trust portfolio achieved recently? Are the fees for administration and services competitive?

Family Trusts

The following section describes a variety of trusts that may be useful in your estate planning. There are others, not described here, that could also be beneficial. Check with an experienced estate planning attorney.

Marital Deduction Trust

Under current tax regulations, no federal tax is paid on property left to a spouse. Up to $600,000 can be left tax-free to a nonspouse. Upon the death of the first spouse, the federal estate tax bite can be avoided by taking advantage of the unlimited marital deduction (check your state laws pertaining to death taxes to see if any state taxes would be paid upon the death of the first spouse). But upon the death of the surviving spouse, any estate worth more than $600,000 could be subject to a hefty federal estate tax bill. One option—of particular interest to those whose estates are large enough to be subject to federal estate taxes—involves the establishment of two separate trusts that come into existence upon the death of the trust maker. The first, the "marital trust," receives the marital deduction and is only for the surviving spouse. The second, known as the "family trust," is created to receive the balance of the estate funds, generally for the benefit of your surviving spouse and children. Using this (latter) plan, often referred to as an A-B Trust, you can reduce or even eliminate the federal estate tax that results after both spouses' deaths.

Qualified Terminable Interest Property (QTIP) Trusts

A QTIP trust is a testamentary trust that qualifies for the unlimited marital deduction but does not give to the surviving spouse the power to bequeath the fund to anyone else. Because it qualifies for the marital deduction, the decedent's estate may incur less tax. Because the QTIP trust does not give to the surviving spouse the power of bequeathal, it also safeguards the decedent's estate from the spouse's possible financial irresponsibility and limits the spouse's power to transfer property to, for example, children from a previous marriage, children whom you wish to disinherit, or a future spouse. After the death of the surviving spouse, the principal of the QTIP trust is distributed according to the provisions of the trust agreement.

For a QTIP trust to be legally acceptable, your (surviving) spouse must have a qualifying income interest for life. Also, your spouse must be entitled to all of the income from the property, payable at least annually, and no one may have the power to allocate any part of the property to any person other than your spouse. The trustee may, however, be empowered to distribute a reasonable amount of the trust's principal to the surviving spouse.

Aside from its planning advantage, a QTIP trust may also save estate taxes. In a QTIP trust, you or the executor of your estate can include the trust fund in either your estate or your spouse's estate. This feature is especially useful if at the time you draw up your will it is unclear whether or not the marital deduction will be overfunded to such an extent that a QTIP inclusion in the spouse's estate would lead to an excessive tax burden. After your death, your executor may re-evaluate the estate and choose to take or decline the marital deduction, whichever results in the lesser amount of taxes. If your surviving spouse's estate is considerably larger than the decedent's, leave your property to other beneficiaries rather than needlessly inflate the larger estate.

Sprinkling Trusts

A sprinkling trust is one by which you grant discretionary powers to a trustee over the disbursement of the trust funds. Such discretionary powers can be used to achieve both tax and nontax objectives. Because the trustee may use his or her own judgment when distributing your trust's funds among the beneficiaries, those beneficiaries with greater financial and material needs can be better served by the trust resources. In addition, trust income that is dispensed in amounts inversely related to each beneficiary's tax bracket can result in income tax savings. Lastly, the trustee can choose to retain income in the trust for future rather than immediate dispersal.

The tax consequences of the sprinkling trust, however, may be far from beneficial. If the trustee can be proved to be related or subordinate to you, the vested power in him or her to sprinkle the trust's income and principal will make the trust taxable to you. However, if the trustee is sufficiently independent from you, he or she may be too far removed from the beneficiaries to appropriately sprinkle income among your beneficiaries.

Crummey Trusts

In order for a trust to qualify for an annual gift exclusion, a portion of the trust fund must be considered by the Internal Revenue Service (IRS) to constitute a gift of a present interest. In regard to a trust under which you wish not to distribute present income to a beneficiary, or a dry trust set up for insurance purposes in which a beneficiary has title only to the policy but no present income, the IRS has ruled that any contribution that you make to the trust (such as a premium payment) does not qualify for the gift exclusion and must be assessed for gift taxes or included in your lifetime exclusion. Clearly, when this sum is considerable, this is an undesirable alternative. To circumvent the IRS ruling, many people have set up Crummey trusts.

A Crummey trust keeps most of the trust funds out of the

beneficiary's hands for as long as you desire, but it qualifies for the gift exclusion by allowing the beneficiary to withdraw each year a set sum equal to the lesser of your annual contribution to the fund or the annual gift exclusion limit of $10,000 ($20,000 with the spouse's consent). The beneficiary must be informed of this right, and the money must be available on demand. In practice, this right is rarely expected to be exercised, nor should you set up the trust if you doubt whether the beneficiary can be trusted to agree with your implied yet unenforceable wish. A child also must be informed of his or her right to withdraw up to the gift tax exclusion amount of $10,000 per year.

Although the IRS has not actively challenged Crummey trusts, their legality has not been definitely established. Indeed, the IRS may be able to overturn your contention that the beneficiary's mere right to withdraw funds constitutes an acceptable present interest. To strengthen your case, it is recommended that the beneficiaries be kept fully informed of their right and that the trust maintain a cash reserve sufficient to satisfy all of the beneficiaries' possible demands for withdrawal.

Charitable Trusts

If you are charitably inclined, you may be able to give to your favorite charity and get more than a thank you and a tax deduction in return. A variety of charitable trust arrangements are discussed below.

Charitable Remainder Trusts

Charitable remainder trusts can provide attractive tax-saving and income-producing incentives for contributing to a worthy charity.

Under a charitable remainder trust agreement, the trust maker puts his or her property into an irrevocable trust with the provisions that the income generated by the property be given to any number of beneficiaries (usually including the trust maker) but that upon the death of the last of the income recipients, the property will be given to a qualified charity for its unrestricted use. In addition to receiving a lifetime income, some important tax savings are gained through a charitable remainder trust. First, as the trust maker, you are granted an income tax deduction based on the value of the property that the charity will eventually receive; this deduction is applicable in the year in which the trust is put into operation. The amount of the deduction is based upon the life expectancy of the beneficiary or beneficiaries if they opt to receive income from the trust for life. Second, your estate is relieved of the property's value from the time the trust begins operation, thus reducing estate taxes that will eventually have to be paid.

Charitable Lead Trusts

A charitable lead trust, also known as a front trust or charitable income trust, allows you to transfer income-producing property in trust to pay either a guaranteed annuity or a fixed percentage, distributed yearly, of the fair market value of the trust property (as determined yearly) to a charity for a period of years. At the end of the term, the property can either be distributed outright to noncharitable beneficiaries (typically family members) or continued in trust for their benefit. In effect, it is the opposite of a charitable remainder trust and is typically used by individuals who have sufficient income but who nevertheless want to pass these income-producing assets on to future generations. Charitable lead trusts are most useful in gift and estate tax planning since you or your estate will be entitled to a gift or estate tax deduction at the time of the creation of the trust based upon the present value of the charitable interest. As a result, the best assets to place in these trusts are those that produce a consistent income and have significant appreciation potential.

Charitable lead trusts may be established during the grantor's lifetime or by will, although they are generally established during your lifetime and terminate at your death. As long as you are able and willing to forego current income, the charitable lead trust is a useful way for the charitably inclined individual to keep property with strong appreciation potential in the family while still providing income for the charity. In addition to the cost of the assets placed in the charitable lead trust, any subsequent appreciation is also excludable from your gross estate.

Unitrusts

A unitrust places income-producing property in trust for a charitable institution and makes regular lifetime payments to a designated beneficiary or beneficiaries, usually yourself and, perhaps, a family member. These payments must be expressed in terms of a fixed percentage, not less than 5 percent, of the net fair market value of the assets, valued annually rather than a certain sum or a specified percentage of the trust's initial fair market value as is the case with annuity trusts.

The law also permits an alternative type of unitrust. Under this type, called the "income-only" unitrust, the trustee is required to distribute to the income beneficiary only the actual income received, if this amount is less than 5 percent of the net fair market value of the assets, valued annually. The trust may, but is not required to, provide that deficiencies in income, if the trust income is less than the stated amount payable to the income beneficiary, may be made up in later years to the extent the trust income exceeds the amount otherwise payable to the income beneficiary for those later years. Either type of unitrust may specify terms and conditions for additional contributions.

Annuity Trusts

An annuity trust differs from a unitrust only by the method used for determining the amount of income payments that are to be made to the noncharitable income beneficiary or beneficiaries. An annuity trust is one which specifies that a fixed dollar annuity is to be paid at least annually to the income beneficiary. The fixed sum must be an amount equal to at least 5 percent of the initial fair market value of all property placed in the trust. Once established, there can be no further contributions to an annuity trust.

Charitable Remainder in a Residence or Farm

A future interest in property can generally not be deducted as a charitable contribution unless it is placed in a charitable remainder trust; however, with the gift of a farm or personal residence, an exception is permitted. With these kinds of property, you may receive an income tax deduction for an irrevocable gift of property that you reserve the right to use for a term of years or for the rest of your life (or that of your spouse). In determining the value of the remainder interest, depreciation and depletion of the property must be taken into account. An allocation between the property's depreciable and nondepreciable portions must be made; if a large amount of the property's value lies in the depreciable portion, then the charitable deduction may be seriously eroded.

Pooled Income Funds

A pooled income fund operates much like a charitable remainder trust. Pooled income funds are becoming increasingly popular with charitable organizations, particularly colleges and universities. These funds accumulate the contributions of many individuals, and, therefore, can provide you with a degree of diversity in the underlying fund that would not be possible in a private arrangement. Another advantage of a pooled income fund is that they require a lower contribution than do charitable trusts. While a charitable trust generally makes sense for contributions in the range of at least $50,000, many charities will accept (indeed, welcome) contributions of $5,000 to $10,000.

Generation-Skipping Transfers

Generation-skipping transfers can be a tax-wise method of shifting one generation's wealth to another, but the onerous generation-skipping transfer tax awaits the unwary.

Generation-skipping transfers—as complex as they are common—enable a grandparent to establish a trust for a grandchild or great-grandchild and, at the same time, possibly avoid or diminish the consequences of paying gift and estate taxes for the interim generation. Each grantor is allowed a lifetime exemption of $1 million for generation-skipping transfers of any type. This exemption applies at the time of transfer. As a result, future appreciation is protected. (However, gift taxes may well be levied at the time of the transfer.)

Each grandparent may take advantage of the $1 million lifetime exemption. That means that a generation-skipping transfer of $2 million per couple is allowed, although again, there may be gift tax consequences on such gifts.

The generation-skipping transfer tax is imposed when there is a taxable distribution (i.e., when trust assets are distributed from a generation-skipping trust to a person assigned to a person two or more tiers below that of the grantor) or when there is a taxable termination. A taxable termination occurs when a termination of the intervening interest in the trust, usually by reason of death in the case of life interest in the trust or by lapse of time in a case in which the grantor created an estate for a specified period of time. If this sounds complicated, that's because it is. If you are blessed with enough money to be concerned about generation-skipping transfers, you need the services of an expert in estate planning.

Suffice it to say that the generation-skipping transfer tax is levied on an inclusive basis. In the case of taxable distributions and taxable terminations, the tax itself is taxed. This aspect of the tax law can have confiscatory consequences for grantors who give large sums of money to their grandchildren or their grandchildren's descendants.

> EXAMPLE: If a grandparent transfers \$10 million to his or her grandson, he or she is treated as making a \$15 million (\$10 million + (50% × \$10 million)) taxable gift. The tax on the gift (without reference to the grantor's available unified credit and assuming that the entire value of the gift is taxed at the 50% rate) is \$7.5 million, which brings the total tax on the \$10 million transfer to \$12.5 million ((50% × \$10 million) + \$7.5 million).

22

FUNERAL PLANNING— DON'T WAIT UNTIL IT'S TOO LATE

Without Preplanning, You Just Might Take It with You

When a family member dies, the survivors all too often stage an overly elaborate and expensive funeral—believing that to economize would be disrespectful to the departed. It is difficult enough to remain level-headed after the death of a spouse, close friend, or family member without having to bargain with a funeral director. If you don't want your family to overspend on your funeral, or if you have strong feelings about how you wish to be interred and memorialized, take the time to preplan your funeral. Preplanning will save your survivors a great deal of trouble and expense during a period when they will already be emotionally strained.

Memorial Societies: A Good Place to Begin

A local memorial society may be helpful in planning your funeral. The one-time membership fee is nominal and often it's transferrable if you move to another city. These societies can offer helpful information on how to plan effectively for your funeral. Often, they are able to obtain lower prices on funeral expenses for members. In addition, memorial societies can recommend reputable funeral homes and ceremony directors. For more information on memorial societies, contact the Continental Association of Funeral and Memorial Societies, Inc., 6900 Lost Lake Road, Egg Harbor, WI 54209-9231 (800)458-5563

Selecting a Funeral Home

Choosing a funeral home is an important step in funeral preplanning. A good way to find a funeral home that will satisfy your needs is to ask friends or a member of the clergy to recommend a funeral home. (You can skip the memorial society if you want, although it may take extra initiative and effort since the arrangements will then have to be made directly with a funeral director.) Also, you can tactfully ask someone who has recently made funeral arrangements. Preplanning provides you the time to observe and compare the different suggestions and various options. The place that will take care of all the details concerning disposal of your body, especially in the case of an earth burial, should meet with your personal and financial approval.

If you are hesitant to haggle over the price of your funeral now, remember that funeral directors aren't immune to seeking financial gain from the bereaved's misfortune. While most won't try too hard to convince them to order the most expensive funeral possible, most won't exhaust themselves pitching the most economical ones either. It is far less likely that they will use this tactic on a preplanning consumer. Funeral directors are businessmen just like anyone else, and they would rather provide you with a simple funeral than see a competitor capture your business.

It is best to use a home that charges separately for each item. This way, you can choose only necessary services, clear of frivolous nonessentials found in "package deals," and, in general, to help prevent overcharging. Also, when planning a funeral in advance, make sure that the funds can be withdrawn or refunded if the funeral arrangements are later changed.

Include Funeral Preferences in Your Letter of Instructions

A letter of instructions supplements, but does not replace your formal will. This document helps ensure that your survivors know exactly how to proceed after your death. Your letter of instructions should include the following information pertaining to your funeral:

- **Notification and pertinent information if you are an organ or body donor.** (Include the location of your uniform donor card.)
- **Names and addresses of the memorial society, funeral home, and/or crematory you have chosen.** The letter of instructions should clearly direct your family to release your remains to the funeral home you have chosen. Changing funeral directors at the last minute could be both emotionally and financially taxing.
- **Type of ceremony and details of service.**
- **Casket and grave-marker preferences.**
- **Preferred death notice.**
- **Whom to notify of your death.** (Chapter 19 further discusses letters-of-instruction.)

In addition, warn your family in advance to be on guard for any frauds or swindlers who often take advantage of the bereaved's state of mind. Such predators often haunt the newspaper obituary column, find the name of the deceased and then call on the family. Common tactics include merchandise sent C.O.D. that has not been ordered, demands for loan repayments on nonexistent loans, forgery of Veterans Administration services designed to swindle the family out of its money, and false notices of life insurance premiums to be paid. Make sure your survivors don't get trapped by frauds.

Evaluating Funeral Alternatives

Everybody should spend some time thinking about the disposition of their remains after death. Don't burden your loved ones with this important decision. By all means consider your beliefs—sacred and/or secular—about the disposition of your remains. Cost of the alternatives should also be factored in so long as you are comfortable with your decision. Before coming to a decision you may also want to discuss your thoughts with close family members. Their opinions are important, too. The various alternatives are discussed below.

Donation to Medical Schools or for Transplant

Donating your body to a medical institution is the most cost-effective way to dispose of remains. Not only does willing your body to a hospital or medical school save your estate a great deal of money, in a small way it may further medical research and thus help other human beings. When considering this option, check with the school or institution of your choice about its detailed requirements. Different medical institutions have different requirements and guidelines for accepting the remains. Some bodies may be unsuitable. Make sure that the institution will accept your body. Also, be sure to have a backup plan for unexpected events, such as death occurring at a place too far away to transport your body.

Usually, embalming is not allowed and the body must be transported immediately to the medical location. Because of this, if you desire a funeral service, it must be held very soon after your death.

An alternative to donating the entire body is to donate only specific organs for transplant. The designated organs must be removed immediately after your death—in order for them to be effective. The rest of your body will be released in time for the funeral. If you are interested in donating organs, ask your doctor for more information. Most organs, with the exception of eyes, have to be age compatible to be effective.

Cremation

Compared with other options, cremation is simpler to carry out and even simpler to describe—your body will be subjected to intense heat and reduced to ashes. Expenses are relatively low (there are no embalming or cosmetic costs.) With rare exception (where a casket is required for the process), a simple fiberboard container, costing about $30, is all that is necessary. (Some crematoria may have their own rules including the requirement of a casket or embalming—avoid them.) If your body is delivered directly to the crematorium, even the presence of a funeral director is unnecessary, further reducing the cost of disposing your body.

After cremation, there are a number of economical ways to deal with your remains. Most families scatter or bury the ashes in a place familiar to the deceased, although local laws may prohibit or restrict this. Niches are also available where a container, usually an urn, can be stored in cemeteries or mausoleums called columbariums or inurements. Another advantage of cremation: ashes can easily be shipped or carried in person without legal complications.

Earth Burial

Although earth burial is the most expensive and complicated way to go, some people still think of it as their only option. Some have their bodies buried immediately after death (which costs less) and others wait for a funeral service. In either case, the largest expense involved in an earth burial is the cost of the coffin. It is important for you to state clearly what kind of coffin you want. That way, if you want a less expensive one, your heirs won't be over-charged by overzealous coffin suppliers. The funeral home might also try to sell you or your heirs burial vaults to enclose the casket or even assert that the cemetery requires it. Even if the cemetery does require a grave lining to prevent cave-ins, a simple metal or concrete liner is more than sufficient and is at most half the cost of a vault. In addition, make your own decision on embalming. Embalming is unnecessary for a normal funeral and is required only when there will be a delay in burial or when the body is to be shipped a great distance. Specify whether you desire embalming because most funeral directors embalm arriving bodies automatically.

CHOOSING A CEMETERY

If you've made up your mind on an earth burial, you have to think about where you want to be buried. Naturally, you want to settle into a place where your family and friends won't be too inconvenienced. Then you have to consider the costs, which vary widely. Municipal cemeteries are usually less expensive than private cemeteries. Urban areas are generally more expensive than rural locations. Above-ground mausoleums tend to be more costly. Different areas within the same cemetery may cost more or less depending on the specific location. If you want to be buried with your spouse, having one coffin placed on top of the other is more economical than placing them side-by-side.

Consider buying your cemetery plot in advance. You may save some money for yourself and your heirs by locking into today's price for tomorrow's plot. It's a good anti-inflation investment. (Burial plots have risen dramatically in price over the last few years, far outstripping inflation rates.) However, advance purchase also has its drawback. If you end up moving to a new place far away from the cemetery where you purchased a plot, it may be complicated to change your plans. Exchange plans are available but often have many restrictions. If you don't have an exchange plan you have to arrange for a private sale. (The salesperson for the cemetery may be able to help you sell it—but not for nothing.) If you want to save yourself from the trouble of resell, you may also consider donating the plot to a church as a tax deduction. Generally, only consider buying a cemetery plot if you are not going to move away from where you're planning to end up.

Religious Services

The second most important consideration after deciding on the disposition of your remains is your funeral service. A great deal of money can either be spent or saved, depending on how well you and/or your family plan. It is important to remember that the service is for the emotional needs of the survivors. Your family may feel that the deceased deserves a big send-off, but the only ones who will appreciate the bowers of roses and the solid bronze casket are the ones who may live to regret the cost of them.

There are basically two types of ceremonies. The first and most expensive type is the funeral service. By definition, a funeral service is one held in presence of your body. If there is a time lapse before the burial, the body will have to be embalmed, and for an open coffin ceremony, cosmetic work is required. Also, if there is a viewing, rental charges may be imposed. The ceremony is usually held at the funeral parlor, but the funeral director may transport the body to another location. The more elaborate the ceremony, the more costly it will be.

Remember, a memorial society can be of great help. If you're not getting assistance from a memorial society, choose a trusted friend or relative to make your preferred arrangements. As with your plot, it's possible to finance your funeral service in advance. (Likewise, do so when you're certainly not going to move away—otherwise it may be hard to get your deposit back.) Also, with the stress and emotional tension that occur at death, unscrupulous funeral homes may attempt to pad bills, especially if your survivors are not sure of the specific prearrangement.

The second type of religious service is a memorial service. It differs from a funeral service in that it typically takes place after the body has been cremated or interred. Because there are no calendar constraints on the disposal of the body, a memorial service offers greater flexibility in location and time. It can be performed at virtually any place that is desired and does not require the assistance of a funeral home. A memorial service can be far less expensive than a funeral service, as all the items required for the funeral service (cosmetic work, elaborate coffin, funeral parlor, and so on) are unnecessary. In general, memorial services tend to be less elaborate and are often more thoughtful than funeral services. A common feature is to suggest that friends make a donation to some specified charitable organization, rather than sending flowers or some other well-meaning but less constructive gift. Your friends will be thankful to you because such donations are both thoughtful and tax deductible.

Financing Your Finale

Death and the medical costs that usually accompany it are such an expensive process that they put a financial strain on many families. Making your family aware of all expenses and any possible special sources of funds you've set aside to cover them can make your funeral less stressful.

There are three main ways of meeting the expenses associated with a death. One is for the funds to come from the family budget. (However, as liquid resources may not be sufficient and the principal assets may be tied up in the probate process, a better alternative is to save for the inevitable expense.) A regularly renewed certificate of deposit (CD) is a good vehicle for this purpose, especially since the penalty for early withdrawal does not apply if the owner dies.

Looking for Outside Sources

Along with your own resources, you may be able to find some outside sources that can help reduce the burden of your "final expense." Among those sources are your insurance, your employee benefits, Social Security benefits, and VA benefits. Let your family be aware in advance that if your death is related to your job, they may be eligible for assistance through workers' compensation plans. In any case, ask them to notify the employee benefits office at your workplace, as there may be some benefit connected with the pension or the company's life insurance or other benefits program.

If you're a fully insured worker under Social Security or have credit for a year and half out of the three years before death, there is a $255 lump-sum death benefit available for you. However, as with other Social Security benefits, you have to apply to the Social Security Administration to receive the benefit. Your surviving spouse and children may also be eligible for survivor benefits.

If you're an honorably discharged wartime or peacetime veteran, you can get a $300 allowance for your funeral expenses. If death is caused by service-related factors, this allowance may be as much as $1,100. In addition, if you're a veteran, you, your wife and your children can obtain free burial in a national cemetery where space is available. If not buried in a national cemetery, you may receive up to $150 towards the purchase of a plot. Simple headstones are available at no cost to veterans, and spouses and children may receive markers free of cost if buried in a national cemetery. If the body requires shipment and (1) the veteran died in or in transit to a VA hospital, or (2) had any service-related disability, then the VA will pay for it. Also, all eligible veterans are entitled to the draping of an American flag over the casket. You can get further information at a VA office or veterans' service organization.

Among the other sources of available benefits are automobile club insurance, liability insurance, state employee survivor benefits, trade unions, fraternal organizations, and specific occupation benefits—for example, benefits available to the survivors of railroad workers. The relevant information about your association with such unions and organizations is yours for the asking—but you have to ask.

Final Expenses and Tax Deductions

When preplanning your funeral, be aware of other expenses in addition to the disposition of your body and the final service. For example, you should take into account the money spent on death announcements and obituaries.

Finally, your loved ones should know that many funeral-related expenses are tax deductible on your estate tax return if they are paid out of your estate. Deductible funeral expenses include all of the funeral's actual expenses, such as the cost of the casket, undertaker's fees, flowers, embalming, and the transferring of the body. Expenses related to the burial site are also deductible, such as the purchase cost of a plot and tombstone or grave marker.

PART FOUR

Making the Most of Your Retirement Years

23

CHOOSING A RETIREMENT LIFESTYLE

FOR SOME INDIVIDUALS, retirement represents an opening up of a broad range of opportunity while for others, it can be a time of dislocation and confusion. If you are approaching retirement, but still have a few years to go before you receive your gold watch, don't postpone taking the time to determine how you would like to spend your later years. For all too many retirees, the end of the last day of work catches them off guard and without plans for the future. Indeed, the lives of many older adults have been so centered on their workplaces that staying at home can feel like staying in exile. Having worked all their lives, these individuals have a hard time adjusting to a life of enforced leisure.

Yet there is little reason why leaving the workforce should be a stressful experience. If you and your spouse take the time to decide how—and where—you'd like to live and what you'd like to do during retirement, your later years will be much more rewarding. The key is thinking hard and planning ahead.

Cultivating a Hobby or Activity

Even the most workaholic of adults usually has some activity that he or she would like to pursue if there were only enough days in the week. Retirement provides the time to pursue these postponed activities, but don't wait until retirement arrives to start to think about exactly how you'd like to get involved. Since one of the main secrets of a happy retirement is being prepared, figuring out how to pursue a particular activity ahead of time will pay off when the time comes to leave the workforce. Suppose, for instance, that you had always wanted to get involved with your town's historical society. Take the time to talk with the society's administrators: they'll be more than happy to discuss how you might become involved, whether it be as a volunteer docent or as a trustee. Indeed nonprofit cultural and historical organizations are always looking to attract active members. If you wanted to, you could make a full-time occupation out of this sort of activity.

Perhaps however, you may have a desire to learn to paint, draw, or sculpt, but have never had the time for lessons. Your preretirement years are a good time to pick up such a hobby so that by the time you retire, you may be proficient enough to really enjoy it. Perhaps you've been intending to take up tennis or golf but never had gotten around to it—or never had the time to get good at it. Why not sign up for lessons now? Once you reach retirement, you'll be that much less of a duffer. Making sure that your retirement years are financially secure is important, but if you don't know what you'll do with yourself when you reach lotus-land, your money won't count for much. By the way, many retirees discover that, for the first time in their lives, they have the time to pay attention to their investments. If you have always wanted to take a more active role in managing your money, by all means start to do so. You undoubtedly have many years of investment experience behind you, including the all-important skill of being able to distinguish between a good investment and a bad one.

Working in Retirement

Increasing numbers of older Americans are working during retirement, whether because of financial necessity or out of an interest in pursuing a line of work wholly different from their old profession. Some retirees find that hobbies, sports, and volunteering simply don't engage them fully enough to be a satisfactory replacement for work. Working during retirement can often boost a retiree's sense of productivity and self esteem and can also provide a source of discretionary funds that may make retirement years more comfortable as a whole. If, however, you are looking forward to a leisure-filled retirement, the fact that financial necessity has prompted more than a few older Americans to reenter the workforce should be an additional stimulus to retirement-oriented saving. For more on working during retirement, see Chapter 27.

Deciding Where to Live

One major decision you will face, one that will go far in determining your retirement lifestyle, is choosing where to live after leaving the workforce. Obviously, if you want to indulge in year-round golf and tennis, staying in Cleveland won't allow you to achieve this ambition. Like many older Americans, a desire to escape winter weather may convince you to move to a milder climate. Or, you may be strongly attached to your local community and decide to stay put.

No matter what you want to do, the fact is that the better your financial situation, the greater your degree of flexibility. For instance, affluent retirees who want to enjoy warm winters can buy a home or a condo in the Sunbelt while maintaining their old home as a spring and summer residence. These individuals don't have to face the unhappy choice of deciding between continued winter blues and leaving their friends and family behind. Chapter 24: Sorting Out Your Retirement Housing Options, and Chapter 30: What to Do with the Family Homestead, will help you make intelligent decisions about future housing.

Later Life Decisions

Not all retirement lifestyle decisions are made before or just after retirement. After all, most of us can look forward to 20, 30, or more years of life after work. Many of these decisions may represent delightful dilemmas—moving to a new locale, taking up new avocations, and so on. Others are the result of some "life events" that are unfortunate but nonetheless inevitable: the onset of senility, chronic illness, death of a spouse or other loved one, and the like. Sometimes, retirees have to adjust their lifestyle as a result of financial exigency. Whatever the cause, the most important thing you can do to cope with later-life lifestyle decisions is to first, anticipate and plan for the downside of old age. You will weather these "life events" much better if they don't catch you completely unprepared.

24

SORTING OUT YOUR RETIREMENT HOUSING OPTIONS

THE AMOUNT OF money you will need to finance a long and comfortable retirement obviously depends on how expensive your tastes are. Your choice of housing, including your choice of community or surroundings, is usually the single most important standard-of-living consideration. Living in a log cabin in Manhattan, Montana, certainly imposes different financial and social obligations from inhabiting a penthouse in Manhattan, New York.

Most retirees choose to live in the same homes they occupied prior to retirement, although from a purely financial standpoint this is often short-sighted. Others will decide they might like to live in another part of the country or try a new lifestyle, such as living in a condominium after years of maintaining a house, or living in a smaller house, a retirement community or a continuing-care community.

Ideally, you should try out—or at least carefully evaluate—any such arrangement before retirement if at all possible. During retirement, when funds are limited, too many people miss their old homes and/or lifestyles.

Housing expenses can present a serious problem for some fixed-income retirees. Many retirees who do not own their homes are confronted with rent or alternative housing costs that can rise faster than inflation and an income that barely keeps up. Even if you bought your home in anticipation of being mortgage-free by retirement, property taxes, which reflect the value of the property rather than your income or ability to pay, may present a serious financial burden. Many people who would prefer to stay in their own homes wind up selling their homes to find a cheaper source of housing.

If you find yourself in this situation, there are a number of ways to stabilize or reduce housing expenses, as there are methods for converting the equity locked in the home into cash income. Fortunately, many states provide relief from property taxes for older homeowners or tenants. Low-income older people may also be eligible for grants to help meet fuel costs and aid in weatherproofing the home.

Many older Americans' most valuable asset is their home, but its value often seems inaccessible to fixed-income retirees who could use additional cash. Sale-leasebacks, reverse mortgage arrangements and deferred-payment loans make it possible for older homeowners to convert the equity in their homes into additional income. However, there are some drawbacks to these arrangements, so use caution and get legal help before employing such techniques—especially since the additional income could adversely affect some retirement benefits. Also keep in mind that second mortgages or refinancings are appropriate only when there is no risk you will outlive your ability to service the debt.

Retirees on fixed incomes who can no longer afford to maintain their homes or pay high rent in private housing and those whose health does not allow them to live alone comfortably are increasingly turning to alternative housing arrangements. Your local office on aging can help in locating specific housing facilities in your chosen community, or your employer may sponsor a consultation and referral service.

The array of housing options available to older Americans are now more extensive than ever before, ranging from homesharing, which enables older people to stay in their own homes, to nursing home care. This chapter provides an overview of some of the housing options currently available to older people in many communities as well as a discussion of options for retirees looking for a new place to live. We'll also take a look at some of the key housing issues confronting anyone considering a big move.

Housing Options for Independent Retirees

Many people choose to move at retirement even though their health or financial circumstances do not compel them to do so. Some wish to adopt new lifestyles by moving into country club communities, for example, or exploring the country in motor homes. Others just want a change of scenery or climate, and some decide to sell their homes and rent or buy smaller ones to tap the appreciation for additional income.

If you do plan to move at retirement, you will certainly want to take advantage of the one-time exclusion from tax on the sale of a home for taxpayers over age 55. (See *Chapter 28: What to Do with the Family Homestead* for details on this once-in-a-lifetime opportunity.)

If you are contemplating a change of residence, you should thoroughly explore the types of housing available and then set your housing priorities. Housing advertisements are often a good place to start to get an idea of what's available. By the time your search starts getting serious—and before you engage the services of a broker—you should have a fairly good idea of what you want, need and can afford. Any decision to buy a house depends on many variables and has significant financial ramifications. That's why you should take your time and carefully choose a home you intend to live in for the next 10, 20 or 30 years. Some common issues to consider:

- Is the home convenient to transportation, shopping and recreation?
- Is the general neighborhood declining or improving?
- How expensive are property taxes and have they been rising at a rapid rate?
- Are there any crime or pollution problems?
- Are older residents offered any local tax breaks?
- Does the community offer programs to senior citizens that may be useful or important to you?
- Is the home of a size and in a location that will facilitate resale?
- What are the advantages and disadvantages of the particular type of housing? Old houses may be less energy efficient and may require ongoing maintenance. Newer houses may be more expensive and of inferior construction. Condos and co-

ops may have less closet and storage space, and some have inadequate soundproofing, allowing footsteps and voices to penetrate from neighboring units.

- Do you plan to live in the home for the rest of your life or only the next few years? If you anticipate spending only a few years in the neighborhood, you should try to pick a home that will be easy to resell and you should make the smallest down payment possible.

Condos and Co-Ops

Many people who still own homes large enough for their whole families decide to sell those homes at retirement, after their children have moved out, and buy smaller houses, condos or co-ops. If the "new" residence is cheaper than the old one this has the obvious advantage of letting them spend the price differential elsewhere. Condos and co-ops have additional advantages for retirees because they often provide all the benefits of owning a home, but without all the maintenance responsibilities.

A condominium owner owns his or her unit outright, as well as an undivided interest in the common areas of the building or complex. A cooperative apartment building or complex is owned by a corporation in which each resident owns stock. Stock ownership entitles the resident to a proprietary lease on his or her unit.

In general, condo and co-op owners get the same tax treatment as owners of traditional single-family homes. A condo owner pays mortgage interest and taxes directly and treats them just as though the condo were a house. A co-op owner makes a monthly payment that covers a portion of interest on the corporation's mortgage and property taxes. The portion that is allocable to these expenses can be deducted by the shareholder.

In addition, if the co-op owner has taken out a mortgage to buy his or her shares, the interest on that mortgage is deductible. Also, just like homeowners, a condo or co-op owner's cost basis for income tax purposes is increased by their share of any amounts paid for improvements.

Note, however, that many condos and co-ops assess a separate monthly maintenance fee to pay for the upkeep of amenities or for services such as trash collection. These fees, which can increase as maintenance costs go up, typically are not deductible.

Retirement Homesite Developments

Over the last decade, thousands of people have been lured by newspaper and magazine advertisements to invest in retirement homesites across the Sun Belt. Developers may put on a hard and elaborate sales pitch, including paying for prospective buyers' airfare and accommodations so they can visit the site.

Buyers paying reasonable amounts to honest developers may be able to find lovely sites they will enjoy in their golden years. However, overbuilding and high promotion costs virtually ensure these lots will not prove lucrative investments. Worse, many real estate development operations are forced to delay building through hard times or tight credit. Occasionally, promised developments, amenities or services never materialize and buyers are left holding the bag to complete the project or promised improvements at their own expense. The following tips can help you avoid having your retirement-housing dollars tied up in years of litigation over some misguided or fraudulent development scheme:

- Don't let yourself be pressured into buying property you can't afford, and don't count on projected appreciation in your calculations.
- Ask the local Better Business Bureau about the property's developer and promoter. Also ask for material to compare the asking price with similar projects.
- Carefully review the required "property report" for details on the project and costs.
- Research the area thoroughly before you put any money at risk. Find out how far the site is from transportation, hospitals, refuse removal services, shopping and recreation. And never buy without visiting the development.
- Have a lawyer review any documents you plan to sign.
- Never be pressured into signing up for any property on the spot—no matter how good the deal sounds or how nice the salesperson is.

Retirement Communities

Retirement communities are a sensible choice for older, healthy retirees who desire social interaction with people their own age. Typically, older individuals rent or purchase an apartment and have access to recreational and other facilities.

However, if you have pets or expect frequent visits from your children or grandchildren, you'll want to pay special attention to any restrictions the community imposes on the use of residents' apartments. Retirement communities often take special pains to ensure serene surroundings for their residents. Thus, by-laws and deed restrictions may bar pets or restrict visits by young children to certain hours of the day or parts of the property.

Motor Homes

For many retirees with extensive travel plans, motor homes represent the ultimate in freedom and convenience: you decide when you're leaving, you set your own pace, and you always get to sleep in your own bed. What's more, you never miss the boat and you never have to wait for the plane. Your home can even follow the seasons.

Today's motor homes are more comfortable than ever before, but they are also more expensive. However, even if you don't plan to spend more than a few months in it each year, your motor home can qualify as a second home for tax purposes. Thus, your mortgage interest payments are deductible as long as it has cooking, sleeping and sanitation facilities and your first mortgage doesn't exceed certain limits.

You can also rent your motor home when you aren't using it. The rental income will help offset your mortgage payments and it may make a portion of your other expenses of owning the motor home (such as insurance, maintenance and repairs) tax-deductible up to the amount of the rent you receive (which, of course, is taxable income). Many dealers who sell motor homes offer programs that assist buyers in leasing their vehicles to others when the owners aren't using them. If you're interested, you'll want to ask about such services when you're shopping for a motor home.

Houseboats

A boat can also qualify as a second home if it has a head, galley and sleeping berth. And just as with a motor home, you can charter it when you aren't using it.

Shared Housing Arrangements and Options for People Who Need Extra Care

As many older Americans have discovered, healthy habits and good medical care have broken the link between advanced age and poor health. With the aging of the nation, more and more alternatives are being developed for the relatively well elderly—that increasingly large group who need a modest amount of help with the chores of daily living but can still manage pretty well by themselves.

These alternatives vary in the lifestyles they promote and in the amount of medical and custodial care they offer. And some are equally well-suited to people in perfect health who merely want companionship or to be close to their children or other family members. The spectrum of options available to relatively infirm older Americans is also broadening. Here's a closer look at some of the most popular options.

Homesharing

Homesharing is a means for an older person to share expenses and household tasks with a younger person who needs affordable housing. A younger person might agree to do cleaning or yard work in exchange for inexpensive or free room and board. There are local community groups or government agencies in most areas that match homeowners with potential homesharers. Be sure to check the references of any potential homesharer and prepare a written agreement spelling out the details of the arrangement.

If you are considering homesharing, you should think carefully about your needs and desires. For example, if you need someone to prepare meals, you should be prepared to address questions such as the following:

- Are you on a special diet that may differ from what the homesharer generally eats?
- Who will determine the menu?
- Who will shop for food?
- How many meals a day will you ask the homesharer to provide?
- Do you expect the homesharer to eat meals with you?
- How will food costs be allocated?

One alternate along these lines is for the retiree to share someone else's home. In many communities, there are organizations to match up interested homeowners with interested retirees. Some will match two retirees who wish to rent and find them an apartment. Zoning regulations that prohibit multifamily dwellings or rentals of part of a house often make exceptions for those over age 65 and those living as one "family" instead of in separate apartments within the same house.

Note, however, that some potential drawbacks apply to homesharing arrangements, including the effects of extra income on Social Security benefits and the adjustments of living with a stranger.

Home Care

Home care is for people who wish to remain in their own homes but for whom the unskilled companionship and guardianship of a homesharer will not be adequate. For people who need help with the daily activities of living, home care is an attractive option because its enables them to remain in familiar surroundings where they feel more at ease, more in control and more comfortable. Furthermore, it's much cheaper than moving into a nursing home or other institution.

Home care is particularly appropriate for people with Alzheimer's or other debilitating diseases and for people recovering from recent hospitalizations who still require nursing care or help with life's daily activities. Different levels of service are available, ranging from custodial care (for people who need some assistance with daily tasks but don't need medical supervision) to skilled nursing care.

Many programs are also available for people who need some help every day but don't need someone to move in. "Meals On Wheels," for example, delivers hot meals or provides transportation to a meal site, and state community care programs provide homemaking services and meals and run errands for homebound persons. Information on these programs is usually published in the local newspaper or is available in your local library or government offices.

Accessory Apartments

This arrangement is similar to homesharing, but each dwelling space has a separate kitchen. In some locales, such housing is known as mother-daughter homes because often the older person is renting or staying in an apartment within a son's or daughter's home. The apartment gives the parents more independence and privacy than he or she would have sharing the child's household.

As with homesharing, this arrangement can be reversed for older people who own their homes and want to take in tenants to give them a sense of security as well as to boost their income.

A new twist on accessory apartments, ECHO (Elder Cottage

Housing Opportunity) allows older people to install and rent self-contained units that are placed in the side or backyard of an adult child's home. The units are removed when they no longer are needed. These must be privately purchased and installed, at a cost of $14,000 to $20,000. They are generally portable and reusable, but many people find the purchase price and installation costs prohibitive. Also, they can raise property taxes and the additional utility costs may exceed those of an apartment. On the other hand, ECHO units offer their residents a degree of independence they would not have in a shared-home arrangement, but with the same closeness and safety of family.

Congregate Housing

This is a group living situation for older people who are basically in good health, but whose functional abilities are somewhat limited. Basic services include one to three meals per day in a central dining area, light housekeeping, laundry services and organized recreational activities. Residents share common areas such as the living room, bathroom, kitchen and dining room. The services of a social worker and/or homemaker, meal delivery, transportation and recreational programs may also be available.

Congregate housing, varying in size and physical design, is sometimes sponsored by nonprofit organizations that offer the housing at a low rate. If you are considering a move to congregate housing, you should:

- Tour the facility, talk with residents and, if possible, participate in a meal and some other activity.
- Examine the lease or contract carefully, checking to see if there is a penalty for terminating the lease. Also, if you are hospitalized, is your room reserved for your return?
- Find out what the monthly fees are and what additional charges for extra services exist.
- Ask about regulations—for example, some facilities place restrictions on visitors or pets.

Many congregate housing facilities are being built in or near the urban areas of the North and Midwest. Thus, they have special appeal for people who don't want to relocate to the "retirement belt" of the Southeast and West and lose touch with their families, friends, clergy and communities.

Fees and Costs: Different congregate care communities make different arrangements for payment, but they typically require a large entry fee ($150,000 to $250,000), for which mortgages are not available, and a monthly charge of $1,000 to $2,000 or more, depending on the size of the unit and other variables. The monthly charge includes meals and most services (but not medical care).

Be sure to ask about extra fees for extra services. The entry fee is normally refundable when the resident leaves or payable to his or her estate, but no interest is paid. Some facilities offer units on a rental basis with no entry fee.

Senior Housing

This kind of housing, subsidized by a branch of local, state or federal government, often offers rents based on the older person's income and ability to pay. As a result, eligibility for the units is typically based on income levels.

Senior housing usually consists of a one-bedroom apartment with a living room, bathroom and kitchen and is accessible to persons with disabilities. Due to the limited number of units available, there will often be a waiting list for admittance to senior housing.

Continuing Care Communities

Designed to meet the changing needs of their residents, these communities offer a variety of housing alternatives in one location: townhouses for independent, active older adults; apartment buildings with meals, homemaker and laundry services; and, in many communities, a nursing home. Continuing care communities usually require a sizable entry payment and a subsequent monthly fee. Because this is a relatively new concept, you should check:

- The financial status of the owners and developers,
- The current level of occupancy,
- Whether the continuing care community has sufficient resources to keep it solvent,
- Whether the down payment is refundable if you move out,
- Whether any of the down payment is refundable to your estate upon your death,
- What services are included in the monthly fee,
- How much the monthly fee has increased over the community's history, and

- Whether the facility is located near public transportation and is accessible to family, friends and shopping.

And as with any housing alternative, you should always visit the community and talk with residents, and have a lawyer review the contract documents. Unfortunately, several such communities have failed, leaving their residents in a lurch.

Many retirees faced with or concerned about declining health and increasing medical costs enter continuous care communities to protect themselves against these risks, because no additional costs will be incurred even if their health care expenses increase. Life-care contracts offer older Americans the advantages of independent living, long-term security and affordable nursing home care.

Adult Day Care

Adult day care is often appropriate for older people who can still get around and take care of themselves for the most part but who may not be entirely self-sufficient. Adult day care is available at a lower cost than residential care, and retirement communities often offer this care daily or several times a week at a much lower cost than nursing home or home nursing care.

Transportation, games and puzzles, exercises, physical therapy, field trips, performances, classes, snacks and hot midday meals are among the staples offered by adult care centers, in addition to having registered and licensed practical nurses on hand to monitor residents' health.

When choosing an adult care center, ask what's included in the daily rate. Program supplies, transportation and excursions may cost extra and individualized services for the severely handicapped, physical therapy and psychiatric care will add substantially to the total cost that's not covered by Medicare or most private medical insurance. Some insurers are beginning to offer policies that cover adult day care, and financial aid may be available to lower-income individuals.

Points to consider in choosing a center include: the center's conformity to state regulations, the sufficiency of available medical staff and services, quality of the meals and the center's ability to accommodate special dietary regimens, client-to-staff ratio and the safety and cleanliness of the facilities. Geriatric social workers and consultants can assist you in evaluating your suitability for this level of care and in identifying an appropriate center.

Nursing Homes

Entering a nursing home is an event of intense personal and financial concern for many retirees and their families. Often the decision to enter a home follows a period of serious illness or loss of a loved one, leaving little time for planning. What's more, the high cost of nursing home care can rapidly deplete the resources of residents, their spouses and families. Nursing homes should be chosen on the basis of location, recommendations, financial arrangements, facilities, a thorough inspection and tour, and according to your specific needs and preferences.

Nursing home care is expensive and private health insurance for such care has only recently become available. Such coverage is itself quite costly and often does not fully cover the full range of nursing home expenses. Medicare generally pays only for skilled nursing care, generally after a hospital stay, in a skilled nursing facility. Patients who need less extensive care must pay for it themselves or qualify for Medicaid reimbursement, often by liquidating assets and exhausting their life savings.

Some prospective nursing home residents try to qualify for Medicaid by transferring assets to a spouse or children or into an irrevocable trust. Be advised, however, that there are clear risks and drawbacks associated with such transfers. (For tips on selecting a home, see *Chapter 32: Choosing a Nursing Home.* For more on nursing home insurance and Medicaid reimbursement rules, see *Chapter 5: Your Protection Against Rising Health Care and Nursing Home Costs.*)

Deciding Where You Want to Live

Since most people's financial resources are not as plentiful in retirement as during their working years, the financial and tax climate are primary considerations for people considering a later-life move. Costs and standards of living vary considerably between urban and rural areas, among different parts of the country and among different countries of the world. Even within the United States, differences between state income and estate tax rates can make a dramatic difference on a retiree's standard of living and on his or her after-tax estate.

In addition to financial considerations, you should evaluate any potential new home or community in terms of the following:

- The extent and quality of services offered by local governments,
- Quality, cost and accessibility of health services,
- Climate,
- Availability and variety of recreational, cultural, and social facilities,
- Proximity to shopping centers, and
- Proximity to houses of worship.

As with any new housing arrangement for seniors, it's best to try living in the new locale for awhile before making an irrevocable move or big financial commitment, such as selling your old home and buying a new one in the new area.

Thinking of Retiring Abroad?

More and more Americans are choosing to retire overseas to stretch their incomes or join their friends or family. Unless you live in certain prohibited countries (you probably wouldn't want to live in countries like Albania or Democratic Kampuchea anyway), your Social Security benefits will not be affected by where you choose to receive them. On the other hand, you will probably lose your Medicare coverage. Of course, many foreign countries have at least partially state-provided health care systems, so you may not need to pay for it anyway.

In addition, your estate may be subject to foreign tax and legal requirements, and your heirs may have difficulty probating your will. Your income tax situation will also probably be complicated. And unless you renounce your U.S. citizenship, you may continue to be subject to U.S. income tax even if your income is earned elsewhere, although some tax breaks are available. You may also be subject to taxes in the foreign country, which may or may not be deductible in the U.S., depending on tax treaties.

Thus, it's vital to consult competent tax and estate lawyers, both here and in the foreign country, to help you avoid potential legal and tax problems and to make sure your affairs are handled right. Among the most important issues to consider is what happens if you take your money abroad only to find after a few years that you don't like living overseas and want to move back to the United States. Some countries have laws that make it hard for you to get your money out.

Currency fluctuations are another big risk if all your retirement income is in U.S. dollars, such as from pensions, annuities and Social Security benefits. If the value of the dollar drops against the currency of your retirement home, your dollar-denominated income won't go as far overseas.

Ways to Test Your Housing Choices

Many people can't wait to sell their homes and move at retirement. Some, however, quickly regret their haste and find themselves missing the old house or neighborhood.

If you are absolutely sure you want to move, you're well advised to sell the old house before buying a new one, even if it means temporarily renting before locating a new home. That's because the cost of carrying two mortgages until the first house is sold can be damaging to your pocketbook.

However, when considering such a drastic and lifelong change, a safer way to test your options is to postpone the sale of your old house until after you're sure the new locale is right for you. Ideally, you might rent at the new location, although this may not be feasible. And since you aren't trying to get rid of your "old" house immediately, you can rent it to help you cover the costs of maintaining two domiciles. Even if the rental income doesn't cover your mortgage payments and property taxes, which it probably won't unless you've owned the home for many years, you may be able to deduct depreciation on the rental property against other income. Check the details with a tax professional.

Even if this plan costs you money for awhile, it may save you from making an expensive mistake. If you're over age 55 and have yet to use your one-time $125,000 house sale exclusion, be sure to limit the rental period to two years. Reason: to qualify for the exclusion, you must have used the property as your principal residence for three of the five years preceding the sale.

25

HEALTH CARE—MORE IMPORTANT THAN EVER

EVERYONE KNOWS THAT health care costs are going through the roof and no one—especially our political leaders—seems to know what to do about it. While the country as a whole may continue bearing the burden of an out-of-control healthcare system for some time to come, there is no reason you and your family can't take action. What the United States can't do collectively, you can certainly do individually: control your healthcare expenses. By practicing preventive medicine, by taking advantage of healthcare expense tax deductions, and by following the money saving tips at the end of this chapter, you **can** protect both your health and your pocketbook.

Preventive Medicine

Many older Americans look with suspicion at the current fitness and nutrition "crazes" and don't appreciate children who nag them about changing their habits. After all, back in the 1940s and 1950s—formative years for many of today's senior citizens, both smoking and the lunchtime cocktail were an integral part of the social scene. Granted, youth, health, and athletic prowess have been worshipped in this country since the late nineteenth century, but it is only comparatively recently that average Americans have started to make physical fitness part of their daily lives. Meanwhile insurance companies have finally come to recognize the fact that good health should be rewarded. Increasingly, Americans who don't smoke, aren't obese, and who otherwise take good care of themselves are paying lower health and life insurance premiums—not to mention fewer doctors' bills—than their devil-may-care neighbors. Quite simply, if you take care of yourself, not only will you enjoy life more and live longer, you'll spend less money on health care.

Eating Habits

The purpose of this section is not to lecture you about healthy eating; you'll have to buy another book to learn the 10 reasons why you'll be better off if you consume less fat and more fiber. The financial liability associated with obesity and bad dietary habits is, however, an issue that no guide to financial planning can ignore. The situation is quite simple: the more sensibly you eat, the less you'll spend on medical care. Not only does an apple a day keep the doctor away; it will similarly repel your insurer's actuaries and adjusters. Eating healthily doesn't preclude all gastronomic pleasure, either: you can improve your diet without restricting yourself to what's available in the health-food store. Nor must you become a teetotaler, either. There is a continuing debate in the medical community about the possible benefits of consuming a glass or two of wine each day, so you probably need not worry if you are a moderate drinker.

The best route toward improving your eating habits is to consult your general practitioner, who should be privy to the most up-to-date information about nutrition. If your doctor is worth his or her salt, he or she will steer you away from eating fads and controversial theories. The only drawback to putting yourself on a healthier diet is the fact that you will live longer. You may have to adjust your retirement income and expense projections—not a bad problem to have, particularly when you consider the alternative.

Exercise

In addition to eating well, the other sine qua non of a strong constitution is exercising regularly. Indeed, no matter how long it may have been since you've gotten any real exercise, it's never too late to start again—gradually. Studies have shown that no matter how much or how long an individual abuses his or her body, turning over a new leaf almost always has a beneficial effect.

Of course, exercise will not whiten soot-blackened lungs, or miraculously clear hardened arteries. Exercise will, however, make you feel better and will allow your body to make up for at least some of the damage that the years may have inflicted upon it. Furthermore, studies have shown that proper exercise is one of the few effective therapies for arthritis—getting those limbs moving again eventually helps to relieve stiffness. Naturally, taking a daily constitutional is not going to cure an acute case of arthritis, and some people may be suffering too severely to be able to exercise. Nonetheless, exercise does have a palliative, and to some extent a restorative effect on older bodies. And a refreshed body, like a well maintained car, will reward you by requiring fewer visits to the mechanic.

What are effective types of exercise? Walking is a good way to begin, since it doesn't require any specialized equipment—all you have to do is open your front door. Swimming and biking, which are much better for one's joints than high-impact exercises like jogging, are appropriate forms of more strenuous exercise for older Americans. Furthermore, the use of exercise machines, like Stairmasters®, exercycles, and Nautilus® machines, has become highly popular in recent years. Despite the youth-oriented image of these devices, there is no reason why seniors cannot take advantage of them. Seasoned health club and gym users usually work their way around a "circuit": they spend a certain amount of time working out on each of a succession of different machines, thereby exercising their whole bodies. If you haven't exercised recently, however, you should consult your doctor before going ahead with a program.

Using the Internal Revenue Code to Cut Your Health Care Costs

While the Tax Code could be more advantageously structured to reduce the expense of health care (and changes may well be on the way) it does offer you limited ways to reduce your medical bills.

The Medical Expense Deduction

If, at year's end, you find that your out-of-pocket medical expenses exceed 7.5 percent of your adjusted gross income (AGI), the IRS gives you some relief. Suppose you tally up your medical expenses and find that they equal 10 percent of your AGI, which is $100,000: everything above the 7.5 percent threshold—in this case $2,500—can be deducted from your tax bill. Remember to count your share of your insurance premiums as an unreimbursed expense. It is very important that you keep records of all your unreimbursed medical expenses if you want to qualify for this tax break, however. While keeping track of all those records may seem an onerous task, it's worth it to cut your health care expenses.

The healthcare travel deduction is often overlooked. If you have to travel any distance to go to a doctor or hospital, you can deduct your travel expenses as medical expenses (subject to the 7.5 percent of AGI threshold). If you use your car, either deduct the actual cost of gas and oil or take a simpler approach by using the standard mileage rate.

The Top Ten Ways to Save Money on Healthcare

These money saving tips will help you chip away at your expenses in ways both large and small. Use them all, however, and the aggregate savings will put a smile on your face and a spring in your step.

1. **Don't get sick.** Preventive medicine is the cheapest medicine. Learn how to stay healthy, then spend all of the money you save on yourself.
2. **Always maintain good health insurance coverage.** The quickest way to lose what you've accumulated over your lifetime as well as, perhaps, a large chunk of your future income, is to suffer an uninsured illness. Do whatever is necessary to maintain adequate health insurance coverage for you and every family member. If you are 65 or older, Medicare gap insurance is a must. Also, make sure your adult children have health insurance coverage through their place of employment or, if they are "between jobs," a temporary health insurance policy.
3. **Get a physical examination at regular intervals.** Preventive medicine is still about the best thing we've got going for us to maintain good health and control health care costs. Follow your doctor's suggestion to get a periodic physical examination. Chances are the poking and stabbing will show you to be in good shape. If there is a problem, it's far better (and cheaper) to know sooner rather than later.
4. **Don't wait until you get too sick to see a doctor.** Most of us are crazy when it comes to our own health. If our car

sputters, we immediately take it to a mechanic. If our dog coughs, it's off to the vet A.S.A.P. But, if we have an apparent health problem, do we go to our doctor? All too often the answer is "no," until the problem worsens. The worse the health problem, the more expensive it is going to be to you, no matter how comprehensive your health coverage. So don't postpone seeing your doctor if you start to sputter or cough.

5. **Investigate health and dental services available at a medical or dental school at no or reduced cost.** If you live near a university medical or dental school, you may be able to take advantage of health and dental services offered by the school as part of its students' training. The price is right—since the charges, if any, are nominal. Rest assured that the student who is examining or treating you is fully supervised and very diligent in treating you.
6. **Don't hesitate to rely on public health nurses for assistance when needed.** If you or a loved one requires some home care, contact your local health dept or Visiting Nurse Association (VNA) to find out what they offer and how you can qualify. You'll be surprised at the number of health programs that are available to people who need them despite all the highly publicized cutbacks in these programs. Don't give up.
7. **Try to lose weight on your own.** Consult with a doctor, buy a couple of diet books, and really try to lose weight on your own before going to an expensive weight-loss clinic. The one thing that's certain about a weight-loss clinic is that it will certainly put your wallet on a diet.
8. **Quit smoking.** Smoking is hazardous to your financial health. The habit can easily cost over $1,000 per year, not to mention what it does to your health and life insurance premiums and dental bills.
9. **Investigate alternative health plans offered by your employer.** If you are still in the workforce and fortunate enough to have an employer that offers a choice of health care plans, don't just assume that the one you have is the best. Review alternatives. Some plans may cost you less while meeting the health care needs of you and your family.

10. **Brush and floss your teeth regularly.** This suggestion can save you a lot of pain, both physical and financial. Many of the calamities that befall our teeth and gums are avoidable with regular brushing and flossing. Just remember the tacky sign that you may have seen staring you in the face as you sat in your dental chair: "You don't have to brush and floss all of your teeth, just the ones you want to keep."

26

MAKING YOUR LIFELONG TRAVEL PLANS COME TRUE

ONE OF THE most striking developments of the twentieth century has been the increasing global mobility of average Americans, a trend accompanied by the rise of a multi-billion-dollar travel industry. After a century of growth and evolution, the travel industry is adapting to the latest important trend—the maturing American population.

The travel industry is determined to make itself attractive to older Americans for the obvious reason: the continuous growth in the number of affluent retirees with disposable income. As you approach your retirement years, you should find yourself presented with a rich array of interesting travel possibilities—often at a discount. This chapter will help you understand and take advantage of the various options available to you.

Plan Ahead

The first question in planning your intended travel: how do you want to go? A prearranged tour? The cost is attractive. Go solo? Too lonely and expensive for most. With a companion? You'd better pick the right one.

Some mature travellers welcome the prospect of a tour. Others find the very idea unbearable. And, while some may find being left to one's devices in a foreign city frightening, others find it exhilarating. Of course, you may prefer a compromise: traveling with a group to desired destinations—countries or cities—while planning your own itinerary once you arrive.

Group Benefits

There is safety *and* savings in numbers. Not to mention the peace-of-mind that comes with traveling via a pre-packaged group tour plan in which professional guides handle the headaches of getting you and your luggage there and back. If you deal with a reputable, established tour company, you should be able to leave your worries behind.

Goodbye, Columbus

If you prefer to plan your own trip, you probably have a particular destination in mind. If, however, you know that you want to travel, but haven't already chosen some specific destination consult the travel pages of the Sunday *New York Times.* It contains practical information about the mechanics of getting you from one place to another, lists of hotels, inns, bed and breakfasts, resorts, and airline ticket deals. Also, it includes features focusing on the art, literature, cuisine, and music of various countries and cities. So, inspire yourself. Visit places about which you had never even dreamt, and get a feel for the character of different destinations. Be careful, however. The travel business is rife with fly-by-night operators who in some instances are downright fraudulent.

Good planning, naturally enough, follows from being well-informed. Be flexible. A great deal of the pleasure in traveling outside of a tour group is to be found in the unforeseen opportunities the do-it-yourself approach presents.

There are many sources of information for planning your trip—home and away. Your local library should have any number of informative travel guides, and a number of informational booklets and pamphlets published by the federal Government are helpful. (See the end of this chapter.) And, of course, don't overlook your local travel agency. A good travel agent should be able to help you plan an affordable and interesting trip whichever way you decide to go.

Before you pack your bags, remember not to throw financial caution to the wind. Nine times out of ten, travel transforms the average savings-oriented couple into big spenders. While abroad, ordinarily frugal Over-50s all too often patronize the best restaurants and shops, spend inordinate sums of money on symphony, theatre and opera seats, and take enough cab rides to make even a New Yorker's head spin. As if that isn't enough, they buy the most expensive exotica for their grandchildren. What's a five-year-old going to do with that silky sarong? Believe me, it could happen to you.

How can you protect your savings from this variety of temporary insanity? You could stay home. But that would be boring. Instead, why not take the following money-saving travel tips. Whether traveling near or far, they'll show you how to get there and back without saying "bon voyage" to your savings.

- **Rent an RV rather than buying one.** Unless you are going to travel throughout the year, you are probably better off renting a recreational vehicle for your vacations and periodic sojourns rather than buying one. They're an eyesore in your driveway anyway.
- **Same goes for boats.**
- **If you plan to rent a car overseas, check with your automobile insurer to see if your coverage can be extended to include cars driven overseas.** If you can avoid having to purchase short-term coverage from the car rental agency, you will most certainly save yourself some money. Make sure, however, that your insurer provides you with complete documentation; you don't want to have the rental agency clerk insist that you buy an overpriced in-house policy and find yourself unable to prove the fact that you are indeed already covered.
- **Take the train or bus instead of a plane.** Airlines are continually raising their prices, so consider surface travel. While Amtrak isn't exactly the Orient Express, even in America you may find traveling by rail to be a sensible alternative to flying. In Europe, of course, rail service is almost always superior. When you add the time it takes to get to and from the airport, surface travel for shorter distances becomes even more appealing. Unlike airports, train and bus terminals are almost always centrally located in cities.
- **Make your airline reservations well in advance.** The cheapest airfares go fast, so plan ahead and make your reservation as soon as your plans are firm.

- **Stay over a Saturday night on airline trips.** Airfares are generally much cheaper if you stay over a Saturday night. The extra night in a hotel is usually a fraction of the airfare savings.
- **Rather than hail a cab, take a bus or subway to and from the airport.** Most airports are accessible via mass transit, so rather than taking a cab or renting a car, you could probably save money by "taking the A-train." If you are unfamiliar with your destination's mass transit system, your travel agent should be able to help.
- **Share cabs to and from the airport or train station.** If you're in a cab queue, you are probably in line with some people who would love to share the cost of a cab with you. Don't be shy about asking.
- **Ask a relative or friend to drive you to and from the airport.** The price is right.
- **If you can wait until the last minute, check with travel discounters.** The airlines, air charter companies, and cruise lines would rather fill a seat or berth for a song than have it remain empty. Several travel agencies specialize in this deeply discounted travel. If time is on your side, it's time to check them out.
- **Fly standby.** If you've got the time, flying standby can result in big savings.
- **Give up your seat if your flight is overbooked.** Airlines regularly overbook flights, so they often ask for volunteers to give up their seats. If you can spare the time, you will get to your destination on the next available flight and you'll be amply rewarded—typically with a round-trip ticket anywhere the airline flies.
- **Use a pay phone to make calls rather than pay the hotel fee for the privilege of making a call from your room.** All you have to do is stroll down to the lobby to make your calls: you will save money (if you have a telephone credit card) by avoiding hotel phone service charges and get some exercise in the process. In fact, some hotel managements charge guests for using the in-room phone even if the call doesn't go through.
- **Go out to get your meals (breakfast, etc.) rather than getting room service at the hotel.** A continental breakfast at the New York hotel can cost $20 dollars! You could walk a

half-block and get the same combination of orange juice, croissant or muffin and coffee for about $2.00. So as soon as you check into your hotel, case out the immediate neighborhood in order to find some good, affordable eateries.

- **Seek out off-beat restaurants favored by locals rather than those catering to tourists.** If you really want to enjoy the flavor of a city or resort area, ask the locals where they go out to eat. The last place they would probably mention are tourist restaurants, establishments offering mediocre fare at high prices.
- **Never use the hotel in-room mini-bar.** I would rather expire from thirst than pay absurdly high prices for pathetically small bottles of aqua vitae.
- **Take snacks on a flight.** So that after a long trip during which they don't feed you enough, you won't be tempted to buy $4.00 hot dogs at the airport when you deplane.
- **Join frequent flyer programs.** You have nothing to lose by joining an airline's frequent flyer program. You never know—you might accumulate enough mileage to qualify for a free flight or some other freebie.
- **Take a good cause vacation.** A growing number of environmental, religious, and other groups are sponsoring trips that combine vacation with good works. You can see interesting parts of the world at low cost while also doing the world some good.
- **Tap your alumni organization for good housing deals.** Many college alumni organizations have reciprocal arrangements with other alumni associations to offer low cost housing in many locales. Educate yourself on any programs offered by your alma mater.
- **Avoid making purchases in tourist/vacation areas.** Souvenirs are wonderful, but you can probably buy the T-shirt or whatever for a lot less if you find a store that is not located in the midst of a tourist/vacation Mecca. The same can be said for other items that you may want to purchase during your vacation.
- **Inquire about discounts when making hotel/motel reservations.** You have to ask, because the reservations agents aren't going to be forthcoming with the information. But often

discounts on room rates are available for members of certain organizations, seniors, weekend stays, and so on. Be sure to speak up and ask.

- **Plan your travel so that you can take advantage of hotel/motel and other travel discounts.** If you are planning a trip, find out whether you might be eligible for various discounts. You may be eligible for discounts depending upon where you travel, the time that you travel, and the duration of your stay. Don't pass up valuable discounts through poor travel planning.
- **Obtain air fare quotations from two or three sources including the airline itself.** The airfare system is a mess, and the consumer is at its mercy. The only way to make sure you are getting a good fare is to check several different sources. You'll be amazed at the differences in the rates that you are quoted, but, by comparison shopping you will be able to buy your ticket with some confidence that you are getting a fair deal.
- **Never buy anything in an airport gift shop.** With the exception of newspapers, magazines, and books avoid buying anything at an airport gift shop. If you want to bestow gifts on family members, the only thing you can be sure of about what you buy in an airport gift shop is that you are paying top dollar.
- **Never buy anything in a hotel gift shop.** See the above comments on airport gift shops. They are equally applicable to hotel gift shops.
- **Buy airline tickets as far in advance as possible.** Generally, the earlier you purchase airline tickets, the more money you will save. Check with your travel agent or the airlines, but the early bird usually flies cheapest.
- **If you're buying bargains overseas, be sure to consider the customs duty on any bargains you want to pay.** Many overseas travelers have encountered a rude awakening when they find out how much in customs duties they will have to pay for purchases made overseas. When you are facing a revenue hungry customs officer, these items won't seem like such a bargain. So be sure to factor in the effect of customs duties when you shop overseas.

- **Before traveling overseas, check the local price of any items you intend to purchase during your sojourn abroad.** What may seem like a bargain when you are several thousand miles from home and basking in a romantic climate may actually have cost significantly less had you purchased it stateside. Therefore, if you plan to make an expensive purchase overseas, check on what it costs locally before you make your trip so that you'll know whether you are truly getting a bargain.
- **Join hotel "frequent stayer" programs.** Just like the airlines, hotels and motels want to build up and reward a loyal clientele. If you travel more than sproadically, join the hotel/motel frequent guest programs. Who knows, you might get some free lodging.
- **Four nights might get you one or more nights free.** If you're going to stay at a hotel or motel for several nights, find out if they offer a free night or nights for guests on an extended trip.
- **Consider trip cancellation insurance.** If you foresee the possibility that a prepaid vacation may have to be canceled, purchasing trip cancellation insurance may end up saving you a lot of money.
- **You don't have to go on a tour to get travel bargains.** While group travel tours are a very economical way to travel, many people don't want to travel in a herd. If you are a rugged individualist, look for travel packages that offer "tour rates" but don't oblige you to spend your vacation listening to some shower curtain ring salesperson tell you about his kids.
- **Go to resorts in the off season.** If you play your cards right, you can visit a resort just before the season rates begin or just after they end. You might enjoy a less-crowded resort when you visit in the off season, and you'll certainly enjoy the money you save.
- **Stay at budget hotels and motels.** There is a lot of difference in the cost of a typical luxury hotel or motel and the rapidly growing cadre of budget hostelries. Most people who have stayed in lower cost lodgings swear by them—that's why budget hotels and motels are thriving in the midst of a flat economy. Remember, when you go on vacation, you generally

spend so little time in your room that you don't really need antique furniture or an entertainment center.

- **Rent a condo or vacation cottage rather than staying in a hotel.** If you are planning to vacation in an area that has condos, vacation cottages, or other types of rental accomodation, compare their prices with those of local hotels or inns. You may find—especially if you have a large brood or group of friends with you—that renting a cottage or house—is a very economical solution. Shop around for the best price, however, and be prepared to haggle with the renter—many resort areas are suffering from overbuilding, and rates are quite competitive. I've known some people who have vacationed for the last five years in Florida and have watched the rental rates for their condo decline with each passing year.
- **Stay with friends or relatives.** Cut way down on vacation costs by staying with relatives or friends. If they reside near a popular vacation destination, they are probably used to having people stay over.
- **Negotiate hotel room rates.** While some people are good hagglers, others are hesitant to plunge into the give-and-take of serious bargaining. Don't let yourself be intimidated: like the sale price of a house, the rental rate on a hotel or motel room is eminently negotiable.
- **Double check your hotel/motel bill.** Don't just blithely accept your hotel or motel bill when you check out. Check it out for errors.
- **Make sure you are adequately insured if you are traveling abroad.** Before you take a trip overseas, check to make sure that your insurance coverage, particularly medical insurance, includes overseas travel. Most policies are effective in foreign countries, but you should double check anyway. You don't want to get appendicitis in Azerbaijan and find out that you have to pay the hospital in cash before the doctors will operate. Senior citizens take note: Medicare provides almost no coverage outside of the United States and its territories. Ask your travel agent or travel organizations about obtaining supplementary insurance for your trip.
- **Don't buy a yearly airline pass unless you are going to use it often enough to justify the cost.** Sometimes what initially seems to be a great purchase ends up becoming a

costly mistake. Yearly airline passes can be attractive to people who can make good use of them. Don't buy one, however, until you have carefully planned your itinerary so that planned travel is sufficient to justify the cost of the ticket.

- **Check into fly-drive packages which combine airfares with accommodations and car rentals.** The airlines are in cahoots with the rental car agencies, and you can benefit from this situation. Fly-drive packages can combine discounted airfares with discounted rental cars. If you are going to need to rent a car when you reach your destination, be sure to investigate some of these convenient packages.
- **Bed and breakfast it—try it, you'll like it.** Some people turn up their noses at bed-and-breakfast establishments, but the better B-and-Bs are the inheritors of the best traditions of the old fashioned inn. They range in size and luxury from a places that consist of a couple of spare rooms in a private home to luxurious establishments that differ from hotels only in their lack of a restaurant. Many B-and-Bs are in restored eighteenth- or nineteenth-century houses and have great historic character. These lodgings have a great deal more charm and personality than most hotels, and their prices have a good deal of charm, too.
- **Find someone to travel with you.** If you are single, you probably realize that traveling alone costs a great deal more on a per-person basis than does traveling with a companion. This is especially true with accommodations, so if you have a friend who is willing to split your planned trip's expenses with you, convince them to come along.
- **When making purchases abroad, find out how to avoid paying local taxes.** If you think that sales taxes are bad in your home state, you will be horrified by the taxes that foreign countries levy upon *their* consumers. In many cases, however, these countries—well aware of the importance of tourist dollars—have established methods to reimburse travelers for domestic taxes like the infamous Value Added Tax (VAT).
- **Interrupt newspaper service if you're going to be away from home for an extended period.** If you're going to be on vacation or on an extended business trip, save some money and, perhaps, avoid a burglary by having your newspaper delivery service interrupted until you get back.

- **Let neighbors know when you're going to be traveling.** One of the best deterrents against burglary is a vigilant neighbor. Be sure to let your neighbors know when and how long you'll be gone. It just may prevent an unwanted and expensive interruption of your travels.
- **Don't Forget:**
  - * Always get a second and even a third opinion on what the most efficient and least expensive way to travel is.
  - * Always carry your prescription medications in your carry-on travel bag, not in the luggage you check through.
  - * Consider trip cancellation insurance. You never know when your children might need a babysitter.

Getting There

Cruising

If you like the idea of traveling, but hate checking in and out of hotels, consider taking a cruise. Once you ensconce yourself aboard your vessel, you can look forward to visiting a number of ports-of-call without having to heft a suitcase once. Despite their popular image, cruises are not limited to the Caribbean either, so if taking a party boat from one tropical island to another does not appeal to you, you could choose amongst ships cruising the Mediterranean, the Baltic, the New England coast, or in a number of inland waterways including the Rhine and Loire rivers.

TAKE A FREIGHTER

If you have the time—30 to 180 days—a tanker can take you to the *most* exotic ports of call for half the hustle and bustle of a cruise ship. The food and accommodations of many freighters rival any ship at sea, and it is a once-in-a-lifetime experience.

TRAVEL TO LEARN

In the eighteenth century, many young aristocrats—often accompanied by a tutor—embarked on a "grand tour" of the continent to complete their education. Now, in the late 20th century, mature Americans of more modest means can similarly combine travel with education. A number of programs, many of them conducted by major universities, give travelers the chance to tour a country or region accompanied by a scholar specializing in its art, culture or history. Because Americans are enjoying longer and longer retirements, many seniors have chosen to continue their education in their later years. If the idea of exploring particular ideas, topics or academic disciplines appeals to you, you may find combining travel with education an exciting possibility. For instance, suppose that you were interested in studying Hellenic architecture. You might be able to cruise the Aegean sea, and visit a number of important ruins, accompanied by a distinguished architectural historian.

If educational tours interest you, you should contact your college's or university's alumni office—many institutions of higher education sponsor tours of this type with faculty members. Another route you could take is to contact the Elderhostel program. Elderhostel sponsors programs based on university campuses; rather than going on a tour, participants travel to a campus and are housed in dormitories there. In the mornings participants take classes; on afternoons and weekends, they can take part in organized trips or travel individually. Elderhostel's address is 80 Boylston Street, Boston, MA 02116.

Traveling with Grandchildren

Taking trips with your grandchildren can be an excellent way of cultivating relationships with the younger members of your family. You should remember, however, that the children's interests will most likely be quite different from yours. You will have to plan your trip carefully, so that all concerned, both young and old, enjoy themselves and don't become bored or irritable. (Avoid long hours visiting art museums.) Do consult with your travel companions (as well as their parents) about itineraries. You might be in for something of a surprise. Children often choose points of interest that will appeal to you too, while other sites, described by adult travel guide writers as "perfect for children," hold all the interest of a deflated balloon.

Useful Government Publications on International Travel

The U.S. government provides some excellent publications that will help you plan your international travel.

Health Information for International Travel is a comprehensive listing of immunization requirements of foreign governments. In addition, it gives the U.S. Public Health Service's recommendations on immunizations and other health precautions for the international traveler. Copies are available for $6.00 from the Superintendent of Documents, U.S. Government Printing Office, Washington, D.C. 20402-9325; (202) 783-3238.

Know Before You Go, Customs Hints for Returning U.S. Residents gives detailed information on U.S. Customs regulations, including duty rates. Single copies are available free from any local customs office or by writing to the Department of the Treasury, U.S. Customs Service, P.O. Box 7407, Washington, D.C. 20044; (202) 927-6724.

Travelers' Tips on Bringing Food, Plant, and Animal Products into the United States explains what you can and can't bring home from your travels. This pamphlet may be obtained free of charge from the U.S. Department of Agriculture, Document Management Branch, Room G110, 6505 Belcrest Road, Hyattsville, Maryland 20782; tel. (301) 436-8633.

Your Trip Abroad provides basic travel information—tips on passports, visas, immunizations, and more. It will help you prepare for your trip and make it as trouble-free as possible. This publication may be ordered for $1.25 from the Superintendent of Documents, U.S. Government Printing Office, Washington, D.C. 20402; tel. (202) 783-3238.

A Safe Trip Abroad gives travel security advice for any traveler, but particularly for those who plan trips to areas high in crime or terrorism. This publication may be ordered for $1.00 from the Superintendent of Documents, U.S. Government Printing Office, Washington, D.C. 20402-9325; tel. (202) 783-3238.

Foreign Entry Requirements lists visa and other entry requirements of foreign countries and tells how to apply for visas and tourist cards. This pamphlet may be purchased for 50 cents from the Consumer Information Center, Dept. 454Y, Pueblo, CO 81009; (719) 948-3334.

Key Officers of Foreign Service Posts gives addresses, telephone, telex, and FAX numbers for all U.S. embassies and consulates. A yearly subscription to this publication, may be obtained for $5.00 from the Superintendent of Documents, U.S. Government Printing Office, Washington, D.C. 20402-9371; tel. (202) 783-3238.

Background Notes are brief, factual pamphlets on each of 170 countries. They give current information on each country's people, culture, geography, history, government, economy, and political conditions. They also include a factual profile, travel notes, a country map, and a suggested reading list. These pamphlets may be purchased for $1.00 each from the Superintendent of Documents, U.S. Government Printing Office, Washington, D.C. 20402-9325; tel. (202) 783-3238.

27

WORKING IN RETIREMENT: IT'S A WHOLE NEW BALLGAME

SOME PEOPLE SPEND their entire working lives looking forward to retirement, and many people enjoy giving up the hassle of the hustle and bustle. I'm sure you've seen the "no hurry, no worry, no boss, no phone" license plates for retirees.

But for many others, the transition from working to the leisure life isn't as easy as putting down a briefcase and picking up a tennis racquet. Having worked for so long, they now find a void that no amount of golf or travel can fill.

Other retirees soon discover that their pensions and personal savings aren't sufficient to support them in the manner to which they've become accustomed. (Contrary to what the advertisements might lead you to believe, if you see anyone over 60 working behind the counter of a fast food restaurant, they probably aren't doing it just for the job satisfaction.)

For one reason or another, many "retirees" at some point return to work, either full- or part-time. Some start their own businesses or return to work for the companies they retired from, either as paid employees, consultants, or volunteers. Others embark on totally new careers. And many others—those driven back into the work force by financial necessity—take any jobs they can find.

Each option has its own benefits and rewards, and each raises different questions and has different financial repercussions. Yet that fact is that more and more "retirees" than ever before are going back to work after they begin drawing pension or Social Security checks. The following table shows the percentage of seniors who are still working by sex and marital status:

Percentage of Persons Age 65 and Over Who Are Still Working

Status	*Percentage Working*
Married:	
Males	17.5%
Females	7.4%
Single:	
Males	20.7
Females	10.9
Widowed, Divorced or Married with Spouse Absent:	
Males	*11.6*
Females	*8.2*

Source: U.S. Bureau of Labor Statistics, 1988 data.

If you intend to continue working (or return to work) in retirement—either because you want to or out of financial necessity—take some time to realistically assess your work experience and marketability. Among the key questions:

- What kind of employment might be available to someone with your experience, desires, skills and needs?
- How long do you want to work?
- When will you want to begin to taper off—and how quickly?
- Do you want to take some new direction in your career?
- Is now the time to try that certain something that you'd always wished you could do?

KEY POINT: The earlier you can start shaping your thoughts into some kind of tangible plan, the better. If you anticipate a work activity that will take some investment on your part (like starting your own business), the earlier you can start setting aside the necessary funds, the better your chances of reaching your goals. If little or no investment will be needed, you'll have that much more time to establish extra reserve funds to see you through should the business venture not work out.

If You Must Work to Make Ends Meet

The need to continue working—or to return to work—out of financial necessity is a situation that faces millions of retirees. Many Americans reach retirement age without having accumulated sufficient resources to be able to afford to stop working. Other retirees watch their incomes being eroded by inflation and return to the workforce to make up for lost purchasing power. Unfortunately, it's quite likely an increasing number of retirees will find themselves in this boat in coming years because of rising inflation, reductions in pension benefits, declining investment returns and increased life expectancies.

If you are now or expect to be in this position, the first order of business is to determine how much you need to earn. Remember: Your goal should be to earn enough both to meet current living expenses and to set aside additional savings for the future so that you can eventually taper off and retire completely.

The extent of your financial needs will dictate the kind and duration of the job you will be seeking. While it's difficult to make these projections at this stage in your life, it's nevertheless crucial—and you will probably discover that your financial situation isn't as bad as you thought.

Once your income needs are clearly defined, you can then begin to search for the appropriate kind of employment. The first place to look is your current employer or, if you have already retired, your former employer. Below are some other ideas to help guide you toward a satisfying job that will meet your immediate and longer term financial goals.

Most Important: Don't get discouraged by your situation. You are by no means alone. What's more, many older Americans have found that working in retirement provides enormous personal satisfaction as well as the obvious financial rewards.

Challenging Jobs for Retirees

Jobs are becoming increasingly available to older Americans as more companies recognize the excellent skills and work habits that retirees offer. Finding a challenging and fulfilling position that pays relatively well is another matter, however. Here are some of the best bets for retirees who want more than just a "job" and a paycheck:

CONSULTING WORK

Whether they retire in their fifties or later, many retirees decide to build on their particular skills and expertise to create new jobs that will challenge them in retirement. One way to do this is by becoming an independent consultant.

Consulting lets you use the knowledge and experience you gained in your preretirement career without returning to your old job. Of course, many consulting jobs result in offers for permanent positions. But in the meantime, you'll have had the chance to "try out" the company (and the company will have had the chance to try you out) before deciding. Many retiree/consultants also like being able to increase their incomes without making any long-term commitments to any one employer.

TEACHING POSITIONS

Another way to use your knowledge is to go into teaching, which many people find interesting and rewarding. Severe teaching shortages have prompted many states to institute alternative certification standards, making it relatively easy for anyone with a college degree to teach. Programs for younger children or children with mental or physical disabilities may be willing to hire assistant teachers with even less formal training. And many colleges are anxious to hire lecturers who bring valuable "real world" experience to the classroom.

EXECUTIVE "TEMPS"

Once limited to secretarial and clerical fields, temporary help agencies today place people in a growing array of executive, professional, and highly skilled positions. What's more, temporary help firms offer a wide range of work arrangements, with different hours and in different work environments.

If you want to make some extra money in a hurry, you may be able to find an assignment where you'll put in 70 hours before the job ends in a week. Or, if you want to play golf every day, you might be able to find a longer-term assignment working afternoons only. And while not all temporary agencies offer interesting, professional-level jobs, temp firms are hard to beat for convenience and flexibility.

Deciding to temp will probably shorten your job search considerably. And you may be eligible for health and life insurance—either company-paid or at a group rate—that you wouldn't be able to get from a part-time employer. You seldom have to make a long-term commitment, although many temporary positions can lead to permanent part-time jobs.

WORKING PART-TIME FOR YOUR PREVIOUS EMPLOYER

A growing number of large corporations has developed programs to hire their own retired employees part-time to fill in on vacations, to train new workers and to lend a hand during busy seasons. If you're lucky enough to have retired from one of these companies, be sure to check out these opportunities.

Key Advantages: You won't have to hunt for a job and learn your way around an unfamiliar company. And the company is spared the trouble and expense of screening, hiring and training a new employee. Some companies also continue life and/or health insurance for their retirees who work part-time and many are willing to let you work limited hours so that your earnings don't reduce your Social Security retirement benefits (see page 381). Many retirees find that returning to work with their former employers gives them steady income, flexible hours, a chance to maintain their social contacts at the office and a satisfying way to fill spare time.

VOLUNTEER WORKING ABROAD

Volunteer work abroad can provide glamour, excitement and satisfaction. Many of these opportunities are associated with churches and organizations that combine private and public programs.

With most of these opportunities, the transportation is free. But once you get to your overseas destination, about all you can count on is subsistence income. Clothing, equipment, utensils and amenities will be your responsibility or that of the sponsoring organization. This is a personal choice that should be regarded as a commitment of your religious belief or humanitarian concern.

For educators, there can be special opportunities through professional organizations. Those associated with the armed forces can teach at military bases. College affiliations provide what amounts to an exchange—you get room and board and a modest stipend while you take over from the local pedagogue who spends a year or so in the United States. These are challenges and extensions of your lifetime work. Increasingly, shorter programs are funded by foundations, trade groups and business firms.

For executives and professionals, some of the best opportunities are offered by the International Executive Service Corps, P.O. Box 10005, 333 Ludlow Street, Stamford, CT 06904-2005; (203) 967-6000. This organization is looking for retirees who have had hands-on experience in business and/or government, are willing to live abroad and can afford to be away for six months or more.

Volunteers act as advisors to private enterprises in developing countries. Among the most challenging assignments today are missions to help privatize and rebuild the former state-run economies of Central and Eastern Europe. The U.S. retirees typically receive no pay but you do get a per diem allowance based on the cost of living in the country of assignment that should be sufficient to permit comfortable living. Knowledge of a foreign language is helpful and special skills are usually a must for these programs.

On the Home Front: The Service Corps of Retired Executives (SCORE) offers similar opportunities for retired executives in this country. SCORE is sponsored by the U.S. Small Business Administration. For more information, get in touch with your nearest SBA regional office.

The Job Search

If you haven't changed jobs in a long time or you've been out of the work force for several years, the idea of entering the job market again can be intimidating, especially when you're so used to your old job that you wouldn't know where else to look.

There's no wrong place to begin. Unless you disliked your job, it might be a good idea to check with your former employer about what sort of opportunities the organization offers and about whether you may be eligible for free outplacement counseling. Other good places to start are your local chamber of commerce, the library, public and private employment agencies and local agencies on aging.

NETWORKING

One mistake that's common among retirees (and unemployed people generally) is hiding their plans from their acquaintances. Don't be afraid to use all your contacts, both personal and professional, to help you in your job search.

Some people call this networking. Ask for help from relatives, friends and fellow members of any groups you've been involved with in your community, your college or professional/business associations. Talk with former co-workers, employers, customers, suppliers, business contacts and neighbors. Compile a list of organizations for which you'd like to work and the names and titles of people to contact for interviews or information. You'll be surprised at how effective networking can be when you're looking for a good job, whether it's a full-time or part-time position.

TAP JOB TRAINING ASSISTANCE PROGRAMS

Many communities offer job training and placement programs for senior citizens. Some are financed by federal and state grants, but most are sponsored by local business groups. Programs' aims and techniques vary, but any should help you brush up on writing cover letters and resumes, as well as interviewing techniques.

When you've defined yourself by your job for so long, it's natural to feel lost and uncertain without it. Job assistance programs explain what jobs are available, how to put your best foot forward and where to look and whom to see for work opportunities. Don't overlook these valuable resources.

Starting a Retirement Business?

What working person hasn't thought from time to time of starting his or her own business? Retired people aren't much different. Some quickly grow bored with the slower pace of retirement and want to get back in the action. Some find their retirement savings inadequate and want to supplement their incomes or increase their nest eggs. Many others leave their jobs earlier than anticipated due to layoffs, early retirement incentives or other business changes. And some people dream all their lives of changing careers, turning hobbies into businesses or pursuing new professional challenges. For the first time in their lives, they have the time to devote to starting a business.

If, for whatever reason, you're one of the growing number of Americans thinking of starting their own businesses later in life, some realistic self-assessment should precede your decision. While the freedom of being your own boss and the thrill of building a business from the ground up can be extremely fulfilling—and sometimes financially rewarding—the challenges and pitfalls of owning and managing a business should not be underestimated. If you go by the statistics, over half of all small businesses launched in the United States end up failing in the first few years of operation.

Before you risk all or part of your life savings trying to turn your dream of starting your own business into reality, consider the following four questions. Each is essential to launching a successful business.

1. *Does your idea fit your experience and desires?* One clear danger sign is having only a desire to go into business for yourself—without a clearly defined idea of the kind of venture you want to start. In order to be successful, you must enjoy the business, be able to manage the business and be able to earn a decent living from the business.

   One clear advantage older people bring to business start-ups is a wealth of experience that should be transferrable to the new venture.
2. *Do you have the stamina?* Business start-ups require an enormous amount of energy. Expect to work 60 to 70 hours a week or more to get your dream off the ground. While the excitement of running your own show can sustain you for many hours, you need to ask yourself if you have the stamina to keep up this pace for a long time, years perhaps.
3. *Are you a good salesperson?* One of the biggest problems that many entrepreneurs encounter is a lack of sales ability. Older workers and retirees often go into business for themselves thinking that their years of business experience are sufficient to ensure success. Many, however, lack the ability to sell because they were never actively involved in marketing before.

   Remember: When you start your venture, chances are you won't be able to afford to hire professionals to sell your products or services. You have to perform a variety of tasks yourself, of which selling is often the most crucial.
4. *Can you afford it?* Sadly, stories abound of retired people who risked their retirement nest eggs to start businesses —only to lose their life savings in the process. You must carefully and realistically estimate the amount of capital you will need to start and grow your business.

   Keep in mind that most entrepreneurs grossly underestimate how much money is really needed. While some businesses are a lot less expensive to start than others, they all require sufficient capital as well as hard work, talent, and luck. As exciting as starting your own business may be, the risk of a major financial setback in your later years is usually too big a risk to take.

Age Discrimination: Know Your Rights

Just about any job that's open to anyone else is open to you. In fact, employers of 20 or more workers cannot fire or refuse to hire anyone age 40 or older simply because of age, except for the rare positions for which age is a bona fide occupational qualification. Employers cannot favor younger workers in pay, promotions or fringe benefits, and unions cannot deny membership to older persons or refuse to refer them for jobs. Nor can employment agencies refuse to refer a job applicant for an opening because of his or her age. And help-wanted advertisements cannot contain statements of age preference.

The federal Age Discrimination in Employment Act also protects most workers from mandatory retirement. And it prohibits employers from using the terms of a pension, retirement, seniority or insurance plan to force people to retire before they're ready. And as long as you continue working, your employer can't force you to sign up for Medicare as your primary health insurance. You must be allowed to choose between Medicare and your employer's health plan for your primary coverage.

In spite of these protections, many seniors sense that they are being discriminated against because of their age. If you think you've been the victim of unlawful age discrimination, contact the nearest office of the U.S. Equal Employment Opportunity Commission or your state fair employment agency.

How Working Affects Your Social Security Benefits

Many retirees who are receiving Social Security retirement benefits work full- or part-time to supplement their income. There's no prohibition against working while you're getting Social Security, but your benefits will be reduced for any year in which your earnings from employment or self-employment exceed certain limits. This reduction, called the retirement earnings test or simply the earnings test penalty, works like an added tax ranging from 33 percent of your earnings if you're between age 65 and 69 to 50 percent of your earnings if you're 64 or younger.

There are, however, two exceptions: (1) Benefits for working people age 70 and older are not reduced, regardless of earnings. (2) A special rule applies in the year you retire, so that your initial benefit payments will not be reduced on account of your last few months of preretirement earnings. (See Chapter 3 for more details on how earnings affect your Social Security benefits.)

28

WHAT TO DO WITH THE FAMILY HOMESTEAD

YOUR OLDER YEARS can be a time of real change and dislocation. Your children finally move out for good (hopefully!). You and your spouse retire from your jobs, and in short you find your whole pattern of living changing. As these changes occur, so do your needs, including your need for housing. Now that your brood has flown the coop, you may have a whole lot of unnecessary living space. It's time to face one of the hardest later-life questions of all—what to do with the family homestead.

There are two main approaches to this question, the hard-headedly rational one and the emotional one. While you should give more credence to the rational voice, don't ignore the emotional one. Otherwise, you may do something that makes a great deal of financial sense, like purchasing a condo in the Sunbelt, and yet find yourself isolated and unhappy in an unfamiliar community. In order to make the right decision, you first need to do a little arithmetic.

The Dollar Price

Add up your current living costs, including mortgage payments, property taxes, and any expenses you incur by continuing to live at your current residence. If you own a home, there is an additional cost of staying there—the "opportunity cost." The more equity you have in your home, the greater your opportunity cost for staying put. Why is this? The more equity you have in your home, the greater the amount of capital you could (if you wish or need to) take out when you sell it. Assuming you then buy a cheaper house or condominium, you could invest the excess capital. By staying put, you are losing the income you would garner by moving into less expensive quarters and investing the savings.

Once you have totalled up all these costs, contrast them with what your living costs would be if you moved to another locale (or to a less expensive home in your current locale). Subtract this sum from the costs of staying in your current residence, and look at the difference. This amount is how much more you will pay to remain at the family homestead.

Finally, you should try to estimate your home's potential for appreciation. Currently the real estate market is depressed in many areas—it is burned out after the overheated 1980s. Yet the market will likely move upwards again during the coming decade. No one knows, however, for how long or by how much the market will rise. If you have good reasons for believing your house may appreciate in value, however, you may find that it's worthwhile to hold onto it. It's conceivable that, in a robust economy, you could get a better return—in appreciation of the price of your home—than you could by investing the profit from its sale.

The Emotional Price

Once you have figured out the cost of staying put, you need to determine—and this is the hard part—whether the emotional costs of moving outweigh the financial costs of staying put. Naturally, this is a subjective decision. If you have moved around a lot already, you may not be particularly tied to a specific house or town. If, however, your family has owned the same house since 1853, you may have very different feelings about leaving. Whatever the outcome, doing this exercise will force you to confront the financial ramifications of whatever course you choose to take. By all means take your time before making the decision.

Selling Your Home

If you decide it is indeed time to move, there are a number of issues relating to the sale of your home of which you should be aware. Some are considerations for anyone selling a home, regardless of age. Other matters, like how to make effective use of the over-55 $125,000 home sale exclusion, are particular to older Americans.

The $125,000 Exclusion

One of the real benefits of passing the half-century mark is that Congress rewards your longevity with a very nice tax break when you sell your home. Like any activity that comes under the purview of the Internal Revenue Code, there are a few complications, but they can be mastered if you take the time to understand the basic concepts.

When an over-55 taxpayer sells a home, as long as it is his or her "principal residence," the first $125,000 of gain made on the sale is tax-free. For tax purposes, a "principal residence" doesn't actually have to be your principal residence at the time you sell it. As long as the dwelling was your real home for three out of the past five years, it qualifies as your principal residence.

You are, however, only given one shot at this tax break—and are automatically disqualified if your spouse has already used it—so use it judiciously. If either you or your spouse do not qualify for the $125,000 exclusion for any other reasons, the IRS will let you take it as a couple, as long as one of you meets the requirements. Remember, however, that state income taxes may still be assessed on the sale of your home. You'll need to consult your own state's tax code to determine how it treats this issue.

Other Ways to Minimize Your Taxable Gain When Selling Your Home

Besides using the $125,000 exclusion, there are a number of other ways for you to keep your tax bill to a minimum. First, maximize your basis (the sum arrived at whan you add the expenses you incurrerd in buying and improving your home). The higher your basis, the less taxable profit you will have when you sell your home, because your gain is the sale price minus the basis. So dig up records of every penny you spent on home improvements—every penny you can prove you spent to increase the value of your dwelling will be one less that can be taxed. Don't confuse improvements with maintenance, however. Putting on a new coat of paint is maintenance; adding dormer windows to increase light and space in your attic is an improvement.

Similarly, you can lower your gain by deducting advertising

costs, appraisal fees, attorney's fees, broker's commissions, title and survey fees from the proceeds of your home sale.

Let's face it, though: unless you've incurred astronomical closing expenses or practically rebuilt your home from the ground up, these methods may save you a few thousand dollars, but they still may leave you with a fair amount of capital-gains exposure. What other tax breaks are available?

The Rollover Break

When you buy a home that is worth more than the one you just sold, you can postpone paying taxes on the proceeds of the previous home sale. Suppose you had used the rollover several times over your adult life to postpone capital-gains taxes, but are now moving into a smaller, less expensive home? Can you limit your exposure to capital gains tax when you finally realize all those years' worth of accumulated profit? If you deploy your $125,000 exclusion properly, you can still benefit from the rollover tax postponement. Suppose you sold your home for $200,000—realizing $145,000 in accumulated profits and planned to purchase a $90,000 condominium. With the $125,000 exclusion, you can claim only $75,000 in profit. Now, the $90,000 condominium costs more than the adjusted sales price of the house. Technically, the condominium costs more than your house's sale price and presto!—you have made a rollover. You owe no tax on $125,000 of the home sale and have postponed tax on the other $20,000.

The Sale-and-Replacement Break

This is a variation on the rollover break. If you sell your principal residence in order to buy a new principal residence, you can postpone paying taxes on the portion of your home sale proceeds that you use to purchase a new home. You only have two years to exercise your sale-and-replacement break, however.

Finally, IRS Publication 523 "Tax Information on Selling Your Home" can provide guidance on other tax aspects of home sales. Consulting this booklet well in advance of putting your home on the market could save you future tax-related headaches.

Maintaining Your Home

You've decided to stay put. Even though your house may be oversized now that your children have left, you owe little on it and, anyway, the real estate market is soft. You are aware that staying has a certain opportunity cost, because your dormant home equity could be invested in income producing investments. But your children—and their children—often visit, so that extra space isn't totally wasted, and you've decided that the economic cost that staying put entails is more than outweighed by the emotional benefits. After all, the goal of the financially sound strategies that this book advocates is your long-term happiness.

Unlike a condo, or a townhouse in a retirement community, however, maintaining your home will continue to be your own responsibility. The following sections highlight areas of concern for the older homeowner.

Keeping up with Household Maintenance Chores

You may be used to doing your own home maintenance such as raking leaves, cleaning out gutters and downspouts, and doing smaller painting jobs. If you keep in good shape, you may be able to keep on doing these homeowner chores for years to come, but you have to face the fact that as you age, you will have greater and greater difficulties doing some manual labor. One item you should thus include when projecting household budgets is the cost of hiring outside help to do routine household maintenance. Of course, you should also try to project what larger repair or cosmetic jobs—like exterior painting may also be necessary in the coming years. If your house was properly "prepped" by good painters, your last paint job should last eight to ten years, so you should be able to estimate when you will next have to paint your exterior.

There are several sources for labor. If you are fortunate enough to live in or near a college town, you have an excellent source of well educated and generally motivated young part time workers. Colleges and universities usually maintain a student employment office where you can place job postings for part time helpers, whether it be for lawn mowing, light carpentry, or other household chores.

If there is no college nearby, you might contact your local high school to see if it has any programs designed to line up students with after-school jobs. While high school students might not be mature enough to take on the more difficult tasks, they certainly can do yard maintenance work.

The following tips may assist you in finding economical solutions to common household maintenance problems.

[ ] **Get several bids on home repair or improvement projects.**

Studies have shown that homeowners rarely take the lowest bid on home repair or home improvement projects. All too often, they fail to obtain several bids although—take my own recent experience—it's profitable doing so.

[ ] **Negotiate fees or ask for competitive quotes.**

After you've decided on the company or person to handle your home repairs or improvements, the quotation may still be negotiable. You may feel awkward trying to get a quotation dropped a bit, but remember, it's your money that you're spending. There may be a little slack in the bid. Don't get too bold, but then again don't pass up the opportunity to save a few bucks.

[ ] **Don't fall for home improvement scams.**

Home improvement scams are on the rise. All homeowners are vulnerable, particularly the elderly. Always take your time in deciding whether or not to go ahead with a home improvement. Always check out the person who wants to do the work. One clear warning sign: the contractor came to you rather than you going to them. If you have elderly parents, encourage them to check with you before committing to any kind of home repair or home improvement no matter how small.

[ ] **Don't make foolish home improvements.**

A home improvement is a project that will add value to the home when you resell it. They include added living space, adding or modernizing bathrooms, and adding kitchens, and so on. Features like swimming pools, boccie ball courts, or home observatories, however, won't add much, if any, value to your house. In fact, some will actually detract from the value of your home.

[ ] **Improve an efficient heating and/or air conditioning system.**

Just because your heating and/or air conditioning system is old doesn't mean you should get rid of it. On the other hand, there probably will come a time where it makes sense for you to bite the bullet. It may take many years for savings through efficiency to pay for the system, but it remains a worthwhile investment.

[ ] **Buy a good home repair manual.**

The easiest way to turn yourself from a klutz into a quasi-competent home repairperson is to buy one of the many good books on home repair. Armed with a good home repair book and a positive attitude, you can save a lot of money by doing small, and perhaps, medium home repairs yourself.

[ ] **Check the foundation of your house annually.**

Don't let an easily correctable problem turn into a financial problem. Check for cracks, bulges, or the presence of moisture in the basement. An ounce of prevention . . .

[ ] **Trim overgrown trees and shrubs.**

Don't let trees and shrubs engulf your home. Trim them back so that they don't damage siding, clog gutters, or harbor pests.

[ ] **Clean out your gutters.**

If you clean out your gutters annually (or pay someone to do it if you don't want to risk a ladder accident), you'll be preventing some big problems later on that are caused when your gutters don't drain properly.

[ ] **Have your sewer pipes cleaned every year.**

Clogged sewers are like clogged arteries. You often don't know there's a problem until it's too late. Spend some money each year and have your sewer pipes cleaned.

[ ] **Install dead bolt locks in your home.**

The first lines of defense aginst intruders are good locks. They will not only give you more peace of mind, but you also may be able to get a deduction in your homeowner's insurance. Also, if they prevent a burglary, they save you money as well.

[ ] **Appeal your property tax assessment.**

Surprisingly, a large percentage of people who appeal their property tax assessments end up with a lower bill. Don't forget, property values have dropped in many areas of the country and will drop in many more as the recession continues.

[ ] **Recycle to lower your trash collection fees.**

If your town doesn't yet have a recycling program, it probably will some day soon. The more that townspeople recycle, the lower the trash collection fees. In fact, many towns are assessing a higher trash collection fee for homeowners who don't recycle.

[ ] **Take in a boarder.**

Has your children's leaving left you with a slew of extra bedrooms? One way to cut your housing costs is to take in a boarder. Depending on your town's zoning ordinances, you may even be able to create an "in-law" apartment with a separate entrance. While taking on a boarder does present some inconveniences, you may be able to find an ideal boarder—someone who travels a lot or is a quiet student. Also, if you are concerned about security, having a reliable, honest boarder around will only help protect you and your home.

[ ] **Defer repairs on your home until a time when they can be included as part of a comprehensive home-improvement project.**

How can a repair be considered a home improvement? Say you want to paint your kitchen ceiling, but also plan to eventually modernize the whole room. If you defer the painting until you are ready to undertake the modernization project, the cost of painting the ceiling can be included as a home improvement.

[ ] **If you live in a prewar house that has any pretensions to architectural interest, you may be able to qualify for federal tax credits by restoring or rehabilitating it.**

If your home could use some major work and you like the idea of preserving or restoring its historic character, you should contact the National Park Service for its preservation guidelines. The Park Service has final say in certifying restoration jobs for the tax credit, and the rules can be stringent. If, however, you have time, patience, and a taste for history, you could get a nice saving on your tax bill while increasing your home's resale value.

Carrying Your Mortgage

Unless you are fortunate enough to have already paid off your mortgage, your mortgage payments may continue to be a large part of your monthly living expenses. If you still have several years of payments ahead of you, consider refinancing your mortgage if you can obtain a new mortgage that is at least 1½ percent to 2 percent below your current mortgage rate. By reducing your monthly mortgage payments, you can painlessly reduce your living expenses.

Because banks can't discriminate on the basis of age, you could also get a longer-term mortgage when you refinance. The longer the mortgage, the lower your monthly payments. However, the longer the mortgage, the longer the time required to pay off the mortgage. Depending on your financial circumstances, taking the opposite strategy to refinancing—paying off your mortgage—may also make sense. If you have more investments set aside than you need to support you during retirement, there's no point in paying a higher rate of interest on your mortgage than you can earn on your investments (which is often the case). If your current mortgage has a low interest rate, or if you have limited savings, prepayment is not recommended.

PART FIVE

A Financial Survival Guide to the Special Trials and Tribulations of Later Life

29

LATE LIFE DIVORCE AND REMARRIAGE

ONE UNFORTUNATE FEATURE of late-twentieth century society is the high-incidence of divorce, even among older Americans. An amicable separation is difficult for any age group, but for over-50s divorce is particularly trying and troublesome. Years of accumulated assets, encumbered with emotional as well as financial value, complicate the necessary process of division.

Current Attitudes Toward Divorce

Attitudes toward divorce and expectations of settlements are important factors to consider. Currently, most divorces are negotiated without regard to "fault" or marital conduct. Property settlements are made on the grounds of fairness and need without reference to moral judgments. The result is that the rationale behind property settlements is changing which, in turn, means that the types of settlements negotiated are also changing. For example, the original reason for alimony was that it enforced the husband's obligation to continue to support his wife, for whom employment opportunities were practically nonexistent. (Authorities have differed as to whether alimony was also intended to compensate the wife for her contribution to the marriage.) The awarding of alimony is within the discretion of the court at a divorce trial, and it is generally only awarded in situations where the divorced spouse cannot support himself or herself or where there are not presently sufficient marital assets to support both spouses. Divorced spouses who are disabled or caring for dependents are often awarded some form of alimony, but this is more and more often taking the form of temporary, or rehabilitative support while the spouse acquires job skills. The court expects most divorced spouses who are of working age to find their way to gainful employment.

Alimony is being replaced by distribution of marital assets. The most common form is called "equitable distribution," although a few states use community property to determine division. Equitable distribution does not mean equal distribution, and the determination of claim to ownership is made by a number of criteria. Basically, community property attempts to divide all marital property between the divorcing spouses, whereas equitable distribution weighs each partner's contributions to the marriage, including nonfinancial considerations, to determine a fair claim. Many divorces negotiate some balance between maintenance and asset division. A spouse who receives a large property settlement, even when he or she is over 50 and has never worked outside the home, can expect to have his or her alimony substantially decreased or eliminated from the settlement. In effect, property is traded for income.

Planning for Divorce

It should be apparent that divorce is a costly undertaking, and one that requires considerable planning and negotiation. Depending upon the complexity if your situation and—to a certain extent—the duration of your marriage, you may need the services of a team of specialized professionals, including your attorney, accountant, vocational expert, psychologist, physician, business-valuation specialist, and mediator.

Don't underestimate the support friends and relatives can provide to help you through what will inevitably be a difficult time. Some people mistakenly withdraw from friendships during this time. Yet, even late-life divorce has become so commonplace that most people should be able to be of emotional assistance to friends who are going through it.

Organizing Your Life

As you know, keeping well organized, accurate records is crucial to managing your finances. A good record-keeping system, which should be carefully maintained during the initial separation, will also ease the process and duress of negotiating an equitable settlement. Good recordkeeping habits should help you and your spouse or ex-spouse determine the real need and expenditures of your households which can enable both of you to structure a fair settlement. In most traditional marriages one spouse is in control of family finances. The result is that the other spouse may not have reasonable expectations or an adequate understanding of a feasible settlement of the marital assets.

Expect your standards of living to decrease at least temporarily after your divorce. The income and assets that once supported one household are now expected to support two. Under the circumstances, you will probably need to place more emphasis on budgeting, planning and revising your financial goals.

Divorce Procedures and Alternatives

If you are going to divorce, you need to consider the significant financial implications of the divorce process itself. Some people may not realize the range of legal fees and related expenses, including such costly minutiae as fees to property appraisers and accountants that may be incurred during divorce proceedings. Depending on the location and size of the firm, legal fees generally range from $75 to $350 an hour. Such fees add up. In New York, for instance, costs for one affluent party of a contested divorce can easily run to $100,000 or more! Indeed, if more separating couples realized the true cost of a contested divorce, they might be more willing to sit down and attempt some sort of negotiated settlement on their own.

Of course, before a final agreement is signed, each party should hire a lawyer who specializes in matrimonial law to review the proposed settlement. Moreover, if your attorney has little tax expertise, you are probably well advised to hire a separate lawyer or accountant to review the divorce's tax ramifications.

If, after considering the daunting costs, you and your spouse can agree to negotiate a less costly solution—both financially and emotionally—so much the better.

Alternatives

Although lawyers should be hired to review the final agreement, alternative professional help is available to mediate an agreeable settlement at a fraction of the legal eagles' cost. The most common alternative is a professional divorce mediator. While mediation is not recommended for hostile couples, it can help nonadversarial couples come to realistic and reasonable terms. Often, it helps both sides to understand and accept the finality of the divorce more easily than they might accept an extensively litigated decision imposed on them by the court. Mediation generally costs $70 to $100 an hour, and uncomplicated divorces can usually be resolved in less than 12 hours.

Another alternative to litigation is doing it yourselves. Amenable couples with no dependent children can, in many states, negotiate their own settlement and file for divorce themselves. Remember, if you choose this route, consult with a lawyer before filing the final agreement so that nothing egregious will be overlooked. Also, don't necessarily jump at a mediated or do-it-yourself divorce if you have been in a long-term marriage and fear that you may get the short end of the stick. Stand up for what you're entitled to, even if it means a more adversarial proceeding.

Dividing Your Assets

The final settlement that you reach with your spouse will be dictated by the state in which you live. As mentioned above, there are two main types of divorce codes which govern property division. If you live in a so-called "community property" state, the court will divide marital assets in half. Unlike "equitable distribution states," which weigh various factors in order to reach an equitable, but not necessarily strictly equal, division of property, community property states occasionally still weigh marital conduct or fault in settling divorces. "Marital property" is defined as all assets acquired since the marriage that were not acquired as a gift from a third party, through an inheritance, or from personal injury. It doesn't matter which spouse originally purchased a certain property if the property is owned jointly.

Equitable distribution states view marriage as an economic and emotional partnership and base their division on the couples' proportionate contributions to the partnership. Contribution to the marriage is weighed as consideration and may include in addition to financial contributions those made as a homemaker or parent in support of the other spouse's career potential. Some of the criteria used by equitable distribution states to guide division are the length of the marriage; the age, health, and position in life of the parties; the occupations of the parties; the amount and sources of income; vocational skills; employability; the estate, liabilities and needs of each party, and the opportunity of each to acquire further capital assets and income; the contribution of each party in acquiring and preserving marital property and assisting in its appreciation of dissipation; loss of inheritance or pension rights; and the possibility of property distribution in lieu of support.

Some property divisions cause specific problems, and some properties are not divisible. If an indivisible property, such as a car, goes to one spouse, the other is generally compensated elsewhere. Sometimes the property, such as a family home, will be sold, and the couple will divide the proceeds. Family businesses also present specific problems.

A divorced spouse can get Social Security benefits on a former husband's or wife's Social Security record if the marriage lasted at least 10 years. The divorced spouse must be 62 or older and not have remarried. For a divorced spouse to receive benefits, the working member of the former couple also must be 62 years or older. If a couple has been divorced at least 2 years, the nonworking spouse can get benefits, even if the worker is not retired. The amount of benefits a divorced spouse gets has no effect on the amount of benefits a current spouse can get.

Making Sure Your Planning Reflects Your New Status

Updating Insurance Coverage

The status of your insurance policies and future coverage will need to be addressed in your final divorce settlement. It is very important that you notify your insurer of your change in marital status. Rates, for instance, may be affected by your revised insurance which reflects your divorce settlement. Where appropriate, you should transfer title and ownership, especially on vehicles and real estate. One bright spot: As long as you have been married for at least 9 months prior to your divorce, you will maintain your eligibility for Social Security benefits upon your ex-spouse's death.

If you negotiate a lump-sum settlement without further spousal maintenance, you may wish to change the beneficiary designation on your existing insurance policies. In cases where life insurance replaces alimony for the recipient spouse after the payor's death, the recipient spouse should insist on a clause in the agreement giving her or him authority to obtain information periodically from the insurance company.

Life Insurance Policies

There are several alternative ways to address the issue of insurance policies in a divorce settlement. The insured can give the ex-spouse the policy outright. The drawbacks for the insured are that he or she loses all ownership rights, including the right to borrow against the cash value, and that the recipient will then get the money if he or she remarries and is no longer entitled to alimony.

The recipient can buy a policy on his or her ex-spouse's life. In this case, the divorce settlement should provide that the insured will comply with the requirements of the insurer (e.g., physical exam) if the ex-spouse ever wants to buy more insurance on his life.

The insured could retain ownership of the policies but name the ex-spouse as beneficiary as long as the ex-spouse remains unmarried. The advantage of this arrangement is that the policy reverts to the insured when the alimony obligation is terminated. The separation agreement should name the particular policy that will be kept in force for the ex-spouse and provide that he or she receive copies of all correspondence relating to it so that the ex-spouse will know it is being kept in force.

If the divorce decree provides that, after the payor's death, alimony payments are to continue by means of life insurance proceeds to replace payments made during the payor's life, the insurance proceeds must be included in the income of the recipient spouse as alimony. If, in accordance with a court decree, you assign an annuity contract for the benefit of your ex-spouse, each annuity payment is taxable to the recipient spouse if the payments are periodic and for support.

Health and Medical Insurance

Divorcing couples need to assure that they are adequately and continuously covered by health and medical insurance. If one ex-spouse is fully insured under Social Security, the other is entitled to

Medicare at age 65 as long as the ex-spouse is also age 65 or over (even if he or she is still working) or is dead. An ex-spouse is entitled to the spouse's full disability benefits.

Borrowing and Credit

Credit may be a new and critical issue as the result of your changed marital status. Many newly single older adults may have to establish credit on the basis of their changed financial position, but in most instances the rating cannot legally be affected by marital status. If, however, your credit was based in any way on your ex-spouse's income, you may have to reapply to the lender for credit. Your application will be accepted, rejected or limited on the basis of several considerations, including current income. A divorcée applying for credit individually can cite as proof of credit-worthiness the credit history of accounts carried in the name of the ex-spouse, if both spouses used them. A divorced person may also have to give reasons why a bad joint credit history does not reflect on personal ability or willingness to pay.

If you receive alimony, you need not reveal that fact to the creditor unless you wish to use it to demonstrate your credit-worthiness. If you do include alimony as part of your income on your credit application, however, the lender is entitled to examine whether your ex-spouse can be depended upon to make regular payments. The creditor might conclude that your ex-spouse is a poor credit risk, in which case, alimony could be legally discounted as income, which could be detrimental to your application. Unless the lenders can prove that your ex-spouse is a poor risk, however, they cannot automatically discount alimony.

You should notify the credit bureau of both your and your ex-spouse's new addresses and specify that those accounts should henceforth be reported separately. Otherwise transactions may be reported on the wrong spouse's account, and the records can get tangled, especially if one of the two remarries. Occasionally, one or both spouses will have credit problems during the separation period preceding the final divorce period, especially if the marital assets are frozen to negotiate the settlement. In this situation, the credit bureau and lenders should be informed of the circumstances. Lenders may be more lenient in restoring the credit ratings of the parties to a divorce once the situation stabilizes.

Tax Planning

While the emphasis in most contemporary divorces is on property division, income division, or alimony, still exists, especially in cases where there are insufficient assets to support both households. For some couples there are significant tax advantages to using ongoing support in structuring a settlement. For others, a lump sum settlement is more advantageous. While the tax implications of your divorce may be the farthest thing from your mind as you undergo the stressful divorce experience, it is important that you understand the various alternatives available to you and your spouse.

A reasonable financial settlement takes projected income and assets into account. The division should provide for necessary and foreseeable expenditures, including the costs of medical or nursing home care. For older couples undergoing divorce, the allocation of pension and retirement plan benefits, which are considered marital property, is obviously a most important issue. If the value of these retirement vehicles is not divided on an equal basis, you should make sure that you are otherwise compensated in your divorce settlement.

Parting Words

Divorce is potentially hazardous to your financial health and should be approached as a financial, as well as a personal, problem-solving venture. What could be worse than living to regret a hasty decision that came to adversely affect your post-divorce financial situation? What could be better than knowing that, at least when it comes to your financial well-being, you made the right decisions?

Silver Lining: Remarriage

Premarital Agreements

Late life remarriage is on the rise. With it, the use of premarital (also known as antenuptial) agreements. These agreements, which should be prepared with the advice and assistance of your lawyer—two lawyers, actually, one for each partner—are particularly useful for wealthier over-50s. These agreements define each partner's separate property being brought into the marriage and describe your financial intentions after you're wed. Premarital agreements may contain a limitation or waiver of alimony should you ever divorce, a provision under which one spouse gives up all rights or limits his or her rights to the other's estate, or it may even go on to discuss more personal matters such as the division of housework. Premarital agreements may also help you overcome some of the anxiety associated with remarriage.

Premarital agreements are advisable if one partner is much wealthier than the other and is concerned with the protection of assets should the marriage dissolve. In these situations, the agreement usually includes a transfer, or the promise of a transfer, of property from the wealthier spouse to the other. The transfer may either be outright or in a trust in exchange for a release of all claims the other may have for support or against the transferor's estate. Also, if you or your partner already has children from a previous marriage, a prenuptial agreement can protect each child's financial security.

Pay attention to your adult children's concerns—whether articulated or subtly hinted at—about the new person in your life. After all, you've been burned once, and could be again: more likely than not, your children's skepticism is motivated by a genuine concern about your well-being. You may feel that your personal life is none of their business. Remember, however, that for at least the first 20 years or so of your children's existences, you made their personal lives very much your business: they are probably only reciprocating the concern you've shown them over the years.

Prenuptial agreements can go a long way toward allaying the fears that your adult children will inevitably harbor. In setting up a premarital agreement, it is often advisable for couples to use a trust instead of an outright transfer. Irrevocable trusts (see Chapter 23) ensure that the property will be kept out of the settlor's estate, and if the spouse is given a life interest with the possible right to invade principal in accordance with a defined standard, with a remainder going to the children or other beneficiaries, then the trust property can be kept out of the spouse's estate as well.

Legal precedent favors adherence to premarital agreements as long as both parties to the contract are open and honest about their assets and liabilities and both have access to legal advice. Most states will allow a spouse to give up or limit interest in his or her partner's estate under certain conditions, but fewer allow contracts that limit or forbid alimony. The concern is that these latter contracts may encourage divorce and therefore violate public policy. Nevertheless, some states have concluded that a properly advised adult should be free to agree to make do without alimony.

Since premarital contracts generally involve a transfer or promise of transfer of property, outright or in a trust, they may have estate, gift, and income tax consequences for the couple. The best estate tax avoidance strategies involve making the transfer irrevocable and unamendable in the present or in the future before death. A lifetime transfer made by one spouse may be includible in his or her estate as long as the property involved is not actually sold to the other spouse. A promise on the part of the receiving spouse to forego all right and claims for support or against the transferor's property or estate does not constitute a purchase of the transferred property. The tax laws treat the transfer in such a situation as a gift, subject to annual exclusion. If the transfer does not actually take place until after the marriage, then the gift tax marital deduction permitting gifts in unlimited amounts applies. Note: There may be income tax consequences depending on whether or not the transfer is determined to be a gift.

Postmarital Agreements

Postmarital agreements can also be used to enable couples to settle beforehand, under more amicable circumstances, what will happen to their property in the event of a divorce. They can be used to clarify which spouse has rights to certain property (e.g., an interest in a closely held business or summer home). Postmarital agreements are also used to update or renegotiate an outdated premarital agreement. Because postmarital agreements can face legal barriers, expert legal assistance is necessary, and each party should be represented by independent counsel.

30

LEARNING TO COPE AS A WIDOW/WIDOWER

LOSING YOUR SPOUSE forces you to reevaluate every aspect of your financial planning. While substantial changes will probably not be required in every area of your finances, some alterations will be inevitable. As a result, you should be prepared to examine every aspect of your financial life. Of course, the first few weeks after a spouse's death are not a good time to make major financial decisions. Nonetheless, it is important that you take matters in hand as promptly as possible. Don't let things drift. Even if you and your spouse did undertake some careful estate planning, you will have to start from scratch in many important respects.

Immediate Problems

Liquidity

The immediate concern that many surviving spouses face is access to funds. Even if your marital assets are considerable, they may not be liquid and/or may be inaccessible during the administration of the estate. Liquidity is necessary not only for your ordinary expenses while your spouse's estate is being settled and/or probated, also it is necessary to enable you to pay extraordinary debts:

funeral expenses, administration expenses, estate taxes, and cash bequests.

If your liquidity needs have not been provided for, there are a number of ways you can obtain sufficient funds:

- In some cases if the executor receives the required authority to do so, he or she can distribute assets in lieu of cash bequests. Such distributions reduce the cash needs of the estate.
- If your spouse created a trust under the terms of his or her will, the executor may elect to place any depressed assets in the trust and sell more marketable assets. If your spouse established a living trust, and it is still funded, a sale of estate assets to the trust might be advisable.
- Your spouse's estate can raise cash by borrowing from a beneficiary or trust.
- If your spouse owned a closely-held business, the tax on his or her business interest may be deferred for up to 14 years. For the first four years after your spouse's death, the estate can make annual payments of interest only and subsequently pay the balance in 10 annual installments of principal and interest. If, however, the value of the interest does not exceed 35 percent of your spouse's adjusted gross estate, the estate won't be able to make payments in this manner.
- If you have joint checking or savings accounts that provide for survivorship, they may help you cover immediate needs.
- Even with the unlimited marital deduction, unforeseen taxes can unduly burden liquidity. To the extent that they save taxes, judicious use of deductions for administration expenses and losses reduce liquidity needs. Consult your accountant to develop an appropriate tax strategy.

Decision Making

While your changed circumstances will call for making some immediate decisions, you should delay making the important ones when possible. Your best bet for the short-term is to be extremely conservative; consider putting all death benefits and/or insurance proceeds into money market accounts, certificates of deposit, Treasury bills, or other safe and liquid short-term investments. After several months have passed, you will most likely be better adjusted to your new circumstances and so be better able to consider major investment decisions.

Be aware that your spouse's death may precipitate an avalanche of attention from brokers and other financial services salespeople attempting to persuade you to sink your money into high-risk investments or to enter into other schemes. Politely but firmly tell these individuals to get lost. You should look out for unusual bills, fraudulent demands for repayment of loans the late spouse never took out, false notices of overdue premiums on life insurance policies, and C.O.D. shipments of merchandise billed to your spouse. Without becoming paranoid, you should realize that all of these ploys have been used to fleece bereaved spouses and they could be used to fleece you. As a general rule, unless you are sure that the merchandise was really ordered, or the debt really incurred, refer the matter to your lawyer. However, to avoid damaging your credit rating, don't delay paying your regular bills.

Budgeting and Recordkeeping

As soon as you are able to do so, sit down and revise your forecast of future expenses and income. A worksheet is provided on the next page to help you (Figure 30.1. Budget for a Surviving Spouse). The results of your revision may affect many decisions, such as whether or not it will be necessary to reenter the workforce if your spouse brought a significant amount of income to the marriage. Your expense projections should take into account any increased expenditures, such as household help. You may also find that you spend an increased amount of money on travel to visit children and other relatives and friends now that you are single. If you have spent the last few months staying at home to tend to your spouse, you may find yourself spending more money on activities that you had put on hold during your spouse's illness.

Right after the death, make sure that you have enough copies of the death certificate (sometimes as many as ten are required) for insurance claims, Social Security benefits, and will probate. Many parties need to be notified of the death, including the Social Security Administration, the insurance company, your spouse's employer (if he or she isn't already retired) and, if the decedent was an honorably discharged veteran, the Veterans Administration. On page 410, Figure 30.2. Checklist for a Surviving Spouse, includes these and other items you'll have to attend to after the death of your spouse.

Figure 30.1. Budget for a Surviving Spouse

You can use this worksheet to budget cash receipts and disbursements as a surviving spouse. Changes in income and expenses are inevitable, and it is important to plan carefully to take into account your new financial status. This budget covers recurring expenses only. The costs of settling your spouse's estate are not included.

Time period (monthly, quarterly, annually): ....

CASH RECEIPTS	*Prior to Spouse's Death*	*Change (Plus or Minus)*	*Estimated Future Level*
1. Gross salary	$......	$.......	$........
2. Bonuses/profit sharing	......	....	....
3. Interest	......	....	....
4. Dividends	......	....	....
5. Alimony/child support received	......	....	....
6. Distributions from partnerships	......	....	....
7. Distributions from closely held businesses	......	....	....
8. Rental income	......	....	....
9. Trust distributions	......	....	....
10. Pension	......	....	....
11. Social Security	......	....	....
12. Gifts	......	....	....
13. Proceeds from sale of assets	......	....	....
14. Life insurance proceeds	......	....	....
15. Other insurance proceeds	......	....	....
16. Employer death benefits	......	....	....
17. Other	......	....	....

Figure 30.1. (Cont'd)

....	......	....	....
....	......	....	....
18. Total cash receipts	$......	$.......	....

CASH DISBURSEMENTS

1. House (rent/ mortgage)	$......	$.......	$........
2. Food	......	....	....
3. Household maintenance	......	....	....
4. Utilities and telephone	......	....	....
5. Clothing	......	....	....
6. Personal care	......	....	....
7. Medical and dental care	......	....	....
8. Automobile/ transportation	......	....	....
9. Childcare expenses	......	....	....
10. Entertainment	......	....	....
11. Vacations	......	....	....
12. Gifts	......	....	....
13. Contributions	......	....	....
14. Insurance	......	....	....
15. Miscellaneous out-of-pocket expenses	......	....	....
16. Furniture	......	....	....
17. Home improvements	......	....	....
18. Real estate taxes	......	....	....
19. Loan payments	......	....	....
20. Credit card payments	......	....	....
21. Alimony/child support paid	......	....	....
22. Tuition/educational expenses	......	....	....
23. Business and professional expenses	......	....	....
24. Savings/investments	......	....	....
25. Income and Social Security taxes	......	....	....

Figure 30.1. (Cont'd)

---

26. Other			
....	......	....	....
....	......	....	....
....	......	....	....
27. Total cash disbursements	$	$	....
Excess (shortfall) of cash receipts over cash disbursements	$	....	....

Notes: ....

....

....

Figure 30.2. Checklist for a Surviving Spouse

This checklist can be used to assist a recent widow/widower in identifying the many financial planning tasks that must be attended to after the death of a spouse.

	Yes	*No*	*N/A*
1. Have you obtained several copies of your spouse's death certificate for filing insurance claims, changing account status, etc.?	☐	☐	☐
2. If your spouse did not prepare an inventory of his or her estate, have you had one prepared yet?	☐	☐	☐
3. Have you or the executor of your spouse's estate hired a lawyer?	☐	☐	☐
4. Have your spouse's credit accounts, mortgage payments, bank, and utility bills been kept up to date?	☐	☐	☐
5. Have your spouse's creditors been notified?	☐	☐	☐
6. Have your spouse's clubs, fraternal organizations, and alumni organizations been notified?	☐	☐	☐
7. Have your spouse's insurers been notified of the death?	☐	☐	☐

Figure 30.2. (Cont'd)

---

8. Have you prepared a forecast of future expenses and income? ☐ ☐ ☐
9. Have you determined how to invest lump sum distributions of insurance policy proceeds, etc.? ☐ ☐ ☐
10. Have you determined how to invest lump sum distributions? ☐ ☐ ☐
11. Have you reviewed and, where necessary, revised your insurance coverage? ☐ ☐ ☐
12. Have you changed joint credit account designations or, where necessary, opened new accounts? ☐ ☐ ☐
13. Have you changed asset ownership designations? ☐ ☐ ☐
14. If your spouse owned any interest in a closely held business, has the disposition of that business interest been determined? ☐ ☐ ☐
15. Have you and your accountant reviewed your tax filing options? ☐ ☐ ☐
16. Have you assigned responsibility for preparing and filing your spouse's final tax return? ☐ ☐ ☐
17. Have you assigned responsibility for preparing and filing the tax returns of your spouse's estate? ☐ ☐ ☐
18. Have you reviewed, and, where appropriate, revised your estate planning documents and strategy? ☐ ☐ ☐

Notes: ....
....
....
....
....
....
....

Many widows/widowers were either uninvolved or not fully involved in managing family finances during their marriage. If this describes your situation, don't simply assume it's too late for you to learn about investments, taxes, budgeting, and all of the other facets of our financial lives. While you may well benefit from seeking some assistance, at least initially, it is incumbent upon you to become familiar with these important matters so you can quickly take control of your financial future. Never, never, never believe that financial matters are just too overwhelming to cope with. As you can see by reading this book, it isn't that complicated. Remember, you are your own best financial planner, investment manager, recordkeeper, and income tax advisor. Even though you may want to rely on others to help you, you should always maintain control.

Insurance

Determining Your Spouse's Death Benefits

You should work with your lawyer and/or the executor of your spouse's estate in order to uncover and track down any death benefits that are due. If your spouse was employed at the time of his or her death, you should contact the company's employee benefits office. Your spouse may be owed a last paycheck, payment for accrued vacation and sick leave, company life insurance, a pension benefit, money in deferred compensation, profit sharing, and/or accident insurance. You should notify your spouse's life insurance agent and file the necessary claims. Finally, as the surviving spouse, you may also be eligible for Social Security and/or Veterans Administration benefits and should contact the appropriate offices.

Disposition of the Proceeds of Your Spouse's Life Insurance

You may have several options on how to receive life insurance proceeds. As long as the disposition of these proceeds meets the requirements for the marital deduction in general, you can take any option and still qualify for the marital estate tax deduction. You and/or the other beneficiaries need not feel pressured to decide immediately on which route to take. You may, if you wish, leave the proceeds with the insurance company—where they will earn interest—until you reach a decision. In general, life insurance proceeds are not taxable to the beneficiary regardless of how he chooses to receive them. Interest generated by the proceeds, however, is subject to income tax. The three general ways a beneficiary can elect to receive life insurance proceeds are described below.

1. **Lump-sum settlements.** Lump-sum payments are usually appropriate for small policies or for beneficiaries who are either themselves capable of sound investment management or who can rely on competent investment advisers. Lump sum payouts occur automatically when insurance proceeds are payable into a trust. If your spouse established a trust to receive a lump sum settlement, you or the executor of your spouse's estate should make sure that the trust's terms allow any property included in the gross estate passing to it to qualify for the federal estate tax marital deduction. The marital deduction is allowed in cases where the lump-sum payment is dependent on your surviving spouse, sometimes for a stated period of time. The use of lump-sum insurance payments, while subject to some restrictions under the Internal Revenue Code, can also help to meet the estate's or survivor's immediate liquidity needs.
2. **Fixed payments.** You can opt to have the insurance company distribute portions of insurance policy proceeds and interest. These payments can be made over a fixed period of time, or in installment payments of a fixed amount paid at stated intervals until the money is used up. Either way, you and any other beneficiaries should retain the privilege of changing your minds and withdrawing the entire remaining sum at a later date. If any of the beneficiaries die before they have received the entire amount due them, the unpaid balance will be payable to either their estates or any other beneficiaries they should choose to name. Alternatively, the insurance company can pay the beneficiary fixed payments of interest only, with the principal payable to either the spouse's estate or named beneficiary.
3. **Annuities.** Many insurance policies allow the beneficiary to purchase an annuity from the policy proceeds. With an annuity, the insurance company agrees to pay the beneficiary a certain monthly sum for life. The amount of the monthly sum depends on the size of the insurance policy and the age of the beneficiary. Purchasing an annuity assures that you won't outlive your insurance proceeds. This option may be particularly useful if your resources and/or investment expertise are limited or if you are concerned that health care expenses could eat up your assets.

> If you decide to purchase an annuity, shop around. The annuity offered by your spouse's insurer may not be the best one you can find: other companies may offer you a higher monthly income. If you do decide to purchase an annuity from a company other than your spouse's insurer, have the insurer transfer funds directly to the annuity provider to avoid adverse tax consequences.

Deciding how to receive the proceeds of a life insurance policy is never easy. Remember that this does not have to be an "either/or" decision. For example, you don't have to choose between taking a lump sum for the entire policy proceeds or an annuity for the entire policy proceeds. Often, beneficiaries are best served by taking both routes. In other words, put part of the proceeds into an annuity with fixed payments, and take the remainder as a lump sum.

Revising Coverage

Review your insurance coverage soon after your spouse's death. You will probably need to revise the beneficiary designations on existing policies and secure continuing coverage, especially for health insurance. You also need to make sure that you are still covered by appropriate automobile, homeowners or renters, and umbrella liability insurance. Depending on your individual circumstances, you may need to acquire or increase the limits of disability (if you are still working) and life insurance coverage.

While the prospect of your having a prolonged illness is hardly pleasant to contemplate, now that you are single, you should consider strategies for dealing with that eventuality. There are several factors to consider. Do you have sufficient resources to pay for uninsured health care costs? Is long-term care insurance appropriate? Could you count on financial support from your children in the event of a debilitating illness?

Borrowing and Credit

Your credit situation should also be reviewed in light of your changed circumstances, especially if your spouse's death has significantly reduced your income. One action you should take is to cancel your spouse's credit cards or convert the accounts to your own name. Also review any outstanding loans: some lenders protect their loans with credit life insurance that will pay the debt in full. Individual credit accounts that were granted solely on the basis of the survivor's income, however, cannot legally be closed without evidence that the survivor will not be able to pay. Skipping two monthly bills may be considered "evidence" of your inability to maintain an account. If, however, the credit accounts were based even partially on your spouse's income, merchants can require you to make a new application. The merchant reserves the right to turn you down, however, if your present financial situation doesn't meet its criteria for creditworthiness.

Investments

Revised Investment Strategies

If your spouse handled your investments, and you now find yourself at something of a loss dealing with money matters, professional investment management may be appropriate. Whether or not you decide that bringing in a professional makes sense, the death of a spouse often warrants a modification of investment strategy. You may have a greater need for investment income and be more concerned about preserving your capital. Such revised financial goals might suggest a more conservative investment approach. For example, it might be appropriate to shift portfolio emphasis from individual stocks to a combination of interest-earning securities and stock mutual funds. Real estate investments may assume less importance for the surviving spouse.

Ownership Designations and Valuation Decisions

If jointly held property and/or joint accounts have passed directly to you without probate, you will need to change their ownership designations. Similarly, security certificate ownership must be changed by contacting the transfer agent or family stockbroker. You will need to show supporting documentation, such as a death certificate, to effect these changes. The transfer is free, but the broker may charge a small fee.

If your spouse owned U.S. savings bonds, they will need special consideration. The interest income on U.S. Series E and EE bonds (or for Series H or HH bonds that your spouse may have traded for E or EE bonds) is usually reported upon the bonds' redemption, unless your spouse elected to report the income on an annual basis. If your spouse did not report the interest on an annual basis, you assume the accumulated income tax liability at the time of your spouse's death.

It may be advantageous, however, to report all of the accrued income on Series E or EE bonds on your spouse's final income tax return, particularly if he or she died early in the final taxable year, before receiving much in the way of taxable income. Even if taking this action results in the imposition of federal income taxes, the tax liability is deductible on the estate tax return.

If there are any receivables or investments that are worthless as of the date of your spouse's death, you or an accountant should determine whether worthlessness occurred during the year of death or in a prior open tax year. If worthlessness occurred during a prior open tax year, you may be able to file a claim for a tax refund.

The Family Business

Was your spouse the owner of a closely held business? If the answer is yes, then it is quite possible that the business comprised a large portion of your spouse's estate, a situation that poses a number of problems and questions. The most obvious question is whether or not to continue operating the business, and if other family members were involved in running it, this is a matter that will have to be decided by the family as a whole. Unfortunately, the death of the owner of a closely held or family business can sometimes precipitate unpleasant battles for control of the firm, especially if your spouse didn't name a successor.

Stock in a family corporation is often illiquid, and its value may be impaired because of your spouse's death. If your spouse didn't resolve the issues surrounding the ultimate disposition of the business before his or her death, you should enlist the assistance of your accountant in developing appropriate strategies. Should you, your family and the executor decide to continue operating the business, the executor will have to administer its reorganization.

If you decide not to maintain the business, liquidation should be avoided if possible, since it almost invariably means severe shrinkage in value. You would be better off to sell the business either to other partners or employees or to an outsider. If you decide to sell the business, it is crucial that it be properly valued by an unbiased expert before you put it on the market. You should be prepared for the possibility that this estimate may be less than what your spouse had stated as the company's worth.

You may have to make many other tough decisions about the disposition of the family business. Many will require professional advice. For example, if the family business had established an Employee Stock Ownership Plan (ESOP), there could be both income and estate tax savings in having the ESOP purchase your spouse's shares. Stock redemptions (in which a corporation agrees to purchase a decedent's stocks) and/or buy-sell agreements, if applicable, need to be carefully administered. Finally, your spouse's estate may also qualify to pay estate taxes on an installment plan.

Tax Planning

If your spouse used to handle your taxes, you may be in for a bit of a jolt as you tackle the Internal Revenue Code for yourself. The following sections are designed to help you cope with the various tax issues posed by both the settlement of your spouse's estate and by your own financial future. There are three tax returns with which you're going to have to deal: your own return, your spouse's last return and the estate's return.

Tax Filing Status of New Widower

You do not lose the right to file a joint return when your spouse dies during the year, if you have been filing joint returns with your spouse *and* you still have dependent children. You can generally file a joint return for the year of your spouse's death and for the two years following. Even if your last return wasn't filed jointly, you can file a joint return now as long as you were *eligible* to file a joint return at that time. (In the first return filed after the death, you can claim a personal tax exemption for your late spouse.)

If you are also the executor of the estate, you may choose to waive the executor's commission, especially if you would otherwise receive an equivalent amount as a bequest or legacy. The inheritance is not taxable, but the executor's commission qualifies as regular income. You may also be better off waiving the commissions if the marital deduction exempts your spouse's estate from estate tax. In that case, a deduction for the commissions won't be needed anyway. However, you can accelerate income to the final joint return by paying partial commissions from the estate before the close of the year in which your spouse died.

Your Spouse's Tax Status

Your spouse's taxable year remains his or her normal tax year regardless of the date of death. Any medical expenses incurred before death and paid within one year after death may be claimed as medical deductions on either your spouse's final return—or on your final joint return—or on the estate's tax return. To prevent a double deduction, the executor of your spouse's estate must file a waiver of right to claim the estate tax deduction if it will be claimed on your spouse's return. Of course, the tax consequences of each option should be weighed, and the option that results in the greatest tax savings should be taken.

Most taxpayers use the cash-basis system to prepare their returns, so all income, whether actually or constructively received up to the time of death, must be reported. Any income earned by your spouse but not included in his or her final income tax return is reported either on the income tax return of your spouse's estate, or on the return of the estate's beneficiary(ies). If the income goes directly to a beneficiary, he or she can take an income tax deduction determined at the highest estate tax rate to which your spouse's estate is subject.

Unfortunately, unabsorbed capital losses from the year of your spouse's death cannot be carried forward to the estate income tax return. The same is true of losses suspended under passive activity rules. Administrative expenses, taxes, interest, business expenses, and other items that have accrued at the date of death can, however, be claimed both as income tax deductions on your spouse's final return and as estate tax deductions.

Tax Status of Your Spouse's Estate

There are many ways to reduce or eliminate death taxes, starting with the unified marital estate tax credit. If, however, after using all the valid deductions, your spouse's estate still owes death taxes, and his or her will does not specify which assets shall be used to pay the taxes (or if there is no will), state and federal laws specify what is required. Most importantly, all taxes must be paid before a beneficiary can receive any property. In states that impose an inheritance tax, the amount of this tax comes directly from the property to be received.

Any estate taxes must be apportioned among all the taxable property in your spouse's estate. When property is left to someone who would be entitled to a deduction because of your spouse's bequest, then that inherited property is exempt from paying the tax. Property left to you qualifies for the marital deduction, and does not pay *federal* estate taxes (but still may be subject to state death taxes).

If your spouse's estate tax year ends more than two years after the date of his or her death, the estate must make estimated payments of income tax. Underpayment of tax could expose the estate to penalties.

Suppose your spouse's estate contains a lot of stock, and it declines significantly in value after your spouse dies. Obviously, you'd be better off if you could pay taxes on the stock's declined price, rather than on its higher, earlier price. By using the so-called "alternative valuation date" to value your spouse's estate, you could reduce the tax burden on your spouse's estate. Essentially, the IRS allows you to value the estate's property for tax purposes at a later date than on the date of your spouse's death. The "alternate valuation date" is defined as being either the day the estate's property is finally disposed of or the six month anniversary of your spouse's death. One caveat: alternate valuation is only available where both the total value of the gross estate and the amount of the estate tax liability are reduced as a result of the election.

Retirement Planning

Your retirement income and expense projections will probably have to be revised to account for the changed circumstances. In revising your retirement plan, err on the side of overestimating your life expectancy—you don't want to run out of money!

As the surviving spouse, you may be eligible to receive retirement benefits in addition to whatever benefits you have earned on your own. The following is a list of sources you should check for possible spouse's benefits:

- **Social Security.** If, when your spouse died, he or she was covered by Social Security, you may be entitled to widow's or widower's benefits, and to a lump sum death benefit.
- **Veterans Administration.** If your spouse was an honorably discharged veteran, you may be eligible for a funeral allowance and/or a pension.
- **Pension plan.** Check with the pension plan administration to see what benefits to which you are entitled to as a surviving spouse.

- **IRA or spousal IRA.** If your spouse died before his or her entire IRA interest has been distributed, the balance is distributable to whomever your spouse named as beneficiary.
- **Qualified employee benefit plan.** These plans may provide annuity or lump-sum death benefits to surviving spouses in place of or in addition to retirement benefits.
- **Other employee benefits.** Your spouse's employer may be obliged contractually to pay death benefits in the nature of extra compensation for services performed, or may choose to make a pure gift. Voluntary payments of death benefits flowing from affection or charity are viewed as a gift and are not subject to income tax. Voluntary payments made in anticipation of some economic benefit to the employer or in recognition of past employee services are taxable.

Estate Planning

Administering Your Spouse's Estate

If your spouse's estate planning was carefully thought through and is up-to-date, the will provisions, specific property beneficiary designations, and joint property laws will probably result in an equitable and agreeable property division and estate transfer. Suppose, however, you or other family members take issue with any or all of the will provisions? There are a variety of ways which your spouse's plan could be revised. Heirs could disclaim part or all of an inheritance, contest part or all of a will, or elect against a provision or provisions of a will.

A disclaimed bequest passes on to an alternate beneficiary as though the designated beneficiary had died before your spouse. This is an option primarily used by surviving spouses who do not need the bequest and who planned to bequeath it to the alternate beneficiary anyway. Disclaiming, also known as renouncing, may allow the transfer to be made under the terms of the late spouse's will, allowing the transfer to be made without incurring gift tax liability. If you make a disclaimer, it is valid even if the will directs that the property disclaimed passes to a trust in which you have an interest. Otherwise, disclaiming the bequest gives up all future interest in the property disclaimed. If you think there is any chance you might later need the property, don't disclaim it, even if you assume that the recipient will support you.

If you are convinced that you have not been adequately provided for under your spouse's will, you may be able to elect against it. In most states, a spouse cannot be disinherited unless he or she assents to it. If you were not disowned entirely, depending on state law, the court may award you a large enough portion of the estate to reach the minimum amount legally due you. The court may also supersede any provisions in your spouse's will to bring it into line with state law.

Generally, either a disclaimer or a right of election taken against the will assume that the will itself is valid, but that a particular clause is not appropriate for some reason. If you believe, however, that a part or all of the will is not valid, you can contest the will or protest probate. Usually only interested parties adversely affected by a codicil or subsequent will are entitled to object to probate of a will. The one who objects bears the burden of proving his or her contentions. Mechanical defects, such as not signing the will in the presence of two witnesses, or substantive defects, such as drafting the will under undue influence or when misinformed by fraud, are grounds for protesting probate.

Your Own Estate

The transfer of the estate occasioned by the death of your spouse will likely have a considerable effect on your own estate planning. You may find your estate is greatly enlarged and/or greatly complicated. At the least, your spouse's name will have to be replaced wherever it appears on family documents. Documents to be reviewed include your will, durable power of attorney, living will, and letter of instructions. Trust documents will also need to be reviewed. If you and your spouse had a joint will, you may be contractually bound to the provisions of the established will. Legal assistance in all of these matters is, of course, necessary.

Your spouse's death will most likely have far-reaching financial consequences. Your income may have been substantially reduced by the death of an income-earning spouse; assets may have been reduced; conversely, your own estate may have been substantially increased by death benefits, insurance proceeds, or bequests. Any of these situations will affect your own financial planning process.

31

THE SINGLE LIFE

INCREASING NUMBERS OF Americans are staying single, and staying single longer. From 1970 to 1990, one-person households increased from 11 million to almost 25 million. But as the number of singles grows, it becomes increasingly difficult to make broad generalizations about them as a group. Singles can, however, be roughly separated into three main groups: singles without children, unmarried individuals with children, and unmarried persons living together. Included in the last category are the ever-growing number of older people who are living together for reasons of economics and/or companionship. Personal financial needs and strategies will often differ at least somewhat depending upon which of the three categories the single person is in. The trend is clear: single persons are becoming more and more of a fixture on the American landscape. While this chapter will deal with issues of general concern to singles in all three categories, other chapters may also be helpful to singles, including Chapter 29, Late-Life Divorce and Remarriage and Chapter 30, Learning to Cope as a Widow/Widower.

Many single people quite correctly complain that the world of financial planning—publications, radio and TV programs,—has not directed sufficient attention to the unique needs of the single person. A common refrain: "Why does everything I hear or read about personal finances assume that I am married with children?" This chapter will help point out some of the areas where the financial planning needs of singles are different.

Unique Problems of Single People

While many people might initially think that the main difference between the financial planning needs of the single person compared with the married person relates to estate planning, differences typically extend to other areas as well, including insurance and investing.

While the most important financial goal of everyone, single or married, is financial security, many single people who are still in the workforce have more difficulty achieving it since, compared with their dual-earner, married counterparts, a higher proportion of the single person's income will probably have to be saved. And saving is comparatively more difficult for singles. Whoever said "two can live as cheaply as one" obviously had never been married. However, a couple living together can live on quite a bit less than two singles supporting separate households. Those who doubt this should speak with anyone who has recently separated from his or her spouse.

Many singles continue to harbor longstanding notions about their personal finances that are at best out-of-date and at worst will result in mistakes that will be financially penalizing for many years. Some of these notions are:

- Single people should not buy (or can't afford to buy) homes
- Single people should invest very conservatively because, among other rationalizations, they have less money available to make up for losses on risky investments (like stocks)
- Single people with no dependents don't need life insurance
- Estate planning is either unnecessary for singles or there is nothing to do beyond a simple will
- Unmarried couples in long-term relationships cannot do very much in the way of providing for the surviving partner after the death of the first partner.

So, while you need to be aware of the differences in your financial planning needs if you are single, you also should be aware of the commonality of financial requirements and planning opportunities that transcend marital and family status. While your needs are different in several respects, they are identical in most others.

Planning and Recordkeeping

Long-term planning is a particularly important component of the financial planning process for many singles because they may not have paid adequate attention to it in the past or they may simply think that planning is not necessary for them. (Partners are likely to encourage each other to discuss shared financial goals, strategies, and priorities with each other. Singles living alone may not be as inclined to plan specifically for the future.) Therefore, if you haven't already, you should make specific plans, both short- and long-term.

You should also organize your personal records so that, in the event of disability, a designated individual (relative, friend, etc.) can readily assume important record keeping chores, including bill paying, banking, and income tax preparation. Ideally, someone should be designated to perform these tasks should the need arise, and the person you have chosen should be shown where the records are located and how they're organized. Also, instructions should be prepared to show what needs to be done in the event someone else has to take over.

Insurance

While the need for comprehensive insurance is as crucial for singles as it is for married couples, there are some differences. While many singles who have no dependents see no need for any life insurance at all (and this could be an accurate assessment), a projection of your financial status at death may reveal a need for coverage. Perhaps your parents or siblings may become financially dependent at some future time. If you were to die without insurance before this need might arise, the opportunity to provide for them would be lost. Also, life insurance proceeds may be useful in providing for a particular charity of your choosing. Another area of insurance that may merit your attention is disability coverage. Singles do not have the luxury of falling back on a spouse's income in the event of an under- or uninsured disability. Therefore, maintaining sufficient disability insurance is particularly crucial for singles.

Investing

While the investment strategies of singles generally do not differ from those of couples of similar financial circumstances, the need to accumulate a financial cushion against financial adversity is more crucial because there is no second breadwinner to take up the slack. Accumulating sufficient investments to meet life's financial adversities as well as to fund a comfortable retirement is perhaps the greatest challenge for singles. Yet many singles do not invest appropriately because, they reason, they can't afford the kind of risks that two-earner families can. If you have been investing too conservatively remember that investing for growth is every bit as important for you as it is for families bringing home two paychecks. See Chapter 11, Basics of Investing.

Estate Planning

Estate planning rules and strategies seem to favor married couples. If fact, they do. Therefore, single people and unmarried persons living together often have more difficulty planning their estates. Selecting fiduciaries (guardians, executors, trustees, etc.) and choosing beneficiaries may be particularly perplexing for you, but it is nevertheless essential. Unmarried couples in long term relationships cannot take advantage of the unlimited marital deduction. Thus, the estate of the first to die may be saddled with a steep estate tax bill. This needs to be planned for in advance.

In spite of the problems of estate planning for singles, opportunities may also be available. If you are charitably inclined and you choose not to leave all or most of your estate to heirs, you should investigate the myriad of lifetime giving strategies that could benefit both the charity and you—during your lifetime. See Chapter 21, Sophisticated Strategies for Larger Estates.

32

CHOOSING A NURSING HOME

THE DECISION TO enter a nursing home or to place a spouse or parent in a nursing home is a particularly difficult one. Once this decision is made, however, an appropriate nursing home must be selected. Few homes will offer everything you want for your loved one. Since any home visited will, of course, put its best foot forward to impress potential clients, it's important to know what to look for and what to ask.

Note that the comments and suggestions in this chapter also apply to selecting a continuing care community or other alternative housing. For a closer look at the various options available to older Americans—both in good health and those in need of special care—see Chapter 22, Sorting Out Your Retirement Housing Options.

Where to Begin

All nursing homes are required to have a current license from the state or letter of approval from a licensing agency. And for nursing homes that serve Medicaid patients, the administrator should also have a current state license or waiver. So, your first step should be to ask for a copy of the nursing home's license, certification for participation in government programs, and reports of any recent violations.

Your impressions while touring the facility will be crucial to your decision. The general atmosphere of the home and staff should be pleasant and cheerful. Most homes are trying to provide the best service they can within the limits of the income they receive, the staff they can afford to hire, and the cooperation they receive from the patients and their families. Pay attention to how patients, other visitors, and volunteers speak about the home and to whether the patients look well cared for and generally content.

Also consider how the staff acts towards the patients. Do they show them genuine interest and affection? Some nursing homes don't allow patients to wear their own clothes or decorate their rooms. Others have and enforce written statements of patients' rights. Make sure there is a place for private visits with family and friends. Visiting hours should be convenient for both patients and visitors.

Some of the things to look for are fairly obvious:

- Is the nursing home clean and orderly?
- Is it reasonably free of unpleasant odors?
- Is it well-lighted?

Do not overlook other perhaps less obvious, items. For example:

- Are toilet and bathing facilities easy for handicapped patients to use?
- Are the rooms well-ventilated and kept at a comfortable temperature?
- Are wheelchair ramps provided where necessary?
- Certain areas should be posted with no smoking signs, and staff, patients, and visitors should observe those signs.

Safety and Health Care

Safety is particularly important where older people are concerned. Toilet and bathing facilities should have grab bars, and hallways should have handrails on both sides. Bathtubs and showers must have nonslip surfaces.

One good indication of how seriously the home takes its patients' safety is how strictly it adheres to standard building safety ordinances. Exit doors should be kept unobstructed and unlocked from the inside, and they should be marked clearly with illuminated signs. Portable fire extinguishers should be accessible, but the sprinkler system and emergency lighting should be automatic. Check to see if an emergency evacuation plan is posted prominently.

Unfortunately, the quality of medical, dental, and even nursing care provided in nursing homes varies widely from facility to facility. An acceptable home will have a physician available for medical emergencies at all times, either on staff or on call. At least one registered nurse or licensed practical nurse should be on duty day and night. A registered nurse should serve as director of nursing services. And, ideally, nurse call buttons should be located at each patient's bed and in toilet facilities.

The home also should have an arrangement with an outside dental service to provide patients with necessary dental care. And many homes have arrangements with nearby hospitals for quick transfer of patients in emergencies. Nursing homes are required to give Medicaid recipients annual check-ups. Find out whether check-ups are also given to patients paying privately.

Pharmaceutical services should be supervised by a qualified pharmacist in a room set aside for storing and preparing drugs. Full-time programs of physical therapy, occupational therapy, and speech therapy should be available to patients who need those services.

Take a Closer Look

Try to check behind the scenes as much as possible. See how clean the kitchen is, if food is refrigerated properly, and whether waste is disposed of appropriately.

Pay special attention to the dining facility and mealtime routine. At least three meals should be served every day at normal hours (with no more than 14 hours between the evening meal and breakfast the next morning), on a schedule that allows plenty of time for leisurely eating. Nutritious between-meal and bedtime snacks should also be available.

Is the food any good? The home will usually allow you to sample a meal—make sure it matches the one on the posted menu. It should look and taste appetizing, and should be served at the proper temperature. The dining room should be attractive and comfortable. Make sure the patients are given enough food and that special meals are prepared for patients on therapeutic diets. You may want to ask how patients who need help eating are assisted.

Insist on visiting patients' rooms, and make sure rooms are shared according to the residents' preferences and compatibilities. Every room should open onto a hallway, and have a window to the outside. Each patient should have a reading light, a comfortable chair, and a closet and drawers for personal belongings. Bathing and toilet facilities should have adequate privacy and be located conveniently, and each bed should have a curtain or screen to provide privacy when necessary. Also ask: Does each patient have a locked drawer or safe box?

CHECK SOCIAL AMENITIES

Once you've established that the nursing home is clean, well-kept, and treats its patients decently, try to determine what the residents do all day. Is there an activities coordinator on the staff who organizes a varied program of recreational, cultural, and intellectual activities? Suitable space, tools, and supplies should be provided for such activities. Activities should also be offered for patients who are relatively inactive or confined to their rooms. Ideally, there should be some kind of activity scheduled each day and some evenings.

Besides the scheduled activities, is there a lounge where patients can chat, read, play games, watch television, or just relax away from their rooms? Is there an outdoor area where patients can get fresh air and sunshine? How easy is patient access to drinking water and telephones?

Also find out what extra services are offered. If any particular service is important, find out how convenient it will be and how much it will cost.

For example, will the resident have access to a barber or beautician, a manicurist, a masseur or masseuse, or a podiatrist? Are social services available to aid patients and their families? Do patients have an opportunity to attend religious services and talk with clergy both inside and outside the home?

Compare Costs Carefully

Finally, consider financial and related matters. Compare the estimated monthly costs (including extra charges) with other homes. Costs can vary widely from one city or part of the country to another—and even from home to home within the same geographic area. You can expect to pay anywhere from $25,000 or $30,000 up to $60,000 annually for nursing-home care, according to the United

Seniors Health Cooperative, a Washington, D.C.-based organization for older health-care consumers.

Make sure that the financial terms are clear and in writing and that the contract specifies that the home will provide a refund for unused days paid for in advance. What's more, the rate you sign on at should be guaranteed for a reasonable period of time.

Another Important Consideration: Is the home certified to participate in the Medicare and Medicaid programs? Will the patient be able to remain if he or she is forced to fall back on Medicaid? (Chapter 5, Your Protection Against Rising Health Care and Nursing Home Costs, explains what costs may be covered by Medicare or Medicaid and the advantages and disadvantages of taking out private insurance to pay for nursing home costs.)

Your Ongoing Relations with the Home

When you have chosen a home and your family member is ready to be admitted, label all of his or her belongings and leave a complete list with the home administrator. Then, on each visit, check to see that nothing is missing. And if there is, report it immediately.

Don't hesitate to discuss any problems you may be having with the supervisor. If your problems or concerns aren't handled properly, file a complaint with the ombudsman council or regulatory authority. These volunteers have the right to visit the home at any time, investigate complaints, and require corrective action and even closure.

> HANDY TOOL: The following checklist (Figure 32.1) is designed to help families in choosing the right nursing home for their loved ones.

Figure 32.1. Nursing Home Comparison Checklist

Nursing Home A:..

Nursing Home B:..

Nursing Home C:..

	Home A		Home B		Home C	
	Yes	No	Yes	No	Yes	No
ADMINISTRATIVE CONSIDERATIONS						
1. Does the nursing home have the required current license from the state or letter of approval from a licensing agency?	☐	☐	☐	☐	☐	☐

Figure 32.1. (Cont'd)

	Home A		Home B		Home C	
	Yes	No	Yes	No	Yes	No
2. Does the administrator have a current state license or waiver (required for nursing homes operating under Medicaid)?	☐	☐	☐	☐	☐	☐
3. Is the home certified to participate in the Medicare and Medicaid programs?	☐	☐	☐	☐	☐	☐
4. If special services such as rehabilitation therapy or a therapeutic diet are required, does the home provide them?	☐	☐	☐	☐	☐	☐
5. Is the administrator courteous and helpful?	☐	☐	☐	☐	☐	☐
GENERAL CONSIDERATIONS						
1. Is the general atmosphere of the nursing home warm, pleasant, and cheerful?	☐	☐	☐	☐	☐	☐
2. Are staff members cheerful, courteous, and enthusiastic?	☐	☐	☐	☐	☐	☐
3. Do staff members show patients genuine interest and affection?	☐	☐	☐	☐	☐	☐
4. Do patients look well-cared for and generally content?	☐	☐	☐	☐	☐	☐
5. Are patients allowed to wear their own clothes, decorate their rooms, and keep a few prized possessions on hand?	☐	☐	☐	☐	☐	☐
6. Is there a place for private visits with family and friends?	☐	☐	☐	☐	☐	☐
7. Is there a written statement of patient's rights that, as far as you can tell, is being carried out?	☐	☐	☐	☐	☐	☐
8. Do patients, other visitors, and volunteers speak favorably about the home?	☐	☐	☐	☐	☐	☐

Figure 32.1. (Cont'd)

	Home A		Home B		Home C	
	Yes	No	Yes	No	Yes	No
PHYSICAL CONSIDERATIONS						
1. Is the nursing home clean and orderly?	☐	☐	☐	☐	☐	☐
2. Is the home reasonably free of unpleasant odors?	☐	☐	☐	☐	☐	☐
3. Are toilet and bathing facilities easy for handicapped patients to use?	☐	☐	☐	☐	☐	☐
4. Is the home well-lighted?	☐	☐	☐	☐	☐	☐
5. Are rooms well-ventilated and kept at a comfortable temperature?	☐	☐	☐	☐	☐	☐
SAFETY						
1. Are wheelchair ramps provided where necessary?	☐	☐	☐	☐	☐	☐
2. Is the nursing home free of obvious hazards (e.g., obstacles to patients, hazards underfoot, unsteady chairs)?	☐	☐	☐	☐	☐	☐
3. Are there grab bars in toilet and bathing facilities and handrails on both sides of hallways?	☐	☐	☐	☐	☐	☐
4. Do bathtubs and showers have nonslip surfaces?	☐	☐	☐	☐	☐	☐
5. Is there an automatic sprinkler system and automatic emergency lighting?	☐	☐	☐	☐	☐	☐
6. Are there portable fire extinguishers?	☐	☐	☐	☐	☐	☐
7. Are exits clearly marked and exit signs illuminated?	☐	☐	☐	☐	☐	☐
8. Are exit doors unobstructed and unlocked from inside?	☐	☐	☐	☐	☐	☐
9. Are certain areas posted with no smoking signs?	☐	☐	☐	☐	☐	☐
10. Do staff, patients, and visitors observe the no smoking areas?	☐	☐	☐	☐	☐	☐

Figure 32.1. (Cont'd)

	Home A		Home B		Home C	
	Yes	No	Yes	No	Yes	No
11. Is an emergency evacuation plan posted in prominent locations?	☐	☐	☐	☐	☐	☐
MEDICAL, DENTAL, AND OTHER SERVICES						
1. Does the home have an arrangement with an outside dental service to provide patients with dental care when necessary?	☐	☐	☐	☐	☐	☐
2. In case of medical emergencies, is a physician available at all times, either on staff or on call?	☐	☐	☐	☐	☐	☐
3. Does the home have arrangements with a nearby hospital for quick transfer of nursing home patients in an emergency?	☐	☐	☐	☐	☐	☐
4. Is emergency transportation available?	☐	☐	☐	☐	☐	☐
PHARMACEUTICAL SERVICES						
1. Are pharmaceutical services supervised by a qualified pharmacist?	☐	☐	☐	☐	☐	☐
2. Is a room set aside for storing and preparing drugs?	☐	☐	☐	☐	☐	☐
NURSING SERVICES						
1. Is at least one registered nurse (RN) or licensed practical nurse (LPN) on duty day and night?	☐	☐	☐	☐	☐	☐
2. Is an RN on duty during the day, seven days a week?	☐	☐	☐	☐	☐	☐
3. Does an RN serve as director of nursing services?	☐	☐	☐	☐	☐	☐
4. Are nurse call buttons located at each patient's bed and in toilet and bathing facilities?	☐	☐	☐	☐	☐	☐

Figure 32.1. (Cont'd)

	Home A		Home B		Home C	
	Yes	No	Yes	No	Yes	No
FOOD SERVICE						
1. Is the kitchen clean and reasonably tidy?	☐	☐	☐	☐	☐	☐
2. Is food refrigerated properly?	☐	☐	☐	☐	☐	☐
3. Is waste properly disposed of?	☐	☐	☐	☐	☐	☐
4. Are at least three meals served each day?	☐	☐	☐	☐	☐	☐
5. Are meals served at normal hours, with plenty of time for leisurely eating?	☐	☐	☐	☐	☐	☐
6. Are no more than 14 hours allowed between the evening meal and breakfast the next morning?	☐	☐	☐	☐	☐	☐
7. Are nutritious between-meal and bedtime snacks available?	☐	☐	☐	☐	☐	☐
8. Are patients given enough food?	☐	☐	☐	☐	☐	☐
9. Does the food look appetizing?	☐	☐	☐	☐	☐	☐
10. Is the food tasty and served at the proper temperature? (The home should allow you to sample a meal.)	☐	☐	☐	☐	☐	☐
11. Does the meal being served match the posted menu?	☐	☐	☐	☐	☐	☐
12. Are special meals prepared for patients on therapeutic diets?	☐	☐	☐	☐	☐	☐
13. Is the dining room attractive and comfortable?	☐	☐	☐	☐	☐	☐
14. Do patients who need it get help in eating, whether in the dining room or in their own rooms?	☐	☐	☐	☐	☐	☐
REHABILITATION THERAPY						
1. Is a full-time program of physical therapy available?	☐	☐	☐	☐	☐	☐
2. Are occupational therapy and speech therapy available?	☐	☐	☐	☐	☐	☐

Figure 32.1. (Cont'd)

	Home A		Home B		Home C	
	Yes	No	Yes	No	Yes	No
SOCIAL SERVICES AND PATIENT ACTIVITIES						
1. Are social services available to aid patients and their families?	☐	☐	☐	☐	☐	☐
2. Does the nursing home have a varied program of recreational, cultural, and intellectual activities for patients?	☐	☐	☐	☐	☐	☐
3. Is there an activities coordinator on the staff?	☐	☐	☐	☐	☐	☐
4. Is suitable space available for patient activities?	☐	☐	☐	☐	☐	☐
5. Are tools and supplies provided?	☐	☐	☐	☐	☐	☐
6. Are activities offered for patients who are relatively inactive or confined to their rooms?	☐	☐	☐	☐	☐	☐
7. Are activities provided each day?	☐	☐	☐	☐	☐	☐
8. Are some activities scheduled in the evenings?	☐	☐	☐	☐	☐	☐
9. Do patients have an opportunity to attend religious services and talk with clergymen both inside and outside the home?	☐	☐	☐	☐	☐	☐
10. Are a barber and beautician available?	☐	☐	☐	☐	☐	☐
PATIENTS' ROOMS						
1. Do all the rooms open onto a hallway?	☐	☐	☐	☐	☐	☐
2. Do all the rooms have a window to the outside?	☐	☐	☐	☐	☐	☐
3. Does each patient have a reading light, a comfortable chair, and a closet and drawers for personal belongings?	☐	☐	☐	☐	☐	☐
4. Is there fresh drinking water within reach?	☐	☐	☐	☐	☐	☐

Figure 32.1. (Cont'd)

	Home A		Home B		Home C	
	Yes	No	Yes	No	Yes	No
5. Is there a curtain or screen available to provide privacy for each bed whenever necessary?	☐	☐	☐	☐	☐	☐
6. Do bathing and toilet facilities have adequate privacy?	☐	☐	☐	☐	☐	☐
OTHER AREAS OF THE NURSING HOME						
1. Is there a lounge where patients can chat, read, play games, watch television, or just relax away from their rooms?	☐	☐	☐	☐	☐	☐
2. Is a public telephone available for patients' use?	☐	☐	☐	☐	☐	☐
3. Does the nursing home have an outdoor area where patients can get fresh air and sunshine?	☐	☐	☐	☐	☐	☐
FINANCIAL AND RELATED MATTERS						
1. Do the estimated monthly costs (including extra charges) compare favorably with the cost of other homes?	☐	☐	☐	☐	☐	☐
2. Is a refund made for unused days paid for in advance?	☐	☐	☐	☐	☐	☐
3. Are visiting hours convenient for patients and visitors?	☐	☐	☐	☐	☐	☐
4. Are these and other important matters specified in the contract?	☐	☐	☐	☐	☐	☐

INDEX

A

Alternative minimum tax (AMT), 252
Annuities, 267–72
  advantages and disadvantages, 271–2
  deferred, 267
  benefits, distribution of, 267–9
  family, 269
  immediate pay, 267
  joint-and-survivor, 33–5; 268
  planning considerations, 269–71
  refund, 268
  straight life, 267–8
  variable, 269
Asset allocation, 168–70; 176–81
Automobile financing and leasing, 129–34
  automobile brokers, 131–2
  collateralized loans, 130–1
  insurance policy loans, 132–3
  leasing, 133–4
  noncollateral loans, 132
  passbook loans, 132
  signature loans, 133
Automobile insurance, 68–9
Automatic teller machine (ATM) cards, 128–9

B

Budgets, personal, 116

C

Capitalization rate, 168
Cash-equivalent investments, 183–9
Certificates of deposit (CDs), 184–5
Common stocks, investing in, 210–3
Consumer fraud, 147–53
Covered calls, 219
Credit,
  bank credit cards, 125–6
  credit bureaus, 122–3
  credit reports, 123

Credit (*cont'd.*)
  creditors' rights, 123–4
  debit cards, 126–7
  debt counseling, 143–5
  home equity, as source of 134–41; *see also* Home equity borrowing
  problems, coping with, 141–5
  tax aspects of, 121–2
  travel and entertainment cards, 126

D

Dividend reinvestment plans, 218
Divorce, late-life, 395–402
  division of assets, and, 398–9
  financial planning implications of, 399–402
  procedures and alternatives, 397–8
  remarriage, 402–4
    postmarital agreements, 404
    premarital agreements, 402–4
Dollar-cost averaging, 217–8
Durable power of attorney, 282–3

E

Estate planning
  basic documents,
    durable power of attorney, 282–3
    letter of instructions, 284–5; 326
    living will, 283–4
    will, 279–82
  minimum needs, 277–98
  strategies for large estates, 311–24
    generation-skipping transfers, 323–4
    gifts, use of in estate planning, 301
    trusts,
      charitable,
        annuity, 322
        lead, 321
        pooled income funds, 322–3
        remainder, 320–1; 322
        unitrusts, 321–2

Estate planning (*cont'd.*)
creating, 315–6
Crummey, 319–20
irrevocable, 313
living, 313–5
marital deduction, 317–8
qualified terminal interest property (QTIP), 318–9
sprinkling, 319
testamentary, 313–5
revocable, 313
trustees, 316–7
Estate taxes,
calculating, 299–300
federal, general issues concerning, 302–4
state, general issues concerning, 304–5
strategies for limiting, 300–2

F

Financial objectives, 3
Financial statements, personal, 106–16
statement of personal assets and liabilities, 115–6
Fixed-income investments, 191–207
strategies, 192–7
Funeral planning
alternatives,
cremation, 328
donation of remains to a medical school, 328
earth burial, 329
religious services, 330–1
final expenses, tax aspects of, 332
financing, 331–2
funeral homes, 326
memorial societies, 325–6

G

Gifts, use of in estate planning, 301

H

Healthcare, reducing costs of, 356–8
Health insurance,
early retirees, 79–80
COBRA, and, 80
Long-term care insurance, 89–91
Medicare, 74–9
Medicare Gap "Medigap" policies, 80–5
Health Maintenance Organizations (HMOs), 86–7
Home,
decision to sell, 383–4
tax aspects of, 384–6
maintenance of during retirement years, 386–90
mortgage payments, and, 390–1
Home equity borrowing, 134–41
home equity secured credit, 139–41
private annuities, 137
refinancing, 137–8
reverse annuity mortgages, 136–7
reverse mortgage, 135–6
second mortgages, 138
Housing, *see* Retirement planning

I

Inflation,
effects on retirement planning, 10; 19
projecting future rates, 19
Insurance,
automobile, 68–9
disability, 61–8
employer-provided, 63–4
comparing policies, 67–8
costs of, 66–7
coverage period, 65–6
definition of disability, and, 65
personal liability, 69–70
professional liability, 70–1
private policies, 64–8
social security coverage, 49; 61–3
life, 95–100
company policies, 96
costs, cutting, 99–100
estate planning tool, as, 98–9
low-load, 100
preretirees and, 95–6
retirees and, 97–9
property and casualty, 54–61
homeowners, 54–61
floaters, 56–7
inventories, importance of, 58–61
renters and condo owners, 57
reducing costs, 57–8
replacement cost coverage, 55
standard exclusions, 56
renters and condominium owners, 57

Investment portfolio,
asset allocation and, 176–81
designing, 173–80
evaluating, 180
Investment products, types of, 158–66
fixed income investments, 159
stock investments, 167
real estate investments, 167–8
Individual Retirement Accounts (IRAs), 261–6
Investments,
certificates of deposit (CDs), 184–5
common stocks, 210–3
blue chip, 213
cyclical, 213
growth, 212
income, 212
speculative, 213
convertible bonds, 206
corporate bonds, 205–6
junk bonds, 206–7
money market deposit accounts, 186
money market mutual funds, 185–6
mortgage-backed securities, 199–202
collateralized mortgage obligations (CMOs), 201–2
Fannie Maes, 202
Freddie Macs, 201
Ginnie Maes, 200–1
municipal bonds, 203–5
municipal notes, 188; 203
preferred stocks, 213–216
callable, 215
cumulative, 216
convertible, 215
participating, 216
straight, 215
voting, 215
real estate, 167; 227–44
evaluating, 238–41
investment alternatives,
commercial property, 237–8
undeveloped land, 234
residential rental property, 235
condos and co-ops, 235–6
duplexes and apartments, 237
investment strategies, 241–4
resort homes, 236
single family homes, 235
time-share units, 236–7
Investments (*cont'd.*)
ownership options, 228–34
direct ownership, 228–9
limited partnerships, 229–32
real estate investment trusts, 232–3
stock options, 224–5
stocks, selling, 222–3
U.S. savings bonds, 198–9
U.S. Treasury bills, 186
U.S. Treasury bonds and notes, 197–8
IRS Publications, 250–2

L

Life events, financial impact of, 5
Life insurance, 95–100
Loans, consumer, 117–21
types of,
brokerage account and margin loans, 120–1
family loans, 119–20
Keogh, 401(k), IRA, and pension plan loans, 120
life insurance policy loans, 118–9
secured, 118
unsecured, 118
Long-term care insurance, 89–91

M

Market uncertainty and volatility,
coping with, 170–2
Medical costs, 87–8
Medical expense deduction, 355–6
Medicaid,
nursing home coverage, as, 91–4
asset shifting, 93–4
spend down rules, 91–3
Medicare, 74–9
enrolling, policies on, 74–6
Part A coverage, 76–7
Part B coverage, 77–8
Medicare Gap "Medigap" insurance, 80–5
Money market deposit accounts, 186
Money market mutual funds, 185–6
Municipal notes, 188
Mutual funds
stock investing and, 221–2

N

Nursing homes
choosing, 427–31
cost of, 88–9
long-term care insurance, 89–94

P

Pensions, see Retirement Plans
taxation of income, 31
Preretirees, 9
Preventive medicine, 353–5

R

Recordkeeping systems,
active file, 105–6
components of, 103–6
developing and maintaining, 102–3
inactive file, 106
safe deposit box, 104–5
Retirement planning,
effects of inflation on, 19
evaluating progress of, 21
home,
decision to sell, 383–4
tax aspects of, 384–6
maintenance of during retirement years, 386–90
mortgage payments, and, 390–1
preliminary examination of financial status, and, 13
preparing a budget for, 19
retirement lifestyles, 335–8
hobbies and activities, 335–6
housing alternatives, 339–352
accessory apartments, 346
adult day care, 349
condos and co-ops, 342
congregate housing, 347–8
continuing care communities, 348–9
home care, 346
home sharing, 345–6
houseboats, 344
motor homes, 344
nursing homes, 350
retirement communities, 343–4
retirement homesite developments, 343
senior housing, 348
retiring abroad, 351–2
Retirement planning (*cont'd.*)
travel, during retirement, 359–71
working in retirement, 336–7; 373–81
timetable for, 11
Retirement plans,
employer-sponsored, 24
employee thrift and savings plans, 24
401(k) plans, 25; 272–3
403(b) plans, 25
pension plans, 24
salary reduction plans, 25
individual retirement accounts (IRAs), 27
annuities, 265
contributions to, 36
designating beneficiaries, 266
managing funds in, 262–3
rollovers and, 24; 32
tax-advantaged investments, as, 261–6
withdrawals from, 35; 263–6
investments, managing, 28
tax rules and, 29
over-funding of, 35
self-employed, 26
Keogh plans, 26; 266
simplified employee pension (SEP) plans, 27; 266–7
withdrawal choices, 29
annuities, 33–5
IRAs, 35
lump sum vs. annuity options, 30
taxation of, 31–2
tax-advantaged, 23

S

Short sales, 219
Singles, financial planning concerns of, 423–6
Social Security,
claims, filing, 41–2
appealing, 52
disability benefits, 49
retirement benefits, 40–4
early retirement, impact on, 44–6
working during retirement, impact on, 381
survivor's benefits, 49
Spouse, death of
financial planning implications, 405–21
Stocks, 209–25
strategies for investing in, 216–21

T

Tax advisors, 248–9
Tax-deferred investments, 247; 255
Tax deductions,
  business expense, 255–6
  medical expense, 257–9; 355–6
Tax-exempt investments, 247–8
Tax planning, 245–59
Travel, during retirement, 359–71
Trusts,
  creating, 315–6
  Crummey, 319–20
  irrevocable, 313
  living, 313–5
  marital deduction, 317–8
  qualified terminal interest property (QTIP), 318–9
Trusts (*cont'd.*)
  sprinkling, 319
  testamentary, 313–5
  revocable, 313
  trustees, 316–7

V

Variable annuities, 269

W

Widow/widowerhood, 405–21; 423–6; see also, Spouse, death of
Working, during retirement, 373–81